THE PSYCHOLOGY
OF LEARNING AND MOTIVATION

Advances in Research and Theory

VOLUME 35

THE PSYCHOLOGY
OF LEARNING AND MOTIVATION

Advances in Research and Theory

EDITED BY DOUGLAS L. MEDIN

DEPARTMENT OF PSYCHOLOGY
NORTHWESTERN UNIVERSITY, EVANSTON, ILLINOIS

Volume 35

ACADEMIC PRESS
San Diego   London   Boston   New York   Sydney   Tokyo   Toronto

This book is printed on acid-free paper. ∞

Copyright © 1996 by ACADEMIC PRESS

All Rights Reserved.
No part of this publication may be reproduced or transmitted in any form or by any
means, electronic or mechanical, including photocopy, recording, or any information
storage and retrieval system, without permission in writing from the publisher.

Academic Press, Inc.
525 B Street, Suite 1900, San Diego, California 92101-4495, USA
http://www.apnet.com

Academic Press Limited
24-28 Oval Road, London NW1 7DX, UK
http://www.hbuk.co.uk/ap/

International Standard Serial Number: 0079-7421

International Standard Book Number: 0-12-543335-2

PRINTED IN THE UNITED STATES OF AMERICA
96 97 98 99 00 01 QW 9 8 7 6 5 4 3 2 1

CONTENTS

MEMORY FOR ASYMMETRIC EVENTS

John T. Wixted and Deirdra H. Dougherty

THE MAINTENANCE OF A COMPLEX KNOWLEDGE BASE AFTER SEVENTEEN YEARS

Marigold Linton

CATEGORY LEARNING AS PROBLEM SOLVING

Brian H. Ross

BUILDING A COHERENT CONCEPTION OF HIV TRANSMISSION: A NEW APPROACH TO AIDS EDUCATION

Terry Kit-fong Au and Laura F. Romo

SPATIAL EFFECTS IN THE PARTIAL REPORT PARADIGM: A CHALLENGE FOR THEORIES OF VISUAL SPATIAL ATTENTION

Gordon D. Logan and Claus Bundesen

STRUCTURAL BIASES IN CONCEPT LEARNING: INFLUENCES FROM MULTIPLE FUNCTIONS

Dorrit Billman

CONTRIBUTORS

Numbers in parentheses indicate the pages on which the authors' contributions begin.

Terry Kit-fong Au (193), Department of Psychology, University of California, Los Angeles, Los Angeles, California 90095

Edward Awh (43), Department of Psychology, University of Michigan, Ann Arbor, Michigan 48109

Lisa L. Barnes (43), Department of Psychology, University of Michigan, Ann Arbor, Michigan 48109

Dorrit Billman (283), School of Psychology, Georgia Institute of Technology, Atlanta, Georgia 30332

Claus Bundesen (243), Psychological Laboratory, University of Copenhagen, DK-2300 Copenhagen, Denmark

Deirdra II. Dougherty (89), Department of Psychology, University of California, San Diego, La Jolla, California 92093

Maxwell Drain (43), Department of Psychology, University of Michigan, Ann Arbor, Michigan 48109

William J. Friedman (1), Department of Psychology, Severance Laboratory, Oberlin College, Oberlin, Ohio 44074

Jennifer Glass (43), Department of Psychology, University of Michigan, Ann Arbor, Michigan 48109

John Jonides (43), Department of Psychology, University of Michigan, Ann Arbor, Michigan 48109

Erick J. Lauber (43), Department of Psychology, University of Georgia, Athens, Georgia 30602

Marigold Linton (127), Mathematics Department, Arizona State University, Tempe, Arizona 85287

Gordon D. Logan (243), Department of Psychology, University of Illinois, Champaign, Illinois 61820

Andrea L. Patalano (43), Department of Psychology, University of Michigan, Ann Arbor, Michigan 48109

Patricia A. Reuter-Lorenz (43), Department of Psychology, University of Michigan, Ann Arbor, Michigan 48109

Laura F. Romo (193), Department of Psychology, University of California, Los Angeles, Los Angeles, California 90095

Brian H. Ross (165), Beckman Institute, University of Illinois, Urbana, Illinois 61801

Eric H. Schumacher (43), Department of Psychology, University of Michigan, Ann Arbor, Michigan 48109

Edward E. Smith (43), Department of Psychology, University of Michigan, Ann Arbor, Michigan 48109

John T. Wixted (89), Department of Psychology, University of California, San Diego, La Jolla, California 92093

DISTANCE AND LOCATION PROCESSES IN MEMORY FOR THE TIMES OF PAST EVENTS

William J. Friedman

I. Introduction

One of the central properties of memories for personal events, and one that distinguishes them from semantic knowledge, is that the events seem to belong to particular times in our past. In this chapter I discuss the psychological processes that contribute to this chronological sense of the past. Using a distinction between two fundamentally different kinds of temporal information, which I call "distances" and "locations," I describe my research on memory for the times of past events on long timescales—on the order of days, weeks, months, and years. A number of the studies support my conclusion (Friedman, 1993) that we rely heavily on our knowledge of temporal locations in remembering the times of past events. But new evidence is presented that shows, perhaps for the first time, that distance information also contributes to our experience of time on these timescales.

The spatial terms distance and location can be used to describe two types of temporal information that are difficult to separate in adults' everyday experience of time but nevertheless are useful for understanding the bases of memory for time. Distance refers to the amount of time that has elapsed between the occurrence of an event and the present. Locations are parts of natural, social, or personal time patterns that we represent. For example we know about the order of the parts of daily or annual cycles, and we know that college comes before graduate school. Intuitively, the distinction between distances and locations seems artificial when applied to memory for the times of past events because we readily translate distances into locations and vice versa: If an event was several weeks ago, we can assign it a range of dates; if we remember the month of an event, it is easy to infer how long ago it was. But the distinction becomes important once one begins to consider the psychological processes that allow us to remember the times of past events.

In a review of research on memory for time (Friedman, 1993), I used the distinction between distances and locations (and a third kind of temporal information, relative times of occurrence) to classify theories and summarize the existing literature. Distance-based theories explain memory for time by positing processes that are correlated with the passage of time, such as the decay of memory traces. The strength of a memory, its accessibility, or, in some theories, its location in the memory store, are used to judge how long ago an event occurred. Location-based theories rely on the recall of information that is associated with an event rather than direct cues to the age of the memory. For example, in reconstructive theories, a type of location-based theory, contextual associations such as the weather at the time of an event are used to infer when the event must have been within the annual cycle.

The review showed that numerous studies (among them the work described in the following section) support the importance of location-based processes. In contrast, there were few findings that pointed to the use of distance-based processes and a number of findings that contradict their predictions. However, in the course of examining the research literature, I concluded that the methods used to study memory for time may have inadvertently biased subjects against the use of distance-based information. In the subsequent section, I explain this reasoning and describe a series of studies using new approaches to the study of distance-based processes. This research shows that distance information does contribute to our sense of the times of past events, and the studies provide information about some of the temporal properties of distance-based processes. A final section discusses the roles of distance and location processes in memory for time.

II. Location Processes

A. THEORIES

According to location theories, we remember the times of past events as unchanging locations in time patterns rather than ever-changing distances from the present. These theories also share the position that the information used to judge the times of past events is laid down at the time when the events are first experienced and later retrieved. Despite the similarities, the three types of location theories make different assumptions about the nature of the temporal information (Friedman, 1993).

A number of theories imply that specific temporal information of some sort is automatically assigned to events at the time of encoding (Flexser & Bower, 1974; Glenberg, 1987; Glenberg & Swanson, 1986; Hasher & Zacks, 1979; Yntema & Trask, 1963). As Brewer (1996) points out, the assumption of absolute time coding is also common among researchers in autobiographical memory. However, the theory suffers from considerable imprecision, and the few empirical implications that can be pinned down (e.g., Hasher & Zacks's, 1979, criteria for the automaticity of temporal coding) have not been supported (Friedman, 1993).

Estes (1972; Lee & Estes, 1977, 1981) proposed a location-based theory of memory for time of brief sequences of stimuli which was later offered as a model of memory for the times of life events (Estes, 1985). In laboratory tasks subjects are presumed to form associations between stimulus items and "control elements" during encoding. Different levels of control elements are hypothesized, so a subject might simultaneously associate an item with the beginning of a stimulus list but the middle of a series of lists. Information degrades independently at each level through a process called "perturbation." This encoding–perturbation theory can explain a number of important phenomena in the time–memory literature (Friedman, 1993), including the "scale effects" that are discussed below. However, some of Estes's claims about how memory searching and perturbation take place seem to assume a representation of the sequential order of events that is not explained by the theory (Friedman, 1993).

The most successful location theories are called contextual association or reconstructive theories. (I will use the latter term.) These theories have been developed to explain both memory for time in laboratory tests (Anderson & Bower, 1972; Guenther & Linton, 1975; Hintzman, Block, & Summers, 1973) and, on much longer scales, memory for the times of personal or news events (Brown, Rips, & Shevell, 1985; Brown, Shevell, & Rips, 1986; Friedman & Wilkins, 1985; Lieury, Aiello, Lepreux, & Mellet, 1980; Linton, 1975; Ribot, 1901; Underwood, 1977). According to the theories, we judge the times of past events by retrieving whatever information is associated with them and, where possible, relating this information to our rich (semantic) knowledge of social, natural, and personal time patterns. For example, the information associated with my memory for a particular hike might help me recall that it was after lunch, during the summer, and the year that I visited a particular country.

Unlike some other location theories, reconstructive theories do not include the assumption that specific temporal information is encoded at the time of an experience; contextual information, coupled with one's general knowledge of time patterns, is all that is required. In everyday memory for time, this contextual information might be percepts, activities, locations, people present, or the proximity of other events whose dates have been learned. Another distinguishing feature of reconstructive theories is that they do not posit that memories are chronologically organized, as some distance theorists propose and many psychologists and nonpsychologists intuitively assume. A third important feature is that time of occurrence is not an integral quantity—amount of elapsed time—as it is, by definition, in distance theories. One can independently remember the time on different scales (as in the hiking example). In the following discussion, I present evidence bearing on reconstructive explanations of memory for time of personal and news events.

B. EVIDENCE

1. Scale Effects

An early demonstration of the nonintegral nature of the information used to judge time was Hintzman et al.'s (1973) study of judgments of the between-list and within-list position in which stimulus words had been presented. The authors discovered that subjects sometimes recalled the within-list position of a word (e.g., that it was near the beginning of a list) but failed to recall in which of a series of lists it had occurred. This finding is difficult for distance theories to explain; if a subject lacks sufficiently refined information to judge distance on a gross scale such as list, how could they judge its distance on a finer scale? Reconstructive theories, which do not assume an integral distance quantity or the representation of a linear chronology, can readily explain this finding. The subject might remember that a new list had just begun but not recall anything that could distinguish that list from others that had been presented. A number of researchers have presented similar evidence for memory for time on much longer timescales (Bruce & Van Pelt, 1989; Friedman, 1987; Friedman & Wilkins, 1985; White, 1982, 1989). I will describe two studies that were specifically designed to show the presence of "scale effects"—cases where subjects are more accurate on a fine timescale than on grosser scales.

Friedman and Wilkins (1985) asked a group of British women to judge the times of 10 news events from the preceding 20 years. All the events were sufficiently notable that the subjects were likely to have learned of them soon after they occurred (e.g., the assassinations of John Kennedy and Lord Mountbatten) or watched them on television as they took place (e.g., the wedding of Prince Charles and Lady Diana, the first manned moon landing). Most studies of judgments of the times of past events use methods that produce a unitary measure of their times of occurrence, typically a month and year (which are integrated into a distance in the past) or a mark on a time line. Arnold Wilkins and I requested, in random order, separate time and confidence estimates on each of the following scales: year, month, day of the month, day of the week, and hour. For each scale we also asked participants to rate their confidence in the estimates and to "List the things you thought of in arriving at your estimate." Subjects were tested in May 1983.

Table I lists the event descriptions and the times that the events occurred. Table II shows the mean error of estimates for each of the events on each scale. The errors for year are expressed as absolute deviations. For example, on average subjects were incorrect by 1.75 years in judging the year of the Kennedy assassination. The other errors can be expressed as proportions of the deviations that would be expected by chance, because there is a particular number of elements on the scale. We made the simplifying assumption that a subject's estimate on a given scale was a deviation from

TABLE I

Stimulus Events and Times of Occurrence[a]

Event description	Day of week	Date	Approximate G.M.T.
1. John F. Kennedy is assassinated.	Friday	November 22, 1963	19:00
2. Donald Campbell is killed in a speedboat accident on Lake Windemere.	Wednesday	January 4, 1967	9:00
3. The first spaceman sets foot on the moon.	Monday	July 21, 1969	3:00
4. Lord Mountbatten is killed by an explosion aboard his boat.	Monday	August 27, 1979	12:00
5. Former Beatle John Lennon is shot.	Tuesday	December 8, 1980	4:00
6. Pope John Paul II is shot.	Wednesday	May 13, 1981	16:00
7. Prince Charles and Lady Diana exchange rings.	Tuesday	July 29, 1981	12:00
8. Egyptian president Anwar Sadat is assassinated.	Thursday	October 6, 1981	13:00
9. Prince William is born.	Tuesday	June 22, 1982	21:00
10. The ship Mary Rose rises above the surface.	Monday	October 11, 1982	9:00

[a] Reprinted from Friedman, W. J., & Wilkins, A. J. (1985), Scale effects in memory for the time of past events. *Memory and Cognition, 13,* 168–175, by permission of the Psychonomic Society.

TABLE II

MEAN ERROR OF TIME ESTIMATES FOR EACH SCALE FOR EACH EVENT[a]

Event	Actual year	Absolute deviation	Proportion of chance deviation					
		Year	Month	Day of month	Day of week	Hour	Mean of the four
1. (Kennedy)	1963	1.75	.98	.79	.62**	.64**	.76
2. (Campbell)	1967	3.78	1.51	1.08	.86	.57**	1.00
3. (Moon)	1969	2.67	.55***	.93	1.06	1.14	.92
4. (Mountbatten)	1979	.71	.10***	.93	1.10	.41***	.64
5. (Lennon)	1980	1.35	.76*	1.18	.86	1.34	1.04
6. (John Paul II)	1981	.76	.65**	.82	1.10	.45***	.76
7. (Wedding)	1981	.06	.04***	.77	.99	.14	.48
8. (Sadat)	1981	.94	.92	1.32	.93	.31***	.87
9. (Prince)	1982	.06	.23***	.76	.65**	.85	.62
10. (Mary Rose)	1982	.29	.73*	.73*	.75	.55***	.69
Mean		1.24	.65	.93	.89	.64	

Note. Significance levels are for one-tailed t-tests with the null hypothesis that entries are equal to or greater than chance deviations.
[a] Reprinted from Friedman, W. J., & Wilkins, A. J. (1985), Scale effects in memory for the time of past events. Memory and Cognition, 13, 168–175, by permission of the Psychonomic Society.
* $p < .05$. ** $p < .01$. *** $p < .001$.

the closest occurrence of the actual time on that scale. For example, a subject estimating March for the Kennedy assassination would receive a proportion of chance deviation of 1, because March is 3 months distant from the true month, November, and 3 months is half of the maximum possible distance, 6 months, under the simplifying assumption. The results of *t* tests against chance levels of responding are also shown in Table II.

Table II shows numerous instances in which estimates actually become more accurate as one moves from grosser to finer scales. For five of the eight events where year is inaccurate by more than .25 (the chance level for the month scale), month accuracy was significantly below chance. More striking is the significant accuracy for hour for 7 of the 10 events. If these estimates were based on integral information about the distances of the events in the past, hour estimates should fall to chance levels once month errors were greater than about .01 or year errors were greater than about .001, that is, for all the events. Two of the day-of-the-week estimates are also more accurate than would be predicted from accuracy on grosser scales, including the 20-year-old Kennedy assassination. Analysis of the confidence that subjects had in their estimates showed that confidence in hour estimates was nearly as great as in month estimates, and both were greater than day of the month and day of the week.

These findings are clearly inconsistent with the possibility that subjects base judgments on distances in the past. On the other hand, the results can be explained by reconstructive theories. The contextual information that subjects recalled might have been sufficient to constrain month but not year, or time of day but not longer timescales. An examination of the method reports showed that the recall of contextual information about the event or the subject's own life was the most common approach, and this contextual information was more likely to be available for year, month, and hour than for the other two scales.

Several findings showed that subjects not only reconstructed times based on their recollections but made inferences that could have been derived simply from the event descriptions. One line of evidence is that they frequently mentioned logical constraints in explaining their judgments. For example, subjects reported that summer weather was likely for the launch of a space mission, and weddings usually take place during the day. Another indication came from instances of systematic distortion away from the true times of occurrence. The greater-than-chance errors of the month estimates for event 2 probably stemmed from the fact that few subjects thought a water speed record would be attempted in midwinter. Third, in a follow-up study, we showed that similar scale effects in judgments were found when subjects dated hypothetical events modeled after those used in the first experiment (Friedman & Wilkins, 1985, Experiment 2).

Although logical inference contributes to scale effects, it is not the only cause. This point is important because of the emphasis that reconstructive theories place on actual memories for the context of events. One line of evidence that true memories can themselves produce scale effects was the finding that many of the unexpectedly accurate month and hour estimates in the study of real events were also significantly more accurate than the corresponding judgments in the study of hypothetical events. Additional evidence comes from a study that used a stimulus event that could occur at any time on any scale, an earthquake.

In January 1986 an earthquake shook northern Ohio, a rare event for this region. About 9 months later, I asked Oberlin College employees who had personally experienced the quake to complete a questionnaire about the time when it had occurred (Friedman, 1987). As in the Friedman and Wilkins (1985) study, participants were asked to provide separate estimates, confidence ratings, and method reports for the scales: year, month, day of month, day of week, and hour. Because earthquakes are not linked to discernible cycles, accurate reports of the time could not be based on logical inference.

The results showed clear scale effects. The mean absolute deviations for the different scales were .11 years, 1.94 months, 9.45 days of the month, 1.57 days of the week, and 1.04 hours. As in Friedman and Wilkin's study, all but year can also be expressed as proportions of chance deviation: .65 for month, 1.22 for day of the month, .92 for day of the week, and .17 for hour. Month and hour were significantly below chance ($p < .001$), but day of the month and week were not. Confidence ratings, on a 5-point scale, were significantly greater for year (3.81) than hour (2.88) and month (2.72), followed by day of the week (1.97) and then day of the month (1.55).

Month estimates were not more accurate than would be predicted from year, but hour was much more accurate than is possible if integral information were the basis. How could subjects for whom the subjective distance in months was inaccurate by nearly two months reckon the time of day within about 1 hr? The accuracy and confidence of hour can be explained by the availability of specific memories that allowed subjects to reconstruct time of day, which happened to be about 11:50 a.m., just before lunch. This explanation is strongly supported by the method reports: 61 of the 99 subjects related the earthquake to their daily routine and another 23 to a nonroutine event whose time was recalled.

Reconstruction was apparent in the methods reported for day of the week and month, too, but it appears that the cues were insufficient to allow precise discrimination on these scales. The many subjects who recalled something about the weather still would have had difficulty identifying a particular month, given the long winters in northern Ohio, and those who recalled that the event was on a workday might still have had difficulty choosing Friday. In contrast, Huttenlocher, Hedges, and Prohaska (1992) found considerable accuracy for day of the week when the probed item had occurred on a Saturday or Sunday, and weekend days were much more accurately judged than weekdays (see also Thompson, Skowronski, & Betz, 1993; for related evidence on temporal orientation, see Koriat & Fischoff, 1974; Koriat, Fischoff & Razel, 1976; and Shanon, 1979). These findings show that accuracy of reconstruction is determined not only by the specificity of the information that is recalled but by the amount of differentiation between elements on a scale.

Although the Friedman (1987) study provides strong support for reconstructive theories, there was one finding that we will return to when considering distance theories. On the year scale, 20 participants reported recalling how long ago the event was; another 20 claimed that they were positive of the time, and many of these subjects may also have been relying on impressions of the recency of the earthquake. Reports indicative of impressions of distance are rare in other studies of memory for time. However, this is one of only two studies in which subjects were asked for a separate estimate of the year. (No similar method category relating to impressions of distance was coded in Friedman and Wilkins's 1985 study.) These reports may reflect the fact that distance-based processes are more likely to be used when the duration of the scale is large relative to the elapsed time.

2. Other Evidence for Location Theories

Scale effects are a clear demonstration that the information that subjects use is not an integral quantity. Another kind of evidence for the nonintegral nature of temporal information was reported by Huttenlocher et al. (1992). The authors analyzed estimates of the time of day and day of the week of a telephone interview that had taken place between 7 and 75 days earlier. Interviews were conducted at varying times of day from morning to evening. If subjects were depending on integral information about the time of the event, interviews conducted in the morning might be especially likely to be misremembered as having occurred on the previous day of the week and those conducted in the evening misassigned to the following day. There was no evidence for such a relation.

Apart from scale effects, method reports, and Huttenlocher et al.'s (1992) findings, a number of other phenomena support reconstructive theories (see Friedman, 1993, for a more thorough discussion). One finding from more than 15 laboratory experiments is that subjects are especially accurate in remembering the within-list position of items presented near the start of a list (e.g., Block, 1982; Guenther & Linton, 1975). The beginning of a list is a distinctive location but an arbitrary distance, so this phenomenon is consistent with remembering locations rather than distances. Another laboratory finding is that temporal judgments are more accurate in conditions where the stimulus lists or the background context has greater structure. An example is blocking the items of a stimulus list by different semantic categories (e.g., Tzeng & Cotton, 1980; Underwood, 1977). Again, this finding cannot be interpreted by distance-based theories of memory for time, but the findings seem to support the position that subjects are using the structure to abstract locations in time.

Finally, there is clear support from both laboratory studies and studies of memory for life events that when events are better remembered, subjects are more accurate in judging the times that they occurred (see Friedman, 1993). Most distance theories seem to imply that the temporal distance of well-remembered events should be underestimated, assuming that similar qualities, such as strength, underlie probability of remembering and apparent distance in the past; but they do not predict greater accuracy. Reconstructive theories can explain the greater accuracy of well-remembered events, because the more that is remembered about an event, the greater the likelihood that some of the information can be used to infer its probable location.

3. Conclusion

A substantial body of evidence supports the position that information about locations is responsible for much of our ability to judge the times of past events. All the phenomena described either are not predicted by distance theories or directly contradict their implications. Even laboratory studies designed to provide a context free of temporal structure, and thereby better reveal the properties of distance-based processes, provide strong evidence for the use of information about locations. Although the research literature weighs heavily in favor of location theories, there is no reason why humans' memory for time need be based on a single process. In the next section, I suggest reasons why the research literature provides so little support for distance theories and describe a series of studies on distance-based processes that have grown out of these ideas.

III. Distance Processes

A. THEORIES

Two main types of distance theories have been proposed to explain memory for the times of past events: chronological organization theories and strength theories. In chronological organization theories (Koffka, 1936; Murdock, 1974), episodic memory is presumed to be intrinsically organized according to the order in which events occur. The times of past events are judged by a kind of distance from the present in the memory store. This theory has been difficult to evaluate because most of its predictions can be explained by other theories as well (Friedman, 1993). However, one unique implication of the theory is that subjects should be able to remember the temporal contiguity of events even when the events are semantically unrelated (Friedman, 1993). If episodic memory is chronologically organized, it is reasonable to assume that one should be able to move backward or forward between adjacent events in the memory store, or at least that adjacent events should prime one another. Two studies provide data on memory for the temporal adjacency of personal experiences: Wagenaar's (1986) study of his memory for personal events from the past 6 years and Friedman and Huttenlocher's (1996) study of memory for the time when the television show *60 Minutes* broadcast particular stories. In both studies memory for temporal contiguity was very poor. In addition, Hintzman, Summers, & Block (1975) have shown that memory for the temporal contiguity of words in a list is poor. These findings, and logical considerations about the amount of time that would be needed to retrieve a memory under such a model (Brewer, 1996), render this type of theory implausible.

Strength theories assume that natural memory processes occurring with the passage of time create clues to the age of a memory. For example, Hinrichs (1970) proposed that the decay of traces, or the interference of later processing, results in progressively weaker traces, thus providing quantitative information about a memory's age (see also Anisfeld & Knapp, 1968; Morton, 1968). In a related theory, Brown et al. (1985) suggest that it is the number of propositions that we remember about an event that is used to gauge the event's distance in the past.

B. EVIDENCE

As mentioned in the previous section, even laboratory studies have provided little support for strength theories, and many laboratory findings contradict the implications of strength theories. Among the small body of supportive evidence is Block's (1982) finding that words from the first of two lists that received shallow (vs. deep) processing were more likely to be judged correctly as belonging to the first (vs. the second) list. The strength explanation is that words that are difficult to recognize at the time of the test would appear to belong to the more distant past. A related finding is that under some conditions pictures from a mixed set of words and pictures were better recognized and judged to be more recent than words of comparable distances in the past (Fozard & Weinert, 1972).

On a much longer timescale, Brown et al. (1985) asked separate groups of subjects (a) to rate how much they remembered about a set of news events (or to recall as many relevant facts as they could), and (b) to judge the recency of the events. In four studies the authors found significant, though usually weak, correlations between knowledge ratings or amount remembered, on the one hand, and how recently the events were judged to have occurred, on the other. However, a later study of news events (Kemp, 1988) and five experiments using personal events (Burt, 1992; Thompson, Skowronski, & Lee, 1988, Experiments 1–4) failed to replicate these findings.

C. LIMITATIONS OF THE EVIDENCE

The meager support for distance theories is not the result of an insufficient number of studies, nor is it an artifact of subjects being asked to provide judgments in the form of locations rather than distances. A substantial body of relevant evidence exists (Friedman, 1993), including many studies in which subjects are asked to judge distances in the past; it simply fails to show that distance-based information is an important cue to the times of past events. However, despite the large number of studies that have been conducted and the frequent request for judgments in the form of distances, it seems possible that the research literature has been restricted in ways that could bias subjects against using distance-based processes.

In formal studies of memory for time, where subjects are repeatedly asked to judge the times of past events—whether as positions in a list, dates, or temporal distances—they might reasonably assume that the experimenters wish them to be as precise as possible. This may lead subjects to use methods that experience has proven lead to the greatest accuracy. Probably most of us have discovered that impressions of distances are relatively imprecise for many purposes, whereas location-based approaches often yield accurate information. Few of us would rely exclusively on distance information in answering important questions about the time of a past event, say, in a criminal investigation; instead we would try to reconstruct the time as best we could based on what we remember and the information provided in the question. This does not mean that we do not have access to distance information, only that it may lack the resolution assumed, by convention, to be required in experiments and other formal contexts. Impressions of distance may play a greater role when it is not important to be accurate (e.g., deciding in which of two restaurants one has dined more recently) or when the scale is large relative to the true distance (e.g., deciding whether some quite recent event, say dining at a restaurant, has occurred within the past year).

If formal studies of memory for time produce a bias to use reconstruction and to avoid distance processes, special measures may be needed to demonstrate the use of distance processes and learn about their properties. Such measures might involve arranging conditions in which subjects would have difficulty reconstructing locations in the past. Three approaches using this strategy are employed in the studies that follow: testing children who are unlikely to be able to reconstruct locations on long timescales, testing adults with stimuli whose times should be difficult to reconstruct, and requiring adults to respond to memory-for-time questions so rapidly that they would have little time to reconstruct the locations of the events. These methods are used to demonstrate that distance-based processes do provide information about the times of past events on long timescales—on the order of days, weeks, and months. They also allow us to learn about the effects of true elapsed time on perceived distance in the past.

D. DEVELOPMENTAL STUDIES

Children develop representations of increasingly long time patterns as they grow older (Friedman, 1990a, Chap. 6). Long-scale patterns such as days of the week, months, and seasons are generally not grasped until after 5 years of age (Friedman, 1978, 1982), and the mental representations capturing these patterns change in important ways with development (Friedman, 1986). Because of their limited knowledge, it is very unlikely that preschool-age children can judge the times of past events on long timescales by retrieving their locations in the calendar or reconstructing their locations. Temporal judgment tasks that are trivial for adults, such as judging which of two holidays occurred more recently, are difficult even for many 8-year-old children (Friedman, 1992). Unless young children have some other source of temporal information available, they should answer questions about the times of past events on long timescales at chance levels of accuracy.

One possible source of temporal information is order codes. According to several theorists (Hintzman et al., 1975; Tzeng & Cotton, 1980; Tzeng, Lee, & Wetzel, 1979), the occurrence of certain events causes the retrieval of an older event, and the order of the two is stored automatically in memory. Research with adults has supported a prediction of order-code theories, that the order of presentation of pairs of items can be judged more accurately when the two items are meaningfully related (Hintzman et al., 1975; Tzeng & Cotton, 1980; Winograd & Soloway, 1985). There is little evidence on the age at which children can use order codes (McCormack, Russell, & Jarrold, 1995) and none in which long timescales are involved. However, the possibility remains that young children can use order codes to judge the order of pairs of events even when their locations cannot be reconstructed.

According to Friedman's (1993) analysis of theories of memory for time, the remaining possibility is distance information. Thus if one controls for the use of order codes, any success that young children show in judging the times of past events on long timescales would be the result of distance information. A first set of studies used this reasoning to test for the existence of distance-based processes in children.

1. Evidence for Distance-Based Processes

In a series of experiments (Friedman, 1991), I examined children's ability to discriminate the recency of two events, one presented 7 weeks and the other 1 week before the test day. The events were not linked to landmarks in the school year, and they were chosen to minimize the likelihood that the occurrence of the second event would remind children of the first. For these reasons it seemed that accurate judgments of their relative recency would depend on the availability of information about their distances in the past.

In the first two experiments, children of 4, 6, and 8 years of age were presented with two stimulus events. One event was a visit by a research assistant who videotaped the children in the playground during recess and showed them the videotape after recess. The second event was a lecture and demonstration of proper toothbrushing technique by the regular classroom teacher, using a large model tooth and toothbrush as props. No strangers were present during this demonstration to remind the children of the earlier event. A control group of children received the events in the reverse order. During the memory test, children were shown cards depicting the two events and asked which of the two was a long time ago and which a short time ago. Children were also asked to recall the day of the week, time of day, month, and season of the more distant of the two events.

Children in all the age groups, including the 4-year-olds, performed significantly above chance in discriminating the relative recency of the two events ($p < .01$ by the binomial test). The older groups were also significantly accurate in judging the time of day, month, and season of the older event, but the 4-year-olds were not. The inability of the 4-year-olds to judge the month or season of the older event suggests that their success on the relative recency task was unlikely to be due to the reconstruction of locations.

A third experiment controlled for extraneous factors that might have influenced the results of the first two experiments. For example, the stimulus events were selected to be sufficiently novel that there was almost no chance that children's judgments would be influenced by confusion with earlier, similar events. Another change was that children were queried about some of the details of the older event, to test for the possibility that they judged it to be a longer time ago because they had forgotten it. For most of the 4-, 6-, and 8-year-old children, the first stimulus event was an invented game involving taking photographs with a Polaroid camera and placing them on game board. The objects photographed were selected to aid reconstruction of the time (e.g., the sun in the sky, a green tree) and to serve among the memory items probed. The other event was a teacher-led science demonstration of sound transmission, using a metal rod which, when rubbed with a chamois cloth, emits a loud, high-pitched tone. Again, a control group received the events in the other order, and again this did not influence the relative recency judgments.

The children were very accurate in judging the relative recency of the stimulus events in each age group (binomial $p < .001$). They also showed excellent memory for a number of the details of the photo game, including the location where it took place and the gender of the person who played it. These findings show that children's ability to discriminate the relative recencies was not the result simply of forgetting the older event.

Even with the provision of special cues to aid reconstruction, the 4-year-olds were unable to recall the season, month, or day of the week of the first event, whereas older children were accurate for month. The 4-year-olds were even unable to identify the current season, month, or day of the week, supporting the conclusion that their success on the relative recency question was not a product of reconstructing locations. Interestingly, though, with the more sensitive time-of-day question used in this experiment, the 4-year-olds were able to reconstruct when during the day the photo game had been played (in the morning, the only time that they attended school). Of course, time-of-day information would be useless in discriminating the relative recencies of the stimulus events. But the finding does show that even young children are capable of reconstructing past locations when they possess appropriately differentiated representations on a given timescale (see Friedman, 1990b).

These experiments demonstrate that children are capable of discriminating the times of 1- and 7-week-old events, even when they were unable to reconstruct locations on a relevant scale and even when the events were unlikely to be related by order codes. If one accepts the premises that location and order-code information were controlled and that only three kinds of information are used in memory for time, then these results support the conclusion that humans can use distance information to discriminate the times of past events on long timescales. The remaining developmental studies were designed to learn more about the temporal properties of distance-based processes.

2. The Effects of Elapsed Time on Judgments of Relative Recency

In this section I describe a series of studies in which the times of the stimuli ranged from recent days to many months in the past. This allows us to learn about the ability to discriminate times from a much broader range of distances in the past. We have already established that 1- and 7-week-old events can be discriminated, but we cannot tell whether the times of events are discriminable for other distances in the past. For example, it is possible that the nearer event must be within the past several weeks or that the ratio of the two distances must be below some value for the distances to be discriminable.

There are no other data that allow us to predict the effects of elapsed time on distance-based judgments, because all the stimuli used in studies of adults' time memory on these timescales would have allowed the possibility of reconstructing locations. There is also little theoretical basis for making predictions about distance effects. The few relevant models were designed to account for results on the brief timescales of laboratory studies. In one model (Muter, 1979), subjects are assumed to scan backwards in a temporally organized memory store. This model implies that accuracy in recency comparison tasks will be affected only by the distance of the nearer of two events to be compared, which is what Muter found for his tasks. Alternatively, strength theorists (e.g., Hinrichs, 1970) usually presume that subjects must evaluate the distance-related quantities of each stimulus event and that these quantities decay at a decelerating rate with the passage of time. For comparisons of relative recency, this implies that the ratio of the two distances will better predict accuracy than the distance of the nearer event alone. But neither model provides any indication of how rapidly distance information decays to an asymptote at which differentiated information is no longer available. Do events continue to appear recent beyond the 1 week of the Friedman (1991) experiments? Can the times of events that occurred 1 or more months in the past still be discriminated from much older events?

In the three studies that follow (Friedman, Gardner, & Zubin, 1995), my students and I investigated children's comparisons of pairs of events from the past year, with large variation in the distances of the events. For practical reasons we used naturally occurring events as stimuli: the child's birthday and holidays. The samples included children who, by virtue of their young age, were very unlikely to have been able to answer the questions accurately using knowledge of the calendar.

In the first study, 718 children between 3 and 12 years of age were asked to judge which was a longer time ago, their birthday or Christmas, and to explain their answers. Testing took place during September, October, and November, so Christmas was between about 9 and 11 months in the past. Children's birthdays, of course, were distributed over the whole year, so by comparing the accuracy of children with different birth dates, we were able to examine the effects of distance on accuracy. Adults, and any age group who possess adequate knowledge of the calendar, would show no such effects: We would provide the correct answer no matter what our birthday. But children who cannot retrieve and integrate information about the locations of the two events would be forced to rely on order codes or cues to the events' distances in the past. Order codes are problematic for cyclic events, and can lead to errors, as we will see. Thus accurate performance for children below some age level should depend on the presence of discriminable information about the two distances in the past.

Figure 1 shows the proportion of children who judged their birthday to be more recent as a function of the distance of their birthday in the past. Curves are plotted separately for children less than and greater than 9 years of age, a near-equal split of the sample. Distances are grouped into

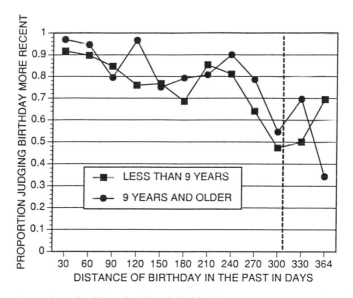

Fig. 1. Proportion of subjects judging their birthday more recent as a function of the distance of birthdays in the past. The mean distance of Christmas is indicated by the dotted line. Reprinted from Friedman, Gardner, & Zubin (1995) by permission of The Society for Research in Child Development.

30-day categories; the actual mean distances per category are roughly 15 days, 45 days, and so on. The dotted line shows the mean distance of Christmas in the past. Because the actual distance of Christmas varied substantially across subjects, the data for birthdays near Christmas are depicted separately in Fig. 2. The October, November, and December categories in this figure only include children whose birthdays were a longer time ago than Christmas. For these three categories, correct responses would lead to means closer to zero, whereas for January, February, and March, accurate judgments are reflected in means closer to 1.

Because of the substantial numbers of errors, it is evident that neither age group was consistently able to use calendar locations to answer the question. The clear decrement in accuracy as birthdays recede in the past is also difficult to explain on the basis of order codes, so it seems likely that these data tell us about the temporal properties of distance-based judgments. Distances of an event from the past several months are readily discriminated from the distance of an event that occurred 9 to 11 months

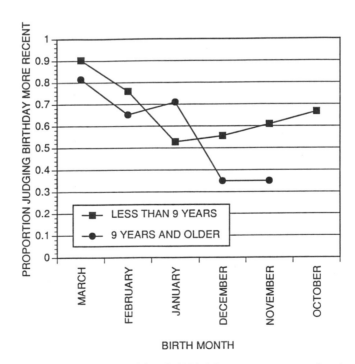

Fig. 2. Proportion of subjects judging their birthday more recent as a function of birth month. Reprinted from Friedman, Gardner, & Zubin (1995) by permission of The Society for Research in Child Development.

ago. The ability to discriminate such distances is well developed even in the youngest age groups: 4- and 5-year-olds were 94% correct when their birthdays fell within the past 2 months (binomial $p < .001$).

The question of how best to describe the relation between event distances and accuracy will be postponed until we examine data from other reference points within the year. But several other findings from this study are worth noting. First, Fig. 2 shows that children younger than 9 years actually tended to display below-chance levels of accuracy when their birthdays were longer ago than Christmas. This and similar data to be presented suggest that young children face special problems answering this question when their birthday is close in the future. The difficulty may be in interpreting the terms used in the question ("a short time ago" and "a long time ago") as referring only to the past or it may be the absence of a cyclic representation of the year (Friedman, 1977, 1986). Second, explanations consistent with an order-code model (e.g., "My birthday is after [or before] Christmas") were given by nearly 20% of subjects. They were especially common when a child's birthday was within about a month or two of Christmas. It may be that this information is the product of some automatic property of memory, as order-code theorists maintain, but it seems equally likely that children simply memorize their parents' answers to a frequently asked question, "When will it be my birthday/Christmas?" In any case these sorts of answers were associated with especially inaccurate answers to the main question, so order codes cannot account for the high levels of accuracy when birthdays fall in the recent past.

In a second study, we repeated the procedure with 255 children of the ages of the younger group in the first study. However, in this study testing took place between April 22 and 30. The change of testing dates allows us to make sure that the presumed distance effects in the first study are not really due to the locations of particular birth months (e.g., children with late summer or early fall birthdays might be especially accurate). The change also allows us to examine particular distances of nearer events when these are different ratios of the farther distance than in the first study. For example, a birthday 3 months in the past would have a ratio of about .30 in the first study but about .67 in the second.

Figure 3 shows the results. Again, children whose birthdays had occurred within the last 2 or 3 months were very accurate. However, the slope for children whose birthdays were more recent than Christmas (to the left of the dotted line) was significantly steeper ($p < .05$) than the corresponding slope in Fig. 1. This suggests that the distance of the farther event also influences accuracy, perhaps in a way described by the ratio of the distances. But the ratio of the two distances cannot explain the flattening of the curve for birthdays beyond about 240 days in the past: When birthdays are more

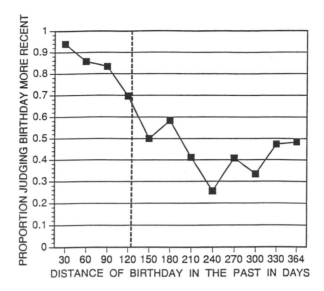

Fig. 3. Proportion of subjects judging their birthday more recent as a function of the distance of birthdays in the past. The mean distance of Christmas is indicated by the dotted line. Reprinted from Friedman, Gardner, & Zubin (1995) by permission of The Society for Research in Child Development.

than twice the distance of Christmas, it should become easier to detect the greater recency of Christmas. A contributing factor may be the difficulty that many children have judging a near-future birthday to be "a long time ago." Finally, as in the first study, children with November and December birthdays were especially inaccurate. The close precedence probably leads to the retrieval of the confusing information that one's birthday is before Christmas.

As in the first study, the frequent errors render it unlikely that these children were relying on representations of calendar locations. Instead, the findings are probably attributable primarily to the properties of distance-based processes. Furthermore, the fact that findings were similar with a different range of testing dates reassures us that the results of the first study were attributable to distances, not particular locations in the year. It appears that when we rely on impressions of distances to compare the times of two events, the distances of both events influence accuracy. This is consistent with the implication of strength models that the strengths of two traces would need to be compared to solve relative recency tasks. In contrast, if backward scanning models were correct, only the distance of the nearer event would affect performance. It also appears that linear decay models cannot provide a full account of the data. Linear decay models imply that it is the absolute temporal separation of the events that should determine their discriminability, not the ratio of their distances. The first point in Fig. 3 and the sixth or seventh points in Fig. 1 are both about the same absolute distance from Christmas, but accuracy is substantially greater in the former case, where the ratio of the distances is smaller.

However, comparison of Figs. 1 and 3 shows that ratio of distances cannot provide a complete account of these findings. Children were less accurate in Study 2 when Christmas was 4 months ago and their birthdays were about 9 months ago than when the two events were the reversed distances in Study 1. One explanation is that in addition to solving the problem by comparing two quantitities that decay at a decelerating rate, children have a bias to perceive their birthday as more recent. This interpretation is supported by the results of the third study, which provides additional evidence about the effects of event distances on accuracy.

In Friedman et al.'s (1995) Study 3, we tested a group of children of ages similar to those of Study 2 shortly before and shortly after Christmas (December 8 to 15 and January 26 to February 3). In addition to the usual birthday–Christmas question, they were asked a similar question about Halloween and Thanksgiving at each testing time.

Accuracy on the birthday–Christmas question was very poor at the pre-Christmas testing, even for birthdays from the past 2 or 3 months, and there were no discernible distance effects. The only noticeable effect was a slight tendency to judge one's birthday to be more recent. It appears that the close future proximity of Christmas disrupted children's ability to compare the previous Christmas with another event, much as birthdays in the near future created difficulties in Studies 1 and 2. However, 79% of the children were correct on the Halloween–Thanksgiving question at the pre-Christmas testing, when Thanksgiving was an average of 16 days ago and Halloween an average of 40 days ago. Even children below 6 years of age were significantly accurate (binomial $p < .0001$). Clearly, the ability to discriminate past distances is not restricted to events as important as one's birthday and Christmas, a conclusion also supported by Friedman's (1991) study of events in school.

The findings for the birthday–Christmas comparison at the post-Christmas testing are shown in Fig. 4. The first thing to notice is the relatively low level of accuracy for children whose birthdays fell within the 30 days before the test. The fact that the comparison item, Christmas, was only an average of 36 days in the past led to significantly lower levels of accuracy than for the 30-day category in Study 2 ($\chi^2[1, N = 55] = 4.78, p < .05$). Apparently, children had difficulty discriminating the distance information associated with their birthday from that of Christmas. This is consistent with

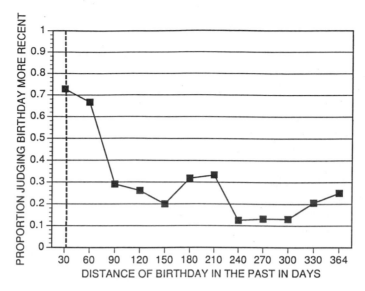

Fig. 4. Proportion of subjects judging their birthday more recent as a function of the distance of birthdays in the past. The mean distance of Christmas is indicated by the dotted line. Reprinted from Friedman, Gardner, & Zubin (1995) by permission of The Society for Research in Child Development.

the position that children are comparing two distance-related quantities and inconsistent with backward scanning models, which would predict that only the distance of the nearer event would influence accuracy. Another finding is that children whose birthdays fell just before Christmas (see the 60-day category) usually judged their birthday to be more recent. This may be due to the interference of retrieving the fact that one's birthday closely precedes Christmas.

Beyond the 60-day category, there is a sharp decrease to an apparent asymptote of approximately .20 of subjects judging their birthday to be more recent. This is quite a high accuracy level, and it shows that children of this age can detect the greater recency of Christmas when it was about 36 days in the past and their birthdays were more than 60 days ago. The asymptote occurs once the ratios of the two distances have fallen below about .30. The failure to approach a proportion of 0 judging their birthday to be more recent may be attributable to the birthday bias.

Distance effects were also present for the Halloween–Thanksgiving comparisons. At the post-Christmas testing, when Thanksgiving was an average of 66 days in the past and Halloween 90 days ago, children's accuracy fell to .68. Again, even children below 6 years were significantly accurate (binomial $p < .01$), but the decrease in accuracy from the pre-Christmas testing was significant (binomial $p < .02$). Given the constant separation of the two holidays, we cannot tell whether the decline is associated with the decrease in the distance of the nearer event (from a mean of 16 to 66 days), as a backward scanning model would predict, or the increase in the mean ratio of distances (from .40 to .73), as an asymptotic decay model would predict. However, the data seem inconsistent with linear decay models, in which a constant separation should remain equally discriminable in the recent and more remote past.

Additional data on the comparison of the recency of two events from the past year come from a fourth study, Friedman, Kemp, Fifield, Goodson, and Sidey's (1995) study of 821 5- to 7-year-old children from Christchurch, New Zealand. Children were tested between November 2 and December 7. The 111 children tested before November 5, Guy Fawkes Day, were asked to compare their birthday and Christmas. The remaining children compared their birthday and Guy Fawkes Day. The former group showed accuracy levels significantly greater than chance (binomial $p < .0001$) and distance effects similar to those found for the children in Friedman, Gardner, and Zubin's (1995) Study 1. Proportions correct for the distance categories 0–90 days, 91–180 days, and 181–270 days were .88, .76, and .72 respectively. With birthdays from the past 3 months and a comparison event about 11 months before the test, children were able to detect the greater recency of birthdays from the past 3 months with high levels of accuracy. The 710 children who compared their birthday to Guy Fawkes day were also able to discriminate the two distances (proportion correct = .78, binomial $p < .0001$), and even 5-year-olds, considered separately, were significantly accurate (binomial $p < .0001$). Accuracy decreased over the 4 1/2 weeks of testing, but a better predictor of accuracy was the ratio of the distances of the nearer event, whether one's birthday or Guy Fawkes Day, to the farther event. Ratio was a significant predictor in a logistic regression analysis ($\chi^2[1, N = 710] = 12.15, p < .001$).

The results of these four studies, like those of Friedman (1991), show that children as young as 4 and 5 years of age can discriminate the distances of events on long timescales. This suggests that distance-based judgments of past times depend on early-developing properties of human memory. Friedman, Gardner, and Zubin's (1995) and Friedman, Kemp, Fifield, Goodson, and Sidey's (1995) data also show strong effects of the distances of the stimulus events in the past. These effects are better described by considering the distances of both stimulus events than by the distance of the nearer event alone. This is consistent with the view that children are comparing two distance-related quantities. The ratio of the two distances appears to be a good predictor of accuracy, whereas absolute separation does not. These findings support the inference that children are comparing two quantities that decay at a decelerating rate with the passage of time.

3. Direct Scaling of Elapsed Time

In a final, unpublished developmental study, I investigated young children's ability to judge the distances of individual events in the past rather than the relative recency of two events. Of course young children cannot judge intervals of time in conventional units, but in an earlier study I found that they can discriminate the magnitudes of intervals of time veridically if time is represented spatially (Friedman, 1990b). The spatial representation used in the present study was a 55-cm board placed on a table at a 45° angle to the child. During pretraining children were taught that the near end of the board represents times that were a short time ago, and a picture of "getting to school today" was placed there. Next, a picture of "when you learned to walk" was placed at the far end of the board, and this was labeled "a very long time ago." After further, similar labeling of different ranges of distances, children placed, one at a time, cards representing six stimulus events: the child's birthday, Valentine's Day, Christmas, Thanksgiving, Halloween, and last summer. The order of the six was randomly determined, and children repeated their placements in the same order. Subjects were 162 preschool children, with a mean age of 4.86 years. Testing took place between March 2 and May 2.

Rating scores were the placements in cm from the near end of the board; high values represent times farther in the past, and 27.5 is the midpoint. The mean correlation between a stimulus's ratings on trial 1 and trial 2 was $r = .565$, indicating that children were moderately reliable in their use of the scale. Figure 5 shows the mean placements as a function of the average distance of an event in the past. Children's birthdays are grouped in 30-day distance categories, and the values on the x-axis are the actual mean distances for the categories. The location of summer was assumed to be July 15.

The curve for birthdays shows that birthdays from about the past 2 months and those that are coming within the next 3 months are judged as a shorter time ago than birthdays from 3 to 9 months in the past. A one-way analysis of variance (ANOVA) showed that distance category was a significant influence on rating score ($F[11, 150] = 2.95$, $p < .01$), and there was strong evidence of a quadratic trend ($F[1, 150] = 17.25$, $p < .001$). Looking at the left half of the curve, it appears that birthdays rise to an asymptote after the fourth data point, suggesting that differentiated distance information is available through about 4 to 5 months, but distances of about 5 to 9 months seem to be undifferentiated. Interestingly, there is also no

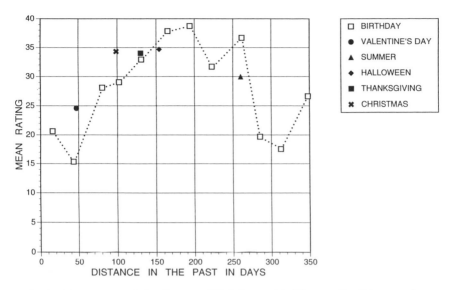

Fig. 5. Mean ratings of the distance of birthdays and holidays on the distance scale as a function of their mean actual distance.

evidence that birthdays of 30 to 60 days in the past are subjectively less recent than birthdays from the past 30 days.

Differentiated information about distances in the past was also available for the holiday stimuli. Tukey tests revealed that Valentine's Day, which was an average of 45 days in the past, was judged to be significantly more recent than Christmas, Thanksgiving, and Halloween ($p < .01$), and summer ($p < .05$). Surprisingly, there was also a trend for summer to receive lower ratings than the mean of Christmas, Thanksgiving, and Halloween. It may be that late in the school year many children knew that summer was coming soon and made the same sort of error as for upcoming birthdays. Another feature of the holiday ratings that warrants mention is that several seem to fall above birthday ratings for comparable distances. Perhaps the subjective recency of events is influenced not only by their times of occurrence but by their salience, a factor that might account for the birthday bias shown in the studies of relative recency.

This study shows that young children can translate their impressions of subjective distances in the past into spatial representations. More importantly, these impressions of the times of events that occurred over extended periods of time are differentiated and partially veridical. The results also provide a useful supplement to the relative recency findings for learning about the temporal properties of distance-based processes. The data suggest that events from the past 2 months strike young children as very recent, those from 3 to 4 months ago as moderately recent, and more distant events as even longer ago and mainly undifferentiated from one another.

The evidence presented in this section shows that distance-based processes provide humans with a sense of the times of past events on a scale ranging up to many months in the past. Young children, who know virtually nothing about relative times of occurrence in the calendar year (e.g., Friedman, 1977, 1992), are able to make differentiated judgments about the distances of events in the past. After considering related data from adult subjects, we will attempt to describe the findings on distance effects in the combined set of studies and consider the role of distance-based processes in humans' memory for time.

E. STUDIES OF ADULTS

Because of their rich knowledge of the calendar and a large number of temporal patterns, causal relations, and the dates of significant events, adults are able to provide accurate estimates of the temporal locations of many personal and public events. It is common in the research literature to find significantly accurate, though not precise, estimates for events that range up to many years in the past (Friedman, 1993). However, there are no data that tell us about adults' sense of past times when they rely on distance-based processes alone. In this section I report a series of studies that use methods designed to make it difficult for adults to benefit from their knowledge of locations in the past.

1. Difficult-to-Localize Events

One way to study distance-based processes in adults is to choose stimulus events whose times should be difficult to reconstruct. For practical purposes, the events must be memorable and distinctive if we are to ask subjects to judge their times long after they occur. But the stimuli must also be free of the differentiated semantic and contextual associations that lead to the reconstruction of locations in the past. In a pair of studies, Friedman and Huttenlocher (1996) selected as stimuli stories that were broadcast on the weekly television news magazine *60 Minutes.*

60 Minutes is broadcast each Sunday evening for one hour and contains three unrelated stories per week. The stories focus on a variety of topics, including crimes, celebrities, and exposés of fraud or misconduct. Most stories are not linked to contemporaneous events and would be germane at least over a period of several years. Furthermore, most viewers probably watch the show in a relatively unchanging context: in the same room, with the same people, and as part of a Sunday-evening routine. The poverty of differentiated contextual or news associations seem to make this content a good choice for studying memory on long timescales, under conditions where reconstruction of locations is unlikely.

In the first study, subjects estimated the times of *60 Minutes* stories that had been broadcast during about the past 9 months. We eliminated from the pool *60 Minutes* stories that had been broadcast before and those that were related to contemporaneous stories in the news. Participants were also asked to provide estimates for a set of major news events from the same period. The news events served as a control condition in which subjects should have access to information that could help them reconstruct locations. In order to find sufficient numbers of regular *60 Minutes* viewers who were willing to participate in our study, we telephoned large numbers of households in middle-class and affluent suburbs of Cleveland and Chicago. The 82 participants (mean age = 50 years) received both news and *60 Minutes* conditions, with order counterbalanced. During the interview subjects were read descriptions of the stories or news events, asked to rate their confidence that they saw the *60 Minutes* story (or learned of the news event when it occurred) on a scale of 1 to 3, and asked to estimate its time. We accepted either distances (e.g., 2 months ago) or locations (e.g., last January), but if estimates were too imprecise (e.g., a season) we asked subjects to provide another estimate in weeks, months, or years ago. All estimates were converted to distances in the past in days. These distances were log-transformed because of the large positive skew, and antilogs of the means are used in the figures and analyses.

Figure 6 presents the mean estimates as a function of the mean true distance for each of the 30-day distance categories for the news events. Only one news event happened to be between 180 and 210 days in the past, so this point is omitted. Figure 7 is a similar plot for the *60 Minutes* stories.

Figure 6 shows a linear function with a slope of near 1 for the news events, with the exception of the 270-day category. The decrease at this distance was due to a single news event, the meeting between Rabin and Arafat at the White House. (The next most frequently presented news event from the same category received a mean rating of 328 days.) The Rabin–Arafat event was estimated to be less than 60 days in the past by 16 of the 52 subjects who received this event, apparently because they confused the target event with the May 4, 1994 meeting between the same two leaders in Cairo to sign a self-rule agreement. When this event is excluded, the correlation for the remaining seven points is $r = .97$, and the best-fitting linear equation is $Y = .92(X) - 5.90$. These findings show that subjects were very accurate in judging the times of major news events from the past 9 months. The findings for the news condition are consistent with those of past studies of news events, which show substantial accuracy over

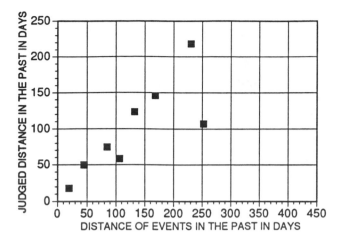

Fig. 6.   Antilog of the mean log distance estimates as a function of the distance of the news events in the past.

periods of years. For example, Ferguson and Martin's (1983) study used major news events ranging up to 2 to 5 years in the past and found correlations between estimates and true dates of $r = .91$ to .97 and slopes of .54 to .79.

In contrast, Fig. 7 shows little differentiation in the estimates of the times of the *60 Minutes* stories. With the exception of the 30-day category, the

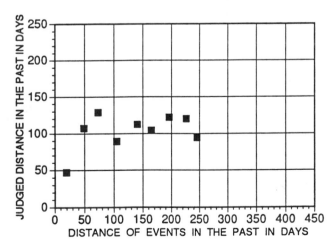

Fig. 7.   Antilog of the mean of log distance estimates as a function of the distance of the *60 Minutes* stories in the past in the first study.

means show a flat curve centering around approximately 100 days in the past. The correlation between true distance and estimated distance for all nine points is $r = .03$. The best-fitting linear equation is $Y = .01(X) + 89.30$. Subjects who received a story from the past 30 days did show significantly shorter estimates for this story than their mean for stories that were longer ago, $t(11) = 2.50$, $p < .03$. This suggests that stories from about the past month are subjectively more recent than older events, although the mean estimated distance of nearly 50 days shows that even here there is little precision. Stories 2 to 9 months old seem to most subjects to belong to an interval of about 3 to 5 months in the past, but the interval is essentially undifferentiated.

One reason the news estimates were much more accurate could be that the news stories were better recognized. In fact, average recognition ratings were substantially greater for news events than *60 Minutes* stories. However, when we repeated the analyses using only trials on which only the highest recognition rating was given, the correlation coefficients and regression equations showed little change.

We conducted a second study to provide more refined information about the effect of elapsed time on estimates of *60 Minutes* stories. Fifty-three subjects were tested on a similar procedure, but in this study we eliminated news events and increased the number of *60 Minutes* stimuli, to provide denser sampling from the recent past and stories from the previous broadcast season. Each subject received, in random order, stories from the most recent Sunday (referred to as 0 weeks ago), 1, 2, 3, 4, 6, 10, 14, 18, 22, and 26 weeks ago, and three stories from about 1 year ago.

Figure 8 presents the mean estimates for the 14 distance categories (the three rightmost points are nearly superimposed). With greater sampling of recent stories and the inclusion of stories from about 1 year ago, the correlation coefficient describing these points, $r = .89$, is much greater than the corresponding coefficient for the *60 Minutes* stories in the first study ($r = .03$). However, the best-fitting linear equation is nearly as flat as that in Study 1, $Y = .17(X) + 37.88$. Examination of the points for distances less than about 60 days shows a discontinuity in the curve, similar to the difference between the 30-day category and the remaining categories in Fig. 7. The addition of a quadratic term to the linear equation increases the variance explained from $R^2 = .79$ to $R^2 = .86$. If the six points of less than 60 days are analyzed separately, the best-fitting linear equation becomes $Y = .96(X) + 15.04$.

To provide inferential tests of the distance effect in Fig. 8 without violating independence assumptions, we conducted within-subjects t-tests between the means for three ranges of distances: less than 60 days, 10 to 26 weeks, and about 1 year ago. The first two means, $t(41) = 4.16$, $p < .001$,

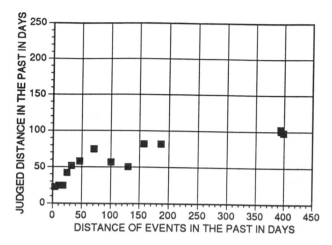

Fig. 8.   Antilog of the mean of log distance estimates as a function of the distance of the *60 Minutes* stories in the past in the second study.

and the second two means, $t(37) = 3.12, p < .01$, differ significantly. Taken together with the descriptive regression analyses, these findings support the following pattern: Generally accurate distance judgments are made for stories from about the past 1 to 2 months. Beyond this there is little differentiation for distances through 6 months, although stories of about 1 year ago are perceived as somewhat more distant than those of 6 months ago. In contrast to the news events in Study 1 (Fig. 6), but like the *60 Minutes* stories in Study 1 (Fig. 7), the ages of stories in this study are greatly underestimated once they are older than about 100 days. It appears that when subjects rely on impressions of distance alone, the subjective ages of events increase little with the passage of time once they are 2 to 3 months in the past.

The distance function found here differs somewhat from the curve obtained when young children gave metric estimates of the distances of their birthdays in the past (Fig. 5). First, the adults showed considerable differentiation within the past 60 days, whereas children in the 31- to 60-day category did not judge their birthdays to be a longer time ago than children in the 1- to 30-day category. However, it is difficult to know how much confidence to place in this difference, because the number of children in a given distance category is relatively small. It also appears that an asymptote is reached at a somewhat shorter distance, about 60 days, in the adult data than in the study with young children, where it appears to set in at about 120 days. Given the differences in methods, stimuli, and samples, it is difficult to know the reason for this disagreement. However, it is notable that despite these many differences a similar function is found for distance estimates on long timescales: an interval of rapid change extending several months in the past, followed by an interval where perceived distance changes little with real distance. Although decelerating decay functions are usually assumed in strength theories, these studies may provide the first indication of the involvement of such a function in distance-based judgments of time and of the temporal parameters of the function.

2. Time-Pressured Judgments

The remaining studies are based on the premise that reconstruction of locations in the past takes more time than the assessment of cues to the age of a memory. This assumption follows from Friedman's (1993) characterization of location-based and distance-based approaches to remembering the times of past events: an active search for information that can constrain the location of an event in the past, and a rapid assessment of distance information. Location-based approaches are assumed to be relatively slow because, unless a date happens to be associated with an event, we must activate contextual associations, search for temporally relevant information among these associations, and interpret that information in light of our semantic knowledge of time patterns. In contrast, distance-based processes are assumed to involve assessing a global quantity, such as the strength or elaborateness of a memory trace. If location-based approaches require more time to execute, then the imposition of brief time limits or the instruction to answer rapidly may lead adults to respond on the basis of their impressions of distances in the past, even with stimuli whose times could be reconstructed (and even in formal experiments, where the goal of precision may be implicit). This method was used in two kinds of studies, comparisons of the relative recency for two events and yes–no judgments of whether a single stimulus falls within a particular distance in the past.

I have conducted three unpublished studies in which subjects were asked to compare rapidly the relative recency of two events from the past year. The subjects were large numbers of undergraduates, 298, 656, and 954 in the three studies, who each made between two and four such judgments. I chose to limit the number of judgments per subject so that they would be less likely to develop a "set" to be precise and also in the hope that they would not activate a representation of the past year that would be used to relate events to locations. Typical instructions were "to respond rapidly, relying on your immediate impressions of which of the two events was a longer/shorter time ago." Stimuli were presented on a computer monitor, and subjects responded by pulling one of two levers. In the first study, subjects compared pairs of events from the academic calendar. One was the spring vacation and the other was either a winter intersemester session or the previous summer. Testing took place in the 51 days after the spring vacation, with comparison data from the second study, conducted in the fall. In the second study, the main stimuli were the subject's birthday and Christmas. Stimuli in the third study were selected to be more difficult to localize. They were news events which, according to a pilot survey, met some minimum level of recognition.

These studies have all resulted in a substantial number of errors, demonstrating that time pressure interferes with location-based solutions. More important, the numbers of errors are related to the distances of the stimuli in the past, although the functions are somewhat noisy. The noisiness of the data may be due to the fact that subjects had too few trials to accommodate to the procedure. However, it is worth noting that higher ratios of the closer to the farther distance were significantly associated with lower accuracy in all the studies (and longer response times (RTs) in most of them). The influence of the distance of the farther event is especially evident in a subset of the news data in which the maximum distance of the farther event was about 100 days. Even here accuracy drops off substantially as the distance of the nearer event approaches that of the farther event, whereas in the other studies, accuracy declines do not set in until greater distances. These findings indicate that both distances influence accuracy, weighing against backward scanning models.

In the final studies, subjects were asked to judge whether or not news events had occurred within the last year. Again, by using pressure to respond rapidly, this time in the form of strict time limits, we decreased the likelihood that subjects would be able to reconstruct the locations of the stimuli. The switch to a single stimulus per trial was motivated by a desire to reduce the contribution of reading times to performance; in the previously mentioned study of comparisons of news events, in which phrase-length descriptions of each of two events had to be read, mean RTs were often about 4 s. News stimuli were selected because, in contrast to birthdays, holidays, and landmarks in the academic calendar, their locations could not be retrieved as dates but would require reconstruction if a location-based approach were to be used.

In the first, unpublished study, 34 undergraduates were presented with phrase-length descriptions of about 70 news events and asked to decide rapidly whether an event was from the past year or had happened a longer time ago. In an untimed post-test, subjects rated each item on the confidence they had in recognizing it. Ten of the events were between 2 and 3 years old, and the remainder were from about the past 9 months. Subjects had 1750 msec to read an item, decide whether it had occurred within the past year, and respond by pressing one of two keys. They reported that the task was very difficult, and exceeded the time limit and received the "too late" signal on about 25% of trials. The actual mean response time for nontimeout trials was less than 1,300 ms.

Despite the difficulty of the task—the mean proportion correct was .63—subjects were significantly more accurate than chance levels in making the discrimination, even for the minority of items from more than one year ago ($t[33] = 3.55$, $p < .001$). This finding suggests that the subjective distances of events from the past 9 months are discriminable from those of events from several years ago. There were also the usual distance effects for the news stories from the past 9 months. Mean accuracy for stories from the past 90 days was .73, for 91 to 180 days .54, and for 181 to 270 days .63. An ANOVA showed that these three means differed significantly ($F[2,66] = 11.00$, $p < .001$). Planned comparisons revealed that accuracy decreased from the first to the second distance category ($t[66] = 4.42$, $p < .001$). There was also a weak but significant increase from the second to the third category ($t[66] = 1.93$, $p < .05$). Distance effects were found even when controlling for the recognizability of news stories. If we restrict consideration only to items with recognition scores of 4 or 5 on a 5-point scale, the means for the three 90-day distance categories are .85, .74, and .76 ($F[2,54] = 6.18$, $p < .01$). Here there is no increase in accuracy from the second to the third distance category, suggesting that the corresponding difference for the unselected stories might have been an artifact of differences in recognizability. Because there was a constant reference distance, 1 year in the past, we cannot tell whether these distance effects are due to the absolute distance of the news stories in the past or the increasing ratios of the stimuli to the distance of the reference point. But in either case there is the suggestion of an asymptotic function in the finding of no decrease in accuracy from the second to the third 90-day category.

Finally, a subsample of subjects who filled out a method questionnaire rated the vividness of the events as a more frequent approach than other listed methods, including those involving reconstruction. Ratings of vividness were followed by another distance-based approach, relying on the amount remembered about an event. These findings are notable because subjects rarely report such distance-based methods in studies of memory for time (e.g., Thompson, Skowronski, & Lee, 1987).

In another, unpublished study, conducted with Simon Kemp, subjects performed a similar task with news events and also judged whether or not particular historical events, whose actual dates ranged up to several centuries in the past, had occurred in the twentieth century. The times of historical events, of course, could only be known as locations, not as elapsed times in one's own life, so they served as a control condition. On a post-test questionnaire, subjects again gave the clarity of memories higher ratings than any of the other methods for the news events, and the mean rating was significantly higher than the same method for the historical-events condition. The second-highest ratings in the news condition again went to another distance-related process, relying on the amount remembered about an event, and this method also received significantly higher ratings in the news than in the historical-event condition. In contrast, a location-based approach, remembering the dates, was significantly more strongly endorsed in the historical-events condition. These introspective data suggest that time-pressured tasks are successful in biasing subjects to rely on impressions of the distances of personally experienced events in the past. They also indicate that vividness, and to a lesser extent amount remembered, are involved in distance-based judgments.

The results from this series of studies support the conclusion that adults have access to distance information, even for events whose locations could be retrieved or reconstructed. The results from the studies in which adults judged which of two events was more recent are compatible with the findings from children's judgments of the relative recency: Higher ratios of distances are associated with a greater proportion of errors. The findings of the studies with single stimuli are also compatible with an asymptotic decay function. These studies, like Friedman and Huttenlocher's (1996) second study, also show that some differentiated information about the ages of memories is present beyond the past several months. Subjects were significantly accurate in discriminating the ages of news events from the past 9 months from those of events from more than 2 years ago. Finally, subjects in the single-stimulus studies reported using the vividness of the news events to judge their times in the past. This suggests that some strengthlike quantity is available to adults and can be used to differentiate the times of past events.

F.   THE NATURE OF DISTANCE-BASED PROCESSES

The findings from the developmental and adult studies support a number of conclusions about the characteristics of distance-based processes in humans' memory for time. When children or adults compare the times of two events using distance processes, the distances of both events influence accuracy. This makes it unlikely that we simply scan backward in time in some temporally organized memory store until encountering a representation of one of the events. Instead, it appears that we engage in a true comparison of two distance-related quantities. Several findings from the paired-comparison studies showed that events of constant separations become more difficult to discriminate as the pair recedes further in the past. This is inconsistent with at least some models in which subjects are comparing two distance-related quantitites that decay at a constant rate. The ratio of the nearer to the farther distance provides a better account of accuracy than absolute separation, and this is consistent with models in which subjects are comparing the magnitudes of two asymptotically decaying quantities.

The developmental and adult studies in which magnitude estimates were obtained also support asymptotic decay functions. The fact that a similar function seems to be present where no comparison was involved suggests that the function corresponds to the nature of the underlying information and is not an artifact of the comparison operation. The scaling studies showed that differentiated information about the times of events was available for the past several months, but after about 2 to 4 months in the past, there was little increase in the subjective ages of events with increases in true distance. However, the curve does not become flat at this distance. The second *60 Minutes* study indicated that discriminations can be made between events from the past 9 months and events that are 13 months in the past. A similar conclusion is supported by the single-event news studies, which showed that the ages of events from about the past 9 months can be discriminated from those of events from about 2 to 3 years ago.

These direct-scaling data can also be used to estimate a kind of "psychophysical function" relating subjective distance to true elapsed time for events ranging from the past weeks to about 1 year ago. One estimate comes from the study in which young children judged the distances of events in the past by placing cards on a board. I used the birthday data from Fig. 5, excluding the three rightmost points which seemed to reflect the influence of upcoming birthdays. The best-fitting power function has an exponent of .2834, $R^2 = .70$. The other estimate comes from Friedman and Huttenlocher's (1995) second study (Fig. 8). Here the exponent is .3532, $R^2 = .88$. Despite the many differences between the two studies, both produce reasonably good fits of the data with power functions that have exponents of about .30. These asymptotic functions differ markedly from the function found in the news condition of Friedman and Huttenlocher's first study, which has an exponent of .9620, $R^2 = .93$. This difference probably reflects the very different processes involved in location-based and distance-based judgments. The functions are also very different from those obtained in laboratory studies of children's and adults' time perception on much briefer scales, which typically have exponents of about .80 to 1.0 (Eisler, 1976). To the extent that distance-based judgments of the times of past events are a kind of perceptual task, then time perception has different functional characteristics on very long timescales than it has on very short scales. Again, this is undoubtedly because very different processes are involved. (See Block, 1990; Block & Zakay, 1996; and Macar, Pouthas, & Friedman, 1992, for discussions of models of time perception.)

However, the functions found in this study resemble those obtained in studies of recall. Several authors have pointed out that recency effects in free recall are influenced by the ratio of the separation of two items to the retention interval (Baddeley, 1986; Bjork & Whitten, 1974; Glenberg & Swanson, 1986), much as the temporal discriminability of two events was a function of the ratio of their distances in the studies reported here. It may be that some common decay or interference mechanism is responsible for the temporal properties of subjective recency and the probability of recall.

Asymptotic decay functions appear to provide a good description of subjects' judgments under conditions in which they rely on impressions of distances in the past. However, the performance data do not tell us what specific mechanism is responsible for these properties (and which, if any, of the strength theories are correct). This is because elapsed time is a correlational variable, and the quantities that might lead to impressions of recency were not experimentally manipulated. We will need new research combining conditions such as those reported here with manipulations such as repetition and priming.

However, these studies provide some clues about the nature of the information used to make distance-based judgments. One source of information is the method reports in the two studies in which adults rapidly judged whether or not a news event had occurred within the past year. The methods most strongly endorsed involved the vividness or clarity of the memory. Another clue is that the quantity underlying impressions of recency does not seem to be the same attribute that is used to assess confidence in recognition. When Friedman and Huttenlocher held confidence of recognition constant, subjects still distinguished the ages of television stories. It appears that we can be very confident that an event happened but still sense that it occurred a relatively long time ago. Third, if distance-based information was indeed the source of the significantly accurate judgments in studies using time pressure, the very brief RTs themselves indicate that this information is almost directly available when a stimulus is presented and is not the product of lengthy evaluation. A final clue about the nature of distance-based processes is the success of children as young as 4 years of age. Again, this finding makes it likely that subjects are judging the recency of events on the basis of some attribute of memories that is directly available and does not require the use of interpretation or strategy-based processes.

To summarize, the findings suggest that some property of memories underlies distance-based judgments, that this property changes at a decelerating rate with the passage of time, and that it follows a power function with an exponent of about .30 on timescales of weeks to many months in the past. It appears that this information is directly available and is associated with the subjective experience of the vividness or clarity of memories, but it is distinguishable from whatever information is used to assess confidence of recognition.

IV. The Roles of Distance-Based and Location-Based Processes

The developmental and adult studies show that humans are able to use both location- and distance-based processes to judge the times of past events. Location-based processes allow us to link past events to time patterns, often with considerable accuracy over long periods of time. In an earlier discussion (Friedman, 1993), I suggested that this kind of memory for time is adaptive because some temporal patterns are recurrent, and knowing when something happened in a pattern can often help us predict when a similar occurrence might happen in the future. The same discussion showed that distance-based processes would be very poor ways of recalling the locations of past events in time patterns. The data reported here also demonstrate that they are of quite limited value even for judging distances of events in the past: Only for the past weeks do we have reasonably accurate information, and beyond a few months only very gross differences in the ages of memories can be detected. Given these limitations, what is the importance of distance-based processes in human cognition?

It may be helpful to turn this question around and consider the benefits of distance-based processes. The principal advantage is that distance-based processes are "inexpensive." If distance-based theories are correct, no special process is required at the time of encoding; distance information is created by some natural correlate of the passage of time. In addition, the present studies suggest that little processing is required at the time of recall. Adults can discriminate distances very rapidly, and even young children are able to make distance judgments that are significantly more accurate than chance levels. The other virtue of distance-based processes is that for many purposes they do create adequate levels of accuracy. When events of a given separation fall in the recent past, or more generally the elapsed time is small relative to the criterion, high levels of accuracy can be achieved. For example, 4-year-old children, who could barely be expected to understand terms like "a long time ago" or "a short time ago," are about 80% correct in discriminating the ages of 1- and 7-week-old events, and they are even more accurate in discriminating birthdays from the past few months from Christmas, when the latter is more than 9 months in the past.

The fact that distance-based processes allow considerable resolution in the recent past makes it likely that we use such processes, probably alongside reconstruction, to judge the times of events from the past days or weeks. But distance information that is easily available and accurate for small ratios would be especially useful for two other purposes: updating and orientation. In their discussion of updating in the *recall* of information, Bjork and Bjork (1988) have argued that it is adaptive to retrieve recent rather than older information when the latter is out of date, and they describe automatic processes in memory that could explain our tendency to do so. Distance-based processes offer another kind of updating mechanism: In cases of *recognition* (or once an item is retrieved), we can readily gauge the approximate age of a memory or, for many pairs of memories, judge which comes from the more recent past. Along with order codes, this distance-based process may help us determine which of our enormous store of memories can be relied on to provide reasonably current information in a constantly changing world.

Distance-based processes probably also play an important role in temporal orientation. In an analysis of the process of temporal orientation (Friedman, 1990a, Chap. 5), I concluded that two kinds of information are primarily involved, semantic knowledge of time patterns and information about the distances of past times. This discussion also showed that having a sense of place in time requires repeated re-orientation. Because of the frequency with which we must re-establish our place in time, it would be advantageous to use processes that do not require extensive processing resources. Having an almost immediate "feel" for the recency of breakfast or the weekend could contribute to the economy of this process. In addition, it seems likely that distance-based processes would often provide the degree of precision that we need, because orienting on a given scale frequently involves comparisons between the most recent occurrence of some type of event with others that precede it by an even greater amount of time. For example, the distance of our most recent meal is usually a relatively small fraction of the distance of the meal that preceded it. These applications suggest that distance-based processes, alongside location-based processes, contribute both to a chronological sense of the past and the closely related sense of our present place in time.

ACKNOWLEDGMENTS

I am grateful to Richard A. Block, Patricia deWinstanley, and Hannes Eisler for their suggestions.

References

Anderson, J. R., & Bower, G. H. (1972). Recognition and retrieval processes in free recall. *Psychological Review, 79,* 97–123.

Anisfeld, M., & Knapp, M. (1968). Association, synonymity, and directionality in false recognition. *Journal of Experimental Psychology, 77,* 171–179.

Baddeley, A. (1986). *Working memory.* Oxford: Clarendon Press.

Baddeley, A. D., Lewis, V., & Nimmo-Smith, I. (1978). When did you last . . . ? In M. M. Gruneberg & R. N. Sykes (Eds.), *Practical aspects of memory* (pp. 77–83). San Diego, CA: Academic Press.

Bjork, E. L., & Bjork, R. A. (1988). On the adaptive aspects of retrieval failure in autobiographical memory. In M. M. Gruneberg, P. E. Morris, & R. N. Sykes (Eds.), *Practical aspects of memory: Vol. 1. Memory in everyday life* (pp. 283–288). Chichester: John Wiley & Sons.

Bjork, R. A., & Whitten, W. B. (1974). Recency-sensitive retrieval processes in long-term free recall. *Cognitive Psychology, 6,* 173–189.

Block, R. A. (1982). Temporal judgments and contextual change. *Journal of Experimental Psychology: Learning, Memory and Cognition, 8,* 530–544.

Block, R. A. (Ed.) (1990). *Cognitive models of psychological time.* Hillsdale, NJ: Erlbaum.

Block, R. A., & Zakay, D. (1996). Models of psychological time revisited. In H. Helfrich (Ed.), *Time and mind.* Kirkland, WA: Hogrefe & Huber.

Brewer, W. F. (1996). What is recollective memory? In D. C. Rubin (Ed.), *Remembering our past: Studies in autobiographical memory* (pp. 19–66). Cambridge: Cambridge University Press.

Brown, N. R., Rips, L. J., & Shevell, S. K. (1985). The subjective dates of natural events in very-long-term memory. *Cognitive Psychology, 17,* 139–177.

Brown, N. R., Shevell, S. K., & Rips, L. J. (1986). Public memories and their personal context. In D. C. Rubin (Ed.), *Autobiographical memory* (pp. 137–158). Cambridge: Cambridge University Press.

Bruce, D., & Van Pelt, M. (1989). Memories of a bicycle tour. *Applied Cognitive Psychology, 3,* 137–156.

Burt, C. D. B. (1992). Retrieval characteristics of autobiographical memories: Event and date information. *Applied Cognitive Psychology, 6,* 389–404.

Eisler, H. (1976). Experiments on subjective duration 1868–1975: A collection of power functions. *Psychological Bulletin, 83,* 1154–1171.

Estes, W. K. (1972). An associative basis for coding and organization in memory. In A. W. Melton & E. Martin (Eds.), *Coding processes in human memory* (pp. 161–190). Washington, DC: V. H. Winston.

Estes, W. K. (1985). Memory for temporal information. In J. A. Michon & J. Jackson (Eds.), *Time, mind and behavior* (pp. 151–168). Berlin: Springer-Verlag.

Ferguson, R. P., & Martin, P. (1983). Long-term temporal estimation in humans. *Perception and Psychophysics, 33,* 585–592.

Flexser, A. J., & Bower, G. H. (1974). How frequency affects recency judgments: A model for recency discrimination. *Journal of Experimental Psychology, 103,* 706–716.

Fozard, J. L., & Weinert, J. R. (1972). Absolute judgments of recency for pictures and nouns after various members of intervening items. *Journal of Experimental Psychology, 95,* 472–474.

Friedman, W. J. (1977). The development of children's knowledge of cyclic aspects of time. *Child Development, 48,* 1592–1599.

Friedman, W. J. (1978). Development of time concepts in children. In H. W. Reese & L. P. Lipsitt (Eds.), *Advances in child development and behavior,* (Vol. 12, pp. 267–298). New York: Academic Press.

Friedman, W. J. (1982). Conventional time concepts and children's structuring of time. In W. J. Friedman (Ed.), *The developmental psychology of time* (pp. 171–208). New York: Academic Press.

Friedman, W. J. (1986). The development of children's knowledge of temporal structure. *Child Development, 57,* 1386–1400.

Friedman, W. J. (1987). A follow-up to "Scale effects in memory for the time of events": The earthquake study. *Memory and Cognition, 15,* 518–520.

Friedman, W. J. (1990a). *About time: Inventing the fourth dimension.* Cambridge, MA: MIT Press.

Friedman, W. J. (1990b). Children's representations of the pattern of daily activities. *Child Development, 61,* 1399–1412.

Friedman, W. J. (1991). The development of children's memory for the time of past events. *Child Development, 62,* 139–155.

Friedman, W. J. (1992). Children's time memory: The development of a differentiated past. *Cognitive Development, 7,* 171–187.

Friedman, W. J. (1993). Memory for the time of past events. *Psychological Bulletin, 113,* 44–66.

Friedman, W. J., Gardner, A. G., & Zubin, N. R. E. (1995). Children's comparisons of the recency of two events from the past year. *Child Development, 66,* 970–983.

Friedman, W. J., & Huttenlocher, J. (1996). *Memory for the times of* 60 Minutes *stories and news events.* Manuscript submitted for publication.

Friedman, W. J., Kemp, S., Fifield, S., Goodson, S., & Sidey, S. (1995). *A test of the effect of retrieval on the subjective recency of events.* Unpublished manuscript. Oberlin College.

Friedman, W. J., & Wilkins, A. J. (1985). Scale effects in memory for the time of past events. *Memory and Cognition, 13,* 168–175.

Glenberg, A. M. (1987). Temporal context and recency. In D. S. Gorfein & R. R. Hoffman (Eds.), *Memory and learning: The Ebbeinghaus Centennial Conference* (pp. 173–190). Hillsdale, NJ: Erlbaum.

Glenberg, A. M., & Swanson, N. G. (1986). A temporal distinctiveness theory of recency and modality effects. *Journal of Experimental Psychology: Learning, Memory and Cognition, 12,* 3–15.

Guenther, R. K., & Linton, M. (1975). Mechanisms of temporal coding. *Journal of Experimental Psychology: Human Learning and Memory, 97,* 220–229.

Hasher, L., & Zacks, R. T. (1979). Automatic and effortful processes in memory. *Journal of Experimental Psychology: General, 108,* 356–388.

Hinrichs, J. V. (1970). A two-process memory-strength theory for judgment of recency. *Psychological Review, 77,* 223–233.

Hintzman, D. L., Block, R. A., & Summers, J. J. (1973). Contextual associations and memory for serial position. *Journal of Experimental Psychology, 97,* 220–229.

Hintzman, D. L., Summers, J. J., & Block, R. A. (1975). Spacing judgments as an index of study-phase retrieval. *Journal of Experimental Psychology: Human Learning and Memory, 1,* 31–40.

Huttenlocher, J., Hedges, L. V., & Prohaska, V. (1992). Memory for day of the week: A 5 + 2 day cycle. *Journal of Experimental Psychology: General, 121,* 313–325.

Kemp, S. (1988). Dating recent and historical events. *Applied Cognitive Psychology, 2,* 181–188.

Koffka, K. (1936). *Principles of Gestalt psychology.* New York: Harcourt Brace.

Koriat, A., & Fischhoff, B. (1974). What day is today? An inquiry into the process of temporal orientation. *Memory and Cognition, 2,* 201–205.

Koriat, A., Fischhoff, B., & Razel, O. (1976). An inquiry into the process of temporal orientation. *Acta Psychologica, 40,* 57–73.

Lee, C. L., & Estes, W. K. (1977). Order and position in primary memory for letter strings. *Journal of Verbal Learning and Verbal Behavior, 16*, 395–418.

Lee, C. L., & Estes, W. K. (1981). Item and order information in short-term memory: Evidence for multi-level perturbation processes. *Journal of Experimental Psychology: Human Learning and Memory, 7*, 149–169.

Lieury, A., Aiello, B., Lepreux, D., & Mellet, M. (1980). Le rôle de repères dans la récupération et la datation des souvenirs [The role of landmarks in the recovery and dating of memories]. *Année Psychologique, 80*, 149–167.

Linton, M. (1975). Memory for real world events. In D. A. Norman & D. E. Rumelhart (Eds.), *Explorations in cognition* (pp. 376–404). San Francisco: Freeman.

Macar, F., Pouthas, V., & Friedman, W. J. (1992). *Time, action and cognition: Towards bridging the gap.* Dordrecht: Kluwer.

McCormack, T., Russell, J., & Jarold, C. (1995). *Developmental changes in temporal memory.* Manuscript submitted for publication.

Morton, J. (1968). Repeated items and decay in memory. *Psychonomic Science, 10*, 219–220.

Murdock, B. B., Jr. (1974). *Human memory: Theory and data.* Potomac, MD: Erlbaum.

Muter, P. (1979). Response latencies in discriminations of recency. *Journal of Experimental Psychology: Human Learning and Memory, 5*, 160–169.

Ribot, T. (1901). *Les maladies de la mémoire* [The maladies of memory]. Paris: Alcan.

Shanon, B. (1979). Yesterday, today and tomorrow. *Acta Psychologica, 43*, 469–476.

Thompson, C. P., Skowronski, J. J., & Betz, A. L. (1993). The use of partial temporal information in dating personal events. *Memory and Cognition, 21*, 352–360.

Thompson, C. P., Skowronski, J. J., & Lee, D. J. (1987, August). *Reconstructing the date of a personal event.* Paper presented at the Second International Conference on Practical Aspects of Memory, Swansea, Wales.

Thompson, C. P., Skowronski, J. J., & Lee, D. J. (1988). Telescoping in dating naturally occurring events. *Memory and Cognition, 16*, 461–468.

Tzeng, O. J. L., & Cotton, B. (1980). A study-phase retrieval model of temporal coding. *Journal of Experimental Psychology: Human Learning and Memory, 6*, 705–716.

Tzeng, O. J. L., Lee, A. T., & Wetzel, C. D. (1979). Temporal coding in verbal information processing. *Journal of Experimental Psychology: Human Learning and Memory, 5*, 52–64.

Underwood, B. J. (1977). *Temporal codes for memories: Issues and problems.* Hillsdale, NJ: Erlbaum.

Wagenaar, W. A. (1986). My memory: A study of autobiographical memory over six years. *Cognitive Psychology, 18*, 225–252.

White, R. T. (1982). Memory for personal events. *Human Learning, 1*, 171–183.

White, R. T. (1989). Recall of autobiographical events. *Applied Cognitive Psychology, 3*, 127–135.

Winograd, E., & Soloway, R. M. (1985). Reminding as a basis for temporal judgments. *Journal of Experimental Psychology: Learning, Memory, and Cognition, 11*, 262–271.

Yntema, D. B., & Trask, F. P. (1963). Recall as a search process. *Journal of Verbal Learning and Verbal Behavior, 2*, 65–74.

VERBAL AND SPATIAL WORKING MEMORY
IN HUMANS

John Jonides
Patricia A. Reuter-Lorenz
Edward E. Smith
Edward Awh
Lisa L. Barnes
Maxwell Drain
Jennifer Glass
Erick J. Lauber
Andrea L. Patalano
Eric H. Schumacher

I. Introduction

Human memory is not unitary. It is composed of a number of systems that are defined by the length of time they store information, the amount of information that can be stored, the form of that storage, and the cognitive functions that the storage serves. This idea of drawing a distinction between long-term and working memory has been honored for over a hundred years (see, e.g., Atkinson & Schiffrin, 1968; Broadbent, 1958; Galton, 1883; Hebb, 1949; James, 1890; Waugh & Norman, 1965). In 1974, Baddeley and Hitch suggested that working memory itself may be composed of a number of subsystems for storing different kinds of information. This is the issue that motivates the present review.

The study of what is now called "working memory" has a long history in psychology. Galton and James described the precursors of this concept

THE PSYCHOLOGY OF LEARNING
AND MOTIVATION, VOL. 35

43

in their discussions of the "presence chamber" (Galton, 1883), and the "specious present" (James, 1890) that constituted what James came to call "primary memory." Their discussions referred largely to the consciousness that observers had of information to which they attended. Much later, Broadbent (1958) and Sperling (1960) described an active perceptual system whose processing outlasted the presence of the stimulus. Building on this, Atkinson and Shiffrin (1968; 1971) first proposed a model of what they called a "short-term store" that emphasized linguistic coding of material stored for a short interval. More recently, Baddeley and Hitch (1974; Baddeley, 1986, 1992) proposed the concept of working memory to include not only short-term storage of information but also the processing operations that make use of this information. To be sure, there are differences among these many conceptions of what we now call working memory, but they all include a common set of characteristics—a memory system that (a) stores information briefly, (b) stores a limited amount of information, (c) is rapidly accessible, (d) is subject to frequent updating, (e) and is used in the service of higher cognitive processes.

These characteristics are the common hallmarks of working memory throughout its entire history of discussion in psychology, during most of which working memory has been conceptualized as a unitary construct. Recent proposals suggest a revision to this conceptualization, however. There is now reason to believe that working memory is composed of a number of subsystems that differ from one another in the kind of information they process, but that are related to one another by their common characteristics of limited capacity, limited duration, frequent updating, and use in higher mental computations (Baddeley, 1986, 1992). The evidence that underlies this view is mainly concerned with the distinction between verbal and spatial working-memory systems, and it is concentrated on the storage rather than the executive aspects of working memory. In this chapter we review this evidence in detail and draw from it a picture of working memory that includes at least two storage subcomponents.

A. A Methodological Note

How does one establish that some psychological processing system is composed of several parts, as we and others would like to argue for working memory? The logic of double dissociation offers a powerful tool for addressing this problem. Originally conceived as an analysis tool for cognitive deficits following brain damage (Kinsbourne, 1972a; Shallice, 1988; Teuber, 1955), the logic of double dissociation has been fruitfully applied to purely behavioral studies as follows:

> If there is a behavioral factor that influences performance on Task
> A but not Task B, and another behavioral factor that influences

performance on Task B but not Task A, then these two tasks are mediated by different processing mechanisms (Smith & Jonides, 1995, p. 1010).

This same logic can be applied to neuropsychological and neuroimaging studies if one allows a rough assumption about localization: that different processing mechanisms will be implemented in different neuroanatomical locations. Note that this additional assumption does not depend on whether a processing mechanism is strictly localized to just one portion of neural tissue or instead is distributed over several locations. What is critical is that the site or sites of implementation of one processing mechanism differ from those of another. When studying the effects of brain damage on behavior, the double-dissociation logic necessitates the study of at least two patients so that the following conditions can be met:

If one patient shows a deficit in performance of Task A associated with loss of function in Brain region a but not Brain region b, whereas another patient shows a deficit in performance of Task B associated with loss of function in region b but not region a, then the two tasks are mediated by different processing mechanisms.

Likewise, the selective activation or deactivation of brain regions evidenced by neuroimaging can use the logic of double dissociation in the following way:

If performance on Task A is associated with changed neural activity in Brain Region a but not Brain Region b, whereas performance on Task B is associated with changed neural activity in Region b but not Region a, then the two tasks are mediated by different processing mechanisms.

When applied in any of these ways, the logic of double dissociation permits one to make strong inferences about the existence of multiple processing systems. It is often the case, however, that the double dissociations one seeks—whether in behavioral data, in neuroimages, or in data from brain injury—are not pure in form. For example, there are behavioral studies in which some experimental manipulation influences performance *more* in Task A than Task B, while another manipulation influences performance *more* in Task B than Task A. In these cases, both factors influence performance in both tasks, and so the strict conditions of a double dissociation are not satisfied. Nevertheless, one may continue to respect this weaker form of dissociation in that it provides evidence of a separation in processing systems, though it might also indicate some overlap in those systems.

One can obtain impure evidence of a double dissociation from neuro-imaging studies as well. This occurs if one finds changed neural activity in response to both Tasks A and B, but more change in the activity of one region in response to Task A than to B, and more change in the activity of another region in response to Task B than to A. Again, this would lead one to conclude that the two tasks recruit some of the same mechanisms in the two regions in common, but it would also indicate that there is some residual specialization of the two regions for the two tasks.

Finally, neuropsychological studies are often cases of somewhat compromised double dissociations (see Shallice, 1988, for discussion). Frequently, one patient may show deficits in both Tasks A and B, with the deficit in Task A being greater, whereas another patient with damage in a different region shows deficits in both Tasks A and B, but with the deficit in B being greater. This sort of finding is possible because tasks recruit more processes than the ones that might be specialized to two areas, and the commonly recruited processes may be the ones that produce common deficits.

While the logic of double dissociation is not without its critics (Caramazza, 1986; Dunn & Kirsner, 1988), it is generally recognized as providing a strong evidential basis for inferring the separability of subsystems (e.g., Coltheart, 1985; Teuber, 1955; Weiskrantz, 1968), which is a fundamental step toward specifying the architecture of any cognitive system. Furthermore, Weiskrantz (1991) has argued that one's confidence in the separability of two systems is solidified if the evidence for double dissociations is derived from multiple populations and multiple techniques. We endorse this argument and extend it to include not only evidence from patient populations and neuroimaging, but also evidence from strictly behavioral studies of the systems in question. Accumulating double-dissociation evidence from all these sources renders quite strong the inference that the dissociated systems are separable, both psychologically and neurally.

In this chapter we review a body of evidence that demonstrates dissociations of both the weak and strong variety to develop the case for multiple processing systems in working memory. Note that the focus of this review is spatial and verbal processing in working memory. Consequently, even though there is a good deal of evidence about working memory in animals other than humans, this evidence does not directly inform us about verbal processing. So, the data we review come exclusively from studies of humans.

II. Dissociating Phonological and Spatial Storage

There are reasons to suspect, even in the absence of empirical evidence, that working memory may dissociate by verbal and spatial qualities. One of the most time-honored generalizations about specialization in the human brain is that verbal functions are lateralized in the left hemisphere and visuospatial functions in the right. It seems reasonable, then, to suspect that working-memory tasks that recruit these two functions may also show selective specialization. Supporting this possibility are introspections of subjects performing verbal versus spatial tasks, such as mental addition of several numbers versus mental rotation of a visual form. These introspections often suggest the use of different sorts of representations in these tasks.

Indeed, for these and other reasons, Baddeley and his colleagues (e.g., Baddeley, 1986, 1992; Baddeley & Hitch, 1974) proposed a model of working memory that explicitly includes the dissociation of spatial and phonological storage. According to the canonical version of this model, working memory is composed of a central executive processor and slave buffer systems that serve the central executive. The central executive is claimed to be the seat of computing operations that permit one to engage in such tasks as mental arithmetic or mental rotation (see, e.g., Hitch, 1978). To implement these operations in any task, the central executive requires information that is fed to it from the slave buffer systems. There are two such buffers: one responsible for information stored in a phonological form and one for information coded visuospatially. These two buffers are assumed to be separate storage systems that feed independently to the common central executive.

A. Behavioral Evidence

Two behavioral techniques have been used to distinguish between verbal and spatial buffers using the logic of double dissociation. Perhaps the more popular one is the *selective interference* paradigm. The assumption underlying selective interference is that introducing a secondary activity during the retention interval of a working-memory task will produce interference on that task. The secondary task is made *selectively* interfering by having the mental code used during this task be either similar to or different from the code used during the main task. A secondary task that involves manipulation of a phonological code should be more interfering on a working-memory task that involves a phonological buffer than on one that involves spatial material. Likewise, a secondary task that involves a spatial code should interfere more with a spatial working-memory buffer than with a phonological buffer.

Various experiments have implemented this rationale (see Logie, Zucco, & Baddeley, 1990; Meudell, 1972; Salthouse, 1974). As one example, consider an experiment by den Heyer and Barrett (1971). They had subjects view 4 × 6 matrices that contained eight letters randomly positioned in eight of the cells of the matrices. After a subject saw a matrix, a 10-second retention interval ensued, during which subjects either did nothing but remember the matrix or engaged in one of two interfering tasks. Then they recalled the matrix by writing in letters on a blank matrix. Thus, subjects had to remember both the *identities* of the eight letters and their *positions*— that is, a verbal and a spatial task. One of the interfering tasks required them to view three 2 × 4 matrices in each of which there were three dots. Two of these matrices were identical and subjects had to judge which of them was different. The other interfering task involved aurally presenting subjects five numbers that they had to add mentally. Consistent with the logic of double dissociation, the rationale behind the experiment was this: If subjects stored the identities of the letters using a phonological code, then the mental arithmetic task should interfere with the stored letters because subjects would have to store a phonological code in part to do their arithmetic (see Hitch, 1978, for elaboration of a model of working memory for mental arithmetic). Furthermore, if subjects stored the positions of the letters using a spatial code, then having to make a spatial judgment during the retention interval should interfere with memory of the letter positions because the spatial judgment would also require a spatial code.

The results support these predictions. Relative to the control condition in which there was no interpolated activity during the retention interval, identity responses were 56% worse when the interpolated task was spatial but 68% worse when it was mental arithmetic. By contrast, position responses were 45% worse than the control when mental arithmetic intervened during the retention interval but nearly 90% worse when the spatial judgment task intervened. This pattern of results establishes a double dissociation in that the interfering task involving arithmetic had a greater effect on phonological working memory than on spatial working memory, but the spatial interfering task had a greater effect on spatial than on phonological memory. The dissociation is of the weak variety, as seen by the fact that both tasks suffered from both kinds of interference to some extent compared to the control.

The second technique used to isolate spatial from phonological buffers in working memory makes use of a logic that is related to that of selective interference. In this case, rather than the variable being the kind of interfering task that intrudes on the retention interval, it is the type of response that the subject must produce. Responses that recruit a spatial processing system are predicted to interfere with spatial working memory whereas responses that recruit a verbal system are predicted to interfere with verbal working memory. The basis for these predictions hinges on an often unstated assumption about working-memory processes—namely, that working-memory processes use mechanisms that plan and produce behavioral responses. The consequence is that having to produce a verbal response in a task that uses verbal-output processes to store information will result in interference. In a similar manner, having to produce a response that requires spatial processing will interfere with working memory for spatial information. A classic example of the use of this rationale is an experiment by Brooks (1968; see also Smyth & Scholey, 1994).

Brooks had subjects engage in one of two tasks that putatively required spatial or verbal working memory. The verbal task was this: Subjects had to memorize a 10-word sentence such as "Rivers from the hills bring fresh water to the cities." The experimenter then cued the subject to make a linguistic judgment about each word in the sentence, for example, Was it a noun or not? In each case, subjects made a positive or a negative response. The spatial task was quite different. Subjects memorized a block figure, such as a block figure of the uppercase letter F. They were trained to scan mentally around the boundaries of the figure, beginning at an asterisk and going in a clockwise direction as indicated by an arrow. On each trial of the experiment, subjects were cued to make spatial judgments about each vertex in the block figure; for example, Was it at the top or bottom of the figure? If so, they responded positively, and if not they responded negatively.

The critical feature of the experiment was that subjects indicated their responses in one of two manners. In one case, they simply verbalized a response for each Yes or No in the string of decisions they had to make, whether in the sentence or the block-figure task. In the other case, subjects were presented with a response sheet that had rows each containing a Y and an N in a staggered arrangement. In this case, subjects indicated their responses by pointing to a Y or an N in each row corresponding to each decision they had made. This procedure forced subjects to monitor the response sheet visually as they indicated their responses, presumably engaging some spatial processes to do so.

The results of the experiment were clear. Responding vocally hindered performance in the verbal task more than responding by pointing; in a complementary way, pointing resulted in poorer performance for the spatial memory task than did vocalizing. There was a clear double dissociation that suggests two streams of processing for the two working-memory tasks. To produce a vocal response, according to Brooks (1968), requires the engagement of a speech-production system so that the output can be formed and executed. To point, however, requires that subjects spatially select the proper letters on the response sheets to produce their responses, which requires spatial localization. These two response modes, then, engage parts of a verbal or a spatial processing system, respectively. The fact that they produce selective impairment on the working-memory tasks is what suggests that these working-memory tasks must be engaging verbal or spatial processing systems as well. It is this line of reasoning that invites the hypothesis of two working-memory modules for verbal and spatial information. In fact, subjects in this experiment reported, "that they 'could say the sentence to themselves' while . . . pointing, but not while saying 'yes' or 'no.' The diagrams could be 'pictured' while subjects were . . . saying 'yes' or 'no,' but not while they were trying to point." These introspections are consistent with the operation of two working-memory modules, one for verbal and one for spatial information.

Taken together, the behavioral demonstrations of double dissociations converge on the view that working memory includes separate subsystems for verbal and spatial information. However, this conclusion must be drawn with caution, for several reasons.

First, a careful examination of the tasks used in the behavioral literature reveals that they are often extremely complex, in the sense that they recruit a range of processes. Recall the selective-interference experiment by den Heyer and Barrett (1971), and consider the secondary tasks that they used: mental arithmetic (which was intended to interfere with verbal working memory) and comparing matrices of dots to find the odd one of three (which was intended to interfere with spatial working memory). While the results were consistent with the existence of separate verbal and spatial working-memory systems, the secondary tasks were sufficiently complex to cloud interpretation of the results. Think about the processes that are involved in mental arithmetic. As Hitch (1978) and others have analyzed this task, it involves not only storage of the numbers to be added, but retrieval of rules of addition, table look-up of addition facts, updating of memory with the intermediate solution, computation of sums when they are not available by table look-up, and so forth. Part of the greater interfering effect that mental arithmetic shows on letter versus position memory may well hinge on these other processes that are necessary to accomplish the mental arithmetic task. A similar problem arises with the secondary task of comparing dot matrices. While it is certainly plausible that this task includes a substantial spatial component, it is also plausible that visual memory of the configuration of dots plays some role in the task, and it may be this configural memory that causes the greater interference with memory for position than memory for letters.

We do not intend to focus on only the experiment of den Heyer & Barrett (1971) in leveling this criticism. Indeed, it is common for selective-interference studies to use tasks with multiple possible sites of interference (e.g., Logie, et al., 1990; Salthouse, 1974). While these studies may recruit spatial and verbal working-memory systems, they surely also recruit other processes that could be the source of selective interference.

Another reason for caution in interpreting the results of strictly behavioral studies has to do with uncertainty about the locus of the processing effects. To illustrate the point, recall the study by Brooks (1968) that showed selective interference on spatial and verbal working-memory tasks as a function of the mode of response. The demonstrated interference was substantial and selective, thus offering support for a double dissociation of spatial and verbal processes. However, what sort of dissociation is implicated? One possibility is that the demands of verbal versus spatial responding intrude on the *storage* of verbal versus spatial information respectively. This would lead to the sort of model of working memory that Baddeley (1986, 1992) has proposed. An alternative, however, is that storage of spatial and verbal information is not different, and the source of response interference is lodged in *retrieval* of information from memory. Subjects may have a more difficult time retrieving verbal information from storage when they are activating a verbal response, but a more difficult time retrieving spatial information when activating a spatial response. Thus, while the double dissociations are clear, they do not unambiguously implicate storage functions of working memory. This problem arises in other behavioral experiments as well (e.g., Smyth & Scholey, 1994) although some experiments have managed to isolate interference effects to storage by presenting interfering tasks only during the retention interval of a working-memory task (den Heyer & Barrett, 1971; Meudell, 1972).

What, then, do we make of the behavioral data that have been accumulated about spatial and verbal components of working memory? A minimal interpretation is that they indicate that some portion of the information processing stream for spatial and verbal material differs in working-memory tasks. This difference may be lodged in encoding, storage, or retrieval processes, or in some combination of these.

B. NEUROPSYCHOLOGICAL EVIDENCE

The behavioral evidence reviewed above suggests that there are differences at some point or points in the processing stream for verbal and spatial working memory. One implication of this is that there should be identifiably different brain pathways that are responsible for these processing differences. In turn, this leads to the interference that there may be patients with brain injury or anomalies who will reveal dissociations between spatial and verbal working-memory systems. Indeed, there is growing evidence to support this inference.

Consider a striking dissociation reported by Wang and Bellugi (1994). They studied two groups of subjects, one with Williams Syndrome and one with Down syndrome. Both syndromes are traceable to genetic anomalies that result in abnormal neurological development and are well known to produce severe cognitive retardation. However, patients with Williams syndrome show remarkably selective preservation of many language functions in contrast to their overall cognitive skills. To study the working-memory capacities of the two kinds of patients, Wang and Bellugi (1994) administered classic tests of verbal and spatial memory. They gave subjects in both groups the Digit-Span subtest from the Wechsler Intelligence Scale for Children-Revised (WISC-R), in which strings of random digits of varying lengths are read to subjects who must repeat them back in order. To test spatial memory span, they administered the Corsi-blocks test, in which the experimenter points to a set of haphazardly arrayed identical blocks in random order, and the subject must then reproduce the order. Scoring the responses either with or without respect to whether the correct order of the strings was preserved, the subjects with Down and Williams syndromes showed a striking dissociation. Subjects with Williams syndrome were superior in their digit span to subjects with Down syndrome, but Down subjects were superior in their Corsi-blocks performance to their Williams counterparts.

While these data are consistent with the involvement of different brain mechanisms in spatial and verbal working memory, they are not specific about either the structural or functional locus of this difference. With regard to neuroanatomical structure, both syndromes are characterized by reduced cerebral volume generally. Relative to this, there is some sparing of the basal ganglia in Down patients and of temporal-limbic structures in Williams syndrome, but this sparing is sufficiently coarse so as not to offer much clue about what structures may be responsible for the dissociations shown in the working-memory tasks.

Moreover, the Down subjects' deficit in verbal working memory and the Williams subjects' deficit in spatial working memory may be secondary to more general difficulties these patients have with verbal and spatial material respectively. That is, these complementary deficits may be material-specific, but not selective for working memory per se. For example, Wang and Bellugi note that Down and William's syndromes are associated with distinctive patterns of perceptual abilities. This raises the possibility that these patients differ in their encoding strategies in addition to, or possibly instead of, their short-term storage of verbal or spatial material. Subjects with Williams syndrome also show poorer memory of visual-spatial than verbal materials over longer retention intervals (Udwin & Yule, 1991), again suggesting a material-specific deficit that extends beyond working memory. The problem is the same here as with the behavioral studies reviewed previously: We cannot be sure that the double dissociation that Wang and

Bellugi report reflects a selective dysfunction in separate verbal and spatial working-memory storage buffers.

Large-scale group studies of patients with focal lesions have the potential to be more revealing about the neural substrates of spatial and verbal working memory. However, the few studies of this kind that exist are also limited in the conclusions that can be drawn about the functional locus of the deficit. De Renzi and Nichelli (1975) examined working memory in patients with left- or right-hemisphere damage using four tests of working memory, three verbal ones and a spatial one. The verbal tests included (a) digit span, with subjects verbalizing their responses; (b) digit span, with subjects pointing to the digits as a response rather than verbalizing them; and (c) a picture–word memory test, in which subjects were given names to store and had to point to the referents of the names in an array of pictures. All three tests revealed the same pattern of results for verbal working memory: Patients with left-hemisphere lesions were impaired more than controls with no brain damage, and also more than patients with right-hemisphere damage. In addition, patients with right-hemisphere damage did not differ in their performance from controls. These results are consistent with the hypothesis that important mechanisms of verbal working memory are lodged in the left hemisphere.

The results for spatial working memory are not so clear from this study, however. To assess spatial working memory, De Renzi and Nichelli (1975) used a version of the Corsi-blocks test described earlier. Overall, the right-hemisphere patients scored lower than the left-hemisphere patients, but not reliably so. In fact, the only statistically significant effect to arise from this test had to do with whether the lesion site was anterior or posterior in either hemisphere. Patients with posterior lesions fared worse on the Corsi-blocks test than patients with anterior lesions. In a follow-up experiment that focused specifically on spatial working memory and that used more taxing variations of the spatial span task (8- or 16- s delays that were filled and unfilled), De Renzi and his colleagues (De Renzi, Faglioni, & Previdi, 1977) did find evidence that only patients with right posterior lesions were significantly impaired relative to neurologically intact controls.

Taken together, these studies suggest a picture of working memory that is consistent with a wealth of information indicating left hemispheric specialization for verbal material and right hemisphere specialization for spatial material. Moreover, a posterior locus is suggested for both types of working memory. Yet, can we be any more certain about the functional locus disrupted in these patients than we were in considering the behavioral and neuropsychological evidence reviewed earlier? Unfortunately, these group studies lack the critical information needed to establish a selective deficit of verbal or spatial working-memory buffers, just as the earlier behavioral and neuropsychological studies did. In particular, we do not know enough about the perceptual abilities of these patient–groups to rule out an encoding problem as the source of the apparent working-memory impairment. There is also the possibility that the deficits reflect generalized memory impairments rather than specific deficits in short-term retention. Indeed, De Renzi et al. (1977) report that their right-hemisphere patients required significantly more trials to learn a spatial sequence to criterion, suggesting that at least the spatial impairment may be more general.

There are several neuropsychological case studies that provide just the sort of information needed to address the question of functional selectivity in addition to providing some indication of structural locus. A classic case, K.F., first reported by Warrington and Shallice in 1969, had mild speech and comprehension difficulties following a head injury affecting primarily the left parietal-occipital area. K.F. had disproportionate difficulty with repetition, as manifested by a dramatically reduced digit span of 2. His limited span could not be attributed simply to speech difficulties since a nonverbal probe-recognition test also indicated a working memory span of 2. Moreover, general comprehension or phonological encoding difficulties could not account for K.F.'s poor working memory since he showed normal long-term memory for verbal material (Shallice & Warrington, 1970). Results from several similar patients, including one patient, J.B., who had minimal comprehension difficulties and fluent nonaphasic speech (Shallice & Butterworth, 1977), offer the same general picture of a deficit that specifically affects short-term retention (Warrington, Logue, & Pratt, 1971; Warrington & Shallice, 1969). There is also some evidence for material specificity of the working-memory deficit, in that K.F. and J.B. were both found to have normal spans when the memory list was composed of nonverbal sounds (Shallice & Warrington, 1974). For these patients, however, information about their spatial working memory is lacking.

This was not so with patient P.V., a more recent case whose verbal working-memory impairment has been studied thoroughly and found to occur in the presence of normal spatial working memory (Basso, Spinnler, Vallar, & Zanobio, 1982; Vallar & Baddeley, 1984a, 1984b). In Basso et al.'s initial report (1982), P.V. was a 28-year-old, right-handed woman who had suffered a stroke 5 years earlier. Her lesion was quite large, extending the full anterior–posterior extent of language areas in the left hemisphere. Given the size of her lesion, her language functions were remarkably intact. Her most notable deficit was an inability to repeat auditorially presented sentences. This observation was amplified by Basso et al. (1982), who showed that on memory-span tests with digits, letters, or words, P.V.'s memory span was noticeably worse than normals'. For example, when she was presented 10 strings of 5 digits each, she was able to recall only 1 string completely correctly (which is far worse than normal). By contrast, her span on the Corsi-block test was 6, which is slightly better than the normal span of 5.7.

We can establish a double dissociation between verbal and spatial working memory by comparing the performance of patient P.V. with that of patient E.L.D., who is the one well-documented case of a spatial working-memory deficit (Hanley, Young, & Pearson, 1991).[1] At the time of the study by Hanley et al. (1991), E.L.D. was a 55-year-old right-handed woman who had suffered an aneurysm of the middle cerebral artery in the right hemisphere, which led to a hematoma in the Sylvian Fissure some 6 years previously. Her major cognitive deficit was an anterograde amnesia for spatial and visual information. When tested on Corsi blocks, she was noticeably worse than normals, indicating a deficit in spatial working memory. For example, E.L.D. correctly recalled no sequences of length 5, compared to a group of normals who recalled 70% of sequences of this length perfectly. E.L.D. showed no deficit in verbal working memory, however, performing comparably to normal controls. When given three sequences of six phonologically different letters to recall, E.L.D. recalled all sequences perfectly, in comparison to controls who recalled only 1.4 of the six sequences on average.

Thus, a comparison of patients P.V. and E.L.D. establishes a double dissociation between verbal and spatial working memory. In addition, for both patients there is evidence to indicate that the working-memory deficits are not secondary to more general difficulties with the perceptual encoding of verbal or spatial material. For P.V., her strong performance on tests of phoneme discrimination, rhyme judgments, and single-word comprehension all converge on the conclusion that her deficit is not due to impaired phonological processing. Her normal verbal long-term memory for items already in her lexicon also strengthens this conclusion and indicates the selectivity of her deficit (Basso et al., 1982). Likewise, E.L.D. performs normally on quite challenging visual tasks. She is able to identify pictures of objects from unusual views, match unfamiliar faces presented in full and

[1] Note that many temporal-lobe patients have been described who have deficits in spatial memory. However, the preponderance of evidence leads to the conclusion that their deficit is not of spatial *working* memory. Smith and Milner and their colleagues (Smith, Leonard, Crane, & Milner, 1995; Smith & Milner, 1981, 1984, 1989), for example, have described groups of patients with temporal-lobe lesions, especially lesions of the right temporal lobe and hippocampal area, who have difficulty with spatial memory tasks. However, Smith and Milner (1989) showed that these deficits did not appear in tasks in which the spatial material in question had to be recalled shortly after presentation, the kind of task that is typically associated with working memory. Rather, they seem to appear only after a significant delay is required before recall, suggesting that the deficit is one that reflects a longer-term representation of spatial material.

profile poses, and judge facial expressions. She also reads normally and shows no signs of visual neglect. Unlike P.V., E.L.D.'s memory deficit does affect long-term memory and the learning of new visual materials (e.g., faces and routes; Hanley et al., 1991). So, while the material-specific deficit is unlikely due to a perceptual problem, E.L.D.'s difficulties extend beyond the short-term storage of visual–spatial material.

These two cases offer the strongest evidence considered thus far for separable verbal and spatial working-memory systems. Beyond that, what do these patients tell us about the brain pathways involved in working memory? The most salient difference in lesion sites between the two patients is hemispheric: P.V.'s lesion is in the left hemisphere while E.L.D.'s is in the right. Both patients show damage in the region of the Sylvian fissure although the damage reported for patient P.V. seems to extend well beyond this site. Elaborating on the nature of this circuitry from an examination of these patients alone is not possible, however. Partly this is a function of the size of the lesions that produced their deficits. Partly it is due to the possibility that even local damage can have global effects (e.g., Farah, 1994). Once a patient has lost a part of a processing circuit, later functions of that same circuit will appear to be damaged as well, a result of upstream processes affecting downstream ones. Based on this type of argument, Allport (1984) has challenged the claim that the problem in patients like K.F. and P.V. is due to a working-memory deficit rather than damage to an earlier processing system for phonological information (see Vallar, Basso, & Bottini, 1990; Vallar, Corno, & Basso, 1992). Similar objections can undoubtedly be raised in the case of visual–spatial working-memory impairments as well. In short, additional information is needed in order to define the functional architecture and localize the circuitry responsible for working memory, and for this reason we turn to neuroimaging data from subjects with intact brains.

C. Neuroimaging Evidence

Two neuroimaging techniques have been used to isolate storage processes of working memory for spatial and verbal material. One technique makes use of event-related potentials (ERPs) that can be recorded with temporal precision during just the epochs when storage occurs, isolating it from encoding and retrieval processes. The other technique uses positron emission tomography (PET) to measure areas of activation in the brain during working-memory tasks. To isolate storage processes in PET studies, experimenters have compared activation during a working-memory task with activation in a task that is similar except for storage. In this way, the difference in activation can be attributed to storage processes alone, following the assumptions of subtractive logic (see Posner, Petersen, Fox, & Raichle, 1988).

1. Event-Related Potentials

One ERP study by Ruchkin, Johnson, Grafman, Canoune, and Ritter (1992) documents a double dissociation in storage processes in spatial and verbal working-memory tasks. They had subjects engage in two different working-memory tasks on different trials. In one task, subjects saw a target string of consonants and vowels of three, four, or five syllables in length and had to store the string for 5 s, after which a probe string was presented and subjects had to indicate whether it differed from the target string. In the other task, subjects saw a target pattern of letter pairs arranged at three-, four-, or five locations in a visual display, and had to store this pattern for 5 s. After the retention interval, a probe pattern of asterisks appeared, and subjects had to indicate whether this pattern occupied the same locations as the target stimuli. During the stimulus presentation and retention intervals, ERPs were recorded from 13 scalp locations covering posterior and anterior locations.

Globally, the pattern of obtained ERPs showed an increasing slow-wave negativity during the retention interval that was sensitive to the memory load of each task. Importantly, this pattern differed in scalp distribution between the spatial and verbal tasks, implying the involvement of different neural sources for the two tasks. For the spatial task, the major effect was a negative slow wave that was maximal over parietal areas and that was sensitive to the memory load of the task. This negativity began during the presentation of the stimulus and continued during the retention interval. It was lateralized during the early portions of the recording interval in that it was maximal over scalp locations on the right. During the retention interval, the slow wave increased in amplitude and became less lateralized and somewhat more sensitive to memory load. This effect may be a signature of several processes related to the memory task. Its initiation during stimulus presentation could be an indicator of its relation to encoding processes. Its increased amplitude during the retention interval and its increased sensitivity to memory load during this interval may be an indicator of its relation to storage processes as well.

The pattern of ERPs in the verbal task was more complex, but only some of the effects persisted during the retention interval, and only these are likely to be related to storage of information in a verbal buffer. One effect was a negativity that was present only early during the retention interval and that was not sensitive to memory load. Presumably, this effect was not related to the storage requirements of the task. A second effect was a positivity that was also present early during the retention interval but not later, but *was* sensitive to memory load. This effect may be related to storage, but the fact that it was nascent during the interval when the stimuli were presented suggests that it may have more to do with encoding of information into memory. Perhaps the most interesting effect for the verbal task was a frontal negativity that was present during stimulus presentation and during the entire retention interval. This effect was definitely sensitive to memory load during its later portions and may have shown some sensitivity to load early on as well. The fact that this effect began during stimulus presentation may lead one to believe that it had something to do with stimulus encoding. However, the fact that it increased in amplitude and that its sensitivity to memory load became more pronounced during the retention interval suggests that it may be a result of storage processes as well. Of clear interest is that this negativity was most pronounced over left and central frontal sites.

To summarize, the effects that seem most related to the memory requirements of the task are these: a largely right-hemisphere posterior negativity in the spatial task and a largely left-hemisphere anterior negativity in the verbal task. These effects clearly differentiate the two conditions of the task, and so they confirm the pattern of double dissociations that the behavioral and neuropsychological evidence has demonstrated. In support of the neuropsychological evidence, these findings confirm the role of lateralized processes in verbal and spatial working-memory tasks. In addition, they suggest that there may be different contributions of posterior and anterior mechanisms to the two tasks. Of course, it is well known that ERP data with as few recording sites as there were in this study may not be unambiguously revealing about the localization of neural generators (see, e.g., Gevins, 1990; Tucker, 1993). In light of this, we turn to data from PET, which are more revealing about the localization of storage processes in working memory.

2. Positron Emission Tomography

Consider first a pair of experiments reported by Jonides et al. (1993) and Smith, Jonides, and Koeppe (1996; also reported by Awh et al., 1996). One of these experiments involved spatial and the other verbal working memory. The Spatial Memory Task is schematized at the top of Fig. 1. Each trial began with a fixation cross for 500 ms which was followed by the presentation of three dots for 200 ms at essentially random locations around the circumference of an imaginary circle. These dots were followed by a 3000-ms retention interval during which the fixation cross reappeared. Following this, a probe stimulus was presented for 1,500 ms; it consisted of an outline

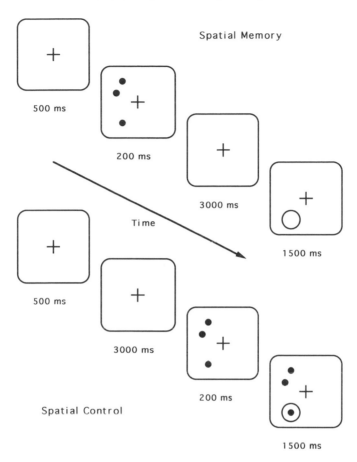

Fig. 1. A schematic of the Spatial Memory and Spatial Control conditions from the experiment by Jonides et al. (1993).

circle. The subjects' task was to determine whether this probe encircled the location of one of the dots presented previously; if so, the subject pushed a response button once and if not, twice. Subjects engaged in a series of such trials during which they were scanned using positron emission tomography (PET).

It is plausible to assume that this task requires the storage of spatial information for a short period of time, thus recruiting spatial working memory. However, the task also clearly requires other processes, such as those needed to: encode the dots, encode the probe circle, attend to the location of the dots, select a response, execute the response, and so forth. These processes were also captured in the PET images of this task because the images were accumulated over a 60-s window of time during which subjects engaged in a number of spatial-memory trials. In order to isolate the storage processes of the task from these additional processes, Jonides et al. (1993) had the same subjects engage in a Spatial Control Task that is shown at the bottom of Fig. 1. In this task, a fixation cross initiated each trial and persisted for 3,500 ms, the duration of the fixation-plus-retention intervals in the Spatial Memory Condition. The cross was succeeded by the presentation of three target dots for 200 ms, which were immediately succeeded by a probe display for 1,500 ms. The probe consisted of the three target dots that had just been presented plus an outline circle. Subjects' task was the same: to indicate whether the circle was superimposed on the location of one of the dots. In this condition, of course, no memory of the dots' locations was required because they were present at the same time as the outline circle. Yet, the condition includes many of the nonstorage processes that were also included in the Spatial Memory Condition. By subtracting the activation images acquired for this Control Condition from the images acquired from the Spatial Memory Condition, then, a relatively pure estimate of activation due to spatial storage could be obtained.

This subtraction revealed four reliable sites of activation, all in the right hemisphere: one in extrastriate occipital cortex, one in posterior parietal cortex, one in premotor cortex, and one in inferior prefrontal cortex. Jonides et al. (1993) attributed these activations to a combination of storage and related processes necessary to create an internal representation of the stimulus to store. It is quite noteworthy that all the reliable activations were present in the right hemisphere. This result is consistent with the data of Ruchkin et al. (1992), Hanley et al. (1991), and De Renzi and Nichelli (1975), who also concluded that right-hemisphere mechanisms were critical to spatial working memory.

Compare this spatial working-memory task to a verbal working-memory experiment that used Sternberg's (1966) item-recognition task (Awh et al., 1996; Smith et al., 1996). The Verbal Memory Condition of this experiment had a structure quite similar to that of the Spatial Memory Condition just discussed. The task is schematized at the top of Fig. 2. Each trial began with a fixation cross for 500 ms that was followed by four uppercase letters arrayed around fixation and presented for 200 msec. These letters were followed by a retention interval of 3,000 ms, after which a probe display appeared for 1,500 ms. The probe consisted of a single lowercase letter presented in the center of the screen. Subjects were to decide if this probe matched in identity any of the letters on that trial. If so, they responded with a single button-push; if not, with a double button-push. Note that the use of a lowercase probe in comparison with uppercase target letters prevented subjects from making a decision on the basis of the shape of the

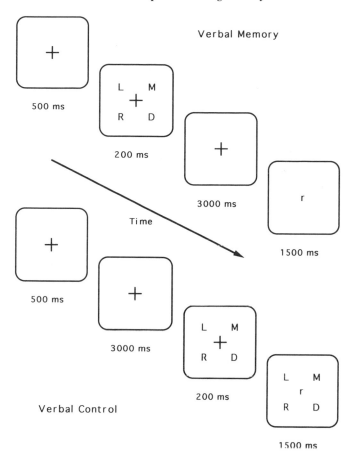

Fig. 2. A schematic of the Verbal Memory and Verbal Control conditions from an experiment reported by Smith et al. (1996) and Awh et al. (1996).

letter; instead, they had to construct a phonological representation of the letters as the basis of their judgment.

This Verbal Memory Condition requires not only storage of letter identities, but additional processes related to encoding of the displays, responding, and so forth. These processes were controlled by collecting activations from a Verbal Control Condition, schematized at the bottom of Fig. 2, and subtracting these from the activations in the Verbal Memory Condition. The Verbal Control is similar in structure to the Spatial Control Condition discussed earlier. The Verbal Control began with a fixation cross for 3,500 ms (the duration of fixation plus retention intervals in the Verbal Memory Condition), followed by the presentation of four uppercase letters for 200 ms. These were followed by the same four letters plus a single lowercase letter in the center of the screen for 1500 ms. As in the Verbal Memory Condition, subjects were to decide whether the lowercase letter matched any of the uppercase letters. In this condition, of course, the judgment did not depend on memory of the uppercase letters because they were present on the screen simultaneously with the lowercase letter. Activations from this Verbal Control Condition were subtracted from those of the Verbal Memory Condition to isolate storage processes.

The PET activations that resulted from this Verbal Memory–Verbal Control subtraction were quite different from those of the Spatial Memory–Spatial Control subtraction. One global difference is that the reliable verbal activations in cortical structures appeared largely in the left hemisphere. These include two sites in posterior parietal cortex (one superior to the other), and three sites in prefrontal cortex: inferior prefrontal, premotor, and supplementary motor. In addition to these, there were also reliable activations in anterior cingulate, right cerebellum, left-hemisphere thalamus, and left-hemisphere insular cortex.

Taken together, the results of the spatial and verbal memory experiments reported by Jonides et al. (1993) and Smith et al. (1996) provide evidence of a double dissociation of spatial and verbal working-memory systems that supplements the evidence reviewed earlier. The reliable activations that resulted from these two experiments did not overlap at all, suggesting two separable pathways for processing information in the two tasks. The spatial task recruited brain mechanisms in the right hemisphere predominantly for the creation and storage of a mental representation of spatial information, while the verbal task recruited largely left-hemisphere mechanisms. Even with this noticeable difference in activation patterns, there were similarities as well. Both tasks resulted in activation of posterior and anterior cortical areas in parietal and premotor cortex respectively, albeit in different hemispheres.

Smith et al. (1996) proposed a pair of hypotheses to account for this pattern of results. One hypothesis is that the activation in posterior parietal cortex was due to the storage of information in the two tasks, with spatial information stored in the right hemisphere and verbal in the left. (The additional occipital activation in the right hemisphere of the spatial task was attributed to the creation of a visual representation of the target locations that was subsequently stored by parietal mechanisms).

The second hypothesis was that the anterior activation was attributed to rehearsal processes in the two tasks, with verbal rehearsal using left-hemisphere anterior structures, and spatial rehearsal using right-hemisphere structures. Rehearsal of verbal information was proposed by Baddeley and Hitch (1974), and Baddeley, (1986, 1992) as an integral component of the phonological portion of working memory. In the case of the verbal task described by Smith et al. (1996), it is plausible to suppose that the anterior structures that were activated (Broca's area, premotor and supplementary motor cortex) participated in rehearsal because these structures are ones that are typically implicated in explicit speech. Indeed, as reviewed later, there is evidence from other PET studies that these structures are involved in implicit speech with little involvement in storage per se. Smith et al. (1996) went on to propose that the right-hemisphere frontal structures activated in the spatial task (premotor and inferior-posterior-frontal areas) accomplished the same sort of rehearsal function for spatial storage. In this case, rehearsal might be, as Baddeley (1986) has proposed, a result of an internal attentional mechanism that reviews each of the spatial locations in turn by directing attention to each. This proposal has anatomical plausibility by virtue of the homology of the premotor and inferior frontal activations in the right hemisphere for the spatial task to the premotor and Broca's area activations in the left hemisphere for the verbal task. There is, however, no additional research that can add to this anatomical case for a right-hemisphere rehearsal function at this time.

Smith et al. (1996) also report an experiment that compares verbal and spatial working memory in more nearly comparable tasks, tasks that load heavily on the storage of information so as to increase the brain activation due to storage. In both the verbal and spatial tasks, subjects were presented a stream of letters during each PET scan, as illustrated in Fig. 3. Each letter was displayed for 0.5 s, with 2.5 s intervening between successive letters. As shown in Fig. 3, the letters were displayed at seemingly random locations around the perimeter of an imaginary circle and they varied in whether they were upper- or lowercase. The presentation conditions for the verbal and spatial tasks were essentially identical. The only difference between the tasks was whether subjects were instructed to remember verbal or spatial information. In the Verbal Memory Condition, shown at the bottom of Fig. 3, for each letter subjects had to decide whether it matched in identity the letter that appeared three previously in the series, regardless of spatial position. Because letter-case was varied, this decision had to be made on the basis of letter identities, not visual shapes. In the Spatial Memory Task, shown at the top of Fig. 3, subjects had to decide whether each letter occupied the same spatial position as the one that appeared three previously in the series, regardless of letter identity. Note that the requirement to consult one's memory of the stimulus "3-back" (the name given to this task) in the series imposes an essentially constant memory load because subjects must store at least the previous three stimuli, constantly updating this representation. Thus, the storage requirements during an entire scan are substantially enhanced over discrete-trial tasks, such as the

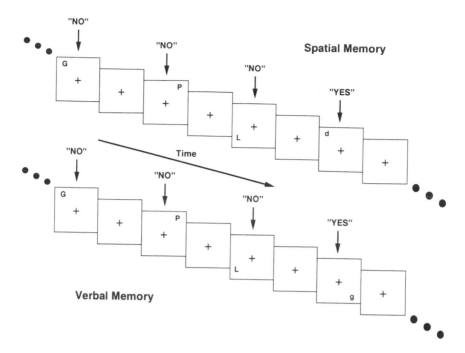

Fig. 3.   A schematic of the Spatial Memory and Verbal Memory conditions from an
experiment reported by Smith et al. (1996).

spatial task of Jonides et al. (1993) and the item-recognition task reported
by Smith et al. (1996).

In order to remove unwanted processes not directly related to storage,
Smith et al. (1996) reported two control conditions, one for the Verbal Memory Task and one for the Spatial Memory Task. In the Verbal Control Condition, subjects were given three target letters at the beginning of a stimulus
sequence that was essentially identical to the sequences shown at the top of
Fig. 3. They were then to decide whether each letter in the sequence matched
one of the three target letters. In a similar way, in the Spatial Control Condition, subjects were shown three target spatial positions at the beginning of
each sequence similar to the sequence shown at the bottom of Fig. 3. They
then had to decide whether each letter in the sequence occupied one of the
three target positions. The activations from these control conditions were
subtracted from those of their respective memory conditions.

The storage requirements of these tasks are high, and this led to substantial activations in the PET images. The patterns of activations were similar
in many respects to those described earlier in this section. Globally, although

there was clear evidence of bilateral activation in both tasks, there was more activation in posterior and anterior areas in the left hemisphere of the verbal task than in the right hemisphere; in a complementary way, the activation in the right hemisphere of the spatial task was higher than that in the left hemisphere. Thus, we have the further evidence of a double dissociation between spatial and verbal working-memory tasks.

At a finer level of analysis, the verbal task resulted in activation in several regions. As in the item-recognition task described previously, there was activation in two regions of the posterior parietal cortex in the left hemisphere. One of these, in the supramarginal gyrus, overlapped almost completely the activation site found in posterior parietal cortex in the item-recognition task of Smith et al. (1996). The other left-hemisphere, posterior activation was in the superior parietal lobule; it may also have been present in the item-recognition task except that that task was conducted on a scanner with a more limited field of view, preventing the collection of data in this portion of the brain. The site in the superior parietal lobule has also been reported in other verbal working memory tasks (see Petrides, Alivisatos, Evans, & Meyer, 1993b). These data contribute to the case that posterior parietal mechanisms are involved in the storage of information in verbal working memory.

Continuing with the verbal task, in addition to the posterior sites, Broca's area in prefrontal cortex showed reliable activation, as in the item-recognition task. By contrast, the other two anterior regions that also showed reliable activation in the item-recognition task, left premotor and supplementary motor areas, did not show reliable activation in the 3-back verbal task. Smith et al. (1996) argue that this may be because the control task in this 3-back experiment was itself somewhat demanding of rehearsal processes, and consequently some of the activation due to rehearsal may have been subtracted out of the Verbal Memory Condition. Alternatively, these other areas may not be integral to rehearsal, and may be involved in some other aspect of processing not yet specified. We shall return to this issue when we later review studies that discriminate between rehearsal and storage functions in verbal working memory.

This verbal task also produced activation in dorsolateral prefrontal cortex in the left hemisphere, an area that has been found by others to play a role in working memory (Cohen, Forman, Braver, Casey, Servan-Schreiber, & Noll, 1994; Petrides et al., 1993b). While studies of working memory in animals have implicated dorsolateral prefrontal cortex in storage functions (e.g., Goldman-Rakic, 1987; Wilson, O'Scalaidhe, & Goldman-Rakic, 1993), this area of the brain is also important in various other cognitive functions, such as temporal coding of stimuli (see Fuster, 1995). The 3-back task of Smith et al. (1996) requires subjects to code the input for the temporal order of the letters that are presented so that subjects can make their memory comparisons to the item that was 3-back. Likewise, the task of Cohen et al. (1994) required a temporal coding operation in that they had subjects determine whether each was identical to the one 2-back in the sequence. Although the task of Petrides et al. (1993b) did not require temporal coding, it did require subjects to manipulate the information in working memory in a way that may also have recruited mechanisms in dorsolateral prefrontal cortex. Thus, the dorsolateral prefrontal activation found by Smith et al. (1996) and others may not reflect storage functions of working memory as much as it reflects "executive functions," as Baddeley (1986) has termed them. If this is the case, there may not be a close analogy between the neural processes of working memory in humans and those in other animals. Although one can make a quite compelling case that the prefrontal neural activity found in animals has something to do with the short-term storage of information (see Funahashi, Bruce, & Goldman-Rakic, 1989), in humans one can find sucessful performance in a working-memory task with little evidence of dorsolateral prefrontal activity if the task does not recruit executive processes (see Jonides et al., 1993; Paulesu, Frith, and Frackowiak, 1993). This issue remains to be more thoroughly investigated.

The pattern of activations found in the Spatial Memory Condition minus its control replicated and expanded on the results of Jonides et al. (1993). First, there was activation in two posterior sites in the right hemisphere, one in the supramarginal gyrus and one in the superior parietal lobule. The site in the supramarginal gyrus agrees well with the site reported by Jonides et al. (1993). The site in the superior parietal lobule is new; however, as in the item-recognition task, the field of view of the PET camera used by Jonides et al. (1993) was not sufficiently large to capture a site this superior in parietal cortex.

The Spatial Memory–Spatial Control subtraction of the 3-back task also revealed activation in dorsolateral prefrontal cortex of the right hemisphere, in an area homologous to that found in the left hemisphere for the verbal task. Once again, we raise the possibility that this area may be involved either in the storage of information or the manipulation of this information by executive processes of various sorts. Activation in this region has also been documented by Petrides, Alivisatos, Evans, and Meyer (1993a) and by McCarthy et al. (1994). Their tasks as well demand not only storage of spatial information, but also its manipulation in various ways that might be characteristic of frontal mechanisms.

While the 3-back spatial task did not show evidence of reliable activation in the right inferior frontal gyrus, as in the study of Jonides et al. (1993), there was activation in a right-hemisphere premotor area that is consistent with the earlier study. Smith et al. (in press) speculate that this activation plus the activation in inferior frontal gyrus may be indicative of a spatial rehearsal mechanism, comparable to the rehearsal of verbal information that has been attributed to similar sites of the left hemisphere. Why the same sites in frontal cortex have not been activated consistently in the spatial tasks we have discussed remains something of a mystery. One possibility (as in the results of the 3-back verbal task) is that some of the putative rehearsal processes in the spatial memory task were subtracted out by the subtraction of the Spatial Control, which itself may have required a modest amount of rehearsal to maintain the three target locations. This explanation, although plausible, remains to be tested.

The results of these various experiments from our laboratory lead to the following conclusions about working memory:

1. Spatial and verbal working memory are mediated by different and separable processing mechanisms.
2. These processing mechanisms are instantiated in different brain circuits.
3. Verbal working memory recruits mechanisms principally of the left hemisphere, including posterior and anterior structures.
4. Spatial working memory recruits mechanisms principally of the right hemisphere, including posterior and anterior structures.

These conclusions are well supported by the neuroimaging data, and they are amplifications of the conclusions that can be drawn from the behavioral and neuropsychological data as well. Thus, we have confidence in the claim that there are different modular systems within working memory for spatial and verbal information.

The neuroimaging studies also support a further claim about working memory, one that was originally proposed by Baddeley and Hitch (1974) and that we shall pursue in detail in the next section. The claim is that the storage functions of verbal and spatial working memory are each mediated by two processes acting in concert: a buffer and a rehearsal process, each of which is specialized for verbal or spatial information. The most compelling basis for this claim is the documentation that verbal working-memory tasks result in activation in posterior parietal and inferior prefrontal cortex in the left hemisphere. The posterior activation is consistent with the site of damage in patients who display deficits in verbal memory span (e.g., Basso et al., 1982; Shallice & Warrington, 1970; Vallar & Baddeley, 1984a; Warrington, Logue, & Pratt, 1971; Warrington & Shallice, 1969), and, thus, this site of activation may underlie the short-term storage of verbal information. The inferior prefrontal site is centered in structures typically associated with Broca's area, structures that neuropsychological evidence suggests are associated with articulation skills (e.g., Goodglass & Kaplan, 1972); this site may underlie the rehearsal of verbal information, using some of the same set of neural mechanisms that mediate explicit speech.

There is tantalizing evidence that this same sort of architecture can be applied to the storage and rehearsal of spatial information as well. Spatial working-memory tasks also produce activation in posterior parietal cortex, in the right hemisphere in an area homologous to the left-hemisphere area activated in verbal working-memory tasks. The symmetry in these two areas leads to the claim that the right posterior activation is reflective of spatial storage processes, just as the left seems to be reflective of verbal storage processes. Also, there is evidence that spatial working-memory tasks at least sometimes produce activation in inferior prefrontal cortex and premotor cortex in the right hemisphere; again, there is a striking parallel here to the left-hemisphere activation produced by verbal working-memory tasks. In the case of verbal working memory, it is plausible to argue that this prefrontal activation reflects rehearsal, given the well-documented functions of Broca's area. In the case of spatial working memory, no such argument can be made at present because too little is known about the function of the inferior prefrontal and premotor structures of human right hemisphere. However, their close homology to the structures activated in the verbal tasks certainly raises the possibility that they may also be mediating rehearsal of some sort (see Awh, Smith, & Jonides, 1995).

Just what this rehearsal may be is not entirely clear. Baddeley (1986) proposed that it may involve an internal allocation of attention to different locations in space, in a kind of parallel to the internal reallocation of attention to different verbal codes in verbal rehearsal. The most straightforward prediction from this sort of account, however, is that brain structures involved in attention or eye-movement control should be involved, and yet we see no evidence of the activation of such structures as the frontal eye fields, the pulvinar nucleus, or the superior colliculus. Of course, absence of evidence is not good reason to conclude that there is evidence of absence, so we must leave it for now that there is simply insufficient basis to say much about the nature of rehearsal of spatial material in working memory.

Let us return to the better justified claim that verbal working memory itself consists of storage and rehearsal processes. This claim has a quite good evidential base in behavioral, neuropsychological, and neuroimaging data, as we will review later in this chapter.

III. Dissociation of Verbal Storage from Rehearsal

A. BEHAVIORAL EVIDENCE

Consider the classic proposal about the architecture of verbal working memory, attributed to Baddeley, Thomson, and Buchanan (1975) originally, and elaborated by Baddeley (1986), among others. The central claim is that verbal working memory is mediated by two subsystems. One is a storage buffer of limited capacity and short duration that is specialized for the storage of information in a phonological code (as opposed to a visuospatial code). The other is a mechanism that is responsible for recirculating the stored information to refresh it. The idea is that recirculation of this information causes its activation to increase, thereby offsetting the decay that afflicts information in the storage buffer. A common example used to motivate this proposal is looking up a number in a telephone book. One finds the number, stores it in the buffer, and then repeats it either aloud or silently until it is dialed. The repetition is identified with this recirculation process, a process sometimes called "rehearsal," "maintenance rehearsal," or "articulatory control." Whatever name is applied to it, this process is typically assumed to be like a tape-recorder loop that runs repeatedly on the material stored in the buffer.

The analogy to a tape loop raises a prediction about rehearsal that was tested by Baddeley et al. (1975): They reasoned that if rehearsal is like a tape loop of limited length, then the number of items one should be able to rehearse should be limited by the length of the items (see also Craik [1968] and Glanzer & Razel [1974] for previous tests of this prediction; Baddeley et al. [1975] for a discussion of these previous tests.). Baddeley et al. (1975) confirmed this prediction in an extensive series of experiments whose composite result was that lists of longer words were more poorly remembered than lists of shorter words (with the same number of words each), where length was measured in either number of syllables or time of articulation by speakers. Quantitative analysis of their results led Baddeley et al. (1975) to conclude that the duration of the tape loop that corresponds to rehearsal is between 1.5 and 2 s.

In addition to the effect of word length, it has been known for some time that the phonemic similarity among verbal items also affects memory-span performance (e.g., Conrad, 1964, 1970, 1972). The effect of phonemic similarity has been attributed to confusion that occurs among items stored in a phonological buffer, such that features of the items become interposed with one another, resulting in a loss of item information, and hence less success in recall (Baddeley, 1986; Baddeley, Lewis, & Vallar, 1984). If word-length and phonemic similarity affect rehearsal and storage, respectively, then one ought to find independent effects of these two variables if they are simultaneously applied in a single experiment (cf. Garner, Hake, & Eriksen, 1956). Longoni, Richardson, and Aiello (1993) tested this prediction and confirmed it. This provides evidence of some functional independence of these two stages in working memory.

Further evidence of the independence of these stages comes from a second experiment by Longoni et al. (1993) that examined the relationship between word length and another variable that has been assumed to affect storage, irrelevant speech. Memory for a string of items is hampered by introducing irrelevant speech that is to be ignored during the presentation and retention of those items (e.g., Colle & Welsh, 1976; Jones & Macken, 1993), and this interference effect has been attributed to a mutual interference between the irrelevant speech and items in the phonological buffer, with little effect of irrelevant speech on rehearsal (Salame & Baddeley, 1982). Two predictions follow from this. One is that the effects of irrelevant speech and phonemic similarity should interact if varied together. They do (Colle & Welsh, 1976; Salame & Baddeley, 1982). A second prediction is that there should be independent effects of irrelevant speech and word length on recall just as there are independent effects of phonemic similarity and word-length. Indeed, there are, as demonstrated by Longoni et al. (1993).

Beyond these tests of the independence of various behavioral manipulations, there is another research strategy that has been explored as a test of the separability of rehearsal and storage in verbal working memory. If rehearsal is a sort of internal articulation, then it should be subject to interference if the mechanism responsible for articulation is also engaged in a secondary, interfering task. This prediction has been tested repeatedly by having subjects articulate something externally, such as "the, the, the . . ." or "one, two, three, four, one, two, . . ." during a memory-span task, thereby suppressing their ability to articulate internally. Of course, doing *any of several* interfering tasks could result in degradation of memory performance. The point of studying the effects of articulatory suppression goes beyond this, however. If articulatory suppression has a selective effect on rehearsal, and if rehearsal is separable from the storage of verbal information, then one should show that articulatory suppression will modulate the effect of a variable affecting rehearsal but it will not modulate the effect of a variable affecting storage. As we have discussed, word length has been implicated as a variable that affects rehearsal, while phonemic similarity has been shown to affect storage. So, articulatory suppression should modulate or interact with the word-length effect but not the phonemic-similarity effect.

Before examining the results of experiments that have tested this prediction, a caution is in order about the mode of stimulus presentation in such a study. Consider an experiment in which material is presented visually and subjects engage in articulatory suppression during the presentation of this material and during the subsequent retention interval. Several studies have found that under such conditions, contrary to the prediction of interest, articulatory suppression diminishes the effects of *both* word length and phonemic similarity on recall (Murray, 1967; Peterson & Johnson, 1971;

see also Richardson, Greaves, & Smith, 1980). With visual presentation, however, suppression may have a pronounced effect on memory not because it exerts its effect on rehearsal, but rather because it interferes with the process of translating visual material into a phonological code before that material is stored. If so, then subjects will not be able to create a phonological code effectively, and any variable that is a sign of this code, such as word length or phonemic similarity, will have its effects diminished.

To meet this caution, investigators have examined the effect of articulatory suppression under conditions in which the material to be remembered was presented by ear. Although a translation process is still required during encoding even with auditory presentation (to turn an auditory input into a phonological code), this translation process is tacitly assumed to be more automatic in character in that it is the staple of natural language processing. In such an experiment, Baddeley et al. (1984) and Longoni et al. (1993) confirmed the prediction of interest: Articulatory suppression eliminated the word-length effect on recall, but it did not affect the influence of phonemic similarity. This points once again to an independence of storage and rehearsal in verbal working memory. (Some earlier studies with auditory presentation failed to find support for the critical prediction, but in these cases rehearsal was not prevented during the entire testing interval: Levy, 1971; Murray, 1968; Peterson & Johnson, 1971.)

B.   NEUROPSYCHOLOGICAL EVIDENCE

Because the selective effects of phonemic similarity and word length are relatively clear, the predicted effects of these variables on patients with verbal working-memory deficits should be rather straightforward. If a memory deficit is due to just impaired rehearsal, then:

1. An effect of word length should be minimal.
2. Articulatory suppression should not influence performance (because presumably there would be no rehearsal to interfere with).
3. Phonemic similarity would be expected to reduce memory for auditory material, as in normals.
4. Phonemic similarity should not influence visual items (since rehearsal is needed to translate these items into a phonological code).

A deficit in the phonological-storage component, on the other hand, should (a) selectively influence the phonemic similarity effect in both the visual and auditory modality, while (b) leaving the effects of word length and articulatory suppression intact.

As straightforward as these predictions may be, the interpretation of verbal working-memory deficits has been less than clear (see Shallice &

Vallar, 1990). For example, the patient P.V. (considered earlier) would appear to display the pattern indicative of a rehearsal deficit—e.g., an absence of word-length and articulatory suppression effects—yet, for a variety of reasons, her deficit has been interpreted as one due to the phonological store (Vallar & Baddeley, 1984b). There are two aspects of her performance profile that pose a particular challenge to a rehearsal-deficit interpretation. First, her overt articulation rate is normal (Vallar & Baddeley, 1984a). Such a sparing of function is inconsistent with a rehearsal deficit because overt and covert speech are generally claimed to depend on common mechanisms; this claim is supported not only by the interference of overt articulation on covert rehearsal (discussed earlier), but also by the high correlation between reading rate and verbal memory span in normal subjects (Baddeley et al., 1975; Mackworth, 1963). Second, there are indications that P.V.'s phonological store is not functioning normally in spite of the normal effect of phonemic similarity with auditory presentation. P.V. shows very rapid forgetting on the Brown–Peterson task which is generally thought to measure the duration of a phonological memory trace (Basso et al., 1982). This task requires a subject to retain a short list of items that is typically well below span (about 2–3), while engaging in counting backward or in simple arithmetic during a retention interval. Because rehearsal is prevented by the secondary task, performance can be used to measure the rate of decay of auditory memory from the phonological store. P.V. forgets everything in 3 s, which is faster than normal. So what are we to make of the absence of word-length and articulatory suppression effects for P.V., which suggest a problem in rehearsal? Vallar and Baddeley (1984b) suggest that though rehearsal is available, P.V. chooses not to use it because of the general ineffectiveness of her verbal working memory.

Other patients, such as C.M. (Nichelli & Cubelli cited in Logie et al., 1989) and G.F. (Vallar & Cappa, 1987), have deficits in articulation (or dysarthria) and do not show word-length effects on span tasks but do show phonemic similarity effects. Although additional information (from the Brown–Peterson test, for example) is lacking, on the surface these cases offer some indication that rehearsal can be selectively impaired. A problem with such cases however, is that they may not have much of a verbal memory deficit; C.M.'s span of 5 is certainly within normal limits.

Belleville, Peretz, and Arguin (1992) reported evidence of case Ro.L., which may offer the clearest indication thus far for a rehearsal component of working memory that can be impaired independently of the phonological store. Ro.L., a right-handed male, sustained a left cerebrovascular accident at the age of 57 which resulted in a lesion of the temporoparietal region. This left him with sensory and motor deficits affecting the right limbs, in addition to aphasia. These deficits showed marked improvement over the subsequent 12-month period. Ro.L.'s language comprehension was relatively intact and his speech was fluent. However, his repetition of single words and sentences was impaired even though his ability to compare auditorily presented phoneme pairs (e.g., "bo" vs. "ro") was normal. His language profile is typical of conduction aphasia, a disturbance that is closely linked with deficits in verbal working memory (see Allport, 1984; Caramazza, Basili, Koller, & Berndt, 1981; Kinsbourne, 1972b; Shallice & Vallar, 1990; Shallice & Warrington, 1977; Strub & Gardner, 1974). Accordingly, Ro.L. has a verbal span of 3 in conjunction with a normal spatial span of 5.

Like P.V., Ro.L.'s span is reduced by phonemic similarity and by using longer words, but is unaffected by articulatory suppression. Unlike P.V., however, Ro.L. has a reduced rate of articulation and appears to perform normally on a Brown–Peterson test of trace decay (though there is some question about the sensitivity of this test). Thus, Ro.L. seems to provide the best neuropsychological evidence thus far for a selective rehearsal deficit as the basis for verbal working-memory impairment.

The study of impaired rehearsal in these and other patients has revealed another potential dissociation that should not go unnoticed. Many have assumed that in addition to recycling information from the phonological buffer to keep it fresh, rehearsal translates information that comes into memory via vision into a phonological code for storage in the buffer. One can now make a case that these two alleged functions of rehearsal themselves may be dissociable. In support of this argument, Nichelli and Cubelli (in Logie, Cubelli, Della Sala, Alberoni, & Nichelli, 1989; see also Della Sala, Logie, Marchetti, & Wynn, 1991) cite the pattern of deficits exhibited by three patients. One, M.D.C., is argued to have damage to the visual-phonological translation process. This patient shows a phonological similarity effect and a word-length effect with auditory presentation, as would be expected if her ability to use phonological storage and rehearsal were intact. However, she does not show either of these effects with visual presentation (Vallar & Cappa, 1987). Nichelli and Cubelli argue that this is because she may have damage to the process that translates visual information into a phonological code. With this damage, she cannot gain access to a phonological buffer from visual input and therefore cannot show effects of variables that affect either the buffer or rehearsal. In comparison to M.D.C., Nichelli and Cubelli cite patients G.F. (Vallar & Cappa, 1987) and C.M. (Nichelli & Cubelli in Logie et al., 1989). These patients are argued to have deficits in rehearsal per se, but a normal coding process to translate visual input into a phonological form. According to this argument, both patients should show a phonological similarity effect for both visual and auditory presentation because they can gain access to the phonological store via either input pathway if their coding processes are intact. However, they should show no effect of word length with auditory presentation if rehearsal is damaged, though they might show some effect of word length with visual presentation if word length affects the ease of creating a phonological code from visual input. All these predicted effects have been documented. To place this argument on a completely firm footing will require the identification of two variables that show clear and independent effects on rehearsal and phonological coding respectively. This remains to be documented.

All in all, a compelling case has been developed on the basis of behavioral and neuropsychological studies that rehearsal and storage of verbal information in working memory are mediated by separable processes. In particular, if the published interpretations of P.V. and Ro.L. are correct, these cases represent evidence for the double dissociability of rehearsal and phonological storage. In addition, as we have just summarized, there is suggestive evidence that the creation of a phonological code for visual input is separable from the process that recycles this code once created. What is not clear from the neuropsychological evidence, however, is the anatomical loci of any of these processes. The anarthric patients discussed have widely different brain regions associated with their deficits. P.V.'s lesion apparently affects the entire language region of the left hemisphere. Ro.L.'s relatively circumscribed lesion affects the posterior language areas—which is very surprising given that its impact is seemingly on the articulatory processes underlying rehearsal. For more evidence about the different brain structures that mediate the processes of interest, we need to consider evidence from neuroimaging studies.

C. NEUROIMAGING EVIDENCE

A classic paradigm for studying the mechanisms of verbal working memory is the item-recognition task that we discussed at length in Section IIC2. Recall that in this task, subjects are presented a short series of items to remember, then a probe item, and they must judge whether the probe is a member of the set they are holding in memory. Paulesu et al. (1993) were the first to search for brain activations that accompanied performance in this task. In their main experimental task, subjects saw a memory set of six consonants, presented sequentially, which they were instructed to rehearse and memorize. These were followed by a probe consonant, and subjects were required to judge whether the probe was a member of the memory set. Trials of this sort were strung together during which PET measurements were taken. Note that this procedure emphasizes the role of storage and rehearsal in that the major portion of each PET recording interval is occupied with storing and maintaining the sequentially presented letters. In order to subtract out task components that were not related to verbal storage and rehearsal, a control condition was included, and activation from it was subtracted from activation in the item-recognition task. The control was identical to the item-recognition task except that the items were Korean letters with which the subjects were not familiar. In this task, subjects were instructed to use a visual code as the basis of their memory. Subtraction of activation in the control task from activation in the experimental task revealed reliably increased blood flow in the left supramarginal gyrus and in Broca's area. Activation of supramarginal gyrus, as reviewed earlier, is consistent with neuropsychological evidence from patients who have deficits in verbal working memory, and again we conclude that activation of this site represents verbal-storage processes in the item-recognition task. The second site, Broca's area, is routinely identified with external speech, and so it is plausible that this is the site of rehearsal processes.

To confirm that the supramarginal gyrus is involved in storage and Broca's area in rehearsal, Paulesu et al. (1993) had subjects engage in a second experimental task. In this task, subjects were presented a sequence of letters and had to judge whether each one rhymed with the letter "B," which was always present on the screen. The control condition for this task was one in which a string of Korean letters was presented on the screen, and subjects had to judge whether each was visually similar to a target Korean letter that was always present on the screen. Paulesu et al. (1993) reasoned that the rhyming task involves some internal articulation compared to its control, and so it should activate Broca's area. However, the rhyming task compared to its control does not involve any verbal storage, and so if the supramarginal gyrus is the structure recruited for storage, it should not be activated in the rhyming task. As predicted, Paulesu et al. (1993) found that the rhyming-minus-control subtraction revealed reliable activation of Broca's area but not of the supramarginal gyrus.

It is also interesting to note another pattern of activations that resulted from the study by Paulesu et al. (1993). They combined activations from the verbal item-recognition task with those from the rhyming task and subtracted from this the combined activations from the two control conditions. Of course, this grand subtraction revealed activation in the supramarginal gyrus and in Broca's area, as reviewed above. It also revealed activation in the supplementary motor area and cerebellum as well, areas that are thought to be involved in the planning and production of overt speech. Paulesu et al. (1993) reasoned that these areas may have been activated as part of a speech-production circuit although no overt speech was required in the tasks. This result leads to the inference that silent rehearsal may engage a circuit of frontal sites just as overt speech does. In this sense, rehearsal may be quite well characterized as "internal speech."

Though the evidence reported by Paulesu et al. (1993) is compelling about the sites of storage and rehearsal, one would like to have additional evidence about these sites for two reasons. First, the data reported by Paulesu et al. (1993) constitute a single, not a double, dissociation. The single dissociation is a result of their showing activation in supramarginal gyrus in the item recognition task but not the rhyming task, while the activation in Broca's area was present in both tasks. Their interpretation of this single dissociation is plausible, though other interpretations may do as well. Suppose, for example, that the item-recognition task was simply more difficult than the rhyming task and so resulted in more activation overall. Indeed, not only did this task show reliable activation in supramarginal gyrus while the rhyming task did not, it also showed a higher level of activation in Broca's area as well, even though the rhyming task produced significant activation in this area. A second difficulty in interpreting the Paulesu et al. (1993) data is that the function of Broca's area in the two tasks may have been quite different. In the item-recognition task it may have been required for internal speech, but in the rhyming task it may have been required for phonological analysis of each letter sound to determine whether there was sufficient similarity to constitute a rhyme with the target.

In light of these concerns, it is comforting that there are two additional reports of PET measurements of storage and rehearsal processes in verbal working memory. One of these is the item-recognition experiment described by Smith et al. (1996) and Awh et al. (1996), which we discussed in the context of spatial–verbal dissociations. Recall that the experiment included an item-recognition task similar to the one presented by Paulesu et al. (1993), plus a control condition in which subjects saw quite similar perceptual events and made responses similar to those in the main condition so that these processing components could be subtracted from the activation images of the item-recognition task. The results showed reliable activation in the anterior part of the brain, including Broca's area, supplementary motor cortex (SMA), and premotor cortex in the left hemisphere. Recall that Paulesu et al. (1993) also reported activation in Broca's area and SMA when they combined activations from their item-recognition and rhyming tasks relative to the controls. Given that Smith et al. (1996) obtained these activations for the item-recognition task alone, they extend the results of Paulesu et al. (1993). The three anterior frontal regions of interest have been implicated in explicit speech production by Petersen et al. (1988). Together with the evidence from Paulesu et al. (1993) about the involvement of these areas in item-recognition plus rhyming, and the evidence from Smith et al. (1996) about their involvement in item-recognition alone, it is becoming quite convincing that these areas are engaged in the processes necessary for silent rehearsal. Together with the activation in right cerebellum that has been associated with these three cortical regions (reported by Paulesu et al., 1993, and Smith et al., 1996), a circuit mediating the production of inner speech is emerging.

As described earlier, Smith et al. (1996) also reported activations in the superior parietal lobule and the supramarginal gyrus. One of these sites of activation is similar to the parietal site reported by Paulesu et al. (1993) for their item-recognition task, which they too associated with storage processes in that task. Indeed, the most common site of damage in patients with deficits in verbal memory span is a posterior site (e.g., McCarthy & Warrington, 1990) that is consistent with the posterior sites discovered by Paulesu et al. (1993) and Smith et al. (1996). Thus, a compelling case is developing that this posterior region is involved in the storage of verbal information in working memory.

A second PET experiment that confirms and extends these results has been detailed by Awh et al. (1996). The main task used in this experiment was one in which subjects had to maintain verbal information in working memory continuously, much as in the 3-back task described in Section IIC2. As such, this experiment emphasized the storage and rehearsal components of working memory more than the item-recognition tasks already described. The paradigm is shown in Fig. 4. The top of the figure illustrates the Verbal Memory condition: Subjects saw a stream of single letters appear centered on a screen, each for .5 s, with 2.5 s intervening between successive letters. As each letter appeared, the subject's task was to decide whether it matched the letter that had appeared two items back in the sequence (hence this is a 2-back task). Note that in order to be successful in this condition, subjects must always maintain in memory representations of the two most recent letters to compare with the current one, constantly updating their representations as new letters appear.

Awh et al. (1996) report two control conditions, one intended to isolate storage and rehearsal processes in the 2-back task, and one intended to isolate storage alone. The Search Control Condition, shown in the middle of Fig. 4, required subjects to search for a single target letter in a sequence similar to that presented in the 2-back condition. The visual and response events in this Search Task were quite similar to those in the 2-back task, but the working memory requirements were minimal. When brain activations in the Search Task were subtracted from those in the 2-back task, there was clear evidence supporting the circuit for working memory that emerges from the item-recognition experiments. In particular, there was activation in left-hemisphere posterior parietal sites as well as in left-hemisphere prefrontal sites, including Broca's area, SMA, and premotor cortex. This constellation of results confirms the involvement of these sites in storage and rehearsal processes, respectively.

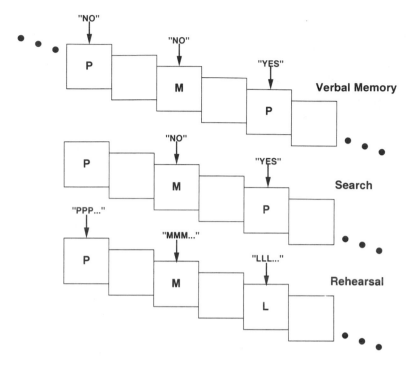

Fig. 4. A schematic of the Verbal Memory, Search, and Rehearsal conditions from an experiment reported by Awh et al. (1996).

The Rehearsal Control Condition from the experiment of Awh et al. (1996) adds more evidence about the circuitry of verbal working memory. In this condition, shown at the bottom of Fig. 4, subjects were presented with a stream of letters, just as in the 2-back task; they had to emit a manual response upon presentation of each letter and then silently rehearse the letter to themselves until the next one appeared. Thus, this condition duplicated the perceptual and response requirements of the 2-back condition, but subjects engaged only in rehearsal, with much less memory load than in the 2-back task. Thus, subtraction of the activations in this Rehearsal control from those in the 2-back task should have yielded left-hemisphere posterior activations if these represent storage, but it should have eliminated left-hemisphere anterior activations if they represent rehearsal. Awh et al. (1996) did find that the posterior parietal activation was still reliable in this subtraction. They also found that the anterior activations in Broca's area and premotor cortex in the left hemisphere were no longer statistically significant, also consistent with their predictions. There was, however, still remnant activation in left SMA and in right cerebellum, both also associated with language production (Paulesu et al., 1993). This remnant activation may well be a result of the heavier rehearsal demands of the 2-back condition than of the Rehearsal condition in that the former demanded constant rehearsal for subjects to be successful in the memory task whereas the latter merely required rehearsal for each letter presented. All in all, the results of Awh et al.'s (1996) experiment confirm nicely the involvement of left posterior parietal cortex in storage, and left prefrontal cortex in verbal rehearsal processes.

IV. Summary and Conclusions

Let us take stock of the large body of evidence presented in this chapter. The central point of our review has been to argue, largely via evidence of double dissociations, that there are at least two storage systems in working memory—one responsible for verbal and one responsible for spatial information. This conclusion seems inescapable in that:

1. One can identify different experimental factors in behavioral studies that separately influence each type of storage.
2. There is at least one pair of patients such that one of them shows a deficit in verbal storage with no deficit in spatial storage and the other shows the complimentary pattern of deficit.
3. Neuroimaging studies find different circuitries for verbal and spatial storage when these storage systems are isolated using subtraction techniques.

We also reviewed evidence that bears on another aspect of working memory, the involvement of rehearsal in addition to storage processes for verbal material. Behavioral studies of normal subjects have yielded a set of variables that seem to exert separable effects on verbal storage and rehearsal. The hypothesis that these two processes are distinct is strengthened by neuropsychological evidence that one or the other process can be selectively damaged. Finally, data from PET studies indicate that rehearsal processes may be mediated by left-hemisphere anterior cortical mechanisms while storage is mediated by left-hemisphere posterior structures.

The PET evidence about dissociations of storage and rehearsal processes for verbal material has implications beyond its value in establishing that these two aspects of processing may be separable. One such implication has to do with the processes of rehearsal. We take it as quite significant that the structures that are associated with verbal rehearsal (Broca's area, premotor cortex, and SMA) are also structures that have been associated with the planning and production of explicit speech. Furthermore, Hinke et al. (1993) have shown that Broca's area is active during internal speech, and McGuire, Shah, and Murray (1993) have shown that this same area is active in schizophrenics during episodes when they report auditory hallucinations (i.e., internal speech). All these lines of evidence converge on the conclusion that some or all of the very same structures that are at the heart of our skill at producing speech are harnessed in the service of internal processes that make use of a speechlike code in other cognitive tasks as well. In particular, it seems as if these structures are involved at least in the internal recycling of verbal information that occurs during the retention interval of a working-memory task. Although we have been assuming that this recycling is done for the purpose of keeping information alive and resistant to forgetting, this issue is not yet settled (see, e.g., Longoni et al., 1993). Whatever the functions of rehearsal, however, it is clearly an integral part of verbal working memory, and separable from the storage of information per se.

There are, however, two caveats to the conclusion that the neural loci involved in covert speech and rehearsal are the same as those involved in overt language production. The first has to do with the uncertain evidence concerning the relationship between damage to anterior regions of the left hemisphere and impaired verbal working memory. To the extent that Broca's area, for instance, participates in rehearsal, damage to it would be predicted to impair short-term verbal memory that relies on rehearsal. The evidence on this point is equivocal. Contrary to the prediction, two large-scale studies examining the relative impact of anterior versus posterior left-hemisphere damage on span tasks found that posterior damage produced significant impairment whereas anterior damage did not (De Renzi & Nichelli, 1975; Risse, Rubens, & Jordan, 1984). On the other hand, more in line with the prediction of interest, Swinney and Taylor (1971) and Vallar et al. (1992) included both anterior and posterior aphasics in their populations and found no differences between them in short-term memory tasks, although neither study mentions any specific comparisons as a function of lesion site. Along these same lines, to the extent that the profile of patient Ro.L. can be taken to reflect a rehearsal deficit, the posterior locus of his lesion is particularly puzzling (though it is possible that the computerized tomography [CT] imaging study of this patient did not reveal the full extent of the lesion). One way to reconcile these findings with the claim that rehearsal is implemented by left anterior regions is to assume that the rehearsal loop cannot function properly if the phonological store is impaired. That is, a deficit in the phonological store may compromise the functioning of rehearsal so that it too is no longer effective. If so, it may *not* be possible to have a pure deficit of storage without an associated, albeit secondary, deficit of rehearsal. By this hypothesis, Ro.L. would be expected to have some (as yet undetected) deficit of the phonological storage system resulting from his posterior left-hemisphere damage.

The second caveat about our localization of rehearsal to anterior regions has to do with the resolution of PET. It is conceivable that the loci identified by Awh et al. (1996) and by Paulesu et al. (1993) are merely in close proximity to areas responsible for overt articulation, but are not these areas themselves. Given that the resolution of PET is no better than approximately 7–10 mm and that the technique requires averaging across individuals, this is certainly a possibility. Indeed, based on the effects of intracranial stimulation during verbal working-memory tasks, Ojemann (1978) concluded that the anterior and posterior loci that participate in such tasks are very close but not identical with the areas involved in naming.

The dissociation of storage and rehearsal for verbal material evident through PET also has implications for the site of storage. Just as anterior structures have been associated with rehearsal, posterior structures, in parietal cortex, have been associated with storage. There are at least two interesting observations to make about this. One is that the many findings in nonhuman animals of storage sites for working memory in frontal lobes (e.g., Funahashi et al., 1989) may not be very telling about verbal working-memory storage in humans. Indeed, this conclusion may apply to the storage of spatial material as well. Given the homology between the right-hemisphere parietal activations in PET studies of spatial working memory and the left-hemisphere parietal activations in verbal studies, it is reasonable to suppose that a key site of short-term spatial storage is the right parietal lobe. While there has been some evidence that monkeys also have parietal sites with spatial storage functions (Chafee & Goldman-Rakic, 1994; Quintana & Fuster, 1993), the dominant conclusion that can be drawn from animal studies is that the frontal lobes are more central to storage. So, here also, there may be an important difference in the anatomical structure of working memory between humans and other animals.

A second observation about the apparently posterior site of storage is more speculative. We consider it interesting that storage mechanisms for working memory are near the anatomical sites at which perceptual processing occurs. For the visual and auditory modalities, the sites of perceptual processing (both very early processes and those responsible for pattern recognition) are all in the posterior parts of neocortex. That working-memory storage also seems to be housed in this same general locale raises the possibility that working-memory mechanisms make use of some of the machinery that is involved in perception of stimuli. This may be true not only of verbal and spatial working memory, as already reviewed, but also of working memory for form (Smith, Jonides, Koeppe, et al., 1995). For example, the spatial-analysis mechanisms that have been identified in parietal cortex (the so-called "dorsal pathway of vision": Ungerleider & Mishkin, 1982) may be among those used in the storage of spatial information as well. Of course, at present it is premature to make much of what may be a coincidence in localization, but the existing data do raise a hypothesis that merits further investigation.

Yet another implication arises from the neuroimaging evidence that shows a dissociation of verbal storage and rehearsal. If there is a homology between verbal and spatial storage in parietal cortex of the left and right hemispheres respectively, perhaps it is worth entertaining the hypothesis that there is also a homology between verbal and spatial rehearsal in frontal cortex of the left and right hemispheres. Several neuroimaging studies of spatial working memory have revealed activations in right inferior prefrontal cortex (Jonides et al., 1993; Smith et al., 1996), in areas that are quite similar to the sites of verbal rehearsal in the left hemisphere. These activations lead one to the hypothesis that there are spatial rehearsal processes as well as verbal ones. At present, this is a hypothesis with little support; however, it is one that merits attention (see Awh, Smith, & Jonides, 1995).

We close with one final comment. The data we have reviewed provide strong support for the architecture of working memory first proposed by Baddeley and Hitch (1974) and since elaborated by others. According to this architecture, the storage of information in working memory is not unitary, but is composed of multiple storage buffers that vary in the type of information they store. The evidence we have reviewed summarizes the case that there are at least two such buffers, one for verbal and one for spatial information. We note, however, that there is growing evidence of more than just two working-memory buffers in humans as well as in other animals. Smith and Jonides (1995), for example, offer evidence of a dissociation between the storage of spatial and visual-object information in working memory. Others offer evidence of the involvement of a motoric working memory as well (see, e.g., Georgopolous, Crutcher, & Schwartz, 1989; Reisberg, Rappaport & O'Shaughnessy, 1984; Saltz & Donnenwerth-Nolan, 1981; Smyrnis, Masato, Ashe, & Georgopoulos, 1992; Smyth & Pendleton, 1989). There is also evidence of an auditory memory that does not store a phonological code (e.g., Colombo, D'Amato, Rodman & Gross, 1990; Zatorre, Evans, Meyer, & Gjedde, 1992; Zatorre & Samson, 1991). In that working memory plays a critical role in various higher cognitive functions, there may well be need to investigate a more abstract working memory as well, one that stores a semantic or propositional code (e.g., Martin, Shelton, & Yaffee, 1994; Shulman, 1971). In all these ways, the architecture of working memory is more complex than our discussion in the bulk of this paper implies. Nevertheless, in that it often has been documented that the human brain is organized around the processing of verbal and spatial information by its hemispheric lateralization, we suspect that the verbal and spatial buffers that we have discussed play a central role in human cognitive functioning.

ACKNOWLEDGMENTS

Preparation of this manuscript was supported in part by a grant from the Office of Naval Research and in part by a grant from the National Institute on Aging, both to the University of Michigan.

REFERENCES

Allport, D. A. (1984). Auditory-verbal short-term memory and conduction aphasia. In H. Bouma and D. G. Bouwhuis (Eds.), *Attention and performance x: Control of language processes* (pp. 313–325). Hillsdale, NJ: Erlbaum.

Atkinson, R. C. & Shiffrin, R. M. (1968). Human Memory: A prepared system and its control processes. In K. W. Spence & J. T. Spence (Eds.), *The Psychology of Learning and Motivation* (Vol. 2, pp. 89–195). Orlando, FL: Academic Press.

Atkinson, R. C., Shiffrin, R. M. (1971). The control of short-term memory. *Scientific American, 225,* 82–90.

Awh, E., Jonides, J., Smith, E. E., Schumacher, E. H., Koeppe, R. A., & Katz, S. (1996). Dissociation of storage and rehearsal in verbal working memory. *Psychological Science, 7,* 25–31.

Awh, E., Smith, E. E., & Jonides, J. (1995). Human rehearsal processes and the frontal lobes: PET evidence. In J. Grafman, F. Boller, & K. Holyoak (Eds), *Structure and functions of the human prefrontal cortex.* The New York Academy of Sciences.

Baddeley, A. D. (1986). *Working memory.* Oxford: Oxford University Press.

Baddeley, A. D. (1992). Working memory. *Science, 255,* 566–569.

Baddeley, A. D., & Hitch, G. J. (1974). Working memory. In G. H. Bower (Ed.), *Attention and performance VI* (pp. 647–667). Hillsdale, NJ: Erlbaum.

Baddeley, A. D., Lewis, V., & Vallar, G. (1984). Exploring the articulatory loop. *The Quarterly Journal of Experimental Psychology, 36A,* 233–252.

Baddeley, A. D., Thompson, N., & Buchanan, M. (1975). Word length and the structure of short-term memory. *Journal of Verbal Learning and Verbal Behavior, 14,* 575–89.

Baddeley, A., & Wilson, B. (1985). Phonological coding and short-term memory in patients without speech. *Journal of Memory and Language, 23,* 490–502.

Basso, A., Spinnler, H., Vallar, G., & Zanobio, M. E. (1982). Left hemisphere damage and selective impairment of auditory verbal short-term memory: A case study. *Neuropsychologia, 20,* 263–274.

Belleville, S., Peretz, I., & Arguin, M. (1992). Contribution of articulatory rehearsal to short-term memory: Evidence from a case of selective disruption. *Brain and Language, 43,* 713–746.

Bishop, D. V. M., & Robson, J. (1989). Unimpaired short-term memory and rhyme judgment in congenitally speechless individuals: Implications for the notion of "articulatory coding." *Quarterly Journal of Experimental Psychology, 41,* 123–140.

Broadbent, D. E. (1958). *Perception and communication.* London: Pergamon Press.

Brooks, L. R. (1968). Spatial and verbal components of the act of recall. *Canadian Journal of Psychology, 22,* 349–368.

Caramazza, A. (1986). On drawing inferences about the structure of normal cognitive systems from the analysis of impaired performance: The case for single-patient studies. *Brain and Cognition, 5,* 41–66.

Caramazza, A., Basili, A. G., Koller, J. J., & Berndt, R. T. (1981). An investigation of repetition and language processing in a case of conduction aphasia. *Brain and Language, 14,* 235–271.

Chafee, M., & Goldman-Rakic, P. S. (1994). Prefrontal cooling dissociates memory- and sensory-guided oculomotor delayed response functions. *Society for Neuroscience Abstracts, 20,* 808.

Cohen, J. D., Forman, S. D., Braver, T. S., Casey, B. J., Servan-Schreiber, D., & Noll, D. C. (1994). Activation of the prefrontal cortex in a nonspatial working memory task with functional MRI. *Human Brain Mapping, 1,* 293–304.

Colle, H. A., & Welsh, A. (1976). Acoustic masking in primary memory. *Journal of Verbal Learning and Verbal Behavior, 15,* 17–32.

Colombo, M., D'Amato, A. R., Rodman, H. R., & Gross C. G. (1990). Auditory association cortex lesions impair auditory short-term memory in monkeys. *Science, 247,* 336–338.

Coltheart, M. (1985). Cognitive neuropsychology and the study of reading. *Attention and Performance XI.* Hillsdale, NJ: Erlbaum.

Conrad, R. (1964). Acoustic confusions in immediate memory. *British Journal of Psychology, 55,* 75–84.

Conrad, R. (1970). Short-term memory processes in the deaf. *British Journal of Psychology, 61,* 179–195.

Conrad, R. (1972). Short-term memory in the deaf: A test for speech coding. *British Journal of Psychology, 63,* 173–180.

Craik, F. I. M. (1968). Two components in free recall. *Journal of Verbal Learning and Verbal Behavior, 7,* 996–1004.

De Renzi, E., Faglioni, P., & Previdi, P. (1977). Spatial memory and hemispheric locus of lesion. *Cortex, 13,* 424–433.

De Renzi, E., & Nichelli, P. (1975). Verbal and non-verbal short-term memory impairment following hemispheric damage. *Cortex, 11,* 341–354.

Della Sala, S., Logie, R. H., Marchetti, C., & Wynn, V. (1991). Case studies in working memory: A case for single cases? *Cortex, 27,* 169–191.

den Heyer, K., & Barrett, B. (1971). Selective loss of visual and verbal information in STM by means of visual and verbal interpolated tasks. *Psychonomic Science, 25,* 100–102.

Dunn, J. C., & Kirsner, K. (1988). Discovering functionally independent mental processes: The principle of reversed association. *Psychological Review, 95,* 91–101.

Farah, M. J. (1994). Neuropsychological inference with an interactive brain: A critique of the locality assumption. *Behavioral and Brain Sciences, 17,* 43–104.

Funahashi, S., Bruce, C. J., & Goldman-Rakic, P. S. (1989). Mnemonic coding of visual space in the monkey's dorsolateral prefrontal cortex. *Journal of Neurophysiology, 61,* 331–349.

Fuster, J. M. (1995). *Memory in the Cerebral Cortex.* Cambridge, MA: MIT Press.

Galton, F. (1883). *Inquiries into the human faculty and its development.* Everyman Edition, London: Dent.

Garner, W. R., Hake, H. W., & Ericsen, C. W. (1956). Operationism and the concept of perception. *Psychological Review, 63,* 149–159.

Georgopoulos, A. P., Crutcher, M. D., & Schwartz, A. B. (1989). Cognitive spatial-motor processes. *Experimental Brain Research, 75,* 183–194.

Gevins, A. S. (1990). Dynamic patterns in multiple lead data. In J. W. Rohrbaugh, R. Parasuraman, and R. Johnson, Jr. (Eds.), *Event related brain potentials: Basic issues and applications* (pp. 44–56). New York: Oxford University Press.

Glanzer, M., & Razel, M. (1974). The size of the unit in short-term storage. *Journal of Verbal Learning and Verbal Behavior, 13,* 114–131.

Goldman-Rakic, P. S. (1987). Circuitry of primate prefrontal cortex and regulation of behavior by representational memory. In F. Plum (Ed.), *Handbook of physiology: The nervous system* (pp. 373–414). Bethesda, MD: American Physiological Society.

Goodglass, H., & Kaplan, E. (1972). *The assessment of aphasia and related disorders.* Philadelphia: Lea & Febiger.

Hanley, J. R., Young, A. W., & Pearson, N. A. (1991). Impairment of visuo-spatial sketch pad. *Quarterly Journal of Experimental Psychology, 43A,* 101–125.

Hebb, D. O. (1949). *Organization of Behavior.* New York: Wiley.

Hinke, R. M., Hu, X., Stillman, A. E., Kim, S., Merkle, H., Salmi, R., & Ugurbil, K. (1993). Functional magnetic resonance imaging of Broca's area during internal speech. *NeuroReport, 4,* 675–678.

Hitch, G. J. (1978). The role of short-term memory in mental arithmetic. *Cognitive Psychology, 10,* 302–323.

James, W. (1890). *The Principles of Psychology, Vol. I.* Authorized Edition, Dover Publications.

Jones, D. M., and Macken, W. (1993). Irrelevant tones produce an irrelevant speech effect: Implications for phonological coding in working memory. *Journal of Experimental Psychology: Learning, Memory, and Cognition, 19,* 369–381.

Jonides, J., Smith, E. E., Koeppe, R. A., Awh, E., Minoshima, S., & Mintun, M. A. (1993). Spatial working memory in humans as revealed by PET. *Nature, 363,* 623–625.

Kinsbourne, M. (1972a). Cognitive deficit: Experimental analysis. In J. L. McGaugh (Ed.), *Psychobiology* (pp. 285–338). Orlando, FL: Academic Press.

Kinsbourne, M. (1972b). Behavioral analysis of the repetition deficit in conduction aphasia. *Neurology, 22,* 1126–1132.

Levy, B. A. (1971). Role of articulation in auditory and visual short-term memory. *Journal of Verbal Learning and Verbal Behavior, 10,* 123–132.

Logie, R. H., Cubelli, R., Della Sala, S., Alberoni, M., & Nichelli, P. (1989). Anarthria and verbal short-term memory. In J. Crawford and D. Parker (Eds.), *Developments in clinical and experimental neuropsychology* (pp. 203–211). New York: Plenum Press.

Logie, R. H., Zucco, G. M., & Baddeley, A. D. (1990). Interference with visual short-term memory. *Acta Psychologica, 75,* 55–74.

Longoni, A. M., Richardson, J. T. E., & Aiello, A. (1993). Articulatory rehearsal and phonological storage in working memory. *Memory and Cognition, 21,* 11–22.

Mackworth, J. F. (1963). The relation between the visual image and post-perceptual immediate memory. *Journal of Verbal Learning and Verbal Behavior, 2,* 75–85.

Martin, R. C., Shelton, J. R., & Yaffee, L. S. (1994). Language processing and working memory: Neuropsychological evidence for separate phonological and semantic capacities. *Journal of Memory and Language, 33,* 83–111.

McCarthy, G., Blamire, A. M., Puce, A., Noble, A. C., Bloch, G., Hyder, F., Goldman-Rakic, P., & Shulman, R. G. (1994). Functional MR imaging of human prefrontal cortex activation during a spatial working memory task. *Proceedings of the National Academy of Sciences of USA, 91,* 8690–8694.

McCarthy, R. A., & Warrington, E. K. (1990). *Cognitive neuropsychology: A clinical introduction.* San Diego: Academic Press.

McGuire, P. K., Shah, G. M. S., & Murray, R. M. (1993). Increased blood flow in Broca's area during auditory hallucinations in schizophrenia. *The Lancet, 342,* 703–706.

Meudell, P. R. (1972). Comparative effects of two types of distraction on the recall of visually presented verbal and nonverbal material. *Journal of Experimental Psychology, 94,* 244–247.

Miyashita, Y., & Chang, H. S. (1988). Neuronal correlate of pictorial short-term memory in the primate temporal cortex. *Nature, 331,* 68–70.

Murray, D. J. (1967). The role of speech responses in short-term memory. *Canadian Journal of Psychology, 21,* 263–276.

Murray, D. J. (1968). Articulation and acoustic confusability in short-term memory. *Journal of Experimental Psychology, 78,* 679–684.

Ojemann, G. A. (1978). Organization of short-term memory in language areas of human cortex: Evidence from electrical stimulation. *Brain and Language, 5,* 331–340.

Paulesu, E., Frith, C. D., & Frackowiak, R. S. J. (1993). The neural correlates of the verbal component of working memory. *Nature, 362,* 342–344.

Petersen, S. E., Fox, P. T., Posner, M. I., Mintun, M., & Raichle, M. E. (1988). Positron emision tomographic studies of the cortical anatomy of single-word processing. *Nature, 331,* 585–589.

Peterson, L. R., & Johnson, S. T. (1971). Some effects of minimizing articulation on short-term retention. *Journal of Verbal Learning and Verbal Behavior, 10,* 346–354.

Petrides, M., Alivisatos, B., Evans, A. C., & Meyer, E. (1993a). Dissociation of human mid-dorsolateral from posterior dorsolateral frontal cortex in memory processing. *Proceedings of the National Academy of Science, USA, 90,* 873–877.

Petrides, M., Alivisatos, B., Meyer, E., & Evans, A. C. (1993b). Functional activation of the human frontal cortex during the performance of verbal working memory tasks. *Proceedings of the National Academy of Science, USA, 90,* 878–882.

Posner, M. I., Petersen, S. E., Fox, P. T., & Raichle, M. E. (1988). Localization of cognitive functions in the human brain. *Science, 240,* 1627–1631.

Quintana, J., & Fuster, J. M. (1993). Spatial and temporal factors in the role of prefrontal and parietal cortex in visuomotor integration. *Cerebral Cortex, 3,* 122–132.

Reisberg, D., Rappaport, I., & O'Shaughnessy, M. (1984). Limits of working memory: The digit digit-span. *Journal of Experimental Psychology: Learning, Memory, and Cognition, 10,* 203–221.

Richardson, J. T. E., Greaves, D. E., & Smith, M. M. C. (1980). Does articulatory suppression eliminate the phonemic similarity effect in short-term recall? *Bulletin of the Psychonomic Society, 16,* 417–420.

Risse, G. L., Rubens, A. B., & Jordan, L. S. (1984). Disturbances of long-term memory in aphasic patients. *Brain, 107,* 605–617.

Ruchkin, D. S., Johnson Jr., R., Grafman, J., Canoune, H., & Ritter, W. (1992). Distinctions and similarities among working memory processes: An event-related potential study. *Cognitive Brain Research, 1,* 53–66.

Salame, P., & Baddeley, A. D. (1982). Disruption of short-term memory by unattended speech: Implications for the structure of working memory. *Journal of Verbal Learning and Verbal Behavior, 21,* 150–164.

Salthouse, T. A. (1974). Using selective interference to investigate spatial memory representations. *Memory and cognition, 2,* 749–757.

Saltz, E., & Donnenwerth-Nolan, S. (1981). Does motoric inagery facilitate memory for sentences? A selective interference test. *Journal of Verbal Learning and Verbal Behavior, 20,* 322–332.

Schweickert, R., Guentert, L., & Hersberger, L. (1990). Phonological similarity, pronunciation rate, and memory span. *Psychological Science, 1,* 74–77.

Shallice, T. (1988). *From neuropsychology to mental structure.* Cambridge: Cambridge University Press.

Shallice, T., & Butterworth, B. (1977). Short-term memory impairment and spontaneous speech. *Neuropsychologia, 15,* 729–735.

Shallice, T., & Vallar, G. (1990). The impairment of auditory-verbal short-term storage. In G. Vallar & T. Shallice (Eds.), *Neuropsychological impairments of short term memory* (pp. 11–53). Cambridge: Cambridge University Press.

Shallice, T., & Warrington, E. K. (1970). Independent functioning of verbal memory stores: A neuropsychological study. *Quarterly Journal of Experimental Psychology, 22,* 261–273.

Shallice, T., & Warrington, E. K. (1974). The dissociation between short-term retention of meaningful sounds and verbal material. *Neuropsychologia, 12,* 553–555.

Shallice, T., & Warrington, E. K. (1977). Auditory-verbal short-term memory impairment and conduction aphasia. *Brain and Language, 4,* 479–491.

Shulman, H. G. (1971). Similarity effects in short-term memory. *Psychological Bulletin, 75,* 399–415.

Smith, E. E., & Jonides, J. (1995). Working memory in humans: Neuropsychological evidence. In M. S. Gazzaniga (Ed.). *The cognitive neurosciences* (pp. 1,009–1,020). Cambridge, MA: MIT Press.

Smith, E. E., Jonides, J., & Koeppe, R. A. (1996). Dissociating verbal and spatial working memory using PET. *Cerebral Cortex, 6,* 11–20.

Smith, E. E., Jonides, J., Koeppe, R. A., Awh, E., Schumacher, E. H., & Minoshima, S. (1995). Spatial vs. object working memory: PET investigations. *Journal of Cognitive Neuroscience, 7,* 337–356.

Smith, M. L., & Milner, B. (1984). Differential effects of frontal-lobe lesions on cognitive estimation and spatial memory. *Neuropsychologia, 22,* 697–705.

Smith, M. L., Leonard, G., Crane, J., & Milner, B. (1995). The effects of frontal- or temporal-lobe lesions on susceptibility to interference in spatial memory. *Neuropsychologia, 33,* 275–285.

Smith, M. L., & Milner, B. (1981). The role of the right hippocampus in the recall of spatial location. *Neuropsychologia, 19,* 781–793.

Smith, M. L., & Milner, B. (1989). Right hippocampal impairment in the recall of spatial location: Encoding deficit or rapid forgetting? *Neuropsychologia, 27,* 71–81.

Smyrnis, N., Masato, T., Ashe, J., & Georgopoulos, A. P. (1992). Motor cortical activity in a memorized delay task. *Experimental Brain Research, 92,* 139–151.

Smyth, M. M., & Pendleton, L. R. (1989). Working memory for movements. *The Quarterly Journal of Experimental Psychology, 41A,* 235–250.

Smyth, M. M., & Scholey, K. A. (1994). Interference in immediate spatial memory. *Memory and Cognition, 22,* 1–13.

Sperling, G. (1960). The information available in brief visual presentations. *Psychological Monograph, 74.*

Sternberg, S. (1966). High-speed scanning in human memory. *Science, 153,* 652–654.

Strub, R. L., & Gardner, H. (1974). The repetition defect in conduction aphasia: Mnestic or linguistic. *Brain and Language, 1,* 241–255.

Swinney, D. A., & Taylor, O. L. (1971). Short-term memory recognition search in aphasics. *Journal of Speech and Hearing Research, 14,* 578–588.

Teuber, H. L. (1955). Physiological psychology. *Annual Review of Psychology, 6,* 267–296.

Tucker, D. M. (1993). Spatial sampling of head electrical fields: The geodesic sensor net. *Electroencephalography and Clinical Neurophysiology, 87,* 154–163.

Udwin, O., & Yule, W. (1991). A cognitive behavioral phenotype in Williams syndrome. *Journal of Clinical and Experimental Neuropsychology, 13,* 232–242.

Ungerleider, L. G., & Mishkin, M. (1982). Two cortical visual systems. In D. J. Ingle, M. A. Goodale, & R. J. Mansfield (Eds.), *Analysis of visual behavior.* Cambridge, MA: MIT Press.

Vallar, G., & Baddeley, A. D. (1984a). Fractionation of working memory: Neuropsychological evidence for a phonological short-term store. *Journal of Verbal Learning and Verbal Behavior, 23,* 151–161.

Vallar, G., & Baddeley, A. D. (1984b). Phonological short-term store, phonological processing and sentence comprehension: A neuropsychological case study. *Cognitive Neuropsychology, 1,* 121–141.

Vallar, G., Basso, A., & Bottini, G. (1990). Phonological processing and sentence comprehension: A neuropsychological case study. In G. Vallar & T. Shallice (Eds.), *Neuropsychological impairments of short term memory* (pp. 448–476). Cambridge: Cambridge University Press.

Vallar, G., & Cappa, S. F. (1987). Articulation and verbal short-term memory: Evidence from anarthria. *Cognitive Neuropsychology, 4,* 55–78.

Vallar, G., Corno, M., & Basso, A. (1992). Auditory and visual verbal short-term memory in aphasia. *Cortex, 28,* 383–389.

Vallar, G., & Shallice, T. (1990). *Neuropsychological impairments of short term memory.* Cambridge: Cambridge University Press.

Wang, P. P., & Bellugi, U. (1994). Evidence from two genetic syndromes for a dissociation between verbal and visualspatial short-term memory. *Journal of Clinical and Experimental Neuropsychology, 16,* 317–322.

Warrington, E. K., Logue, V., & Pratt, R. T. C. (1971). The anatomical localisation of selective impairment of auditory verbal short-term memory. *Neuropsychologia, 9,* 377–387.

Warrington, E. K., & Shallice, T. (1969). The selective impairment of auditory verbal short-term memory. *Brain, 92,* 885–896.

Waters, G. S., Rochon, E., & Caplan, D. (1992). The role of high-level speech planning in rehearsal: Evidence from patients with apraxia of speech. *Journal of Memory and Language, 31,* 54–73.

Waugh, N. C., & Norman, D. A. (1965). Primary memory. *Psychological Review, 72,* 89–104.

Weiskrantz, L. (1968). Some traps and pontifications. In L. Weiskrantz (Ed.), *Analysis of behavioral change* (pp. 415–429). New York: Harper and Row.

Weiskrantz, L. (1991). Dissociations and associates in neuropsychology. In R. G. Lister & H. J. Weingartner (Eds.), *Perspectives on cognitive neuroscience.* New York: Oxford University Press.

Wilson, F. A. W., O'Scalaidhe, S. P., & Goldman-Rakic, P. S. (1993). Dissociation of object and spatial processing domains in primate prefrontal cortex. *Science, 260,* 1955–1958.

Zatorre, R. J., & Samson, S. (1991). Role of the right temporal neocortex in retention of pitch in auditory short-term memory. *Brain, 114,* 2403–2417.

Zatorre, R. J., Evans, A. C., Meyer, E., & Gjedde, A. (1992). Lateralization of phonetic and pitch discrimination in speech processing. *Science, 256,* 846–849.

MEMORY FOR ASYMMETRIC EVENTS

John T. Wixted
Deirdra H. Dougherty

I. Introduction

Several independent lines of research have tested an animal's ability to discriminate, retrospectively, events that are inherently unequal. Examples include investigations of (a) memory for the presence versus absence of an event (such as a keylight), (b) memory for event duration (e.g., 2-s vs. 8-s samples), and (c) memory for stimuli from different sensory modalities (e.g., tone vs. light). These procedures are unlike the standard delayed matching-to-sample (DMTS) task, which arranges memory tests for events that are approximately equal in salience (e.g., red vs. green keylights).

A variety of theories has been advanced to explain an interesting pattern of results common to studies in all three of these areas. Specifically, in all cases, the retention function on one kind of trial decays much more slowly (if at all) than the retention function on the other kind of trial. In the presence-versus-absence memory literature, these results are usually explained on the basis of a default response/asymmetric coding theory. In the event-duration literature, similar results are explained based on the notion of subjective shortening (according to which the remembered duration of an event shrinks with the passage of time). In the sensory-modality literature, the same result has been explained by assuming that memory for events in one modality fade more slowly than memory for events in the other modality.

THE PSYCHOLOGY OF LEARNING
AND MOTIVATION, VOL. 35

89

Dougherty and Wixted (1996) argued that a single set of principles defined in the context of signal detection theory can accommodate the major results from these separate literatures (and, by extension, to the general case of memory for asymmetric events). Initially, these ideas were applied to delayed presence-versus-absence discriminations in pigeons, so we begin our treatment there. In subsequent sections, we describe how similar ideas can be extended to other areas, most notably memory for event duration and memory for different stimulus modalities.

II. Memory for Presence versus Absence

Most animal memory procedures require a delayed discrimination between two events of roughly equal salience. For example, in a typical DMTS procedure involving pigeons, the stimuli to be discriminated consist of red and green keylights. Following the presentation of one of those two stimuli (the *sample*), subjects are presented with both the red and green stimuli simultaneously. A response to the choice stimulus that matches the sample yields a reinforcer, while a response to the nonmatching stimulus terminates the trial. An interesting variant of this procedure requires a delayed discrimination between events that are unequal in salience. One of the first procedures of this kind used samples consisting of food versus no food, followed by a choice between red and green keylights. If food was presented at the beginning of the trial, a response to the red choice key was reinforced (with more food). If no food was presented at the beginning of the trial (e.g., if an empty hopper was briefly illuminated), then a response to the green choice key was reinforced. Intuitively, one would expect the presentation of food to a hungry pigeon to be an especially memorable event, while the presentation of no food would be a rather forgettable event. It was, therefore, somewhat puzzling when studies consistently showed that the proportion of correct responses following a food sample decreased rapidly as the retention interval increased (to below 50% correct) while performance following no-food samples remained accurate even at very long retention intervals (Colwill, 1984; Grant, 1991; Sherburne & Zentall, 1993; Wilson & Boakes, 1985).

Subsequent research revealed that the reason for this seemingly anomalous finding was that pigeons did not solve the delayed food/no-food discrimination by remembering which of those two events occurred. Instead, they responded based on the presence versus absence of food (with the no-food sample being tantamount to a nonevent). Thus, exactly the same pattern of results is observed in procedures that explicitly arrange a discrimination between the presence versus absence of other kinds of events. In the procedure used by Grant (1991) and by Dougherty and Wixted (1996), for example (which is illustrated in the upper panel of Fig. 1), the intertrial interval (ITI) was followed by a sample stimulus (a red center keylight in the illustration) or by nothing at all. A response to one choice alternative (red) was reinforced on trials that included a sample stimulus, and a response to the other choice alternative (green) was reinforced on trials in which no sample was presented. Performance on no-sample trials was accurate and did not decline as the retention interval increased. Performance

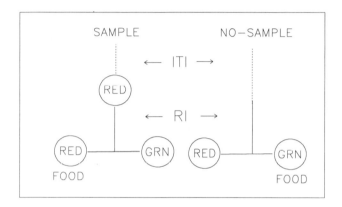

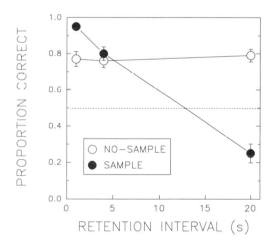

Fig. 1. *Upper Panel.* Graphical illustration of the sample/no-sample memory procedure. The dashed vertical line represents the intertrial interval (ITI) and the solid vertical line represents the retention interval (RI). *Lower Panel.* Proportion of correct responses as a function of retention interval for sample and no-sample trials (averaged over eight subjects). The error bars represent the standard errors associated with each mean value.

on sample trials, by contrast, decreased rapidly to well below 50% correct. The lower panel of Fig. 1 presents typical results from this procedure. The data represent the average performance of eight pigeons and are taken from Dougherty and Wixted (1996). Note that results like these are obtained even when the end of the ITI is demarcated by a brief warning stimulus (e.g., Grant, 1991).

A.   THEORIES OF MEMORY FOR PRESENCE VERSUS ABSENCE

1.   Default Response/Asymmetrical Coding

Why does this procedure (and the food/no-food procedure) yield asymmetric forgetting functions? Most theoretical accounts of findings like those shown in Fig. 1 have been based on an intuitively appealing idea. Specifically, pigeons are assumed to choose the no-sample (or no-food) choice alternative by default. Thus, if the green key is the correct choice alternative on no-sample trials, then choosing the green key represents the default strategy. That strategy is overridden only if a memory trace of the sample is present. In the presence of such a memory trace, the other choice alternative (i.e., the red key) is correctly selected. This default response model has also been called the asymmetric coding model because it assumes that qualitatively different mental codes exist on sample and no-sample trials (e.g., Grant, 1991).

How does this model account for the data shown in Fig. 1? First, accurate no-sample performance merely reflects the operation of the default response strategy. Because no sample is presented at any point during the trial, nothing interrupts the bird's default strategy of correctly choosing the no-sample choice alternative (green) most of the time (no matter how long the retention interval is). On sample trials, a more dynamic set of events takes place. If the retention interval is short, a strong memory trace of the sample is likely to exist. As a result, the default strategy is abandoned and the bird correctly selects the choice alternative associated with the sample (red). As the retention interval increases, however, the memory trace fades. When it fades completely, nothing deters the pigeon from once again executing its default strategy. If the default strategy involves choosing the no-sample alternative 75% of the time, then, on trials in which the memory trace has faded completely, the pigeon will choose *incorrectly* 75% of the time. This basically captures the results shown in Fig. 1, and it seems fair to say that the default response account is the dominant theory of performance on this task (Colwill, 1984; Grant, 1991; Sherburne & Zentall, 1993; Wilson & Boakes, 1985).

2.   High Threshold Theory

Though usually not described as such, the default response/asymmetrical coding model is formally equivalent to an old account known as *high-*

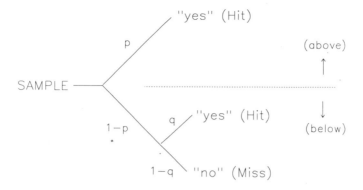

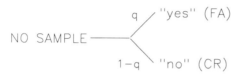

Fig. 2. A graphical representation of the discrete-state high-threshold model for sample and no-sample trials. The dashed line represents the threshold that defines the two mental states (above threshold implies a memory trace, below threshold implies no memory trace). The symbol p represents the proportion of sample trials in which the sample is remembered, and q represents the probability that the Yes alternative will be chosen by default in the absence of a memory trace.

threshold theory. Figure 2 illustrates the events that govern performance on sample and no-sample trials according to the high-threshold model. On a sample trial, there is some probability, p, that the pigeon will remember that a sample was presented and correctly report "Yes" (a *hit* in the parlance of signal detection theory). The other possibility on a sample trial, which occurs with probability of $1-p$, is that the pigeon will not remember that the sample was presented. Under these conditions, the default response strategy is implemented. That is, in the absence of a memory trace, there is some probability, q, that the pigeon will respond yes by default, again resulting in a hit. Alternatively, with probability $1-q$, the pigeon will incorrectly report No by default, resulting in a *miss.* The same analysis can be applied to no-sample trials. If no sample was presented, then no memory trace exists, and the default response strategy will be implemented every time. Thus, the pigeon will incorrectly respond Yes with probability q, a response known as a *false alarm* (FA), and, with probability $1-q$, the bird will correctly report No, resulting in a *correct rejection* (CR). The probability q is the same for the subset of sample trials involving a forgotten memory trace and for all no-sample trials because the high threshold model allows for only two mental states (presence vs. absence of the memory trace).

This kind of model has a long history in psychology, and it provides the theoretical justification for the "correction for guessing" formula once used extensively in the human memory literature. As indicated in Fig. 2, hits consist partially of responses based on memory, which occur with probability p on sample trials, and partially on correct guesses when memory has faded, which occur with probability $1\text{-}p$ times q on sample trials. In other words, the hit rate (H) equals $p + (1\text{-}p)q$. The value of q (the probability of choosing Yes by default) is given directly by the false alarm (FA) rate. To solve for p (the measure of interest), one simply replaces q with FA followed by some algebraic rearrangement. The result is the traditional correction for guessing formula, $(\text{H-FA})/(1\text{-FA})$. In the human memory literature, high-threshold theory's main competitor was signal-detection theory, which eventually won the day. Indeed, the correction for guessing formula has been largely abandoned in favor of the dependent measure suggested by signal detection theory, namely, d'. In what follows, we argue that the evidence from animal memory studies suggests that signal-detection theory offers a better account there as well.

3. Signal-Detection Theory

Wixted (1993) and Dougherty and Wixted (1996) proposed an altogether different account of the sample/no-sample findings shown in Fig. 1. This theory, unlike the default response model, assumes that the same, imperfect, decision strategy is involved on both sample and no-sample trials (i.e., there is no asymmetry in the bird's decision strategy). Figure 3 illustrates the basic assumptions of the signal-detection model they proposed. The analysis assumes that choice responding is governed by the subjective strength of evidence that a sample was presented. On both sample and no-sample trials, strength of evidence is assumed to vary from trial to trial according to Guassian distributions (which need not have the same variance). The average strength of evidence on sample trials is generally higher than that on no-sample trials because of the delayed effect of the sample stimulus. However, even on no-sample trials, some evidence for the presence of a sample is assumed to exist due to the cumulative effect of many previously presented samples (cf. Wright, Urcuioli, & Sands, 1986). That is, extending the argument advanced by Wright et al. (1986), the pigeon is aware that samples have often been presented in the experimental situation. That awareness yields some strength of evidence that a sample appeared on the current trial, though not as much evidence as if the sample had actually appeared. Because strength of evidence is a continuous dimension, and

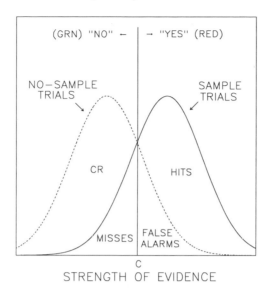

(GRN) "NO" ← | → "YES" (RED)

NO–SAMPLE
TRIALS

SAMPLE
TRIALS

CR

HITS

MISSES | FALSE
ALARMS

c
STRENGTH OF EVIDENCE

Fig. 3.   A graphical illustration of signal-detection theory. The dashed distribution represents strength of evidence on no-sample trials and the solid distribution represents strength
of evidence on sample trials. The vertical line at point c represents the decision criterion.

because the signal and noise distributions partially overlap, no errorless
decision strategy exists.

Signal detection theory assumes that, to solve the task, the subject sets
a criterion value above which the Yes (i.e., red) alternative is selected and
below which the No (i.e., green) alternative is selected. The decision criterion is placed to maximize more or less the number of reinforcers obtained
over the session and can be theoretically manipulated by varying the relative
payoff for correct Yes and No responses. For example, if correct Yes and
No responses yield reinforcers with probabilities of 1 and .20, respectively,
the decision criterion would be placed relatively far to the left to avoid
missing the many reinforcers arranged for correct Yes responses (Wixted, 1993).

How does this model account for the pattern of results shown in Fig. 1?
With regard to the flat retention function on no-sample trials, the important
point is that the position of the no-sample (i.e., noise) distribution is not
determined by factors occurring on a given trial. For that reason, the
distribution remains fixed as the retention interval on a particular trial
increases. In the simplest case, the decision criterion is also assumed to be
fixed at the point that roughly maximizes the number of reinforcers obtained
during a session. This allows the bird to use one simple discriminative

strategy on every trial (i.e., if strength of evidence exceeds c, choose Yes, otherwise choose No). Because both the noise distribution and the criterion are fixed, the area beneath noise distribution to the left of the criterion (which corresponds to the proportion of correct responses on no-sample trials) remains constant across within-session variations in the duration of the retention interval.

The sample (i.e., signal) distribution, on the other hand, does not remain fixed as a function of retention interval because the delayed effect of the sample presumably weakens as a function of time since the sample was presented. Figure 4 presents hypothetical distributions for three retention-interval conditions (1-, 4-, and 20-s). When the retention interval is short, the mean of the signal distribution greatly exceeds the mean of the noise distribution. Under these conditions, the signal is easily distinguished from noise and accuracy should be (and is) high on both kinds of trial. As the retention interval increases, the signal distribution moves toward (and increasingly overlaps) the noise distribution because of the weakening memory trace. In the limiting case, the signal and noise distributions will overlap such that performance on sample trials will actually fall significantly *below* chance. As indicated earlier, below-chance performance has often been observed at long retention intervals on sample trials (Fig. 1).

The signal detection analysis offers a fundamentally different interpretation of memory for presence versus absence than the default response model. In what follows, we describe the results of several experiments designed to differentiate between these two theories.

B. EXPERIMENTAL ANALYSES

1. Between-Condition Manipulation of Retention Interval

All the experiments considered to this point involved within-session manipulations of the retention interval. Under these conditions, the default-response hypothesis and signal-detection theory make the same (correct) predictions. When the retention interval is varied across conditions, however, theoretical predictions diverge. If pigeons simply rely on a default-response strategy of choosing the comparison associated with the absence of a sample on no-sample trials, then the pattern of results should not differ whether the retention interval is varied within or between sessions. A signal-detection analysis, by contrast, suggests that the between-condition manipulation of retention interval will affect performance on both sample and no-sample trials. More specifically, the between-condition manipulation of retention interval should eliminate the asymmetry observed in Fig. 1.

To see why this is so, consider the distributions shown in Fig. 5. This figure again presents hypothetical trace intensity distributions for three

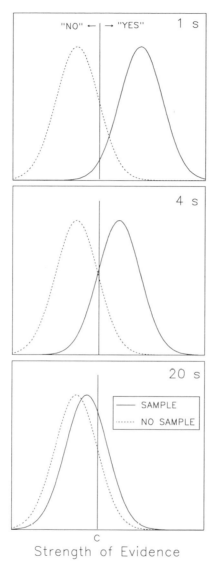

Fig. 4. Hypothetical sample and no-sample distributions for three retention intervals (short, medium, and long) manipulated within session. The location of the decision criterion, c, remains fixed as a function of retention interval.

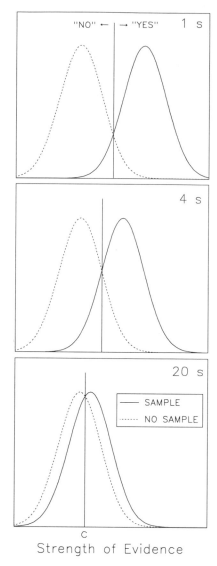

Fig. 5.   Hypothetical sample and no-sample distributions for three retention intervals (short, medium, and long) manipulated between conditions. The location of the decision criterion, c, changes with each condition.

retention-interval conditions, but now the retention interval is varied between conditions rather than within a session. The only difference between this figure and Fig. 4 is the placement of the decision criterion. Neglecting the effect of inherent response biases, one might assume that the criterion will generally be placed at the point that maximizes the reinforcer payoff averaged over trials (i.e., directly between the two distributions). Thus, unlike the within-session case, each retention interval will be associated with a different value of c.

Why is the criterion fixed in the within-session case but free to move in the between-condition case? Because its placement is determined by experience aggregated over many trials. If those trials involve multiple retention intervals (as in the within-session case), then a single criterion will necessarily be in effect for all of them. If the trials instead involve only one retention interval (as in the between-condition case), then the birds have an opportunity to set a different criterion for each retention interval. In each case, they will experience a sufficient number of trials at a single retention interval to determine the criterion placement that maximizes reinforcement.

The anticipated change in the placement of c now suggests that performance on no-sample trials will not remain constant as the retention interval increases. As c moves leftward, more of the noise distribution falls to the right of c such that more false alarms (and correspondingly fewer correct rejections) should occur. Thus, performance on both sample and no-sample trials should decline as the retention interval increases. The existence of a retention interval effect on no-sample trials would at least raise the possibility that a memory decision occurs on these trials as well.

To test this prediction, four pigeons were exposed to the between-condition retention-interval procedure. The procedure was identical to that normally used except that each retention interval was in effect for an extended period of time to allow performance to reach stability. The pigeons were exposed to an ascending series of retention intervals (0.50, 2, 6, 12, and 24 s), with each condition in effect for 15 sessions. An ascending sequence was used because the random selection of retention-intervals tended to produce disruptions in performance when a long retention interval condition immediately followed a short one (the most notable problem being the complete cessation of responding to the sample stimulus). Also, the use of an ascending series seemed unlikely to disrupt any default response strategy that may have developed at the shorter retention intervals. At the end of the sequence, all birds were returned to the 0.50-s condition for 15 sessions.

Figure 6 shows the mean proportion correct as a function of retention interval for both the sample and no-sample trials averaged over the last

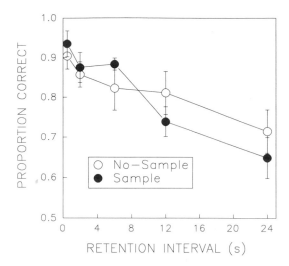

Fig. 6. Proportion of correct responses as a function of retention interval on sample and no-sample trials (averaged over four subjects) when the retention interval was manipulated between condition. The error bars represent the standard errors associated with each mean value.

five sessions of each condition (the data are taken from Wixted, 1993). In contrast to the results of all other sample/no-sample experiments, performance now declines on both kinds of trial. An analysis of variance performed on these data revealed a significant effect for retention interval, $F(4, 12) = 9.32$, but the effect of trial type and the interaction between trial type and retention interval did not approach significance. Although performance at the 24-s retention interval had declined to 65% and 72.6% correct on sample and no-sample trials, respectively, accuracy increased to 92.4% and 85.6% correct over the last five sessions of the final condition (with the retention interval again set to 0.50 s).

The results shown in Fig. 6 are, for the most part, representative of the performance of individual subjects. One bird exhibited the pattern predicted by the default response hypothesis (i.e., the absence of a retention interval effect on no-sample trials) and three exhibited the pattern predicted by signal-detection theory. Theoretically, because each retention interval was in effect for an extended period of time, the decision criterion (c) was, according to this account, adjusted in such a way as to maintain more favorable payoff probabilities (averaged across trials). As a result, performance on both signal and noise trials should diminish as the retention interval increases.

The default response hypothesis, which readily explained the results from all prior sample/no-sample experiments, cannot explain the data from this experiment unless it is assumed that pigeons altered their default response strategy when the retention interval was increased across conditions. That is, when a short retention interval was in effect, the pigeons may have adopted a default strategy of choosing, almost exclusively, the alternative associated with the absence of a sample (indeed, this is the default strategy that is usually assumed). As the retention interval increased across conditions, however, they may have chosen to adopt a less exclusive default strategy (for whatever reason) and divided their responses more evenly between the two alternatives. If that were true, then perhaps one could still argue that performance on no-sample trials did not involve memory in spite of the fact that the forgetting functions on sample and no-sample trials declined at essentially the same rate. The viability of this account obviously depends on an adequate explanation for why a new default strategy was implemented with each retention interval.

Wixted (1993) argued that at least one fairly straightforward modification of the default-response hypothesis can accommodate the results of the between-condition experiment. According to high-threshold theory, a Yes response always occurs on sample trials if the strength of the signal exceeds a fixed sensory threshold. On no-sample trials, however, Yes responses (i.e., false alarms) are merely guesses that do not arise because of any sensory process. Instead, the subject is assumed to adopt a default response strategy of saying Yes or No a certain proportion of the time in the absence of an above-threshold sensation. Wixted (1993) showed that if the default strategy is one that distributes responses in such a way as to match reinforcement probabilities associated with the two alternatives, the results shown in Fig. 6 could be accommodated.

Consider, for example, high-threshold parameter values that might be in effect following a relatively short (e.g., 1 s) retention interval. Under these conditions, p (the proportion of sample trials yielding an above-threshold sensation) might be very high (e.g., .95). On all these trials, a reinforcer is arranged on the sample (or Yes) choice alternative. Similarly, whenever a memory trace is absent, odds are that a reinforcer is arranged on the no-sample (or No) alternative. The only exception to this is the 5% of sample trials involving a subthreshold trace strength. Under these conditions, it makes good sense to adopt a default strategy of always choosing the no-sample alternative when no memory trace is present (because a reinforcer is very likely to be waiting). On the other hand, consider the situation in effect when a long retention interval is used such that p (the proportion of trials involving an above-threshold trace) is only .30. It is still the case that whenever a memory trace is present (that is, on 30% of the sample trials) a reinforcer is arranged on the sample choice alternative. Where is the reinforcer arranged on trials not involving an above-threshold trace? Now, even in the absence of a memory trace, a reinforcer will often be arranged for choosing the sample alternative. Indeed, on 70% of the sample trials (which are functionally equivalent to no-sample trials from the bird's point of view) the reinforcer is arranged on the sample choice alternative. If birds are sensitive to that fact, they might adjust their default strategy at longer retention intervals in order to pick up the reinforcers that are often available on the sample alternative even when no memory trace is present. This change in strategy would account for the drop in no-sample performance at longer retention intervals.

This revised default-response analysis is also consistent with the results of the within-session retention interval experiments (in which a flat no-sample function was observed). The reason is that the probability of reinforcement for a Yes response in the absence of a memory trace does not change on a trial-by-trial basis. Instead, the default-response strategy (like the placement of the signal-detection criterion) is determined by experience with reinforcement probabilities averaged across trials. Thus, the default strategy will not change from trial to trial and a flat no-sample retention function should be (and is) observed.

2. Eliminating Sample Trials

Dougherty and Wixted (1996) addressed the default-response versus signal-detection debate from yet another angle. Specifically, they argued that if performance on no-sample trials really reflects a memory-free default-response strategy, then performance on those trials should not be affected by the inclusion (or exclusion) of other trials that *do* involve memory (specifically, the sample trials).

As indicated earlier, the default-response model is a discrete state account that holds that the pigeon is in one of two states when confronted with the choice stimuli. In one state, a memory trace of the sample stimulus is present. After many training sessions, the bird presumably knows the probability of reinforcement for choosing the Yes and No choice alternatives when in that state. Typically (though not necessarily), these probabilities would be 1 and 0 respectively, so the pigeon should invariably choose the Yes key. In the other state, there is no memory trace (either because the sample was forgotten or because no sample was presented) and choice performance should be governed by the relative probability of reinforcement for choosing Yes and No under *these* conditions. Because most of the no-memory-trace trials will be no-sample trials (with reinforcement arranged for choosing No), the probability of reinforcement for choosing

No will exceed that for choosing Yes. As indicated earlier, the exact values depend on how often a memory trace is present on sample trials.

How should a pigeon behave in the no-memory-trace state assuming that the probability of reinforcement for choosing No exceeds the probability of reinforcement for choosing Yes? That depends on how the reinforcers are arranged. To see why this might be true, it is instructive to compare no-sample trials to a discrete-trials concurrent choice procedure. Topographically, they are identical in that, in both cases, two stimuli appear simultaneously on the side keys on each trial (without being preceded by a sample), and a single response to either stimulus terminates the trial. Thus, for example, each trial in the concurrent choice procedure might consist of the simultaneous presentation of red and green choice keys, with red associated with a .7 probability of reinforcement and green associated with a .3 probability of reinforcement. A single response to either key, which may or may not produce a reinforcer, terminates the trial and initiates an ITI of some duration (e.g., 15 s). Thus, the discrete-trials choice procedure is essentially a series of no-sample trials that are not intermixed with sample trials.

Behavior on this task is controlled by the reinforcement probabilities associated with the two keys. Typically, pigeons are more likely to choose the stimulus associated with the richer schedule of reinforcement. However, the way reinforcers are arranged on this procedure determines the degree of preference for the richer alternative. In a discrete-trials procedure involving probabilistic reinforcement, the probability of a reinforcer being presented for pecking a key remains constant throughout the session, so the optimal strategy is to choose exclusively the key associated with the higher probability of reinforcement (which is what pigeons do). For example, Bailey and Mazur (1990) used a discrete-trials procedure with reinforcers arranged probabilistically to determine the rate of acquisition of preference for one key over the other. The phrase "arranged probabilistically" merely refers to the fact that the two keys were associated with some probability of reinforcement that did not change during the session. Initially, the two choice keys had equal probabilities of reinforcement, and the pigeons divided their responses roughly equally between them. As the probabilities of reinforcement associated with the two keys were made asymmetrical in subsequent conditions (e.g., .7 vs. .3), the pigeons showed near-exclusive preference for the key with the greater payoff after several hundred trials, with the rate of approach to exclusive preference being determined by the degree of asymmetry. Herrnstein and Loveland (1975) also found that once steady-state behavior was reached, most pigeons showed near-exclusive preference for the alternative with the higher probability of reinforcement when reinforcers were arranged according to variable-ratio schedules of reinforcement. Thus, when reinforcement is arranged probabilistically, pigeons tend to maximize reinforcement by always selecting the alternative with the highest momentary probability of reinforcement (Shimp, 1966).

Note that the default-response model assumes that no-sample trials are not only topographically identical to the discrete-trials choice procedure, but that they are *functionally* equivalent as well. On both no-sample trials and on every trial of a discrete-trials concurrent choice procedure, responding is determined by the scheduled reinforcement probabilities, not by a memory decision. If that is the case, then performance on no-sample trials should be near 100% correct when reinforcers are arranged probabilistically (because, in the absence of a memory trace, the probability of reinforcement for choosing the no-sample alternative is always higher than the probability of reinforcement for choosing the sample alternative). Indeed, exclusive preference for the no-sample alternative on no-sample trials is how the default response strategy is usually described. However, as indicated earlier, exclusive preference (which would mean performance in the vicinity of 100% correct on no-sample trials) is not always observed.

In the experiment designed to test these ideas, a standard sample/no-sample task was arranged in Phase 1. Retention intervals of 1, 4, and 20 were used (varied within session), and the results, which were typical, were shown earlier in Fig. 1. After the pigeons' behavior reached stability, Phase 2 was implemented. This phase was identical to Phase 1 except that the sample trials were eliminated. That is, in this phase, all trials were no-sample trials (which means that the procedure was changed into a discrete-trials concurrent choice procedure). Scheduled reinforcement probabilities in this phase were calculated to match those obtained on no-sample trials in the first phase according to the discrete state model (see Dougherty & Wixted, for details, 1996). If no-sample trials and discrete trials are functionally as well as topographically identical, performance on these trials should be the same in both conditions when the reinforcement schedule parameters are kept constant between the conditions.

On the other hand, as indicated earlier, prior research suggests that birds will show near-exclusive preference for the richer choice alternative in Phase 2, and that is what they did. Under the same conditions in Phase 1, however, exclusive preference was not observed. In other words, something about the presence of sample trials prevented exclusive preference for the no-sample alternative on no-sample trials in Phase 1. The results are displayed in Fig. 7. The solid bars represent the choice proportion for the stimulus associated with the richer schedule of reinforcement (i.e., the stimulus that was the no-sample choice alternative in Phase 1). For comparison purposes, the proportion of correct choices on no-sample trials from Phase 1 are also shown (hatched bars). Three of these four subjects showed

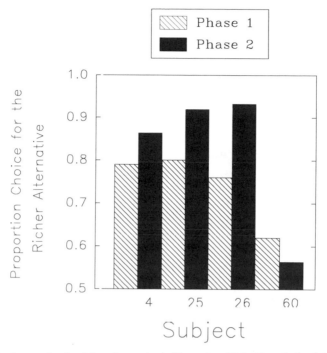

Fig. 7. Preference for the richer alternative in Phases 1 and 2. In Phase 1, the data represent preference for the no-sample alternative on no-sample trials. In Phase 2, the data represent preference for what was the no-sample alternative in Phase 1 (and what is simply the richer choice alternative in Phase 2).

near-exclusive preference for the richer alternative in Phase 2, but none did so in Phase 1. The one exception was Subject 60. This bird developed an extreme left-side bias which drove preference down toward indifference.

The discrete-state model has no provision to explain why performance on no-sample trials changes when the other half of the trials in the session shift from sample trials to no-sample trials (although the theory could perhaps be modified to correct that problem). Signal-detection theory, though, provides a natural account of these results. What prevents the occurrence of exclusive preference on no-sample trials, according to this account, is the effect of sample trials on the placement of the decision criterion. If the decision criterion were adjusted to pick up all reinforcers arranged on no-sample trials (by moving it far to the right in Fig. 3), the cost would be to lose reinforcers arranged on sample trials. This opposing force prevents the appearance of exclusive preference on no-sample trials. When the sample trials are removed (as in Phase 2 of the present experiment), this opposing force is removed as well, thereby resulting in near-exclusive preference. Although it might be possible to again adjust the default-response model to accommodate these findings as well, on the whole the data appear to be more easily reconciled with the signal-detection account.

3. Receiver Operating Characteristic (ROC) Analysis

As detailed by Swets, Tanner, and Birdsall (1961), the high-threshold model predicts a linear function when the probability of a hit is plotted as a function of the probability of a false alarm (i.e., a linear ROC curve). An ROC plot is generated by manipulating response bias (the overall tendency to choose Yes or No). One way to do that is to vary the payoff for correct Yes and No responses. If the payoff for a correct Yes response exceeds that for a correct No response, then, according to signal-detection theory, the criterion should no longer be placed midway between the signal and noise distributions. Instead, it should move to the left, which increases both the hit rate and false-alarm rate. According to high-threshold theory, that manipulation changes the default-response strategy such that q (the tendency to guess Yes) increases.

Referring to Fig. 2, high-threshold theory holds that the hit rate (H) is equal to $p + (1-p)q$ and the false-alarm rate (FA) is equal to q. Thus, $H = p + (1 - p)FA$. This is an equation of the form $y = b + mx$, which means that a plot of hit rate versus false alarm rate should be linear across biasing conditions. Signal-detection theory, by contrast, predicts a characteristically bowed ROC curve that extends upward from the origin to the upper right corner.

Swets et al. (1961) used the form of the ROC curve to rule out a high-threshold theory of auditory signal detection, and Murdock (1965) used a similar approach to reject a high-threshold account of human short-term memory. ROC curves have rarely been examined in the animal memory literature, although an apparently curved ROC function was obtained by Harnett, McCarthy, and Davison (1984) using a standard DMTS procedure. Wixted (1993) generated ROC curves for four pigeons by manipulating the probability of reinforcement for hits and correct rejections across conditions. The procedure was similar to prior sample/no-sample experiments (i.e., the retention interval was varied randomly within session) except that the reinforcement probabilities for hits and correct rejections were varied across conditions. The retention intervals within each condition were 0.5, 2, 4, and 12 s. Each reinforcement condition was in effect for 15 sessions. Following baseline training during which the probability of reinforcement was .60 for both hits and correct rejections (.60/.60), the values were changed to .20/1 for two birds and 1/.20 for the other two birds. After 15 sessions under these conditions, these values were reversed for 15 sessions. In the final phase of the experiment, the reinforcement probabilities were reset to their baseline values (.60/.60).

Figure 8 presents the obtained ROC functions (i.e., hit vs. false-alarm probabilities) for each retention interval averaged across subjects. Each point represents the average performance for the four birds during the last five sessions of each condition (the values for the pre and post .60/.60 conditions were averaged together). For each plot, the middle of the three points reflects the hit and false-alarm probabilities obtained when the probability of reinforcement for a correct Yes response equaled that for a correct no response (.60/.60). The point higher and to the right in each graph reflects the hit and false-alarm probabilities obtained when the probability of reinforcement for a correct Yes response exceeded that for a correct No response (.20). Under those conditions, both correct and incorrect Yes responses (hits and false alarms, respectively) were relatively high. The

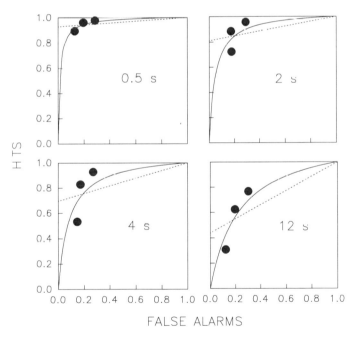

Fig. 8. Empirical receiver operating characteristic (ROC) curves for the four different retention intervals. Each graph depicts the hit rate versus the false alarm rate (averaged over four birds) for three reinforcement outcome conditions. The solid curves represent the best-fitting ROC functions based on signal-detection theory, whereas the dashed lines represent the best-fitting linear functions based on high-threshold theory.

point lower and to the left in each graph reflects the hit and false-alarm probabilities obtained when responding was biased in the opposite direction (.20/1).

As indicated earlier, one reasonable version of the default-response theory requires a linear ROC function of the form H = p + (1-p)FA, where p represents the proportion of sample trials in which trace intensity falls above a fixed threshold. This one-parameter line extends from the upper right corner to a point, p, on the left vertical axis. Signal-detection theory, by contrast, requires a curved ROC function. This one-parameter function follows a curvilinear trajectory from the lower left corner to the upper right corner. The larger the value of d', the more bowed the function becomes.

The two models were fit to these data using maximum likelihood estimation (Macmillan & Creelman, 1991; Ogilvie & Creelman, 1968). The solid curves shown in Fig. 8 represent the best fitting ROC functions based on signal-detection theory, whereas the dashed lines represent the best-fitting linear functions based on the default-response account. In all four cases, the performance of the curvilinear function is far better than that of the linear function. Indeed, the linear fits are so inaccurate that the version of high-threshold theory under consideration here can be safely rejected.

The failure of default-response (or high-threshold) models to predict the shape of the ROC function is the main reason why they were abandoned as plausible theories of human-recognition performance. These results suggest that the model may have similar trouble accounting for animal memory performance.

Although the fits based on signal-detection theory are far better than those based on the default-response account, some systematic deviation is apparent. In particular, the range of variation in false-alarm probabilities was generally less than would be expected given the fairly wide range of hits induced by manipulating the reinforcement outcomes (this is especially true for the 2- and 4-s retention intervals). Similar deviations are often apparent in the data from auditory signal-detection studies involving human subjects. As noted by Swets et al. (1961), such deviations might arise because the assumption that the signal and noise distribution are of exactly equal variance may be too strong. Indeed, a second reason to examine the shape of an ROC function (in addition to testing a key prediction of the default response model) is to obtain a quantitative estimate of the relative variances of the underlying signal and noise distributions. To test for this, a more complete model must be fit to the data. This model includes a parameter that allows for the possibility of unequal variances of the sample and no-sample distributions.

The data from each retention interval was subjected to a maximum likelihood analysis using the full signal-detection model (i.e., allowing for the possibility of unequal signal and noise distribution variances). Each fit of the full model involved estimating five parameters: σ (the standard deviation of the signal distribution), d' (the distance between the means of the signal and noise distributions), and three decision criteria, $c1$, $c2$, and $c3$ (one for each condition). The mean of the noise distribution was arbitrarily set to 0 and its standard deviation to 1. Because each fit involved five parameters and six data points (three hit rates and three false-alarm rates), the chi-square goodness-of-fit statistic for a given retention interval was associated with one degree of freedom. The resulting chi-square values for retention intervals one through four were 0.02, 3.99, 0.93, and 2.21, respectively such that the overall test, $\chi^2(4) = 7.15$, was not significant (meaning that the deviations from the model were not greater than would be expected on the basis of chance).

The maximum likelihood estimates of σ, $c1$, $c2$, and $c3$ did not vary systematically as a function of retention interval. The mean value of σ across the four retention intervals was 0.33, which implies that the standard deviation of the signal distribution was approximately one third that of the noise distribution. This would account for the fact that hit rates changed more rapidly than false-alarm rates across conditions (Fig. 8). Also, as would be expected, $c1 < c2 < c3$ for conditions 1/.20, .60/.60, and .20/1, respectively. In other words, the decision criterion moved up as the payoff for a correct No response increased relative to that for a correct Yes response. The mean maximum likelihood estimates of $c1$, $c2$, and $c3$ (averaged across retention intervals) were 0.59, 0.86, and 1.08, respectively. The only parameter that did change systematically as a function of retention-interval was d' (which is to be expected). The maximum likelihood values for this parameter were 2.54, 1.92, 1.81, and 1.39 for retention intervals one through four, respectively.

Figure 9 shows the signal detection model that corresponds to the ROC data shown in the lower right panel of Fig. 8 (i.e., the 12-s retention interval condition). The three criteria ($c1$, $c2$, $c3$) show the maximum likelihood estimates of the placement of the decision criteria in the three biasing conditions. Note that the maximum likelihood analysis also revealed that the variance of the no-sample distribution is much wider than that of the sample distribution. This suggests that the experience of "nothingness" is a more variable experience than that of a 5-s sample.

The fact that the variance of the noise (no-sample) distribution was nearly three times that of the signal distribution is interesting. Why would that be? Actually, in retrospect, equal signal and noise variances would have been the more surprising finding. The two kinds of trial (sample and no-sample) are inherently unequal. The trial-to-trial variability in the experience of nothingness is apparently more extreme than the trial-to-

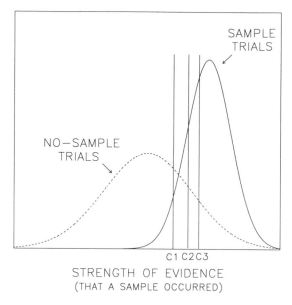

Fig. 9.   Form of the sample and no-sample distributions and placement of the decision criteria in the three biasing conditions based on maximum likelihood parameter estimation of the 12-s ROC function in Fig. 8.

trial variability in the experience of a 5-s keylight. Although not yet tested, similar distributional inequalities may be evident whenever asymmetric sample stimuli are used.

The results of the ROC analysis provide especially compelling support for the signal-detection account over the high-threshold model. Nevertheless, the present results do not rule out all possible default-response models. A variety of more complicated models can be proposed that will fit an apparently curvilinear ROC function even though responding is assumed to occur by default on no-sample (or no-signal) trials (Lockhart & Murdock, 1970). For example, Luce's (1960) low-threshold model holds that default Yes responses can occur when trace intensity falls below threshold (as with the high-threshold model) and that default No responses can occur when trace intensity falls above threshold. This model predicts a bitonic function with two linear segments that can often fit an ROC curve as well as the curvilinear function derived from signal-detection theory. With regard to the two models under consideration here, however, the signal-detection account offers the more parsimonious and quantitatively accurate account.

III. Memory for Long versus Short Durations:
The "Choose-Short" Effect

The discussion to this point has been concerned with a theoretical analysis of perhaps the most extreme asymmetric memory task (i.e., one that arranges memory of something vs. nothing). A variety of other tasks have arranged a delayed discrimination between less extreme asymmetric events. Prominent among these is memory for event duration. In a typical experiment of this kind, a sample stimulus is presented for either 2 or 8 s and is later followed by a choice between red and green. A response to red is reinforced following the long sample and a response to green is reinforced following the short sample. The usual finding observed on this procedure is that performance following the long sample decreases rapidly to below chance levels as the retention interval increases while performance following the short sample remains accurate regardless of the duration of the retention interval (Fetterman, 1995; Spetch, 1987; Spetch & Wilkie, 1982, 1983). Figure 10 presents representative data from this literature.

A. SUBJECTIVE SHORTENING

The dominant interpretation of these results is that the remembered duration of an event shrinks with the passage of time. Thus, immediately after it is presented, a long-duration sample will be accurately represented (leading to accurate performance). After a long retention interval, however, that representation will shrink and the long-duration sample will actually be remembered as a short-duration sample (eventually leading to below chance performance). The theoretical decrease in the representation of event duration with the passage of time is known as *subjective shortening* (Spetch & Wilkie, 1982, 1983).

B. SHORT DURATION EVENT AS A FUNCTIONAL NONEVENT

A different theoretical interpretation of the results shown in Fig. 10 is based on the idea that memory for "nothing" plays a prominent role, a point initially made by Kraemer, Mazmanian, and Roberts (1985). One simple application of this idea might be to assume that pigeons solve the event duration task by remembering whether or not the long-duration sample was presented (and by regarding the short sample as a nonevent). However, while this idea could explain the persistent tendency to choose the alternative associated with the short sample, a somewhat more complete account is needed to deal with the fact that the data shown in Fig. 1 (sample/no-sample) and Fig. 10 (short/long) are not identical.

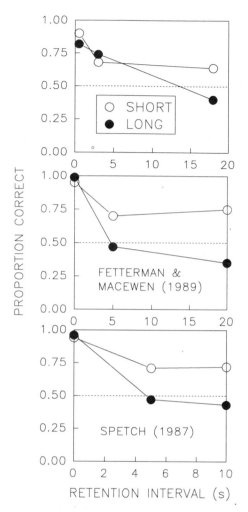

Fig. 10. Proportion correct as a function of retention interval in an event-duration memory experiment. The open symbols represent performance on trials involving the short-duration sample while the solid symbols represent performance on trials involving the long-duration sample. The data in the upper panel were averaged across four pigeons from my laboratory. The data in the middle panel were taken from Fetterman and MacEwen (1989), and the data in the lower panel are from Spetch (1987).

Unpublished findings from my laboratory reflect subtle but important trends that are apparent in many studies on event duration. In our procedure (which is similar to the procedure used by others), the sample stimulus was either a 2-s or 8-s illumination of the houselight. Following a 0.5-s retention interval, red and green choice stimuli were presented (with a response to red being reinforced on long trials and a response to green being reinforced on short trials). In occasional test sessions, retention intervals of 0.5, 3, and 18 s were implemented. The results averaged over three birds are shown in the upper panel Fig. 10. The typical "choose-short" bias is evident in that performance falls to below 50% correct following the long sample and reaches an asymptote well above 50% correct following the short sample. An important feature of these data is that performance following the 2-s sample declines noticeably before leveling off. The next two panels in Fig. 10 show data taken from other representative studies, and exactly the same trends are apparent there. In each case, a choose-short bias is apparent, but, before leveling off, performance following the short sample declines as the retention interval increases.

That decline in performance is significant because it rules out the simplest alternative explanation for these findings based on memory for nonoccurrence. If pigeons solve the event-duration task by simply remembering whether or not the 8-s sample appeared, then a 2-s sample trial would be tantamount to a no-sample trial, and performance should remain well above 50% correct as the retention interval increases (because that is what happens on actual no-sample trials). However, this account also predicts that performance should remain *flat* on 2-s sample trials, just as it does on no-sample trials (cf. Fig. 1). The fact that performance does not remain constant indicates that the situation is not as simple as that (i.e., something must explain the drop in performance on 2-s trials).

In the next section, we argue that the connection between memory for presence versus absence and memory for event duration lies in the fact that a 2-s sample is more like (but is not equivalent to) nothing than an 8-s sample is. Moreover, following a very long retention interval (such that the memory trace has faded completely), pigeons will respond as they would if no sample had been presented. These simple notions can account for a wide array of findings from the event-duration literature. Kraemer et al. (1985) were actually the first to propose and to test ideas like these. In that experiment, they arranged a three-way discrimination between a 2-s sample (short), 10-s sample (long), or no-sample and found that pigeons tended to choose the no-sample choice alternative as the retention interval increased following both short and long sample trials. These results are consistent with the idea that pigeons decide that nothing occurred when the memory trace (for either the short or the long sample) has faded. However, this kind of analysis was never worked out in the context of a formal theory, nor was it evaluated against the wide array of interesting results from this literature. The signal-detection analysis described in the previous section offers one way to formalize these principals and to guide the evaluation of them.

C. SIGNAL DETECTION MODEL OF MEMORY FOR EVENT DURATION

What accounts for the drop in performance on 2-s sample trials (and the even more precipitous drop on 8-s sample trials) evident in most studies on event duration? Figure 11 presents one theoretical analysis that can account for these results. The decision axis in this case is appropriate to an either/or choice task (i.e., did the short sample appear or did the long sample appear?). The zero point on the scale, which represents the placement of the decision criterion, is the point of subjective indifference. Values along the x-axis moving to the left of the zero point represent increasing subjective evidence that the 2-s sample appeared. Values to the right of the zero point represent increasing subjective evidence that the 8-s sample appeared. Whenever strength of evidence exceeds the decision criterion, the pigeon is assumed to choose the alternative associated with the 8-s sample (red), otherwise the 2-s alternative is chosen (green).

The solid distribution on the left represents subjective strength of evidence created on trials in which a 2-s (short) sample is presented. Most of

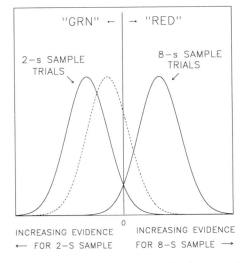

Fig. 11.   The solid distribution on the left represents subjective strength of evidence created on trials in which a 2-s sample was presented. The solid distribution on the right represents subjective strength of evidence created on trials in which the 8-s sample was presented. The dashed distribution represents subjective strength of evidence that might occur if no sample was presented. Values along the x-axis moving to the left of the zero point represent increasing subjective evidence that the 2-s sample appeared. Values to the right of the zero point represent increasing subjective evidence that the 8-s sample appeared.

the time, that sample creates evidence to the left of the decision criterion such that the correct alternative is chosen. Occasionally, however, subjective strength of evidence on these trials exceeds the criterion and an incorrect response is made. The solid distribution on the right represents subjective strength of evidence created on trials in which the 8-s (long) sample is presented. Most of the time, that sample creates evidence to the right of the decision criterion such that the correct alternative is chosen. Once again, however, subjective strength of evidence on these trials occasionally falls below the criterion and an incorrect response is made.

The dashed distribution represents subjective strength of evidence that might occur if no sample is presented. It can be loosely referred to as the mental state of "nothingness," that is, the mental state in effect when no exteroceptive events are arranged by the experimenter (although, as indicated earlier, that state is not assumed to be a mental vacuum). That distribution is closer to the 2-s distribution than to the 8-s distribution. Why? Because the model assumes that pigeons can more easily discriminate an 8-s sample from nothing than they can discriminate a 2-s sample from nothing. If that is true, then the appropriate signal detection analysis requires that the 2-s and no-sample distributions be placed closer to each other than the 8-s and no-sample distributions (because the distance between the distributions reflects how easily the two situations can be discriminated from each other). Note that the no-sample distribution must be placed *between* the 2-s and 8-s distributions. Placing it to the left of the 2-s distribution would imply that no sample creates more evidence that a 2-s sample occurred than a 2-s sample itself (which could not be correct).

How does this theory explain the pattern of results consistently observed in experiments on memory for event duration (Fig. 10)? An assumption inherent in this analysis is that when a long retention interval is introduced in a test session, whatever memory trace was established has faded (thereby resulting in the same mental state that would be in effect on no-sample trials). That is to say, the 2-s and 8-s distributions in Fig. 11 both converge on the nothingness (or no-sample) distribution as the retention interval increases. Eventually, both distributions coincide with the dashed distribution (just as the sample distribution eventually merges with the no-sample distribution in the presence-versus-absence memory experiments discussed earlier). If so, then performance following a 2-s sample should decline as the retention interval increases, but only to a point well above 50% correct. Performance following an 8-s sample, by contrast, should decline to a point below 50%. This is exactly the pattern of results shown in Fig. 10.

Note that this model not only accounts for data typically explained on the basis of subjective shortening (viz., the "choose-short" bias), it also uniquely explains the consistent drop in performance on trials initiated by the short duration sample. This model also clearly predicts that the use of a no-sample probe trial will result in a strong bias to choose the short alternative, a finding that has been well established (Fetterman & Mac-Ewen, 1989; Spetch & Grant, 1993). Neither of these findings is easily reconciled with the subjective shortening account.

1. Long Baseline Training Retention Interval

As described earlier, a simple discrimination strategy based on the presence or absence of the 8-s sample cannot adequately explain the data shown in Fig. 10 because that model predicts a perfectly flat retention function on 2-s sample trials. Indeed, it is difficult to imagine how a bird trained to attend to the houselight could selectively attend to an 8-s sample while treating the 2-s sample as a nonevent. On the other hand, it does seem possible that birds could, given the right circumstances, adopt a strategy based on the presence versus absence of *any* houselight sample, regardless of its duration. Such a strategy can be defined by the following decision rule: If memory for the houselight is strong, choose red, otherwise choose green. Note that this decision rule is not the one the experimenter has in mind for the subjects. Whether this decision rule or the one shown in Fig. 11 is used may depend on the size of the retention interval used in baseline training.

When the baseline retention interval used during training is very short (as in most event-duration studies), it stands to reason that a simple presence versus absence strategy would not work and that the birds would use the strategy shown in Fig. 11 instead. That is, after only 0.5 s, subjective evidence that a houselight sample recently occurred is likely to be very high on both 2-s and 8-s trials. Thus, the only effective discriminative strategy would be to decide whether it was the short or long sample that occurred. However, if the baseline retention interval were significantly longer than 0.5 s (e.g., 10 s), then a different discriminative strategy becomes possible. The memory trace for the 2-s sample presumably fades to nothing more rapidly than that for the 8-s sample. If so, then an appropriately long baseline retention interval will effectively result in a mental state of nothing on approximately half the trials (the 2-s trials) and something on the other half (the 8-s trials). Under these conditions, a discriminative strategy based on event duration is no longer possible (because the information for the less salient event is usually not available by the time the choice stimuli are presented), but a presence-versus-absence strategy would be quite effective.

Figure 12 shows the signal-detection interpretation of this state of affairs. Note that the decision axis has changed and now reads "Strength of Evidence that a Sample Occurred," because that is the dimension along which

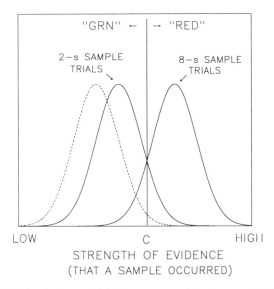

Fig. 12. The solid distribution on the left represents subjective strength of evidence created on trials in which a 2-s sample was presented. The solid distribution on the right represents subjective strength of evidence created on trials in which the 8-s sample was presented. The dashed distribution represents subjective strength of evidence that might occur if no sample was presented. Values along the x-axis represent increasing evidence that a sample was presented (moving from left to right).

the decision is assumed to be made under these conditions. Whereas the analysis illustrated earlier in Fig. 11 represents an *either/or* recognition strategy (i.e., was it the short sample or the long sample?), Fig. 12 represents a *Yes/No* decision strategy (i.e., did a sample occur or not?). The analysis shown in Fig. 11 involves a bidirectional decision axis, but the decision axis here is unidirectional because it represents monotonically increasing strength of evidence for occurrence (moving from left to right).

By the end of a 10-s retention interval, a 2-s sample presumably leaves less evidence that something happened than an 8-s sample. Thus, the 2-s distribution is reasonably placed to the left of the 8-s distribution in Fig. 12. The dashed distribution again shows the expected strength of evidence that should prevail on, say, a no-sample probe trial. This distribution is now placed to the left of the 2-s distribution. Why? Because nothing (i.e., no sample) creates even less evidence that something happened than a 2-s sample. As the retention interval increases, both the short and long distributions converge on the stationary no-sample distribution (as in Fig. 11).

The predictions of this model are often exactly the opposite of the predictions derived from Fig. 11. For example, this model predicts that performance on 2-s sample trials should, if anything, *improve* as the retention interval increases beyond the baseline training retention interval. Why? Because any residual trace strength from the short sample will fade away, making it that much more likely that the pigeon will decide that nothing occurred (and choose what is from the bird's point of view the no-sample choice alternative and what is from the experimenter's point of view the short duration choice alternative). This pattern of results has been observed before by Spetch (1987), who used a 10-s baseline retention interval in an event-duration procedure. The data showed that performance on short sample trials improved significantly as the retention interval increased beyond 10 s (while performance on long sample trials worsened as usual).

It should be noted that this result also happens to be consistent with the subjective shortening model because, as the retention interval increases beyond 10 s, the representation of the sample is assumed to shorten, making it even more likely that the bird will select the short choice alternative. The key difference between the subjective shortening model and that shown in Fig. 12 is how the choice alternatives are interpreted. The subjective shortening model always assumes that a response to one alternative implies a decision that the sample was short whereas a response to the other alternative implies a decision that the sample was long. The model proposed here instead assumes that the use of a long retention interval (during baseline training) alters the bird's discriminative strategy such that the decision is no longer short versus long but is now Yes (a sample occurred) versus No (a sample did not occur).

Both models can explain the curious increase in accuracy on short sample trials as the retention interval increases. An even more curious result is observed when the retention interval is reduced to less than the 10-s interval used during baseline training. Usually, decreasing the retention interval improves performance. However, Spetch (1987) showed that performance on short sample trials *worsened* as the retention interval decreased, a result that was taken as evidence of "subjective lengthening." That is, just as remembered duration should shorten as the retention interval increases, it should lengthen as the retention interval decreases (leading the pigeon to choose the incorrect long choice alternative).

On the other hand, the theoretical scheme outlined in Fig. 12 also predicts a worsening of performance on short sample trials as the retention interval decreases. Why? Because, theoretically, the birds are relying on a presence-versus-absence discriminative strategy such that they choose the short (i.e., No) choice alternative when strength of evidence that something happened is low enough. If the retention interval is reduced, strength of evidence that something happened on short sample trials increases (because memory for the houselight will still exist), leading the subject to choose the wrong (i.e., Yes) alternative. Of course, accuracy on long sample trials should increase under these conditions because strength of evidence that something happened is especially strong on long sample trials involving, say, a 3-s retention interval.

The subjective shortening analysis always predicts subjective lengthening when the retention interval is reduced and "subjective shortening" when it is lengthened. The signal-detection analysis advanced here predicts such effects only when the baseline retention interval used is sufficiently long to induce the birds to change their discriminative strategy from one based on event duration to one based on presence versus absence. Otherwise, exactly the opposite effects should be observed. Indeed, throughout this section we have argued that, when the baseline retention interval is short, increasing the retention interval leads to a reliable *decrement* in performance on short sample trials (contrary to what a subjective shortening model would predict). When the baseline retention interval is long, increasing the retention interval leads to a reliable *increment* in performance on short sample trials (which is what a subjective shortening model always predicts). Figure 13 shows data from my laboratory (averaged over three birds) showing the trends that are representative of the findings from this literature.

2. Very Long Retention Intervals and the Mental State of Nothing

A critical assumption of this entire analysis is that, after a long retention interval (i.e., after any memory trace established at the beginning of the trial has faded completely) birds respond as if no sample had been presented. This idea was originally proposed by Kramer et al. (1985), who also provided some empirical support for that idea. It should be noted that a finding reported by Spetch and Grant (1993) was taken as evidence against this idea. Because that is a central assumption of the present analysis, the issue needs to be further considered. The finding of interest to Spetch and Grant (1993) was that performance on no-sample probe trials was similar for birds trained on a choice procedure and birds trained on a successive procedure. In a successive DMTS procedure, a sample of 2- or 8-s (short vs. long) is followed by either the red or green choice stimulus (not both) for 5 s. A response to red is reinforced on 8-s trials and a response to green is reinforced on 2-s trials. In both cases, a choose-short bias was observed on no-sample probe trials. On the other hand, performance following a long retention interval (a situation supposedly analogous to the no-sample case) differed in the choice and successive tasks. The choice group exhibited the usual choose-short effect, but the successive group apparently did not.

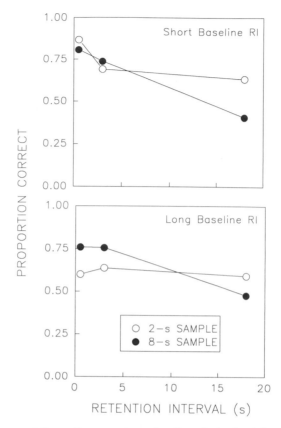

Fig. 13. *Upper panel.* Proportion correct as a function of retention interval for an event-duration experiment conducted in my laboratory. The open symbols represent performance on trials involving the short (2-s) sample while the solid symbols represent performance on trials involving the long (8-s) sample. The baseline retention interval in effect prior to probe testing was short (0.5 s). The data are averaged over three birds. *Lower panel.* Data from the same birds when the baseline retention interval in effect prior to probe testing was long.

Actually, the pattern of data from the successive group did reveal a choose-short effect because the interaction between retention interval and sample duration was significant (i.e., performance on long trials dropped faster than performance on short trials). The difference was that an initial bias (i.e., at the 0-s retention interval) was evident for responding to the test stimulus associated with the long sample in the successive group, whereas for the choice group no bias for either alternative was evident at the shortest retention interval. From a signal-detection point of view, this difference merely reflects a difference in the placement of the decision criterion, but the situation is not otherwise fundamentally altered. In both cases, performance on short-duration trials dropped more slowly than performance on long-duration trials. Moreover, unless the retention interval used during a test session is long enough to produce chance responding (which it was not in this case), one cannot say if obtained no-sample performance matches what would happen when the memory trace fades completely.

In any case, these issues are certainly debatable, and others have reported an absence of a choose-short effect on the successive task (e.g., Grant & Spetch, 1991; Wasserman, DeLong, & Larew, 1984). Thus, an experiment explicitly testing the idea that performance on no-sample trials matches performance on sample trials involving a long retention interval (on both choice and successive tasks) needs to be conducted.

IV. Memory for Stimulus Modality

Wallace, Steinert, Scobie, and Spear (1980) tested memory for stimulus modality in rats by using a procedure in which one choice response was reinforced following a tone and another was reinforced following a light. The forgetting functions following light and tone samples were asymmetric: Whereas performance following the light sample dropped rapidly as the retention interval increased, performance following the tone remained flat. These results were taken to suggest that a visual code decays more rapidly than an auditory code. An alternative interpretation, however, is that the rats solved this task by selectively attending to the presence or absence of the visual stimulus (with the auditory stimulus being effectively a nonevent). If so, the use of no-sample probes should have resulted in a strong bias to choose the alternative associated with tone. However, such probes were not included.

In the earlier discussion of memory for event duration, it was argued that pigeons trained to attend to the houselight are unlikely to selectively attend to an 8-s houselight while treating the 2-s houselight as a nonevent. By contrast, when one sample is visual and the other auditory, selective attention to one modality would not be particularly surprising. Indeed, a study by Cohen, Fuerst, and Roberts (1991) supported the hypothesis that rats in this procedure tend not to attend to the tone unless explicitly trained to do so (by requiring them to press a lever when the tone sample was presented). Instead, the rats responded based on the presence or absence of the light, creating the impression that no forgetting occurred on tone trials. Interpreted in terms of signal detection theory, the results reported by Cohen et al. suggest that Fig. 3 and Fig. 4 apply to this situation, with trials involving light being the sample trials. The tone was effectively a nonevent, conceptually identical to a no-sample trial. If so, then no-sample probe trials should reveal a bias toward the tone alternative that is equal to the bias observed when a tone is actually presented.

Kraemer (1991) reported an interesting phenomenon that bears on the analysis proposed here. In this experiment, pigeons were exposed to 2-s versus 10-s houselights and 2-s versus 10-s tones. One set of choice stimuli (red and blue) followed houselight samples and another set (green and yellow) followed tone samples. Presumably, the usual choose-short effect would have been observed on both kinds of trial had the retention interval been increased, but that was not the purpose of this study. The experimental manipulation involved inserting occasional probe trials in which the choice stimuli associated with one modality were presented following samples from the other modality. Thus, for example, the red and blue choice stimuli were presented following tones, and the green and yellow choice stimuli were presented following houselights. Kraemer found that on these cross-modality probe trials, pigeons tended to choose the short alternative whether the signal was short or long. This result bears an obvious similarity to the choose-short effect obtained when retention interval is manipulated.

Because accurate performance did not transfer when the choice stimuli were switched (instead, a choose-short bias emerged), the author concluded that choice decisions made in the presence of the two sets of comparison stimuli were modality specific. The connection between this result and the signal detection account offered here becomes apparent if that conclusion is worded in a slightly different way. For example, if the red and blue choice stimuli were presented, Kraemer's (1991) data suggest that pigeons make a retrospective decision about whether the short or long houselight occurred (as usual). That remains true even if the trial began with a tone. Because no houselight actually occurred, the trial is functionally equivalent to a no-sample trial, and the situation outlined in Fig. 11 should apply. The fact that a tone occurred is irrelevant because the retrospective decision pertains only to the houselight samples, neither of which occurred. Thus, on these trials, a bias toward the short alternative should be observed, but the bias should not be as strong as that observed when a short houselight is actually presented. This is precisely the pattern reported by Kramer (1991). On the short trials used during baseline training, pigeons chose the correct (short) alternative 82% of the time. On cross-modality probe trials (which are assumed to be functionally equivalent to no-sample probe trials), pigeons chose the short alternative an average of 75% of the time (averaged across short and long trials).

Kraemer (1991) used a short baseline retention interval during training, so the scheme illustrated in Fig. 11 should apply. Although the size of the retention interval was not manipulated in that study, the theoretical analysis proposed here makes some strong predictions about what should happen under those conditions. If a series of retention intervals are added in test sessions, performance on cross-modality trials should remain flat (not increase or decrease) because that is what happens on actual no-sample trials (Fig. 1). On the other hand, performance on short training trials should drop somewhat (to the level obtained on the functional no-sample trials), while performance on long trials should drop precipitously to below 50% correct. Thus, to use a concrete example, had Kraemer (1991) introduced a series of retention intervals in a test session, the expectation here is that performance on cross-modality probe trials would remain constant, with 75% of responses directed toward the short alternative. Performance on short training trials would be expected to drop from 82% correct to 75% correct, whereas performance on long training trials would be expected to eventually drop to 25% correct (i.e., they would choose the short alternative 75% of the time).

If a long baseline retention interval were used in this kind of study, the relevant theoretical scheme should change from that shown in Fig. 11 to that shown in Fig. 12. Moreover, cross-modal probe trials should now yield a choose-short bias that is even greater than that observed when a modality-consistent short sample is presented because a tone creates even less evidence that a light happened than a short light sample. Whether these predictions are borne out remains to be seen.

V. Conclusion

A number of issues currently under investigation in the event-duration literature have not been addressed here. For example, several studies have shown that the usual choose-short effect can be eliminated when a many-to-one procedure is used (Santi, Bridson, & Ducharme, 1993; Grant & Spetch, 1993, 1994). Thus, if one choice alternative is correct following either a 2-s houselight or a red keylight, and the other choice alternative is correct following either a 10-s houselight or a green keylight, a choose-short effect may not be obtained. The generally accepted reason for this is that by associating two samples with a single choice, a common code is created (the nature of which is unknown at the present time). That code could be isomorphic with the color sample (e.g., both the 2-s houselight and the red keylight create a representation of red). In that case, the memory task would no longer be asymmetric and the specific analyses described here would not apply.

When an asymmetric memory test is employed, the following principles may help to explain why animals behave the way they do:

1. The less salient event is more like nothing than the more salient event. Operationalized, this means that it will be harder to discriminate a less salient event from nothing than it will be to discriminate a more salient event from nothing.

2. The mental state of nothingness can be created either by inserting trials in which the sample is omitted or by using a very long retention interval such that any memory trace created by the sample fades completely. In either case, pigeons should be inclined to choose the alternative associated with the less salient event (because of principle 1).

3. If the retention interval used during baseline training is short, then information about the presence of a sample will be available on every trial. As a result, the task must be solved by remembering whether the more salient (e.g., 8-s) or less salient (e.g., 2-s) sample was presented. If the retention interval used during baseline training is long enough to allow the memory trace associated with the less salient sample to fade (but not the more salient sample), then a presence-versus-absence strategy will be adopted.

These ideas serve to connect a disparate array of findings currently explained on the basis of separate models that assume a default response strategy, subjective shortening, and modality-specific decay rates.

Acknowledgments

This research was supported by Grant IBN-9122395 from the National Science Foundation. Address correspondence to John T. Wixted, Department of Psychology, 0109, University of California, San Diego, La Jolla, CA 92093-0109.

References

Bailey, J. T., & Mazur, J. E. (1990). Choice behavior in transition: development of preference for the higher probability of reinforcement. *Journal of the Experimental Analysis of Behavior, 53,* 409–422.

Cohen, J. S., Fuerst, D., & Roberts, R. (1991). The role of stimulus modality in rats' short-term memory reconsidered. *Canadian Journal of Psychology, 45,* 288–302.

Colwill, R. M. (1984). Disruption of short-term memory for reinforcement by ambient illumination. *Quarterly Journal of Experimental Psychology, 36B,* 235–258.

Colwill, R. M., & Dickinson, A. (1980). Short-term retention of "surprising" events by pigeons. *Quarterly Journal of Experimental Psychology, 32,* 539–556.

Dougherty, D. H., & Wixted, J. T. (1996). Detecting a nonevent: Delayed presence-vs.-absence discrimination in pigeons. *Journal of the Experimental Analysis of Behavior, 65,* 81–92.

Fetterman, J. G. (1995). The psychophysics of remembered duration. *Animal Learning & Behavior, 23,* 49–62.

Fetterman, J. G., & MacEwen, D. (1989). Short-term memory for responses: The choose-small effect. *Journal of the Experimental Analysis of Behavior, 52,* 311–324.

Grant, D. S. (1991). Symmetrical and asymmetrical coding of food and no-food samples in delayed matching in pigeons. *Journal of Experimental Psychology: Animal Behavior Processes, 17,* 186–193.

Grant, D. S., & Spetch, M. L. (1991). Pigeons' memory for event duration: Differences between choice and successive matching tasks. *Learning & Motivation, 22,* 180–199.

Grant, D. S., & Spetch, M. L. (1993). Analogical and nonanalogical coding of samples differing in duration in a choice-matching task in pigeons. *Journal of Experimental Psychology: Animal Behavior Processes, 19,* 15–25.

Grant, D. S., & Spetch, M. L. (1994). Mediated transfer testing provides evidence for common coding of duration and line samples in many-to-one matching in pigeons. *Animal Learning & Behavior, 22,* 84–89.

Harnett, P., McCarthy, D., & Davison, M. (1984). Delayed signal detection, differential reinforcement, and short-term memory in the pigeon. *Journal of the Experimental Analysis of Behavior, 42,* 87–111.

Herrnstein, R. J., & Loveland, D. H. (1975). Maximizing and matching on concurrent ratio schedules. *Journal of the Experimental Analysis of Behavior, 24,* 107–116.

Kraemer, P. J. (1991). Absence of immediate transfer of training of duration symbolic-matching-to-sample in pigeons. *Animal Learning & Behavior, 19,* 276–282.

Kraemer, P. J., Mazmanian, D. S., & Roberts, W. A. (1985). The choose-short effect in pigeon memory for stimulus duration: Subjective shortening versus coding models. *Animal Learning and Behavior, 13*(4), 349–354.

Lockhart, R. S., & Murdock, B. B. (1970). Memory and the theory of signal detection. *Psychological Bulletin, 74,* 100–109.

Luce, R. D. (1960). Detection thresholds: A problem reconsidered. *Science, 132,* 1495.

Macmillan, N. A., & Creelman, C. D. (1991). Detection theory: A user's guide. New York: Cambridge University Press.

Murdock, B. B. (1965). Signal-detection theory and short-term memory. *Journal of Experimental Psychology, 70,* 443–447.

Ogilvie, J. C., & Creelman, C. D. (1968). Maximum-likelihood estimation of receiver operating characteristic curve parameters. *Journal of Mathematical Psychology, 5,* 377–391.

Santi, A., Bridson, & Ducharme, M. J. (1993). Memory codes for temporal and nontemporal samples in many-to-one matching in pigeons. *Animal Learning & Behavior, 21,* 120–130.

Sherburne, L. M., & Zentall, T. R. (1993). Asymmetrical coding of food and no-food events by pigeons: Sample pecking versus food as the basis of the sample code. *Learning and Motivation, 24,* 141–155.

Shimp, C. P. (1966). Probabilistically reinforced choice behavior in pigeons. *Journal of the Experimental Analysis of Behavior, 9,* 443–455.

Spetch, M. L. (1987). Systematic errors in pigeons' memory for event duration: Interaction between training and test delay. *Animal Learning & Behavior, 15,* 1–5.

Spetch, M. L., & Grant, D. S. (1993). Pigeons' memory for event duration in choice and successive matching-to-sample tasks. *Learning and Motivation, 24,* 156–174.

Spetch, M. L., & Wilkie, D. M. (1982). A systematic bias in pigeons memory for food and light duration. *Behavior Analysis Letters, 2,* 267–274.

Spetch, M. L., & Wilkie, D. M. (1983). Subjective shortening: A model of pigeons memory for event duration. *Journal of Experimental Psychology: Animal Behavior Processes, 9,* 14–30.

Swets, J. A., Tanner, W. P., & Birdsall, T. G. (1961). Decision processes in perception. *Psychological Review, 68,* 301–340.

Wallace, J., Steinert, P. A., Scobie, S. R., & Spear, N. E. (1980). Stimulus modality and short-term memory in rats. *Animal Learning & Behavior, 8,* 10–16.

Wasserman, E. A., DeLong, R. E., & Larew, M. B. (1984). Temporal order and duration: Their discrimination and retention by pigeons. In J. Gibbon & L. Allen (Eds.), *Timing and perception* (Vol. 423, pp. 103–115). New York: Annals of the New York Academy of Sciences.

Wilson, B., & Boakes, R. A. (1985). A comparison of the short-term memory performance of pigeons and jackdaws. *Animal Learning and Behavior, 13,* 285–290.

Wixted, J. T. (1993). A signal detection analysis of memory for nonoccurrence in pigeons. *Journal of Experimental Psychology: Animal Behavior Processes, 19* (*4*), 400–411.

Wright, A. A., Urcuioli, P., & Sands, S. F. (1986). Proactive interference in animal memory. In D. F. Kendrick, M. E. Rilling, & M. R. Denny (Eds.), *Theories of animal memory* (pp. 101–125). Hillsdale, NJ: Erlbaum.

THE MAINTENANCE OF A COMPLEX KNOWLEDGE BASE AFTER SEVENTEEN YEARS[1]

Marigold Linton

I. Introduction

Long-term memory (LTM) has not been studied with the systematic care allotted to short-term memory. The present largely atheoretical study was designed to fill some gaps in our knowledge about LTM, to suggest some changes in memory that occur over time, and to highlight some questions that can be raised in this context. In the present study a single subject (the researcher) has learned items from a large complex knowledge base and through periodic rehearsals has attempted to maintain that knowledge in an accessible state over a period of many years. The study examines both the acquisition and long-term maintenance of scientific and common plant names learned as responses to color photographs of the plants. Designed in part to assess the impact of differing maintenance schedules on very long-term recall, the study also provides a framework of acquisition and retention against which other questions can be explored.

The present paper focuses on several themes from this 17-year old study:

1. How well do encoding difficulties and errors predict recall difficulties and errors months or years later? Are difficult-to-learn items also difficult to maintain? Are the same errors made?

[1] This paper is dedicated to the memory of my father, Walter Alexander Linton, who after a long and eventful life died during the final weeks I was writing this paper.

THE PSYCHOLOGY OF LEARNING AND MOTIVATION, VOL. 35

127

2. How does the structure of the knowledge base relate to its recall? That is, which elements of complex well-learned information are best recalled and what changes in recall patterns, if any, occur as expertise is acquired?

3. What can such a a long-term study tell us about tips-of-the-tongue (TOTs)?

In addition, a variety of less systematic reflections on changes that occur in memory over time are also included.

Although the materials were rotely learned and repeatedly underwent rote rehearsal, reorganization and other "smart" processes can be identified in the protocols almost at once. Evidence for such changes are detected by comparing errors made during encoding trials with those made during the years of maintenance rehearsals. Accuracy of recall decreased with increases in delay before recall, but shifts in relative accuracy of different item elements also occurred. These changes are explainable in terms of the subject's increased expertise in the knowledge domain.

I describe an effort to learn (encode) a body of information and then to maintain it (keep it available through rehearsal) for a period of decades. The following introductory sections attempt to set the stage for this effort.

A.   An Historical Note

In 1972 while spending a sabbatical leave with the Center for Human Information Processing's Lindsay, Norman, and Rumelhart (LNR) Research Group at the University of California, San Diego, I embarked on a study I hoped would answer some puzzling questions concerning complex very long-term memory. The topic of this investigation has come to be called "autobiographical memory." Guided by Professor Donald Norman and the LNR group's interest in temporal codes in memory, the study examined temporal codes as well as a number of other variables. As I have indicated elsewhere (Linton, 1975), I did not originally intend to serve as the sole subject in this study. That decision emerged when I considered issues of compliance and reliability of alternative subjects that must be faced in any study that lasts for long periods of time. This first long-term-memory single-subject study continued for 8 years. A factor that contributed to my abandoning that paradigm was Neisser's (1978) cogent observation that repeated testing of items (an inextricable feature of my autobiographical study) in fact comprised unintended researsals resulting in artificially inflated recall levels. As I write this paper I have already completed my 23rd year of serving as my own subject in studies examining long-term memory, and have spent 17 years examining "maintenance of knowledge" (MOK)—the focus of this paper. Because MOK focuses on deliberately memorized items, and because carefully controlled rehearsals become an interesting variable, the unavoidable confounding of tests and rehearsals that posed difficulties for the autobiographical study cease to be a major problem.

B. SOME QUESTIONS

In setting the framework I find it instructive to consider some of the questions raised by the curious and the critical about my implementation of this long-term-memory paradigm. This question-and-answer format permits me to summarize information that does not conveniently fit elsewhere.

Question: What of importance is likely to be learned from examining memory for 10 or 20 years that cannot be observed in days, weeks, months, or fewer years?

Answer: Although I do not have a simple answer to this query, this study was originally motivated by the perceived opportunity to track complex changes that we know occur in memory because each of us observe them in our lives and because cognitive psychologists have studied the phenomenon under such labels as metamemory, expertise, and the like. Evidence of expertise may not emerge in shorter periods and may not be apparent with more traditional methods. Thus, I believe knowledge about additional regularities in memory will emerge from examining memory with novel paradigms that extend over longer time periods. The present study is only one instance of this genre.

Question: Is this paradigm an optimal one for studying long-term memory?

Answer: I wish this were so, but first ventures—however long lasting—rarely provide best answers. The results I obtain, like the results in every other study, are highly dependent on the specific, quite idiosyncratic research choices I have made. Moreover, in this study the results are dependent as well as on the characteristics of the ever-changing memory—aging but more expert—I bring to bear.

Question: Do you, the researcher/subject, believe your memory is representative of "the average memory"?

Answer: I must begin with the disclaimer that we know remarkably little about the overall texture and mix of skills that make up individual memories. Some extraordinary memories have been studied and we see, most notably in Luria (1968), that exceptional abilities in one arena may reside uneasily with mediocre memorial talents, or even deficiencies in other areas. While conceding the dearth of metrics on this score, I do not judge my memory to be typical or average. A frequent comment from both psychologists and laymen on learning the thrust of my research may be roughly paraphrased: "Oh, you have been studying memory for 20 years, you must have a great memory." Regretfully, this does not follow. In comparison with a typical college population I judge my memory to be quite mediocre.

Were this not true my career might have been very different—and I would almost certainly not have become as interested in the memory failures that ultimately led to this study. Although I can make no claims for exceptional memory in any area, I fare better placing events and items temporally and spatially—an aspect my autobiographical memory study capitalized upon—than with any other aspect of memory.

Question: If your memory cannot be demonstrated to be average, what value does it serve to have a wealth of data on this single memory?

Answer: Memory has been studied from many perspectives. Each paradigm provides unique insights into how mind and memory perform and together provide a more complete picture than can any alone. A single-subject study that examines several facets of a memory over very long periods of time may permit us to identify regularities that would otherwise be overlooked. I believe the world would be poorer without a few single-subject very-long-term-memory studies.

Question: What advantage does a continuous testing paradigm such as the present one have over the assess and test procedures used so effectively by Bahrick (1979, 1984) and Bahrick and Karis (1982).

Answer: Some methodological advantages to the present continuous testing paradigm (well described by Bahrick et al., 1993) include better control over rehearsal, an opportunity to examine spacing effects and separating effects of amount and distribution of practice. To these there must be added the development of expertise. Among the disadvantages must be listed difficulty in obtaining subjects, need to rely upon fewer subjects, the devastating effects of lack of subject compliance, and the potential for contamination among experimental conditions.

Question: How long do the experimental procedures in your paradigm require?

Answer: The amount of time required has varied over the course of the study. More time is required when items are being newly encoded. At present with most rehearsals widely spaced and no new encoding being undertaken, experimental procedures consume between 30 min and an hour a day.[2] On the average each minute I perform three rehearsals and complete records of response times, order, errors, and the like. More time is required in general maintenance of the files: dating, sorting, filing, and tracking items. Over the 17 years data collection has probably consumed more than 12,000 hrs.

Question: Do you record your data directly into a computer database?

Answer: No.

---

[2] This is true only because, at present, Phase I and Phase II files are partially "hibernating." When regular testing in these phases resume, an additional 30 min to 1 hr will be required each day.

Question: Why not?

Answer: Basically, paranoia. But there are a number of reasons I have been reluctant to rely on electronic databases. First, databases were not widely available when I initiated the study and creating a sophisticated database was easier said than done. Second, I have always traveled regularly, and such travel, until recently, would have separated me from any database. From time to time I have entered (or have had entered) large amounts of data. More than once, substantial databases have disappeared into the ether. Up to the present, I am pleased to report, no hard copies have ever permanently disappeared. To provide balance, many thousands of the estimated 20–30 million scoreable bits accumulated over this time period are in one or another database.

Question: Why have you spent almost 25 years engaged in these solitary studies?

Answer: Motivation is complex and my perceptions about my motivation are not the final answer to why my behaviors occur. However, I offer the following considerations. I cherish things that last and will have meaning and (potential) value over long periods of time. I find periods of solitary activity relaxing. I prefer independent activities where I do not have to rely upon other individuals to complete tasks. I am a contrarian financially and this trait may be related—if everyone is "selling," "buy," and if everyone is doing short-term memory projects, do long-term-memory projects. I like plants (the stimuli employed in the study) and it makes me feel good to have a remarkable database of plant names in memory (although one loses friends rapidly if this knowledge is shared with any regularity). Finally, I think this study may ultimately provide a modest scientific contribution.

C. RESEARCH INTRODUCTION

Kenneth Spence (1958) repeatedly harangued his students that no one conducts research without theory, explicit or implicit. Where theory is implicit and informal, as is the case in the present study, ties to earlier literature are often tenuous.

1. Single-Subject Designs

Although few experimental or cognitive psychologists have followed his lead, Ebbinghaus's seminal pioneering work lends an air of respectability, perhaps combined with nostalgia, to the use of single-subject designs to examine learning and forgetting. Ebbinghaus (1885/1964) in his precedent-setting work was concerned with a number of issues that, in different guises, have continued to interest psychologists for more than a century. Among these topics are included the relationships of item length (his measure of difficulty) to the speed of learning, retention as a function of the number and spacing of repetitions, forgetting as a function of delay, retention as a function of repeated learning, and retention as a function of order of succession. Each of Ebbinghaus' major topics, except the last, have been touched upon within the context of the present study. A few of these themes are reflected in this paper.

In the late 1960s and early 1970s when my studies were being conceptualized, experimental/cognitive psychologists were just beginning to step beyond the confines of the paradigms deriving from Ebbinghaus' (1885/1964) legacy and the scientific traditions of the first half or more of the 20th century. Within this older tradition a number of features were understood: Definitions of long-term memory set the lower bound at about an hour. Materials were "scientifically" stripped of meaning.[3] Where motivations were not ignored, research settings minimized them. In an effort to step out of these confines I designed my autobiographical and later my maintenance of knowledge studies. A major impetus to my original decision to perform a very-long-term single-subject study was the wish to wed Ebbinghaus's methods with an alternative tradition that emphasized real-world materials. Cognitive psychology, of course, has undergone significant changes since the 1960s as well as during the more than two decades since I began my long-term-memory research and such criticisms are less cogent.

A number of studies are related thematically to the research described in this chapter. One summary is provided by Bahrick and Karis (1982) who cogently argued that whereas most earlier memory studies have involved episodic memory, the study of semantic information is a more appropriate focus for cognitive psychology. Most studies described in their careful review of semantic memory, however, are concerned with retention, rather than acquisition of information. Researchers, they say, have eschewed studying the step-by-step development of semantic knowledge "because semantic knowledge accumulates over a long time span [and] the process of acquiring generalized knowledge is not readily observed or manipulated in the laboratory" (Bahrick & Karis, 1982, p. 428).

They describe four methods used by psychologists to study memory after long delays. The most time consuming of these requires the subject to acquire a body of knowledge under carefully monitored conditions and examines changes in recall by implementing systematically spaced tests and rehearsals. This method is employed in the general research program described in this report. It was also used by Bahrick and Phelps (1987) and Bahrick et al. (1993).

The Bahrick et al. (1993) study on many dimensions closely resembles the present effort. In a 9-year longitudinal investigation, four subjects

---

[3] This phrase does not adequately convey Ebbinghaus's genius. Although Ebbinghaus chose to use nonsense syllables, he also carried out "several tests with six stanzas of Byron's *Don Juan.*" Not surprisingly he reports that Byron's verses were retained/relearned (his savings method) more easily than were nonsense syllables (Ebbinghaus, 1885/1964, p. 82).

learned, were tested on, and relearned 300 English-foreign language word pairs. Either 13 or 26 relearning sessions were administered at intervals of 14, 28, or 56 days. Retention was tested for 1, 2, 3, or 5 years after training ended. The researchers concluded that longer intersession intervals slowed acquisition slightly, but this disadvantage during training was offset by substantially higher retention. For example, 13 retraining sessions spaced at 56 days yielded retention comparable to 26 sessions spaced at 14 days.

The Bahricks' and the Linton studies are similar in that both are concerned with very-long-term memory (9 and 17 years respectively). Both employ semantically rich materials. Both rely on a small sample of subjects (four vs. one). Both include spacing of rehearsals and tests as an important element in the studies. Both depend heavily on rote learning. The studies differ in the following significant ways:

1. The Bahricks' study is designed to test specific hypotheses while the Linton study is largely atheoretical but provides a background against which a variety of hypotheses or speculations may be examined.

2. The Bahricks' study involves a close-ended very-long time period while the Linton study involves an open-ended long-term effort.

3. The Bahricks' study uses relatively simple (bilingual) semantic materials while the Linton study employs more complex internally structured materials.

4. The Bahricks' study involves word–word learning while the Linton study employs picture–word pairs.

5. The Bahricks' study uses a "drop-out procedure" while the Linton study uses extensive overlearning on every trial.

This glance at the literature does not fully set the stage for the MOK study. A crucial issue was, how is memorial information made useful in daily life? If knowledge were to be useful in real-world settings, acquisition and maintenance procedures must render it readily accessible. For this reason strict response time criteria were imposed and spacing of rehearsals became an important aspect of the study. An additional assumption in the study's design was that permanent rehearsals would be required to maintain knowledge in an accessible state. Because materials difficult to remember at first would become easier to recall with study, it followed that delays between successive tests could be increased gradually without impairing performance.

The rough model of memory that guided this research was that rotely learned material is held in an active memory system. It was thought that repetitions would improve specific recall but, in addition, the context surrounding any target material, both locally and more generally, would change as additional relevant material was learned (or forgotten). These changes would have two countervailing effects: (a) permitting the reorganization of materials into a set of efficient streamlined structures as expertise is acquired, but also (b) in some cases making it more difficult to retrieve items. Although these aspirations for the research bear only slight fruit in this paper, it is hoped that eventually the interactions between expertise and the acquisition and retention of knowledge may be more fully mapped. The emergence of smoothly polished skills from halting performance is not ordinarily examined in the context of simple acquisition and retention of verbal behaviors and this study may eventually contribute to filling this lacuna. How general knowledge is acquired, how material that is awesomely difficult at one point in life becomes routine deserves greater attention than it has been accorded.

II. A Developing Paradigm: Method and More

The findings presented in this paper are drawn primarily from two of the study's four phases. The experimental context, however, is provided by all the phases. For that reason, and because the methodological changes are informed by observations from the earlier phases, I provide a description of the paradigm, method, and materials covering all phases combined with rationale and commentary. For greater clarity, a brief résumé of the experimental phase and specific conditions involved accompanies each analysis in the section on findings.

A. Gradual Emergence of the Final Paradigm

Because this study leaped into the relatively unexplored domain of very-long-term memory, some assumptions and guesswork (but little formal theory) were involved in developing the design. Many of the choices were informed by my observations about the workings of my own memory (experimentally and in daily life). Some choices were poor, in itself not surprising, but certainly suggestive of the hazards of such an approach.

B. Stimuli and Why They Were Chosen

What constitutes an appropriate corpus for a long-term investigation of semantic information? I correctly understood that to mirror natural memorial processes optimally the materials chosen for a long-term memory study must have several characteristics: (a) attractiveness: If I were to work with stimuli on a "voluntary" basis for a number of years, it was crucial the materials be attractive, else the "subject" was likely to defect; (b) size of pool and degree of difficulty: The frequent rehearsal of the stimuli as well as the long time periods over which training and retention were proposed necessitated a large and appropriately difficult corpus if both ceiling and floor effects were to be avoided.

1. What Should the Materials Be?

At no time did I consider performing this study on the materials of Ebbinghaus. As experimenter I simply lacked the coercive power over myself as subject to obtain performance on such materials over any period of time. An additional reason for rejecting "nonsensical" materials of any sort was that such a choice eliminated the opportunity to examine developing expertise.[4] I considered a variety of word–word learning options (perhaps the world's largest vocabulary building test), but rejected these alternatives for a variety of reasons. Based on my knowledge of ease with which I learn such materials, I judged learning pairs of single meaningful words to be too easy. Using a single word paired with a sentence, phrase, or a group of words was rejected because this procedure, while it increased complexity, seemed to invite numerous scoring difficulties. I never considered using foreign language/English pairs (as the Bahricks have) although from time to time I have attempted (unsuccessfully) to learn Spanish vocabulary using the drop-out method they employ.

2. Pictures and Names

One way to increase the complexity of learning materials is to mix modes, for example, associating names with pictured materials. Such a procedure has a number of features to recommend it. Such pairings eliminate stimulus-response verbal chaining and require that objects be identified and linked with specific labels. These processes have been studied by a number of researchers including Rosch (1978) and Jolicoeur, Gluck, and Koselyn (1984).

As I narrowed my choices, I considered, among other possibilities, pictures of plants paired with their names. There are an estimated 35,000 species of flowering plants in the world as well as a variety of other flora. I ultimately selected as my target corpus colored pictures of plants (the

---

[4] My interactions with the late William Chase at Carnegie Mellon University in 1980–1981 during my sabbatical leave (from the University of Utah to the University of Pittsburgh's Learning Research and Development Center) reinforced this thought and interest, and confirmed a strongly held belief that governed these early choices. While I emphasized the memorial quality of the study I was conducting, he emphasized the development of expertise he was convinced was at the core of the cognitive process. Our conversations enriched my understanding of the relationship of expertise and memory.

stimuli) paired with the names (the responses).[5] This corpus met the criteria I had set, of interest, and of the pool's size and difficulty. The choice was facilitated by the publication of a set of commercial materials that fulfilled the requirements of the proposed research. In the four phases of the study I encoded and presently maintain more than 1,500 items from this potential pool. Largely because of the time-consuming nature of the study, especially during encoding, items were introduced gradually into the study.[6] This number of stimuli paired with the complex responses and the rate at which they have been added satisfactorily challenge my memory, but considerably larger or smaller sets or faster or slower addition of items may be appropriate for other subjects. Two distinct sets of materials, both pairing pictures of plants with their names, have been employed in the study. In Phase I and Phase II the stimuli are materials then commercially available from Western Publishing Company: in Phase I, *The Greenhouse* (1978), and in Phase II, *The Green Thumb* (1980). The response terms comprise the scientific (genus and species) names and a single, sometimes compound, everyday common name. In Phases I and II the stimulus cards are 10.6 × 17.6 cm. The pictures are 8.9 × 13.1 cm. The names appear above the picture with everyday common names above scientific names. The everyday common name appears in large and small letters (0.4–0.5 cm high), the genus in all cap letters 2 cm high, and the species in lower case of the same type. For some items varietal names follow the species names. A number, used as the experimental identification code, is printed in the upper right-hand corner of each card.

The stimulus materials used in Phases III and IV were constructed by laminating colored photos of plants pictured in the Audubon Society's popular *Field Guide to North American Wildflowers: Eastern Region* (1979)

---

[5] My students who have engaged in "long-term-memory" projects over the years—most efforts lasting a matter of months—have selected a variety of different subject matters. One who selected pictures of minerals strongly advocated my adopting this fascinating (to him) subject matter. He greatly enjoyed learning these materials. Another, at my instigation, created a marvelous stimulus pool of waterfowl. She reported being unable to learn them, and 10 years later, a Ph.D. in another discipline, still has negative associations with the whole experience—and decidedly does not like ducks. Only a few actual or potential long-term-memory subjects have expressed interest in learning names of plants. Conversely, had I been forced to learn items from most of their preferred domains (minerals, birds, insects, baseball cards, etc.), my study would have been very short term indeed. On the other hand, had I been able to find a tractable set of art representations I would have leapt at the opportunity to learn the works of the masters from around the world. I used "works of art" as stimuli in a study with one child over a number of years and observed important and long-lasting changes in her cognitions.

[6] An additional reason for keeping the number small was the high degree of interference that occurred among items learned at the same time.

paired with appropriate names.[7] A set of 4 × 5 in (11.25 × 15.4 cm) plain white cards provide the base. The pictures are 9.5 cm wide and are either 5.5 or 8.5 cm high. Some representations include an inset detail of flowers or leaves. Pictures appear toward the bottom of the cards with the typed names above them. Cards were laminated to preserve them. The following moderately difficult item exemplifies the names learned in Phases III and IV. The names were typed in three rows in 12-point type with much the appearance of the example.

TRUE FORGET-ME-NOT
Myosotis scorpioides
Forget-me-not family (Boraginaceae)

The everyday common name appears in full caps in the first row. The species and genus appear in the second row in upper and lower case, and the family name (common and then scientific) in the third row, again in upper and lower case. As many as three different common names are listed for some items.

The elements of these names differ obviously in difficulty (length, phonemic complexity, and rarity) and their degree of organization (their association with each other and with their pictorial representations). This is an issue to which I shall return.

3. Storing Materials

Items for all phases are stored in "sleeves" cut from heavy manila envelopes to cover them exactly front and back. In Phases I and II items are stored collectively in sleeves that indicate the previous test date together with the next retest date. For convenience in testing they are stored by anticipated retest date. In Phases III and IV items are stored in *individual* sleeves, once again by anticipated retest date. Because the individual sleeves in Phase III are used to record the exact date on which items are to be next tested, each item's sleeve contains the cumulative history of test dates for that item. Double sleeves are used in Phase IV. The inner sleeve permits either the item's name or picture to be separately viewed. The outer sleeve serves the same function described for Phase III sleeves. The materials from the four phases are stored separately all by the date on which they

[7] The choice of the Eastern Region guide materials was deliberate. Because I have always lived in the West, I thought to minimize contamination resulting from nonexperimental exposure by choosing stimulus materials I would not see regularly. This nicety was probably wasted since, to give only the most flagrant example, for 8 years I had an instantiation of one experimental item in a pot beside my bed—and failed to learn the name.

are next to be tested. Thus, on any day by moving to each file in turn it is possible to perform appropriate tests of all the items scheduled to be tested that day.

C. ENCODING PHASES

Over the course of the study acquisition has occurred in four discrete phases. In Phase I, a total of 540 items were learned from January 1979 to approximately September 1979. These dates are not precise because the criteria for encoding were not well defined in this phase. In Phase II, 428 items were learned from April 1981 to September 1982. In addition, 49 items were learned in three discrete groups between December 1982 and December 1983. In Phase III, 406 items were learned from May 1985 to July 1986. Finally, in Phase IV, 105 items were learned from August 1992 to February 1993.

D. GENERAL PROCEDURES

1. Presenting Stimuli

For both encoding and testing, items from Phases I, II, and III are removed from their storage sleeves and placed in a large concealing folder. With the left hand, items are drawn from the folder by the lower edge, rapidly exposing the entire picture but not the item name. A battery-run digital stopwatch held in the right hand is simultaneously started. The watch is stopped as the last syllable of the name is pronounced. The names are given subvocally or softly aloud, but every syllable is pronounced on each recall. The sole exception occurs if more than one common name occurs with two or more names sharing a single term. In such cases the overlapping term is ordinarily pronounced on only one occasion, for example, the common name "Japanese bamboo, Japanese knotweed" would be given as "Japanese bamboo, knotweed." This procedure has the effect of shortening somewhat the long multiple common names.

2. Encoding

A number of differences distinguish the encoding methods of the study's four phases. The procedures standardized in Phase II are described. Items ordinarily are encoded in relatively small groups (e.g., 8–20 stimuli). The picture is rapidly exposed and, even on the first exposure, an effort is made to provide the item's name as quickly as possible in any order. When all available information has been given, the plant name is exposed. The item name is read one or more times; the name is then covered and an effort is again made to repeat the name correctly. Early in encoding this latter procedure may be repeated a number of times before a speedy, correct response is given. In Phases I and II items were rehearsed in scientific then common order, because at the time it was easier to give the responses in that order.[8] In Phases III and IV names are ordinarily practiced in the standard order given above: common, genus, species, and family. In Phases I and II encoding trials, separated by delays of at least one hour, occurred as often as was convenient throughout the day. These trials had to fit into a busy schedule and the number of daily encoding trials ranged from 0 to 12 but would occur on successive days until the criterion of encoding—perfect performance in 5.5 s or less on the day's first or *primary test* and on at least two subsequent trials on that day—were met. During initial encoding in Phase III and IV, rehearsal/tests were fixed at three to five a day with rehearsals separated by at least an hour.

3. Scoring the Responses

Responding "at criterion" both during encoding and during maintenance trials involves giving all response elements correctly in fewer than 5.5 s. Any sequence is counted correct that includes all elements correctly marked for order (e.g., the species name may be given before genus with no error recorded unless there is confusion, *as sometimes happens,* about which is the species name and which the genus). The order in which response elements occur, together with errors of omission, commission, and the overall time to respond, are recorded. When there are delays in the flow of giving a response, I indicate where the pauses occur.

4. Commentary

When I began the MOK study, my focus was fixed firmly on long-term recall and the maintenance of knowledge. I thought interesting and exciting results would emerge only after many years, and saw learning/encoding as being trivial, a well-studied phenomenon that was somehow irrelevant to the approach I was taking. I was like the athlete, looking forward to several hours of vigorous workout, who parks as close as possible to the front door at the gym to avoid the walk across the parking lot. For Phase I as a consequence, I have virtually no information on the (what I now perceive to be interesting and crucial) encoding period. In Phase I, items appear in

[8] At that time I experienced considerable difficulty accessing the scientific name after giving the common name but little difficulty with the common name after giving the scientific name. Recalling the common name first appeared to delay access to the scientific name. There was no discernible interference of scientific name with recall of the common name. Rehearsing and recalling names in the preferred order eliminated most intraitem interference. Several years into the study this order-related difficulty disappeared and thereafter items were studied in the order in which they were listed: common, scientific, family.

the maintenance study "fully encoded." This is particularly unfortunate because during this early period I was engaged in the most complex task I faced in this study, learning how to encode complex Latinate words: learning to parse, pronounce, and link them together. In later phases a separate formal encoding period exists and detailed information on errors, response times, and order of responses was recorded on every trial. For this subject and this class of materials, however, the opportunity to study very early acquisition, as I moved from novice to slightly expert, is lost forever.

5.   Maintenance Trials/Rehearsals

Although in Phases II, III, and IV there are carefully defined encoding periods, the methodology blurs the distinction between acquisition and retention as is the case in everyday life. As indicated, encoding trials end and maintenance rehearsals begin when the criteria of accuracy and latency are met both on the first test of the day and on at least two additional tests during a single day. When the encoding criterion is met the regime of daily testing ends, items are assigned to a maintenance schedule and the cycle of spaced rehearsals begins.

When an item is first tested after a designated maintenance delay, the speed and accuracy of the response on this primary test determine whether further rehearsals will occur on the next day and the number of rehearsals on the first test day. Items must be completely correct and given in fewer than 5.5 s on the *first test of any day* and that criterion must be met two or three of five possible times during a day of tests.[9] If an item is perfectly recalled, the response is given speedily and accurately on the primary test as well as on two additional spaced tests. Such items are then returned to the file to await their next scheduled test—days, months, or years later.

If items are imperfectly recalled on any test they are relearned to the original criterion. It must be emphasized that, as with encoding occasions, maintenance rehearsal occasions are all potentially complex transactions.

Intratrial Rehearsals.   As in encoding, if the response term is recalled incompletely, inaccurately, or if the time exceeds criterion,[10] the stimulus is immediately studied and retested. Retests, seconds or minutes apart, are repeated until the criterion of speed (when applicable) and accuracy are met. An hour or more later the item is retested. Again, if the response is

---

[9] In Phases I and II the number of required correct trials is two, while in Phase III and IV the number is three.

[10] This detail is omitted to simplify exposition but some items are repeated until they reach the response time criterion of 5.5 s on every trial, and others are not. This latter condition is not germane to any results in this paper.

speedy and accurate a single test occurs; if not, intratrial rehearsals continue until criteria have again been met. After perfect performance on the primary test, if an error is made or a slow response given on later tests, appropriate intratrial rehearsals occur and additional spaced tests occur to bring the total number of perfect tests to three (of five). If continued errors are made, the item is retested on the next day. When performance is not perfect on the primary test, regardless of the performance on the remaining trials (frequently four perfect trials follow), the item is retested on the next day. The first test on the subsequent day is again treated as the primary test and the procedures described above are repeated.

6.   To Summarize

At criterion on Trial 1 and on 2 of remaining 5 trials	Item moves on
At criterion on Trial 1 but on fewer than 2 additional trials	Retest next day
Incorrect or slow on Trial 1	Retest next day

7.   Commentary

These complex procedures emerged to deal with two problems. Most importantly, a single maintenance rehearsal, or even the two rehearsals described for Phases I and II, are not adequate to keep knowledge available and rapidly accessible over the long delays employed in the study. Early in Phase I a surprising number of errors occur on trial X + 1 for items receiving only one or two rehearsals on maintenance trials, even if the responses were correct on both occasions.

E.   Spacing of Rehearsal Trials

1.   Customized Schedules

Bjork (1988) suggests provocatively: "If one were able to do so one should schedule each successive retrieval just prior to the point where one would otherwise lose access to the item in memory." Although as this study was being designed the guiding principal was "efficiency," it seemed plausible that more rapid learning and better recall would be obtained if "customized" schedules were employed (i.e., ones that responded to how rapidly and well an individual item was recalled) rather than "lock-step" schedules for all items (i.e., ones that ignored individual item difficulty). There remained the issue, highlighted by Bjork, of assessing the optimal time for the next rehearsal. The "customizing" procedure adopted in Phase I assumed that time to respond was a measure of the "strength of response," hence, fastest (read: strongest) responses could be safely followed by the longest delays. In other words, if a rapid response were given on Test X, then a longer delay would precede Test X + 1. If the response on Test X were slow, then a shorter delay would precede Test X + 1. I imagined that using this "sensitive" indicator of strength I could delicately keep each item at exactly the "delay" that suited its own "difficulty" and that, as prescribed by Bjork, the retrieval would occur close "to the point where [I] would otherwise lose access to the item." This implementation, the only customized schedule attempted during the course of this research, led down a nonproductive path. This procedure was abandoned after a matter of months and produced no coherent or usable results. Individual reaction times were extremely erratic.[11] Rapid responses were frequently followed by very slow responses (a phenomenon presumably produced by the long delays preceding Test X + 1 for items rapidly responded to on Test X). The schedules for Phases I and II continue to be controlled by the *accuracy* of performance. A proposed schedule exists, but delays are increased only when performance is speedy and accurate. In this modified procedure accuracy, not time, controls the length of delay an item attains. If items are missed, they are tested at shorter or equivalent delays rather than longer ones.

2. Standard Schedules

The issue of the optimal schedule continued to loom large. Several kinds of schedules are employed across Phases III and IV. I begin by describing the schedules, and then provide a rationale for them. The three basic schedules are *even, progressive,* and *accelerated.* The latter two would be described by Bjork (1988) as "expanded" schedules.

3. Even Schedules

Even schedules have at their base a single consistent delay between mainte-nance rehearsals. These relatively short delays are repeated 10 times. Fol-lowing these evenly spaced rehearsals, there is a "test delay" which ranges from the original base delay length to 10 times that delay. Following the tests delay, 6 months or a year intervenes after which the cycle is repeated. The base delays for the even schedules are one of the following: 6, 12, 18, 24, and 30 days. Let me provide two examples of even schedules before explaining them in greater detail. The values given below indicate the days since the last test:

    6, 6, 6, 6, 6, 6, 6, 6, 6, 6, 36, 365, 6, 6, 6 . . . and
    24, 24, 24, 24, 24, 24, 24, 24, 24, 24, 48, 180, 24, 24, 24 . . .

---

[11] Within this paradigm at least, speed of responding on a single trial was not a good predictor of later performance.

In the first ("6 even") schedule, the 6-day base delay is repeated 10 times. This part of the cycle requires only 60 days if the criterion is met on each primary test. These evenly spaced tests are followed by a test delay of 36 days. Test delays are invariant for each item so an item on this schedule always has a 36-day test delay. For other "6 even" items the test delays would be 6, 12, 18, 24, 30 . . . 60. Finally, this schedule includes a 1-year intercycle delay after which the cycle is repeated. The entire cycle requires a minimum of 461 days, or about 15 months. In 10 years, 8 cycles have been completed and a total of almost 100 rehearsal occasions have occurred.

The second ("24 even") schedule is similarly constructed. The basic 24-day delay is repeated 10 times, followed by a test delay of (in this case) 48 days. Finally, there is a 6-month intercycle delay. A cycle for an item on this schedule is completed in a minimum of 468 days (about 15 ½ months). In 10 years almost 8 cycles have been completed and a total of 94 rehearsal occasions have occurred. The shortest cycle for any even schedule has a base delay of 6 days, a test delay of 6 days, and a 6-month intercycle delay. The cycle requires 246 days. On this cycle in 10 years almost 15 cycles and 180 rehearsals have been completed. The longest cycle for any even schedule has a base delay of 30 days, a test delay of 300 days, and a 1-year intercycle delay. For this schedule a cycle requires a minimum of 965 days (or 2 years, 8 months). In a 10-year period fewer than 4 cycles are completed with fewer than 50 rehearsal occasions.

4. Progressive Schedules

Progressive schedules use a base value by which the length of delays between maintenance rehearsals are increased. The base values are the integers from 1 to 10. All these functions are linear with differing slopes. The delays for a progressive schedule with base value 1 are 1, 2, 3, 4, 5, 6, 7 . . . 56, 57, 58 . . . 83, 84, 85 . . . In each case 1 day is added to the length of the preceding delay. The values given are not cumulative! It takes about 10 years to reach a delay of 85 days and items on "1 progressive" schedules during that time have received 85 spaced maintenance trials. The base 1 ("1 progressive") schedule is the "richest" of the progressive schedules (although with 85 trials in 10 years not as rich as most of the even schedules described above). The "leanest" progressive schedule has 10 days as a base value. Test delays for this schedule are 10, 20, 30, 40, 50 . . . 80, 90, 100 . . . 250, 260, 270 . . . In each case 10 days is added to the length of the preceding delay. At the end of a 10-year period delays are approximately 270 days, and items have received only 27 spaced maintenance trials.

5. *Accelerated Schedules*

The accelerated schedule is most easily listed. The intervals between successive rehearsals increased throughout the experiment (Landauer & Bjork, 1978). Delays for the accelerated schedule were as follows: 2, 4, 8, 14, 22, 32 . . . 158, 184, 212 . . . 422, 464, 508 . . . Once again, these values are not cumulative. That is, a first test is given at the end of 2 days; 4 days later (at the end of a total of 6 days) the second test occurs; 8 days later (at the end of a total of 14 days) the third test occurs, and so on. In contrast to the progressive schedule where the delays increase but the size of the increments remain constant, in the accelerated schedule the increments, too, increase systematically. *Increments to delays* were 2, 4, 6, 8, 10 . . . 36, 38, 40 . . . More specifically, the *increments* were 2 (between delays 2 and 4 days), 4 (between delays 4 and 8 days), 6 (between 8 and 14) . . . 14 (44–58), 16 (58–74) . . . 36 (308–344), 38 (344–382) . . . In 10 years delays reach 464 days with items experiencing a total of 22 rehearsal occasions.

6. *Motivation for These Schedules*

Spurred on by the practical wish (nicely described by Bjork, 1988) to maintain the maximum amount of knowledge with the minimum number of rehearsals, I sought the "leanest" schedule that also allowed good retention. In addition, I wondered whether the *pattern* of rehearsals would have significant effect on the development of long-lasting memory for items. The even schedules in combination with the progressive schedules help to answer the question: Is it the number of rehearsals or the gradual increase in spacing that best predicts improved recall. The even schedule was loosely modeled on my undergraduate experience. Fairly regular practice occurred on materials during class and information would become quite secure. The end of the class often meant that ideas were no longer rehearsed regularly. Was this material still available a year or so later? The use of the even schedules was seen as an extension of studies (such as Bahrick, 1993) indicating that while wider spacing slowed learning it improved recall later. Both the progressive and the accelerated schedules are influenced by and related to Landauer and Bjork's (1978) schedules.

III. Findings

A. SOME UNINTENDED CONSEQUENCES

Performing 25 years of long-term-memory studies has been associated with a number of unintended and sometimes unexpected personal memorial consequences detectable within and outside the study:

1. The thousands of repetitions of the scientific names has resulted in a valuable transferable skill: comfortably and consistently pronouncing scientific names in a variety of contexts. I have not included "accurately" in my list of descriptors because I have not identified a consensus on the pronunciation of some scientific words.

2. A major change has taken place over the course of the study. Early in the study scientific names were difficult for this novice learner. However, learning Latinate names take many fewer trials now than it did when the research began. Over the study's course improvement occurred in (a) pronunciation of elements, (b) linking of elements both within and between names, and (c) proper placement of accent. Although I can learn new scientific names much more rapidly, the source of the improvement is not clear. Have I learned a skill or has my task become easier because after learning 1,000 items I know a significant number of the likely Latinate combinations. There is considerable overlap in word elements. For example, all plant scientific family names end in *aceae*. Once learned, this rule was applied effortlessly to each new family name and no errors are ever made on this element of any response.

3. Each day more evidence of the potential for maintaining cognitive skills with age is reported, as a result it is not surprising that permanent changes are apparently occurring in my ability to encode and remember materials. One such instance: I have always been at the bottom of the class in remembering names of specific persons and objects. It is pleasant, therefore, to observe my aging friends bemoan the loss of their once fine memories and to observe that my own memory, while no miracle of accuracy, continues to become modestly more effective in many memorial tasks, including remembering people's names. I can report no improvement in my ability to recognize faces but I would bet money (but not the 25 years necessary for a proper demonstration) that a lengthy study on identifying and applying names to faces would improve my real-world ability to distinguish and remember faces.

4. When I initiated the MOK study I fondly imagined that for the first time in my life I would have a large body of "trivia" in a highly accessible form. The real-life outcomes are not quite what I anticipated. To begin with, there is no certainty that transfer will occur to real-life instances of a plant/tree/flower even if I consistently recognize and can label the plant pictured in my experimental files. Perhaps the most dramatic example involved my first view in Puerto Rico of *Ficus lyrata*. My file showed a single stalk perhaps an inch in diameter, 3 ft tall, and covered sparsely with perhaps 50 leaves. The Puerto Rican version was 25–30 ft tall, densely covered with enormous leaves, with a trunk a foot in diameter. My failure to recognize this magnificent specimen is repeated regularly in chance

encounters with other plants. On the upside, walking through a botanical garden even when I do not immediately recognize a plant I show marvelous savings. I can rapidly reinstate the name by reading the label and may have the information available for hours, days, or weeks—a feat unheard of before I began the study.

B.   ENCODING AND ITS RELATION TO LATER RECALL

These analyses examine the relationship of original encoding difficulty to difficulty in maintaining information over long time periods. In addition, they examine the persistence of specific errors, or types of errors, over the course of the maintenance study. More simply: Is an item that is difficult to encode also difficult to maintain? And, do the same errors that occur during encoding reoccur during the years that material is maintained?

Data for this set of analyses come from Phase III summaries. This data set was selected because Phase III provides careful records of performance on encoding trials which are lacking in earlier phases. A total of 406 items were encoded in Phase III between May 1985 and July 1986. The first maintenance trials began in May 1985 and have continued to the present (1996).

Acquisition for 110 items in this phase (a 27% sample) was examined to determine the number of trials required to reach criterion. (The criterion was perfect performance in less than 5.5 s on three of five trials on a single day.) The average number of trials to reach this criterion of learning was 31.2 for the 110 items. The smallest number of trials required to reach this criterion was eight (this item had appeared in a similar guise in an earlier phase of the study). The largest number of encoding trials required was 70. A detailed analysis of encoding trials was performed for 34 items subsequently maintained on the progressive schedule. The analysis examined the number of errors made on each encoding test.

Finally, the performance of 12 of these items was examined over the next 9 years. Five items with an average of 56.2 encoding trials comprised the "difficult encoding group." Seven items with an average of 18.7 encoding trials comprised the "easy encoding group." Although there was a 3–1 difference in the number of trials required for encoding, there were only minimal differences in difficulty of maintaining items. Over the 9-year maintenance period the average number of trials required overall was 156.4. For the difficult group 157.2 trials were required; for the easy group 155.8 tests were required. Although the small sample size precludes a definitive statement on the subject, it appears that over this time period the rather substantial (3–1) differences found for these items during encoding has been erased. Thus, we appear to have an answer to the first question: Do difficult items permanently remain difficult? At least for items on the most severe (progressive) schedule where the greatest opportunity for differences, the answer would appear to be no. It seems unlikely that larger discrepancies would exist for items that have experienced more rehearsals.

Do the same errors encountered during encoding reoccur during the years that material is maintained/rehearsed? The original assumption was that errors that occurred during encoding would reoccur at least from time to time throughout maintenance of specific information. Errors, however, did not persist beyond the encoding stages among any of the stimuli that were closely observed. Of the many hundreds of errors recorded during encoding, only two or three were repeated in a similar form during maintenance rehearsals. Is there an explanation for this lack of consistency in errors? A typical encoding error occurred when a name was difficult to access or to pronounce. Such errors were eliminated during the sometimes lengthy encoding sessions. However, encoding sessions were never more than a day apart and were usually separated by mere hours. It is somewhat surprising that under the pressure of the considerably longer retention periods that when the response chain weakened, different failures occurred than had been noted during encoding.

If the same errors did not occur, did the errors during either encoding or maintenance follow a simple consistent pattern? Again, the answer is no. In retrospect, however, the results are not surprising.

Let me provide two specific examples. The first: EWF #73: *Grass of Parnassus; Parnassia glauca; Saxifrage, Saxifragaceae.* During encoding, after a series of errors based on physical similarities of the plant to others, there occurred a succession of mispronunciations of the scientific family name: *Saxifragaceae.* After 19 encoding trials these mispronunciations were eliminated. On eight maintenance trials the correct name was given. On 11 of the 22 primary tests an incorrect family name was given. Five times the item was mistakenly identified as a member of the grass family, three times as a lily, but also once each as a buttercup, a primrose, and a bedstraw. One weak point in the item from the beginning has been the rarity of the family in the stimulus pool. The expression of difficulty changed from *pronunciation* during encoding (with numerous *Saxifragaceae* in the pool the resolution of pronunciation difficulty would have been shared over family members) to *identification* of the family during maintenance (the item is frequently identified as a member of a more frequently occurring family).

The second example, EWF #286: *Common sunflower; Helianthus annus; Sunflower, Asteraceae.* This item required only 10 trials during encoding to reach the criterion. No errors were ever listed; the item was given correctly on the second trial, but required additional trials before the response was given speedily. During maintenance trials errors of the following four sorts occurred:

1. *Visually controlled:* This sunflower has a very large head, apparently leading to the responses "giant" or "tall," and *giganteus* (all labels appropriate for other sunflowers); "giant" occurred four times; "tall" occurred once (in combination with "giant"); *giganteus* occurs four times, twice in combination with "giant;" overall, this "size" error occurs six times. It is of some interest that five of the six responses occurred on or before the 184-day delay (that is, during the first 2 ½ years).

2. *Semantic errors:* As indicated, the species name is *annus;* although *annus* appeared correctly virtually every time, a variation of this name appeared as part of the common name, hence, "annual" sunflower. This combination occurred six times, with all six of these errors occurring after a minimum of 212 days' delay. One of these errors (at 382 days) occurs in conjunction with the only late "giant"/*giganteus* error.

3. *Phoneme shift: Helianthus* (genus name) was replaced by *helianthemum* at the 92-day delay.

4. *Importation:* "Compass plant" (the common name of another sunflower) replaced the common name at the 308-day delay.

For many of the other items that were carefully examined, errors during maintenance trials involved confusions among species. For example, EWF #54's common name is "wood anemone." Although other errors occurred during the first months, after the 58-day delay, "rue anemone," "false rue anemone," and "sweet anemone" were substituted on 13 of 14 trials. EWF #198: *Flowering spurge; Euphorbia corollata; Spurge, Euphorbiaceae* made a somewhat dramatic shift at the 58-day delay. Prior to this time the specimen was clearly recognized as an *Euphorbia.* Subsequently it was confused with several plants which (to a novice and at a distance) bear some resemblance to this plant. Thereafter, 10 of 14 times it is identified (incorrectly) as a "buttercup" (*Ranunculaceae*). Of particular relevance to the present argument, however, thereafter the common name cycles among "meadow rue," "tall meadow rue," "sweet meadow rue," and "early meadow rue" with a strong bent toward "tall" and "early." Similarly, EWF #261's common name is "moneywort." Again, beginning at about 58 days the names "creeping Charlie" and "creeping Jenny" (names of closely related species, or alternative names for this species) were substituted on 8 of 14 primary tests.

Does something special and potentially interesting to cognitive psychologists happen throughout the course of memory's recall? This analysis, which examined the relationship of original encoding difficulty to difficulty in maintaining information over long time periods, suggests that difficulty is relative and that whatever may predict difficulty of items late in recall, original difficulty of the item is not significantly implicated. In addition, the examination of persistence of specific errors, or types of errors from encoding to maintenance, again suggests that some evolutionary changes take place during the acquisition and maintenance of knowledge. It seems clear that the kinds of errors that are made throughout the course of recall depend on the characteristics of the specific item being recalled and very importantly upon the surrounding body of information. *Saxifragaceae* is a rare family in this pool. Not surprisingly, there continue to be difficulties in identifying the item, but few difficulties resulting from confusing with another genus or species within or outside this family. In contrast, over time (58 days showed up with some regularity in this small analysis) confusions among species/genus within common families begin to occur with considerable regularity. For these items, identification of the families is relatively easy and confusions among family name for such items are rare and more often than not are simply slips of the tongue.

C. How Does Recall of Item Elements Change over Time?

In this study items are overlearned and then recalled after a delay. This cycle is repeated with continued overlearning and ever-lengthening recall delays. Under these conditions how does recall of subelements of complex stimuli change over time? Stimuli as a whole may become inaccessible, that is, the entire response may be available or lost as a unit. On the other hand, as with the Cheshire cat, the ghostly smile may remain after the cat has disappeared. If the latter is the case, is the lingering presence a consistent element? Are some elements of the stimulus compound highly resistant to forgetting? If so, which elements are these? Do elements that are resistant early in the study remain resistant over the course of the study? How much reconstruction goes on for these rotely learned items? And how stable are these processes? If we look at patterns for individual items do the same elements reappear occasion after occasion when responses are partially forgotten? Finally, if responses are remembered, do the elements occur in the same order or is order itself variable?

1. The Procedures Employed

In order to begin to answer these questions an analysis was performed on a portion of Phase III items maintained with the accelerated schedule. This schedule is the leanest employed in this research and was selected for this analysis because errors are more likely under austere than under rich conditions. The analysis is based on the rehearsal trials over a 10-year period for 58 items (a 40% convenience sample).

2. Predictions

Which elements of a plant's name are remembered most persistently? There are at least two simple bases for predicting difference in learnability and recall of elements of these complex stimuli: (a) the difficulty of a name, represented roughly by the difference between English and Latin terms (the more complex or difficult the item, the longer it takes to learn and the more rapidly it is forgotten), and (b) organization, the degree to which information is systematically linked to the visual stimulus and to other response elements (the greater the linkages or organization, the faster the learning and the better the recall).[12] If item difficulty as defined is assumed to have greater weight, the predicted order of performance for the items would be: common family > everyday common > scientific family > genus > species. A greater weighting of organization would result in the following ordering: common family > scientific family > genus > everyday common > species.

The following rationale, while not dismissing organization as a factor, assumes that item *difficulty* is more important and hence provides the arguments for the first order above. Best performance was predicted for the plant's *common family name.* The common family names are relatively easy: "lily," "sunflower," "forget-me-not;" and because only 70 or so families appear in the present study, choices are severely limited. Moreover, because family names generally refer to classes of plants that share some visual features, an easily identified scheme often links them to the plants' appearances. The *everyday common names* are most often familiar common-sense configurations: "daylily," "salt marsh aster," "rose vervain." Although not systematically linked to the plants, common names are usually highly meaningful, and sometimes capture visual features of the plants (e.g., "trout lily" leaves have the coloration of the fish). It seemed that their familiarity would produce easy learning and good recall. *Scientific family names,* although sharing the organizational properties of common family names, involve complex Latinate forms. These were expected to be recalled somewhat less well than common names (either family or everyday). Poorest performance was predicted for *species names.* Species designations, almost always Latin terms, have little to tie them to the physical appearance of the corresponding plants. The meaningfulness of these terms varies widely. They are highly varied, ranging from Latinized proper names (e.g., *Thompsonii*) to Latin descriptors (e.g., *griseoargentea*) and to a novice the organizational scheme is not sufficient to serve as an effective memory aid. It was

---

[12] Other, more complex, bases for predicting recallability suggest themselves, including sheer length (e.g., number of syllables) or more careful analyses of difficulty, as the *degree of difference* between English and Latin, or the rarity of phonemes in English, and so on. Analyses based on these complex indicators have not been performed.

thought that *generic names* would be somewhat easier than species names to learn and retain. Although difficult because of their Latinate form, they should be recalled more accurately than the species because generic names occur more often, are more systematically applied, and are more consistently related to the visual appearance of the plant than are specific names. For example, a name like *helianthus* is associated with some (but not all) plants that "look like" sunflowers. Otherwise, generic names share the properties/difficulties of specific names.

A preliminary examination of this question was undertaken in 1987 (Linton, 1988). The analysis summarized the recall of elements for 38 stimuli over the first year and a half of the study. Three levels of performance emerged. During this period the accuracy for family names (there was no difference between the scientific and common names) was greater than for all other elements. This dramatic difference did not emerge immediately. In fact at 2- and 4-day delays, performance for plant names overall was virtually perfect. By 8- and 15-day delays, however, there was a drop (to about 70%) in accuracy for all elements except family names. Over the next year common and genus names remained closely similar, ultimately dropping to about 50% accuracy. As predicted by both rationale, the accuracy for species names was the poorest, at about 40%.

Figure 1 presents the data for this analysis over the 10-year period from 1985 to 1995. This long-term analysis involves 37 of 38 stimuli included in the original analysis; the addition of 21 items increased sample size to 40%. A curve for overall item accuracy is also shown. Most conspicuous in this curve of long-term memory is the continued accurate recall of family names. For delays up to 464 days (15 months) performance remained between 80% and 90%. It seems likely, although this suggestion has not been examined with the appropriate schedules, that were the schedule less stringent, accuracy for family names would approach 100%.

It was predicted that common family names would be recalled better than scientific family names because they are less difficult. For the rehearsal conditions and delays of the present sample, however, recall for scientific and common family names was virtually identical and performance was represented by a single curve. Why should accuracy of family and common names be so similar during maintenance trials? The reason is obvious in hindsight. Common family names are uniquely linked with their corresponding family names. The overall family names are learned as a simple verbal chain. They are given as a pair many hundreds of times over the course of the experiment in the fixed order: common/scientific family name. No interference with this link occurs. If one name is available, about 98% of the time the other is as well. It took significantly longer to learn scientific than common family names, but once encoding was complete, scientific

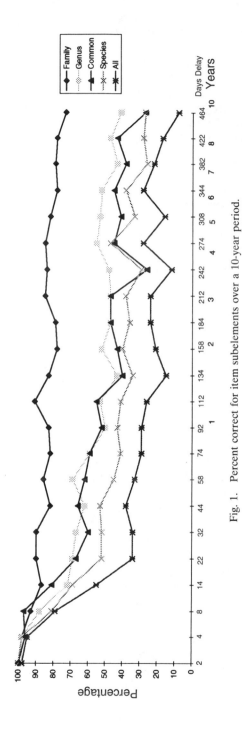

Fig. 1. Percent correct for item subelements over a 10-year period.

family names were available virtually whenever the common family names were.

Recall levels of the remaining subelements were much more similar. If one considers only years 6 through 10 (tests at delays of 308 days and longer), recall for species names was consistently poorest. For delays of 242 days (8 months) and longer, recall for genus names was superior to recall for common names. For these names as well as for family names, it appears that scientific names, though difficult to learn, once learned are maintained as readily as elements of the names that were originally easier.

In short, contrary to an expectation that item difficulty would be the controlling factor in very long-term maintenance of knowledge, the results mirror exactly the predictions weighing organization over difficulty. Common and scientific family names are identical in terms of organization and because only a limited number of families appear in the present study, choices are severely limited. Moreover, because family names generally refer to classes of plants that share visual features, an easily identified scheme often links them to the plants' appearances. Although the remaining subelements are more similar, genus shows more structure than the other elements and produces superior performance.

The pattern of results suggests in addition that common names were unexpectedly difficult. There may be a mundane explanation for this discrepancy. A number of plants have closely similar names—for example, "annual sunflower," "common sunflower"—or have nondistinctive elements such as "common" affixed to a name that is otherwise easily memorable. Moreover, a number of the plants have two or even three names by which they are commonly known and each name may have two or more elements, for example, "wild coffee, feverwort, tinkerweed" comprise the everyday common names of a single plant; "beach heath, false heather, poverty grass" are the names of another plant. If any element in the compounds is omitted during recall, an error is recorded. These units form "slippery" chains because there are no natural links between elements and there is no strong cue to search for a second or a third name when the search for the common name appears to have been satisfied by the identification of a first or a second name. In contrast, the generic names always comprise a single term. Scientific names are more likely to contain rare phonemes, and on the average, are longer than common names but there is always only one of them, and once learned they may be more securely recalled than the easier, but slippery compound chains found in the common names. It appears then that with infrequent rehearsals and with increasingly long delays, organizational features of stimuli become more important determiners of recall even for rotely learned and maintained materials.

As indicated, the results support the *importance of organization* over that of difficulty in determining recall, at least after a number of years. Difficulty is clearly a significant factor in learning and memory and the extent of loss of its influence (at least as defined) over the years is surprising. The highly similar performance of common and scientific family names cited above is another finding that emphasizes how ephemeral the concept of "difficulty" becomes in long-term maintenance of knowledge studies.

To what extent may these results be extrapolated to other schedules and to longer delays for the present schedule? It seems likely that with less stringent schedules the separation of curves found for the accelerated schedule would occur years later or not at all. For the accelerated schedule it also seems likely that the present trends should become more pronounced with time but it must be recognized that the trends found for this schedule and for these intervals may themselves prove to be slight perturbations when recall is examined after 20 or more years.

The question we have just considered may be abbreviated: Is there differential loss of information among the elements of the plant names? The preceding analysis suggests the answer is clearly yes. There is differential loss, and the nature of the loss changes somewhat over time. In fact, some of the differences take weeks, months, or years to appear.

A closely related question is, How stable is recall of elements for individual items? A scan of the specific elements correctly given for any item show remarkable variability. We are dealing here with two countervailing forces. Numbers of rehearsals continue to accumulate while over time each item experiences increasing lengths of delays. A perusal of the data indicate there is no simple loss of additional information over the years. There are few cases where it may be said, for example, either the response is completely correct or there is an error on the species (or some other element) name. One way to examine the degree of stability is to evaluate the specific combination of elements that are recalled on each trial. If the two elements of the family name are taken as a unit, there are 16 possible combinations in which elements may be recalled.[13] Over all 58 items the average number of combinations that occurred for each item was 5.6. The preferred combinations, aside from all and none correct, were 5 of the 7 combinations that included family name. The two items recalled with the greatest consistency occurred in 2 of the 16 possible different combinations. For item #33, for example, it was equally likely that all names would be correct, or that all except the species name would be remembered. The least consistent item, in contrast, was recalled in 9 of the 16 possible combinations.

[13] There are four elements—common, genus, species, family—that may be remembered one at a time (four possibilities), two at a time (six possibilities), or three at a time (four possibilities). In addition, all or none of the items may be remembered (one possibility each).

What can we make of the fact that any item is recalled with nine different combinations of elements? For this item about 40% of the time (9/22) all elements were recalled correctly, one combination was recalled five times but on the remaining eight trials seven different combinations of elements occurred. Even for a well-learned item, over the years, it can be said that something is likely to be recalled, but it is not clear what that something will be. For many of these items it appears that recall has a mind of its own.

3. How Does Order of Recall Change Over Time?

A query about order of recall was based on the data from the first year and a half of the same sample. Is there a standard order in which item elements are recalled, or does order change over time? Because all items in Phase III were learned rotely in a standard order (common, c; scientific (genus/species), s; family, f) recall in that order (c, s, f) seemed most probable. Thus, an alternative way to understand stability and changes in memory relies on an examination of the way in which the order of these compound responses change over time. If strictly rote processes are involved, that is, if the item can be accessed in memory exactly as it was entered, recall order should closely mimic the encoding/learning order. To the extent that fluctuations in order occur from trial to trial, more complex searches or reconstructive processes that randomly or systematically modify the sequence are implicated.

The following summary is based on primary test performance at each delay. (The probability of items being given in the standard order is much higher on nonprimary tests.) On the first test, after a 2-day delay, 60% of the names were recalled in the original standard order (c, s, f). However, each of the other five possible orders occurred for at least one stimulus. On the next test, at a 4-day delay, only 29% of the names were recalled in the original order and this percentage remained quite constant for all trials up through 112 days except the 8-day delay, when inexplicably 50% of the responses were in the standard order. The second most popular order overall, s, c, f, occurred on the average 20% of the time. The orders f, c, s and f, s, c each occurred 16% of the time. The order c, f, s occurred 14% of the time, and the least frequent order s, f, c occurred only 5% of the time.

Although it is clear that variability in order/sequence occurs, this summary focusing on order at different delays addresses only part of the issue of order. We may also ask: How consistently are elements of a particular plant name recalled? Appropriate counts reveal that for no item were responses always given in the same order across all tests, but 21% of items were recalled in only two orders and for half of these items only a single deviation from the preferred order occurred. Twenty-nine percent were recalled in three orders, 32% in four different orders, and the remaining 18% in five or six different orders. Order analyses were not performed on data beyond the first year and a half because analyses becomes less comprehensible when all name elements are given only 20% of the time.

For the conditions reported, recall order was highly flexible and variations in order began to occur almost immediately. Order in which information was recalled fluctuated for all items and for all delays. It should be noted that as subject, I have little sense of these fluctuations and as I record data I am sometimes surprised to observe changes. The fact that recall is so rushed probably accounts for some of the variability. Frequently, especially with well-known items with relatively short delays, the response simply comes to me without any thought. Often, however, I am confronted with a problem-solving situation: emitting the appropriate response within 5.5 s. In a standard deliberate solution to the problem, I begin with the common name. If I fail to recall quickly the common name, I move rapidly to the genus, then to the family name. Once any name element becomes available, the remaining elements are likely to become available. That is, to meet the criterion I must grab hold of some part of the item as quickly as possible. For some items there emerges what might be called the "entry point," (Jolicoeur et al., 1984). The entry point, which may or may not be the common name, is the most immediately accessible part of the response. For some items, order is of little importance. Other items, especially long complex ones, may be easily accessed in only one order.

We have examined a number of indicators that suggest that the recall, even of well-learned items, is quite unstable. If we consider order of recall of elements we find considerable inconsistency. Even if all elements of a name are recalled individual elements are accessed in a variety of orders. We must conclude there is considerable variability in the accessibility of the pool—or in the retrieval strategies that are employed—and that access is affected both by the characteristics of the individual item and by other information in the subject's memory.

D.   TIPS-OF-THE-TONGUE IN EXPERT MEMORY

If we peruse typical definitions of a tip-of-tongue (TOT), we encounter such statements as people are "unable to produce a word although they are certain it is known. Its representation in memory can be verified by correct recognition or spontaneous retrieval of the target at a later time" (Cohen & Burke, 1993). An examination of TOT-like phenomenon within the context of the present study seemed very attractive. First, the present study explores TOT-like responses in an expert knowledge base. Second, information is available about the number of rehearsals each item has experienced together with a reasonably complete history of both the number and kind of errors that have occurred for the item. Particularly promising was the opportunity to track recall failures with the repeated tests over periods of years. Within this context it was possible to examine the extent to which TOTs persist, or are endemic to particular words. How frequently did TOT-like states occur? How frequently were they resolved? How accurately were the success of memory searches predicted?

1. Redefining Tips-of-the-Tongue

In this study a wide variety of states, all roughly signifying "I know it, but I can't remember it," are lumped together under the rubric, "tip-of-the-tongue." Perhaps in part because of the complexity of the stimulus materials, I only rarely experienced the classic TOT made famous by Brown and McNeill's (1966) description of subjects who cannot recall the name, but have considerable information about the word's characteristics. A careful set of queries to the subject regarding length and initial letters might elicit more comparable data, but information in this form was never explicitly requested. Instead, best efforts at providing the response were made. The following list, although not exhaustive, suggests some conditions under which TOTs are noted:

1. Classic TOT—the item seems to be on the tip of the tongue.
2. Correct name (whole or in part) is given, but is thought to be erroneous and is rejected.
3. Part of the name is available, but large or small elements are missing and recovery seems likely.
4. No association to stimulus is available (occasionally the stimulus is not recognized).
5. A Latin word or phrase is slightly wrong (e.g., "mariana" is sought; "maritima" is given but does not seem quite right).

In this context it should also be noted that simple errors (those detailed in the preceding sections) occur frequently: A response is given, and is accepted as appropriate although it is incorrect. If there were uncertainty I might treat the response as a TOT, but in these cases the response is erroneously judged to be correct.

2. A Note about the Method

TOT-like phenomena have been recorded since 1986 for items in Phases I and II. The present analysis examined Phase II data collected after 1987 when TOT notation became regularized. By 1987 Phase II items were no longer the primary target of the research and were often tested later than their prescribed test date. Excessively long delays before testing increase both errors and number of TOTs, hence these Phase II materials provide a particular rich field for this exploration. When a TOT-like occasion occurs, an estimation of the probability the item will be remembered during the subsequent trials is indicated. During the first year and a half a simple Yes, No, or "?" notation was employed. During the next 6 years numeric estimates of probability of completely correct recall of the item were given. During the final 2 ½ years a more detailed specification, indicating degree of confidence about specific item elements, was added but about this final more refined set of data nothing more will be said.

3. Some Baseline Data

A total of 477 Phase II items tested between 1987 and 1995 were examined to determine the number of TOT-like blocks experienced. To provide a context for TOT performance, an indication of overall accuracy on these items during this period is provided. A total of 3,331 rehearsal tests occurred in Phase II during the almost 9 years spanned by this examination. Of these tests, 2,192 or (66%) of the tests did not produce TOTs; that is, for these tests responses given were accepted as correct.[14] On 854 (39%) of these non-TOT tests, responses were given correctly at criterion speed; on 548 (25%), responses were given correctly but required longer to produce; errors were made on 790 (36%) responses. The remaining 1,137 (34%) tests resulted in TOT-like states (two items could not be scored). Of the TOT items, 538 (47%) were positively resolved while the remaining 599 (53%) items were ultimately missed.

Let us move to the question: Are some items, even of a well-practiced set, more likely to be repeatedly inaccessible over the years? An examination of the probability of a TOT reveals the following distribution. For 110 (23%) of the 477 items tested no TOTs occurred on any test. From 1 to 11 TOTs for other 367 items occurred over this period. The distribution of frequencies of TOTs per item is shown in Table 1. Some items were tested more frequently than others during this 9-year period but this additional detail is not available.

For over half of the items TOTs occurred only rarely or not at all. Only for a small number of items was it necessary to search through memory

---

[14] One difficulty with these assessments is that criteria for being satisfied with an existing response may change both during a single experimental session, between sessions, and certainly is susceptible to change over a decade. During a single session if numerous errors are made early in the session it becomes easier to reject items about which there is any uncertainty. The result of such a criterion shift is that the number of immediate errors decrease and the number of reported TOTs increase. Over the years, knowledge that better recall results if responses are delayed when there are questions has almost certainly increased reported TOTs.

TABLE I

FREQUENCY OF OCCURRENCE OF TOTs

# of TOTs	Frequency	Total
1	94	94
2	82	164
3	63	189
4	46	184
5	38	190
6	17	102
7	13	91
8	6	48
9	6	54
10	1	10
11	1	11
Total	367	1,137

repeatedly to find or reconstruct material that had been available fluently in the past.

E.   HOW ARE THE TOTs RESOLVED?

1.   A Note about the Method

In order to answer this question the 14 items on which TOTs most frequently occurred (the number of TOTs ranged from 8 to 11) were examined. Detailed responses for 122 of the 123 rehearsal occasions were recorded. Scoreable data was yielded by 108 primary tests, and it was on these tests that the following observations were made: A total of 33 (27%) TOTs were positively resolved. A comparison of this accuracy with the overall 47% TOT resolution rate indicates that these items are considerably less accessible than the general pool of 367 TOT items from which they are drawn.

2.   How Accurately Were Correct TOT Resolutions Predicted?

The accuracy of predictions (estimated probabilities) that TOTs would be correctly resolved were unimpressive; the average estimated probability for the 29 correctly resolved items was 45.3% while the estimated probability for the 79 incorrect items was 38.2%. This difference, although in the correct direction, is not persuasive especially if the data are perused more closely. The correct response was given but not recognized a number of times. The average estimated probability for resolving these already correct items was less than 50%. More concerns are raised if individual items are examined. For example, for #151 the average estimate of a correct resolution on the primary test on the 7 scoreable occasions was 43%. The item was never correctly resolved! For item #594, which was correctly resolved on 4/7 scoreable occasions, the predictions that the item would be correctly resolved averaged 58%. For the four occasions on which correct resolutions occurred, the mean probability was 51% while on the three occasions on which the item was not recalled the mean probability was 67%.

3. What Kind of TOT Responses Are Given and Do They Change Over Time?

Errors on the 14 items for which the largest number of errors occurred can roughly be divided into phonetically related and meaning-related. Meaning-related errors were of a number of types. Frequently, an inappropriate species name was given in combination with the appropriate genus. In a number of cases an alternative common name—one appropriate for a related species—was persistently given. In several cases there was a general (perhaps family) recognition of the item that produced a range of responses over the years that, for example, fitted the description: "scale-leaf tree." In general, phonemic errors occurred only when the target was an unusual or difficult word. For example, when "*Centaurea cyanus*" was sought, the following responses were given: *Catananche, campanula,* and *caerulea* were given, mostly early in the 8-year period. The first two are genus names. The latter, *caerulea*, like *cyanus*, means blue. *Centaurea* and *cyanus* were also given a number of times and not recognized as correct. Plausible species names not similar in sound, *montana* and *americana*, also occurred throughout the 8-year period. Another item, interesting because of the variety of responses generated on the way to occasional correct solutions was #594: *Alder buckthorn; Rhamnus frangula.* TOTs were resolved correctly 5/8 times in the 8-year period. One persistent class of errors was the substitution of *Rhapheolepsis indica* for *Rhamnus frangula.* This substitution occurred on 6/8 occasions with the correct response obtained on three of them. This substitution was accompanied 4/6 times by "Indian hawthorn." A second repeated search for an "animal name" was triggered by the common name, "alder buckthorn." Such searches were initiated on 5/8 separate occasions resulting in responses such as "wolfbane," "wolf," "rabbit," and "fox". Correct responses were obtained on three such occasions. Finally, the term "alder" appears to have triggered its own set of associates: *Alnus* as the proposed genus name, "*black alder*" (repeatedly) as the common name, and other variations such as "*black buckthorn.*" Item #230: *Crape myrtle; Lagerstroemia indica,* correct 3/9 times, produced a hodge-podge of responses similar to the target mostly in length: *cryptomeria, cryptotenia, alstromeria, auriantica, austromeria, cereopegia, chamadorea,* and *lereostigma.*

The answer to the second question: Do responses change over time? is not a great deal. In this small sample of extremely difficult items a wide range of responses occur, but as nicely depicted by #594: *Alder buckthorn, Rhamnus frangula,* these items appear to cycle through, appearing not on every occasion but at least from time to time over this rather lengthy period. Many of these meaning-related responses reflect the subject's growing expertise.

At least part of the difficulty with analyzing these TOT results is that they provide a little insight into what the researcher was thinking as the responses were produced. Within the last year an effort was begun to document associations in greater detail. This exploration, while still in its infancy, holds some promise for indicating the persistence of TOTs and their potential changes over time. These records may also help to answer the question, How do these "resolutions" occur, to distinguish information that gradually becomes available over trials from that which suddenly, "out of nowhere," appears to leap upon the scene.

IV. The Future

The present analyses comprise a first step in analyzing a database that has been accumulating for 17 years. When I think about the future of this research, I ordinarily think about moving to examine another body of materials, for example, the art of the world, examining changes that have occurred with age in both the acquisition and retention of materials, and trying to understand some intricacies of the encoding process. However, writing this paper has made it very clear that much remains to be done to better understand the existing 17 years of data.

As Bahrick et al. (1993) point out, although Ebbinghaus investigated spacing effects his research has little to tell us about the effects of spaced practice on *long-term maintenance* of knowledge. I had hoped to complete an analysis of the impact of the numerous schedules that provide the broad framework for the present research. At present I can say that many rehearsals are better than few, but I am years away from comparing the impact of the numerous schedules more completely. In this paper I have focused on very severe schedules. I must now return to examine the relationship between encoding difficulties and later recall under a variety of other schedules. Similarly, changes in recall of item elements must be examined for a variety of other schedules.

There also remains, completely unanalyzed, an effort to examine circadian rhythms within the context of Phase III. For a decade items have been tested alternatively in the a.m. and in the p.m. For five years, in a masochistic frenzy, tests occurred at all hours of the day and night.[15] My intuitive sense is that young items (especially during encoding) are best recalled in the morning, and mature items (during later years of maintenance) best in afternoon and evening. It seems likely that circadian rhythms may have different impact for items of different levels of initial difficulty and for items experiencing different maintenance schedules.

One assumption I did not question for many years was the directionality of learning. It always seemed obvious that the picture was the stimulus, and the words were the response. Perhaps 10 years into the study I began to realize that sometimes when I recalled a plant name I could not conjure up the picture with which for many years I had been associating the name. This difficulty was especially problematic when I seized upon a name, wondered if it was correct, but had no way of confirming the accuracy of the "guess" by approaching it in the alternate direction. After almost 15 years I devised a simple exploration of the impact of learning items in more than one direction and found time to add a simple study investigating the issue. In Phase IV, I look more closely at the bias introduced into the experiment by always using the plant picture as the stimulus and the names as the response. In a preliminary way, it appears that I lose the visual information more rapidly than the verbal, but flaws in the present methodology bias the results.

I imagine that I will continue encoding (learning new plant/name pairs) items periodically over the next decades. In part this effort is motivated by considerable curiosity about the ways in which age impacts both speed of encoding and ease of maintaining knowledge. We know that age has considerable impact on encoding new materials, and that recall for well-learned materials is less affected. Does material that is learned and over-learned later in life follow the same decay as similar materials learned earlier in life?

As the years pass my conception of the ideal length of a very-long-term memory study continues to move ahead of me into the distance. In my optimistic periods a 50-year examination of a memory seems feasible and worthwhile.

REFERENCES

Audubon Society (1979). *Field guide to North American wildflowers, eastern region.* New York: Knopf.

---

[15] Kudos to my husband, Robert E. Barnhill, who, after five years of my quietly slipping out of bed in the middle of the night to "run my experiment," commented only once on the procedure. When I announced I would not be doing round-the-clock testing any more he asked, using the old soccer phrase: "May I check your ID?"

Bahrick, H. P. (1979). Maintenance of knowledge: Questions about memory we forgot to ask. *Journal of Experimental Psychology: General, 108,* 296–308.

Bahrick, H. P. (1984). Semantic memory content in permastore: Fifty years of memory for Spanish learned in school. *Journal of Experimental Psychology: General, 113,* 1–26.

Bahrick, H. P., Bahrick, L. E., Bahrick, A. S., & Bahrick, P. E. (1993). Maintenance of foreign language vocabulary and the spacing effect. *Psychological Science, 4,* 316–321.

Bahrick, H. P., & Karis, D. (1982). Long-term ecological memory. In C. Puff (Ed.), *Handbook of research methods in human memory and cognition* (pp. 427–465). New York: Academic Press.

Bahrick, H. P., & Phelps, E. (1987). Retention of Spanish vocabulary over eight years. *Journal of Experimental Psychology: Learning, Memory, and Cognition, 13,* 344–349.

Bjork, R. A. (1988). Retrieval practice and the maintenance of knowledge. In M. M. Gruneberg, P. E. Morris, R. N. Sykes (Eds.), *Practical aspects of memory: Current research and issues: Vol. 1. Memory in everyday life,* pp. 396–401). New York: Wiley.

Brown, R., & McNeill, D. (1966). The "tip-of-the-tongue" phenomenon. *Journal of Verbal Learning and Verbal Behavior, 5,* 325–337.

Cohen, B., & Burke, D. M. (1993). Memory for proper names: A review. In G. Cohen, & D. M. Burke (Eds.), *Memory for proper names* (pp. 249–263). Hillsdale, NJ: Erlbaum.

Ebbinghaus, H. (1885/1964). *Memory: A contribution to experimental psychology.* New York: Dover.

Jolicoeur, P., Gluck, M. A., & Kosslyn, S. M. (1984). Pictures and names: Making the connection. *Cognitive Psychology, 16,* 243–275.

Landauer, T. K., & Bjork, R. A. (1978). Optimum rehearsal patterns and name learning. In M. M. Gruneberg, P. E. Morris, & R. N. Sykes (Eds.), *Practical aspects of memory* (pp. 625–632). New York: Academic Press.

Linton, M. (1975). Memory for real-world events. In D. A. Norman & D. E. Rumelhart (Eds.), *Explorations in cognition* (pp. 376–404). San Francisco: Freeman.

Linton, M. (1988). Maintenance of knowledge: Some long-term specific and generic changes. In M. M. Gruneberg, P. E. Morris, & R. N. Sykes (Eds.), *Practical aspects of memory: Current research and issues: Vol. 1. Memory in Everyday Life.* New York: Wiley.

Luria, A. R. (1968). *The mind of a mnemonist.* New York: Basic Books.

Neisser, U. (1978). Personal communication.

Rosch, E. (1978). Principles of categorization. In E. Rosch & B. B. Lloyd (Eds.), *Cognition and categorization.* Hillsdale, NJ: Erlbaum.

Spence, K. (1958). Personal communication.

The greenhouse. (1978). Racine, Wis.: Western Publishing Company.

The green thumb. (1980). Racine, Wis.: Western Publishing Company.

CATEGORY LEARNING AS PROBLEM SOLVING

Brian H. Ross

I. Introduction

Categories are crucial for intelligent thought and action. If we had no representation of categories, we would have to deal with each item as if it were new and we knew nothing about it. Instead, we are usually able to decide what category an item is in, and then we can access knowledge about that category. This accessed knowledge can be used for a wide variety of purposes, such as making predictions about unseen features, explaining the situation, or understanding why something happened. Therefore, we can think of the category-related processing as being composed of two parts. First, we *classify* the item, assigning it to a particular category (or perhaps, categories). Second, we access knowledge about the category and *use* this knowledge to do something else. That is, the classification is often done in the service of accomplishing some goal.

Over the last 25 years, category research has focused principally on classification (e.g., Medin & Smith, 1984; Ross & Spalding, 1994; Smith & Medin, 1981). This research has addressed a number of important issues about classification and classification learning, and has led to many formal models able to account for a wide variety of findings (e.g., Estes, 1986; Kruschke, 1992; Medin & Schaffer, 1978; Nosofsky, 1986, 1988). The use of the category has received much less attention, though it has not been ignored. This work focuses on how people use the knowledge of the categories to accomplish some other task, such as making predictions about properties of new instances (e.g., Anderson, 1991; Heit, 1992; Murphy & Ross, 1994) or determining the strength of inductive arguments (e.g., Gelman & Markman, 1986, 1987; Osherson, Smith, Wilkie, Lopez, & Shafir, 1990; Sloman, 1993).

In this chapter, I will review some recent research of mine that examines classification learning when people are also using the instances and categories. The lesson is simple: People's category representations (including the classification knowledge) depend upon *both* the classification and the use. Thus, an understanding of the use of categories is crucial for a theory of categories not only because the use is often the goal of the classification, but also because the use may affect the classification.

II. Classification Learning and Category Learning

To better explain the motivation for this work, it is helpful to begin with a contrast between classification learning and category learning. Consider a typical *classification learning* experiment. An item is presented, the subject is asked to respond with one of the few (usually two) experimenter-defined category labels, feedback is given, and the subject studies the item until he or she is ready to continue. Then, the next item is presented and the same response-feedback-study cycle continues until some criterion is met. In these experiments, classification is *the* goal and the only way in which the items are used. There is no additional category-related processing in which the classification accesses category knowledge for some other purpose. When the goal is classification, people try to find diagnostic features that will allow them to assign category membership of new items.

Although classification learning is a *crucial* part of category learning, it is not *all* of category learning. As we learn many categories, we learn a variety of additional information beyond that necessary for classification. A child might be able to learn to classify cats and dogs on the basis of a few features, such as size, head shape, and purriness, but if the child spends time playing with the animals, his or her knowledge of the categories goes far beyond these diagnostic features. A student learning new types of math problems may learn to distinguish the types by keywords in the problems, but as the problems are solved, the student may learn much more about the structure of each of the problem types.

No one would argue that we do not know additional information about categories beyond that necessary for classification. However, the view to be discussed here makes two further claims. First, the knowledge gained by such use can affect not only how the category is used, but also the classification of new instances. Second, and relatedly, we need to consider classification as an integral part of how people access and use relevant knowledge about categories, rather than as an isolated process.

III. Category Learning As Problem Solving

Before beginning a more thorough explanation of these ideas, let me briefly digress to explain the two motivations behind the title, "Category Learning As Problem Solving." One motivation was a restaurant experience. Although they are not so common anymore, many Chinese-American restaurants, in my childhood, used to have a special type of menu in which the foods were listed in columns and you could choose one food from column A (say an appetizer or soup) and one food from column B (say a main course). As a child, I was intrigued by this idea (though I must admit that I am not sure if it was the combinatorics or the food that I found interesting).

The second motivation is a creativity technique to force one to think differently about a topic. This technique, which is used by many creativity programs, is to pair together ideas that are not usually paired, by constructing a column of adjectives, a column of nouns, and then randomly repairing. For example, Finke, Ward, and Smith (1992, p. 111, Table V.3) list adjectives and nouns from psychology (e.g., perceptual, conceptual, associative; memory, problem solving, attention) and suggest that pairings often lead to interesting views.

These two motivations have led to my own research menu, shown in Table I. Column B, as in the Finke et al. table, has a list of cognitive topics that often are chapters in cognitive psychology textbooks, such as problem solving, category learning, memory, and attention. The one change (if one

TABLE I

COLUMNS FOR GENERATING
DIFFERENT PERSPECTIVES

Column A		Column B
Perception		Perception
Attention		Attention
Memory		Memory
Comprehension	as	Comprehension
Category Learning		Category Learning
Problem Solving		Problem Solving
Reasoning		Reasoning
Decision Making		Decision Making
Language		Language

can call it that) is that Column A has exactly the same list of topics. Each chapter is a random pick from Column A, a random pick from B, and "as" between them. (One should probably add the qualification of sampling without replacement since if the same topic is picked from both columns, it could be a boring chapter. But maybe not.) With luck, this technique could well supply me with chapter ideas for the rest of my career.

These combinations may provide a very different perspective for research, and many of them have been done already. For example, the early work in problem solving contrasted the associationist view (problem solving as learning) with the Gestalt view (problem solving as perception). Some of James Gibson's contributions can be viewed as cognition as perception, while some of Eleanor Gibson's work can be characterized as learning as perception. More recently, the instance views have examined attention as memory (Logan, 1988), classification as memory (e.g., Brooks, 1978, 1987; Medin & Schaffer, 1978), and problem solving as memory (e.g., Ross, 1984). It is fun to think about this and one can go on for quite a while, but I hope the point is clear. The different perspective does not just provide a catchy title, but brings in new ideas, methodology, and interpretations that one might not otherwise think about.

With this general motivation, let me consider the more specific parallels between category learning and problem solving. The modal view of expert problem solvers is that they have a large variety of problem schemata—knowledge structures that allow them to identify problems of that type and associated procedures for solving such problems (e.g., Reimann & Chi, 1989). Routine problems are solved not by intensive problem solving, but rather by recognizing the type of problem (i.e., classifying) and then using the stored knowledge about how to solve problems of that type. Thus, a large part of problem solving is classifying. However, the difference from the situation examined in most classification research is that this classifying is done in the context of making use of the classification to solve the problem. Solving the problem is the goal. The problem is classified because doing so provides relevant knowledge for solving it.

Learners in a problem-solving domain have experience with both classification and use. In addition, it is easy to see how the use might affect classification. It is often in the use (the solution) that one sees how the parts fit together and what is crucial for classification. For example, if one has two similar problem types such as permutations and combinations, the difference in solutions relates back to the difference in the problem types and may make it clearer what the important classification distinction is.

The point to be espoused in this paper is that there are clear parallels between category learning and problem solving, if one includes in category learning not just classification, but the use of categories as well. Often when we classify, we are not simply classifying the item, but classifying it in order to do something. We do not classify an approaching animal simply for our edification, but so we can know how to react to it. Even in classification situations, such as diagnosis, the reason for the classification is to allow a determination of how to fix the malfunction. To the extent that such uses are similar to the problem-solving situations, they may influence what is known about the category, including classification knowledge. As we make use of a classification, we may learn additional information about the category, its structure, and the relations of the relevant features. Such knowledge may be important for a wide variety of category-related processing, including classification.

The research program to be described has a number of different methodologies, but a typical experiment is as follows: Subjects learn to classify the items, but also do something with the items, such as manipulate them or access category knowledge to make a further inference. A later classification test shows that these uses affect the classification (compared to a group that does not use this classification or uses it differently). A focus of this research is to examine how classification learning proceeds in the context of a larger process. Thus, there are three parts to this idea. First, there is a standard classification-learning task. Second, this classification learning is interleaved with another task related to the categories. Third, the final test shows that the other task has affected classification performance. Although there is much work related to each of these ideas (or at least the first two), I know of no work that has examined all three. A brief examination of related research may help to make this point more clearly.

IV. Related Work

The ideas just presented have been partially examined in work on classification, unsupervised learning (in which classification information is not provided), and the use of categories. In addition, some research has examined the learning that may result from interleaved classification and use.

A. CLASSIFICATION RESEARCH

Much classification research examines how knowledge used to make classifications changes during learning. A number of papers on classification allow some means by which classification knowledge can change as a function of feedback about the classifications (e.g., Kruschke, 1992; Medin & Edelson, 1988; Ross, Perkins, & Tenpenny, 1990; Spalding & Ross, 1994). In addition, the goals or strategies of the learner can affect the perceived similarities among the instances and can affect classification (e.g., Allen & Brooks, 1991; Brooks, 1987; Jacoby & Brooks, 1984; Lamberts, 1994; Medin & Smith, 1981; Waldmann & Holyoak, 1992; Ward & Becker, 1992; Wattenmaker, 1991; Wisniewski, 1995). In some studies, the researchers have manipulated whether classification learning is the intentional goal or whether the classification learning is incidental to some other processing objective, such as to memorize the instances (e.g., Brooks, 1978; Kemler Nelson, 1988; Ward & Scott, 1987; Wattenmaker, 1993; Whittlesea, 1987). The intentionality of the task affects performance by influencing what stimulus information is attended to (e.g., Ward & Becker, 1992; Wattenmaker, 1991). Although these studies on classification do show that the particular processing of a category instance can affect the classification performance, they have not examined cases in which a second task, such as an interaction or category use, is interleaved with the classification learning.

B. Unsupervised Learning

In *unsupervised*-learning tasks, the categories are not provided to the learner (e.g., Anderson, 1991; Billman & Heit, 1988; Billman & Knutson, 1996; Clapper & Bower, 1994; chapters in Fisher, Pazzani, & Langley, 1991; Heit, 1992; Lassaline & Murphy, 1996; Medin, Wattenmaker, & Hampson, 1987; Wattenmaker, 1992). The motivation for this work is that much of our natural learning of categories occurs without explicit labeling and feedback. Some of the empirical work is closely related to the current research in that it shows that the particular interactions people have with the items may affect later formation of categories (e.g., Lassaline & Murphy, 1996). However, because the learners do not participate in a classification-learning paradigm (i.e., they get no feedback about classifications), this work does not examine how the interactions or uses affect the classification.

C. Category Use

A number of investigators have asked how people use categories to make inductive inferences. The inductions may be between categories (e.g., Osherson, Smith, Wilkie, Lopez, & Shafir, 1990) or from a category to a new category member (e.g., Gelman & Markman, 1986, 1987; Kalish & Gelman, 1992). For example, if you learn some new information that is true of both robins and eagles, how likely is it to be true of all birds? Other researchers have examined predictions about particular features when the categorization is uncertain (e.g., Malt, Ross, & Murphy, 1995; Ross & Murphy, 1996; Murphy & Ross, 1994). For instance, if you see an animal approaching but are uncertain about what type of animal it is, how do you predict how it will behave (and, thus, what you should do)? Although these investigations do examine category use, they do not examine learning. The categories being asked about are well-learned ones (or are available) and the question of interest is how they are used to make some inference.

D. LEARNING AND USE

Some research has examined how people learn to classify and use categories. Much of this research shows that experts' extensive use of categories can affect their category representations. For instance, Boster and Johnson (1989) had novice and expert fishermen sort various types of fish and found that while the novice judgments relied upon the obvious morphological characteristics, the experts' judgments were also influenced by the similarities in how the experts interacted with the different types of fish (e.g., superb sport fish). Tanaka and Taylor (1991) found that dog experts were as fast to classify a dog at the subordinate level (e.g., collie) as at the basic level (dog), unlike the usual basic level advantage found with nonexperts. In problem solving, experts not only are better at solving the problems, but appear to have very different means of classifying the problems (e.g., Chi, Feltovich, & Glaser, 1981). Novices rely upon surface features for classifying problems, while experts often use deeper features related to the underlying principles (though the surface features can be used heuristically, Blessing & Ross, 1996). Murphy and Wright (1984) showed that experienced clinicians had derived a different set of typical features for diagnostic categories, with more emphasis, compared to novices, on the common features of these categories. Medin, Lynch, Coley, and Atran (1995) found that the categorization judgments of some tree experts were strongly influenced by the particular goal-derived (as opposed to taxonomic) categories (Barsalou, 1985, 1991). Although some goal-derived categories may be constructed to deal with a particular situation, frequent use of a goal-derived category may lead to it being represented much like taxonomic categories are (Barsalou, 1991; Barsalou & Ross, 1986). Thus, experience with using the categories can lead to very different category structures. However, because these studies examine experts, it is difficult to know whether it is the category use that has affected the category representation, rather than some other correlated property of expertise (such as much more experience at classification).

Finally, some work closely related to the current project has been conducted by A. B. Markman and his colleagues (Markman, Yamauchi, & Makin, in press; Yamauchi & Markman, 1996). They have been examining how nonclassification tasks may influence what is learned about the category. They find that classification learning leads to less learning about feature relations than does an inference learning task, feature prediction. Most interestingly, for the purposes here, when the two tasks are learned successively, the inference-first group appears to do at least as well on classification as the classification-first group, and better on inference (Yamauchi & Markman, 1996, Ex. 4). This result suggests that what is being learned in each task may affect what is learned about the category from the other task. However, this research does not include cases in which the learning is interleaved, nor was the purpose of the experiment to examine what classification knowledge was being affected by this use.

E. SUMMARY

Although there is much related research, the effects of interactions and category uses on classification are still not well understood. The classification research has generally not included classification as part of a category use task, but instead has focused on the classification. The unsupervised learning work has involved uses of categories and their effect on category formation, but has not examined how this learning may be integrated with classification learning. The work on how people use categories for inferences has focused on prior categories, not ones learned experimentally. Finally, the work examining expertise has shown that experts' classifications appear to be a function of the interactions and uses they have, but the specific effects of these uses on learning of the category have not been examined.

V. Overview of the Research Project

I have been stressing the need to examine classification in the context of a larger task. When classification is not the goal, but rather a means to accomplish some other goal, how people learn to classify may be partly a function of diagnostic properties (as examined in classification research) and partly a function of the properties important for the larger task. In this paper, I will be presenting research about two different, though related, situations.

First, when people learn to classify instances, they often *interact with the instances* beyond the classification. A child learning about dogs does not always just get the dog labeled by a parent, but may have the opportunity to play with it. Learning about different tools is usually accompanied by practice in using each of the tools. In most problem-solving domains, one does not learn the different problem types by extensive classification experience. Rather, the classifications are learned in the context of solving the problems. A new problem is given, classified, and then solved. The point of these examples is, I hope, obvious: Classification learning often also involves interacting with or using the instances. These interactions allow learners to gain further knowledge about the instances, which may, in turn, affect later classifications.

Second, when people learn to classify instances, they often *use the classifications* to perform some additional category-dependent task. For example, when one is learning to diagnose a malfunction in a complex system, the diagnosis serves as a way of accessing relevant knowledge about the malfunction, which can then be used to help fix it. Again, the goal is not the diagnosis per se, but rather to fix the malfunction. The diagnosis (classification) is important in helping to point out the relevant knowledge, but it is not the end goal.

This second use of categories is clearly closely related to the interactions, but for now I keep them separate by how they make use of the classification. The interaction does not depend much upon the classification—one can play with a dog the same way whether it has been classified as a dog or not. However, the category uses do depend upon the classification. How one treats a disease or fixes a car malfunction presumably depends upon what type of problem one has diagnosed. The next two sections describe experiments addressing each of these situations, interactions with instances and uses of categories. Following these descriptions, I discuss the implications of these effects.

VI. Interactions with Instances

As just mentioned, people often do not just learn to classify new instances—they interact with the instances during learning. For example, a person taking a math course learns about new types of problems, but also spends much time trying to solve the problems. The classification is important, but it is not the only goal nor is it the limit of the interaction with the instance. These interactions beyond the initial classification are important for two reasons. First, they are common occurrences, but we understand little about how the interactions depend on the classifications or what is learned about the instances and categories. Second, these interactions may affect the category representations, including knowledge used to make classifications. As people interact with the instance, they may learn additional information, which might in turn affect the category representation. Learning to classify may depend not only on information and feedback directly relevant to the classification, but also additional information about the interactions with the instances. In classification experiments, however, there are no such interactions and classification is the only goal.

Ross (1996) examined how interactions following classification may affect the category representation. The paradigm was to adopt the usual classification procedure, but after each item was classified, subjects *interacted* with it before proceeding to the next item, as shown in Table II. This interaction introduced a second goal (besides learning to classify). The hypothesis was that the interaction would lead learners to focus more on properties relevant to the interaction and that this focus might affect the category representation, including knowledge used for classification.

The materials used in these first experiments were simple equations. Three reasons motivated this choice. First, I thought it important to have the interaction involve the item, not just a picture or description of the item. Second, this choice relates the effects of interactions more closely to the work on learning in problem solving. Third, these equations allow a clear separation of different types of properties (mathematical and non-mathematical surface properties), which allows a clean test of the hypotheses.

The main manipulation was whether subjects had to learn only to classify the equations (*classify group*) or to classify and solve each equation (*solution group*). The solution group was expected to pick up more on the mathematical properties, so the prediction was that the solution group's performance on later classification tests would be more influenced by the mathematical properties than would the classify group's performance.

Let me make this concrete by going over one of the experiments in more detail. In Experiment 1a, equations differed on both the method of solution and the surface properties, as shown in Table III. Consider first the Type 1 equations, such as $f = (cnx/6) + 1$. To solve this equation for x, one would subtract 1 from both sides, multiply by 6, and then divide by cn. Thus, the solution method will be referred to as SMD for subtract-multiply-divide.

TABLE II

General Procedure for Interaction with Instances Experiments

Item is presented.
Subject responds with category.
Feedback on category is given.
Subject interacts with item.[a]
Subject studies item.
Next item is presented.

[a] Italicized step of procedure is one that differs from usual classification learning procedure.

TABLE III

Sample Materials for Interaction with
Instances Experiments

	Type	
	Type 1 (SMD)	Type 2 (MSD)
Study	$a + \left(\dfrac{bx}{c}\right) = p$	$\left(\dfrac{q + mx}{b}\right) = s$
	$f = \left(\dfrac{cnx}{6}\right) + 1$	$r = \left(\dfrac{dx + 7}{sp}\right)$
Sample Test	SMD	MSD
	$n = \left(\dfrac{3x}{t} + p\right)$	$e = \dfrac{(7x) + 6}{9d}$

(The last two operators could be applied in either order, but that will not matter for this experiment.) In addition to this solution method, Type 1 equations all had two surface characteristics in common: They used mainly letters from early in the alphabet and had a parenthesis that covered only part of one side of the equation.

Type 2 equations had a different solution method and different surface characteristics. As shown in Table III, one equation might be

$$r = \left(\frac{dx + 7}{sp}\right).$$

To solve this equation, one would multiply by sp, subtract 7, and divide by d. This solution method was MSD for multiply-subtract-divide. The Type 2 equations also had mostly letters from later in the alphabet and had a parenthesis that covered one whole side of the equation. Thus, Type 1 and Type 2 equations differed in both mathematical properties (solution methods) and surface properties (letters and parentheses).

All subjects were given the equations one at a time, classified them as Type 1 or Type 2, and were given feedback. The classify-group subjects studied the equation and then were shown the next equation, as in a typical classification experiment. The solution-group subjects had to solve each equation before going on to the next equation. The hypothesis was that solving the equations (one type of interaction) would lead these subjects to represent the equation categories differently from the group that only classified them, and that this difference would extend even to how they classify later items. To test this idea, later classification tests were given, the most diagnostic type of which is provided at the bottom of Table III. In this test, the solution method for one type was combined with the parenthesis and letters for the other type. For example,

$$e = \frac{(7x) + 6}{9d}$$

has the solution method for Type 2 (MSD) combined with the Type 1 parenthesis (that covers only part of one side of the equation) and Type 1 letters (early in the alphabet).

   If the solution group subjects were using the mathematical properties for classification more than the classify group subjects were, then they should classify this test equation as a Type 2 more often. They did, with proportions of such classifications of .81 versus .60 for the solution and classify groups, respectively. Thus, the interaction led the solution group to learn something additional about the equations that affected later classification. Classification learning is not influenced only by feedback about the classification task, since both groups received the same feedback. Rather, classification learning is part of category learning and is not isolated from what else is learned about the category.

   The later experiments in Ross (1996) extended the generality and scope of this idea. One experiment showed similar effects with different mathematical properties (whether the two x terms have similar or different coefficients so could be combined simply or required the use of the distributive property).

   Two additional experiments showed that it was not just whether there was an interaction or not, but the *type* of interaction that affected later classification performance. In these experiments, subjects solved the same equations but for different unknowns (x or y). For example, the Type 1 equation

$$\left(\frac{tx}{a}\right) + d = \frac{(6c + 7y)}{p}$$

is solved by the solution method SMD when solved for x, but by the solution method MSD when solved for y. Type 2 equations used the solution method MSD when solved for x and SMD when solved for y. The later classification tests (with the variable z) showed the subjects solving for the different variables had very different category representations. In particular, the group that solved for x tended to classify any SMD equation as a Type 1, while the group that solved for y tended to classify these equations as Type 2 (overall, across two experiments, more than 75% of the time). Thus, these effects are not just due to greater time with the items for the solution group. Different interactions lead to different category knowledge, which in turn may differentially affect later classification. Additional experiments found that these interactions affected the formation of categories, the typicality gradient of each category, and the memory for the specific equations. However, these studies are not as relevant for the current point so will not be elaborated.

Although it is clear that people *could* use knowledge gained in one task when performing in a later task, it is not obvious they *would*. In these experiments, the mathematical characteristics that can be used for classification are not pointed out to the subject, but have to be noticed during the solution of the equations. In addition, the subjects have to realize that these mathematical properties are predictive of the categories and know how these differences can be observed in the equations at test without solving the equations. At the same time, the classify group is also picking up some mathematical properties (or other properties correlated with mathematical properties, such as whether there are one or two addends on each side of the equation), since even in the conflict tests, more than half the classify group's responses were consistent with the mathematical properties. Thus, solving the equations is leading to a greater influence of the mathematical properties.

These experiments show that interactions with classified instances affect category representations, including the knowledge used to make classifications. Even though the equations contained readily available surface characteristics that were perfectly predictive of the equation categories, the people who solved each equation were more likely to classify on the basis of the solution method than were people who did not solve the equations. Thus, classifications are not solely a function of feedback about the classification, but can be influenced by other knowledge the learners are gaining while learning to classify the instances.

VII. Use of Categories

People not only interact with particular instances, they also use their knowledge of the instance's category to bring relevant knowledge to bear for accomplishing their particular task. The studies just described focused on how interactions with instances may affect the category representation, but the category of the instance was not critical in determining the interaction. That is, for the materials in Ross (1996), subjects could solve the equations without knowing which category the equations were in. In many other cases, however, what we do with the instance depends critically upon the knowledge we have of the category. For example, seeing an animal coming toward us, our decisions about whether to flee or not depends upon our classification of the animal and the knowledge we access about that type of animal.

Categories are useful because classification provides access to much other knowledge that is likely to be relevant for the situation. To foreshadow the experiments, consider medical diagnosis. Diagnosis does not solve the medical difficulty, but it is important because it allows a determination of possible treatments and their efficacy.

As we use categories, our knowledge of the use may affect our category representations. For example, as we learn more about how different treatments affect a disease, we may change our understanding of the disease. We may learn to view some symptoms as being more important. Not only might this affect our understanding, but it could even affect how we classify later instances. Patients with this important (for treatments) set of symptoms may be more readily classified than they were before the knowledge was gained from the use.

Some recent experiments test this idea of whether the use of categories might affect the category representation, including knowledge used to make classifications. The general procedure is given in Table IV. The usual classification procedure is interleaved with a second task in which people make use of the classification to make a further judgment (and get feedback on it). In these experiments, the classification task is one of assigning patients to different disease categories. In addition, after each classification, the

TABLE IV

GENERAL PROCEDURE FOR CATEGORY-USE EXPERIMENTS

Item is presented.
Subject responds with category.
Feedback on category is given.
Subject uses classification to make some other judgment or inference.[a]
Feedback on other judgment or inference is given.
Subject studies item.
Next item is presented.

[a] Italicized steps of procedure are ones that differs from usual classification learning procedure.

person must decide what drug treatment should be given to each patient (the treatments depend upon the disease category). The question is whether deciding about treatments for each patient might affect how one comes to classify later patients. The patient-disease task is a common one for classification studies (e.g., Gluck & Bower, 1988; Medin & Edelson, 1988), but the hypothesis was that including an additional task that depended on the category might influence what subjects knew about the category, which in turn might influence later classifications.

Again, to be more concrete, I will present one of the experiments in detail. Table V shows the category structure. There were two disease categories, *terrigitis* and *buragamo,* but I will call them Disease A and Disease B here to make the design clearer. For each disease category, there were four symptoms (e.g., fever, dizziness, abdominal pain, itchy eyes), which I will label a1 to a4 for Disease A and b1 to b4 for Disease B. Each of these critical symptoms was sufficient for category membership. That is, whenever any symptom a1 to a4 occurred, the patient had Disease A, and whenever any symptom b1 to b4 occurred, the patient had Disease B. All critical symptoms were presented equally often. The manipulation of category use, however, was that two of these symptoms for each disease, a1 and a2 for Disease A, were also perfectly predictive of the treatments, A1 and A2. Whenever a patient had symptom a1 (e.g., nausea), the correct treatment was always A1 (e.g., galudane). The hypothesis was that as subjects learned about the diseases and treatments, those symptoms that were predictive of the treatments (called *relevant-use symptoms*), a1 and a2, would also come to be viewed as more predictive of the disease than would the other equally disease-predictive symptoms (*irrelevant-use symptoms*), a3 and a4. (The

TABLE V

PARTIAL DESIGN FOR CATEGORY USE DISEASE EXPERIMENT:
SAMPLE STUDY MATERIALS FOR ONE DISEASE[a]

	Patient 1	Patient 2	Patient 3	Patient 4
Relevant-use symptom[b]	a1	a1	a2	a2
Irrelevant-use symptom	a3	a4	a3	a4
Nonpredictive symptom[c]	c1	c2	c3	c4
Treatment	A1	A1	A2	A2

[a] The diseases and treatments had fictitious names, but the symptoms were real symptoms, such as abdominal pain and nausea. The cards given to subjects contained just the three symptoms listed for each patient.

[b] a1 is a relevant-use symptom for subjects getting these materials because whenever it occurs, the treatment to be given is A1. Symptom a2 always is treated with A2.

[c] The nonpredictive symptoms are presented equally often with the other disease.

particular symptoms were counterbalanced between relevant-use and irrelevant-use symptoms.) As can be seen in Table V, each "patient" consisted of three symptoms: one relevant-use symptom, one irrelevant-use symptom from the same disease category, and a nonpredictive symptom (i.e., a symptom that is presented equally often with both diseases).

Table VI shows the procedure and sample test items. A patient is presented to the subject who responds with one of the diseases. Feedback is given and then the subject uses this correct disease to decide which treatment the patient would receive. Note that each disease has different treatments, so the treatment choice depends upon the disease category. Subjects participated in six study blocks of 16 patients each.

The test trials assessed whether the relevant-use symptoms were viewed as more important for the disease than the irrelevant-use symptoms (see Table VI for examples). In the single-symptom tests, each symptom was presented individually, and subjects responded with the likely disease if this symptom were all they knew about a patient. If the relevant-use symptoms had come to be more important for the disease representations than irrelevant-use symptoms, the subjects should be better able to classify from the relevant-use symptoms than the irrelevant-use symptoms. The results show that they are, with correct disease classifications .96 of the time for

TABLE VI

Specific Procedure for Category Use Disease Experiment (Using Abstract Notation from Text and Table V)

STUDY TRIAL: (italicized text describes steps of a study trial)

Procedure for each trial	Sample trial
Present patient	a1 a3 c1
S responds with disease	Disease A
Feedback	Correct, Disease A
S responds with treatment: (must be A1 or A2 if Disease A)	Treatment A2
Feedback	No, Treatment A1
Next patient presented	

TEST TRIALS (no feedback given on any test trials)

Single Tests	
present single symptom	a2
S responds with disease	Disease A
Double Tests[a]	
present two symptoms	a2 b3
S responds with disease	Disease A

[a] Critical double tests had a relevant-use symptom from one disease paired with an irrelevant-use symptom from other disease.

relevant-use symptoms compared to .80 of the time for irrelevant-use symptoms. In the double symptom tests, two symptoms were presented, with a relevant-use symptom of one disease paired with an irrelevant-use symptom of the other disease. If relevant-use symptoms are viewed as more predictive than irrelevant-use symptoms, the prediction is that the subjects should choose the disease of the relevant-use symptom over the disease of the irrelevant-use symptom. They do .73 of the time, almost a 3 to 1 advantage. Thus, the treatment decisions had a strong influence on later classifications. Knowledge about classification is not isolated from other aspects of category learning.

Again, later experiments expanded the generality and scope of this idea. The effect of relevant-use symptoms being viewed as more predictive than irrelevant-use symptoms does not depend upon the exact category structure or procedure. The effect occurs when the symptoms are not perfectly predictive of category, which also shows that people can take both the symptom and the disease into account when making treatment judgments (since the relevant-use symptoms occurred in both diseases, but were only predictive of the treatment in one disease). Even if the second task is not deciding about treatments (a task which may be closely related to disease diagnosis), but rather just deciding about an arbitrary set of letters for last names, those symptoms predictive of this latter task come to be viewed as more predictive of the diseases. The results of two additional experiments suggest that what is being learned is more general than the symptom-to-disease connections and may transfer to a variety of other tasks. For example, when subjects are asked to generate the symptoms associated with each disease, relevant-use symptoms are much more likely to be generated than are irrelevant-use symptoms (.75 vs .53), and relevant-use symptoms are judged to have occurred more often in the experiment (18.6 vs. 16.2).

The experiments described so far have examined situations in which the category and use were learned together. Sometimes, however, the use may occur after people have already learned to classify the items well. For example, one might learn about some different types of objects or situations and only later come to use them. Or, one might learn a new use for a previously learned category. It is difficult to assess how common such a situation is relative to situations in which the classification and use are learned together, but they may both be common enough situations to warrant examination.

Intuitively, it seems that if one learns the use after the classification, there may still be an effect on the category representation, but the classification may be less affected. That is, if one already has a means of classifying instances, later learning of a use might influence it less. However, the effect may depend upon the availability of the features, the difficulty of the classification, and what is learned from the use. For instance, if two types of situations or objects are difficult to distinguish, the use might provide an easier means of classifying them. The effects of expertise in a domain may possibly be of this "post-classification" type. That is, one might learn to distinguish different types of situations or problems, but the means of classification (and the category structure) might change with extended use of the categories.

The effect of learning to use the category following classification learning was examined by changing the original disease experiment, with subjects first learning about diseases and only later introducing treatments (after they had met a learning criterion on the disease categories). Following the treatment learning, the generation task was given, in which they were asked to generate the symptoms for each disease. Again, the relevant-use symptoms were more likely to be generated, with an average of .80 versus .58 for the irrelevant-use symptoms. A subsequent forced-choice classification test showed a marginally reliable difference (with .59 of the choices for the relevant-use symptom disease), but later work will examine the effect on classification without an initial generation task. However, based on the generation results, even when the classification is learned first, the use of a category can affect the category representation.

These experiments show that how we use categories can affect our representations of the categories, including the knowledge used to make later classifications. Those symptoms that were predictive of the treatments came to be viewed as more predictive of the disease as well. Although more work is needed to understand better the limits and cause of this effect (especially with the use learned after the classification), these results do show that the category learning, including classification learning, depends upon the category use.

Before discussing the implications of these experiments, one additional point needs to be addressed. So far, I have only looked at this one particular use of categories. I chose the disease-treatment paradigm both because of the earlier classification work using disease categories and because it provided a way of having a further inference or feature prediction (of treatments) that seemed to "naturally" follow a diagnosis. Although I intended the treatment decision to be a type of inference, it has been pointed out to me that it can also be viewed as an additional classification that divides each disease category into two subcategories. (Though note that this possibility is not true of the interaction with instances experiments.) It may be that consistent uses of a category often lead to a conceptual organization, such as subcategories, that reflects the use (e.g., Medin et al., 1995). However, future work will examine various different uses of categories to examine the generality of the claims made from this category use.

VIII. Discussion of Category Use

In this chapter, I have proposed viewing classification as part of a larger process. I have reviewed two projects that examine how interacting with instances or using categories affects what is being learned about the category, including the classification. In this section, I consider the implications of this work, speculate about why category use might be important for classification, and discuss further the parallels between category learning and problem solving.

A. IMPLICATIONS

1. What Has Been Shown?

The experiments sketched in this chapter show that classification learning is integrated with what is being learned from other cognitive activities. When people are interacting with the instances being classified or making use of the categories being learned, the category representation, including knowledge used for classification, may be affected. The classification is more likely to include features and relations that are important for the interaction and category use.

When people interact with instances as they are learning to classify, they appear to learn much about the instances, at least some of which can affect the classification. This effect occurs not only on the classification, but also on decisions about the typicality gradient and on the formation of new categories.

When people learn to use categories to make additional decisions, the features important for these additional decisions also come to be viewed as more important for the classification. Again, the effect is not limited to classification judgments. These features are also more likely to be generated from the category and are judged to have occurred more frequently, suggesting that the effect is not simply due to an increased weighting in the feature-to-category connection. Finally, this effect does not depend on the interleaved learning of classification and category use. Even when the classification was learned first, the category use affected how people made later classifications (also see Yamauchi & Markman, 1996).

Thus, classification learning depends not only on the diagnosticity of features for assigning category membership, but also the way in which these features may play a role in the interactions and category uses during learning. Given this influence, it is important to go beyond tasks in which classification is the goal, and to consider how category learning includes both classification and use. The work presented here examines what may be more usual category learning, in which the classification is learned along with instance interactions and uses of the category.

2. What Is Being Learned?

When people are learning to classify, there is a tendency for them to find a few diagnostic features that accurately separate the categories involved in the learning task. When people are also using the category, the use often forces them to consider how the different features go together (i.e., relations). Even in the simple disease experiments presented earlier, the learner had to understand which symptom was important for which treatment within which disease. This learning is already more relational than the simple feature-to-category connection required in most classification studies. If a more complicated use of the category knowledge (e.g., explanations) had been required, then there would have been far greater opportunity to learn about the relations among the features. Related work by Lassaline and Murphy (1996) shows that one use, making predictions about features, may promote learning about the relations between the features.

When people are learning to classify items and use knowledge about the category, it is likely that those features important for the use will be included in the classification. Even when people learn to use a category after having learned to classify, there is still an effect on the category representation, as shown in the final experiment reported here. In this case, the people already know how to classify the items before learning the use, so what is being learned here changes a prior representation. One possibility is that the means of classification changes toward emphasizing the features relevant for the use, such as a change in weight. For example, the relevant-use symptoms may get increasing weight because of their predictiveness for deciding on the treatments, and this increased weight makes them more readily accessible for other tasks (such as classification) as well. A second possibility is that the use provides a second set of classification features, so that subjects have alternative means of classification. The subjects who had not originally used the relevant-use symptoms in their disease classifications might add them after the treatment decision phase. The addition of alternative means of classification may be especially useful if people need to classify later on the basis of only partial information.

3. Implications for Theories of Categorization

The focus in research on categories has been on classification. One reason for this focus is that classification appears to be a generally separable process that provides access to the knowledge for the other category-related processes, such as prediction, explanation, and understanding. However, based on the studies sketched here, it appears that these later processes can in turn affect the classification. What are the implications? In particular, do theories of categories need to be more than theories of classification? The results here suggest that they do, even to account for classification performance. Thus, rather than viewing classification as an isolated part of our use of categories, it may be fruitful to consider how classification may affect, and be affected by, other category-related processes.

Classification does not depend only on classification feedback, but also on other category-related information. One cannot simply examine a category structure (or even multiple contrasting category structures) and determine how the classification judgments will be made, because the category uses and interactions might affect the classifications. If such interactions and category uses are common in real-world categorization, then theories of categorization need to incorporate the effects of such uses.

Many classification theories allow features weights to be adjusted as a function of the classification learning, but they do not generally allow the weights to be affected by nonclassification information (e.g., Kruschke, 1992). One possible modification is to allow information learned in a different task to affect the classification learning. That is, rather than think of classification learning as being separate from other category knowledge, have it make use of whatever else might be known about the category. Although this is an attractive possibility for extending the range of knowledge used for classifications (and accounting for the current findings), there may be a variety of uses, each of which is influencing the knowledge used for classification. It is necessary to have the classification influenced by other knowledge about the category, but a theory that does this is going to have to be much more complex than the current theories of classification.

I am not claiming that classification theories are wrong, but rather that they are incomplete. Is this incompleteness of classification theories in accounting for the effects of use a serious problem or just an acknowledgement that we do not fully understand cognition?

The final answer will come with attempts to incorporate classification theories into more complex tasks, but I clearly think that such use effects are important to include in classification theories. The use is often integral to the learning of categories. That is, the uses of categories are not some separate activities that happen to affect similar knowledge as does classification, but rather may be a primary reason we have the categories we do. Category learning involves learning to classify new instances *and* learning to use the categories. There are many situations in which we do make use of the classifications.

This integration of classification and use does not rule out the possibility (and probability) that there may also be situations in which the classification theories do well without incorporating the use. Classification may sometimes be the goal, with little or no use made of the classification. For example, people can learn to classify animals from pictures, such as African and Indian elephants, without any clear use made of the classifications. In other cases, perhaps the use is not important for the classification or there may be a variety of uses with none dominating the others.

Although there may be cases in which classifications do not depend upon the use, there may also be cases in which the use is necessary to learn the classification. As one speculative example, the use may affect the interpretation of features. Theories of classification assume that the items each consist of a given set of features (or structured representations), and the theories explain how these feature sets are assigned to categories. However, it is not clear a priori what should count as a feature (see Murphy & Medin, 1985, for an extended discussion). A variety of results suggest that classification is not simply a computation using fixed features, but rather that the classification can affect the features seen (e.g., Goldstone, 1995; Schyns & Murphy, 1994; Spalding & Ross, 1996; Wisniewski & Jung, 1996; Wisniewski & Medin, 1994). It is possible that the uses to which we put items may affect what features we "see" in the items. For example, experts do not simply weight features differently than do novices, but rather use different features that they have "discovered" from using these categories (e.g., Chi et al., 1981). If the use of the category affects the features used for classification, then theories of classification that do not incorporate the use will often make incorrect predictions in these situations.

B.   WHY MIGHT CATEGORY USE AFFECT CLASSIFICATION?

Learning to classify items in the world is complicated. There are three problems of particular concern for this chapter. One is that an item usually consists of a large number of features, only some of which are relevant to the classification. A second problem is that one needs to avoid learning to base classifications on features that are incidentally predictive in the sample, but are not predictive for the full category. A third problem is that one sometimes needs a large number of items to learn the appropriate predictive features. If category use influences classification, then all three of these problems may be alleviated. First, those features that are important for the use get more heavily weighted, so the use is acting as one selection criterion for which features might be used in the classification. Second, it seems probable that features involved in the use of the category are generally less likely to be incidentally predictive than are features not involved in the use. That is, these features have proven to be useful in at least one use of the category. Although the features could still be incidental to the category, their importance for a use makes it less likely (unless it was a very unusual use for the category). For example, in diagnosis, those features that predict how best to fix a particular problem of Type X seem more likely to be predictive of Type X than do features in the sample that are equally frequent but are not involved in the use. In problem categories, the features that are important for the solution are unlikely to be poor predictors of the category (compared to equally frequent features that are not important for the solution). Third, the number of examples that one might need to see to learn a new category may be reduced, because, as just described, the use provides a way of more quickly focusing on features more likely to be predictive for the category.

A common view of categories is that they consist of clusters of correlated features (e.g., Rosch, Mervis, Gray, Johnson, & Boyes-Braem, 1976). Why do we have categories? One possibility, consistent with the Rational Model of Anderson (1991), is that categories allow people effectively to make use of the category knowledge, such as to make predictions or inferences. From this perspective, the categories formed *should* depend upon the uses made of the categories. The apparent reliance on feature clusters may be due to their heuristic value for the uses—items with similar feature clusters are likely to be used similarly. This scheme would be a good one *only* if the earlier uses were predictive of the later uses. That is, the effects of category use of the category representation, including knowledge used to classify, helps the learner only if the category will be used in similar ways in the future (or if the features important for current use are also important for later uses). Thus, if past use is a good estimate of future use, then the influence of use on classification may be helpful.

C. PROBLEM SOLVING AND CATEGORY LEARNING

I began this chapter by trying to draw parallels between category learning and more complex problem-solving situations. Problem solving is very different from the usual experimental classification tasks, but it provides a clear case in which categories are used to accomplish some nonclassification goal. I will close the chapter by going back and considering this parallel in more detail. In particular, I will consider three points about learning in problem-solving domains and how they relate to category learning: the goal, the feedback, and the complexity of the classification and use.

First, as mentioned often in this chapter, in problem solving (and in many cases apart from classification experiments) classification is not the goal, but rather the classification is done as part of achieving a larger goal. The classification is important because it provides access to knowledge that is relevant for the use and because different classifications lead to different uses. What are the implications of considering classification as only a means to attaining the goal? One is that the knowledge relevant for the classification may not be the same as the knowledge relevant for the use. For example, one might classify by a similar exemplar, but then make use of summary information about the category for making an inference (e.g., Ross & Murphy, 1996). A second implication is that how particular items are classified may depend upon the use. During learning, the classification may be greatly affected by the goals (e.g., Lamberts, 1994; Medin & Smith, 1981; Waldmann & Holyoak, 1992; Ward & Becker, 1992). Even after this initial learning, items may become classified with respect to goals that they frequently help achieve (Barsalou, 1991). For example, Medin et al. (1995) show that the conceptual organization of trees by landscapers differs considerably from the scientific taxonomy, because it incorporates specific utilitarian features for their job (e.g., shadiness).

Second, feedback about the classification is not always immediate or direct in problem solving. The solvers may get the incorrect solution and only then find out they had the wrong problem category. In some cases, finding out they had the incorrect solution may not allow the solvers to be sure whether their classification was correct or not. What are the implications for classification if one cannot know how to assign blame for an incorrect use (i.e., to the classification or the application of the category knowledge)? A simple readjustment of connection weights will not be easy, given that the reason for the failure is not clear. One possibility is that learners provide an explanation for why the use was incorrect. This explanation might help them to learn what the underlying structure of the category representation is, as well as to note similarities and differences to other categories.

Third, in problem solving, the knowledge needed for classification and use can be quite complex. The classification often depends upon relational features and an appropriate classification is not sufficient to achieve a solution. The use (solution) may often be quite complex and require an understanding of structural (e.g., temporal and causal) knowledge. In most work on classification, a simple representation is assumed. What are the implications of including more complex knowledge? If a category has one or a few common uses, an understanding of the use may provide an understanding of the category (i.e., why these items go together).

These parallels all seem to point to a common idea—category use may lead learners to learn more about the structure underlying the category. If the use then influences the classification, the classifications will include more conceptual aspects of the category rather than just perceptually salient or easily available features. Although in many cases classification by perceptual features may be sufficient, this more conceptual understanding may help to select some diagnostic features among many potential ones, provide an alternative means of classification when the usual perceptual features are not available, and help one to classify new items that do not have the usual perceptual features, but are of the same type (at least with respect to the particular use). Viewed in this way, considering the use may provide one means by which people's theories for particular concepts might develop and be used (e.g., Murphy & Medin, 1985). To the extent that helps people to "explain" the category, the use features may be highlighted.

IX. Summary

In this chapter, I have examined how the use of instances and categories affects category representations, including the knowledge used to make classifications. The parallels to problem solving were meant to point out that classification needs to be viewed as part of a larger set of processes for attaining some goal, not as a goal in itself. Classification is an integral part of many cognitive activities, and the experiments examine a more usual category learning situation in which the classification is learned along with the interaction and use of the category. This idea and the empirical research presented here suggest that classification learning is not isolated from the learning of how this category is used, but rather the classification and use may interact. These ideas do not mean that theories of classification are irrelevant to theories of categories, nor that the results of classification research will not be important for such theories. Rather, the goal is to understand how theories of categories might be extended to include both classification and the use of categories.

ACKNOWLEDGMENTS

Brian H. Ross, Department of Psychology and the Beckman Institute, University of Illinois.

This research was supported by Grant 89-0447 from the Air Force Office of Scientific Research and conducted at the Beckman Institute for Advanced Science and Technology. I thank Gregory Murphy and Valerie Makin for discussions and comments on the manuscript. I also thank Lawrence Barsalou, Dorrit Billman, Gary Dell, Mary Lassaline, Arthur Markman, Douglas Medin, Edward Shoben, Edward Smith, Thomas Spalding, and Thomas Ward for comments and discussions on this research. Michelle Kaplan, Amanda Lorenz, and Amanda Schulze are gratefully thanked for their help in testing the subjects for the experiments described here. Correspondence may be addressed to Brian H. Ross, Beckman Institute, University of Illinois, 405 N. Mathews Ave., Urbana, IL 61801 or via email to bross@s.psych.uiuc.edu.

REFERENCES

Allen, S. W. & Brooks, L. R. (1991). Specializing the operation of an explicit rule. *Journal of Experimental Psychology: General, 120,* 3–19.

Anderson, J. R. (1991). The adaptive nature of human categorization. *Psychological Review, 98,* 409–429.

Barsalou, L. W. (1983). Ad hoc categories. *Memory & Cognition, 11,* 211–227.

Barsalou, L. W. (1985). Ideals, central tendency, and frequency of instantiation as determinants of graded structure in categories. *Journal of Experimental Psychology: Learning, Memory, and Cognition, 11,* 629–654.

Barsalou, L. W. (1991). Deriving categories to achieve goals. In G. H. Bower (Ed.), *The psychology of learning and motivation* (Vol. 27). New York: Academic Press.

Barsalou, L. W., & Ross, B. H. (1986). The roles of automatic and strategic processing in sensitivity to superordinate and property frequency. *Journal of Experimental Psychology: Learning, Memory, and Cognition, 12,* 116–134.

Billman, D., & Heit, E. (1988). Observational learning from internal feedback: A simulation of an adaptive learning method. *Cognitive Science, 12,* 587–625.

Billman, D., & Knutson, J. (1996). Unsupervised concept learning and value systematicity. *Journal of Experimental Psychology: Learning, Memory, and Cognition, 22,* 458–475.

Blessing, S. B., & Ross, B. H. (1996). The effect of problem content on categorization and problem solving. *Journal of Experimental Psychology: Learning, Memory, and Cognition, 22,* 792–810.

Boster, J. S., & Johnson, J. C. (1989). Form or function: A comparison of expert and novice judgments of similarity among fish. *American Anthropologist, 91,* 866–889.

Brooks, L. (1978). Nonanalytic concept formation and memory for instances. In E. Rosch and B. B. Lloyd (Eds.), *Cognition and categorization* (pp. 169–211). Hillsdale, NJ: Erlbaum.

Brooks, L. (1987). Decentralized control of categorization: The role of prior processing episodes. In U. Neisser (Ed.), *Concepts and conceptual development: Ecological and intellectual factors in categorization* (pp. 141–174). New York: Cambridge University Press.

Chi, M. T. H., Feltovich, P. J., & Glaser, R. (1981). Categorization and representation of physics problems by experts and novices. *Cognitive Science, 5,* 121–152.

Clapper, J. P., & Bower, G. H. (1994). Category invention in unsupervised learning. *Journal of Experimental Psychology: Learning, Memory, and Cognition, 20,* 443–460.

Estes, W. K. (1986). Array models for category learning. *Cognitive Psychology, 18,* 500–549.

Finke, R. A., Ward, T. B., & Smith, S. M. (1992). *Creative cognition: Theory, research, and applications.* Cambridge, MA: MIT Press.

Fisher, D. H. Jr., Pazzani, M. J., & Langley, P. (Eds.) (1991). *Concept formation: Knowledge and experience in unsupervised learning.* San Mateo, CA: Morgan Kaufmann.

Gelman, S. A., & Markman, E. M. (1986). Categories and induction in children. *Cognition, 23,* 183–208.

Gelman, S. A., & Markman, E. M. (1987). Young children's inductions from natural kinds: The role of categories and appearance. *Child Development, 58,* 1532–1541.

Gluck, M. A., & Bower, G. H. (1988). Evaluating an adaptive network model of human learning. *Journal of Memory and Language, 27,* 166–195.

Goldstone, R. L. (1995). Effects of categorization on color perception. *Psychological Science, 6,* 298–304.

Heit, E. (1992). Categorization using chains of examples. *Cognitive Psychology, 24,* 341–380.

Jacoby, L. L., & Brooks, L. R. (1984). Nonanalytic cognition: Memory, perception, and concept learning. In G. H. Bower (Ed.), *The psychology of learning and motivation* (Vol. 20). New York: Academic Press.

Kalish, C. W., & Gelman, S. A. (1992). On wooden pillows: Multiple classification and children's category-based inductions. *Child Development, 63,* 1,536–1,557.

Kemler Nelson, D. G. (1988). The effect of intention on what concepts are acquired. *Journal of Verbal Learning and Verbal Behavior, 23,* 734–759.

Kruschke, J. K. (1992). ALCOVE: An exemplar-based connectionist model of category learning. *Psychological Review, 99,* 22–44.

Lamberts, K. (1994). Flexible tuning of similarity in exemplar-based categorization. *Journal of Experimental Psychology: Learning, Memory, and Cognition, 20,* 1003–1021.

Lassaline, M. E., & Murphy, G. L. (1996). Induction and category coherence. *Psychonomic Bulletin & Review. 3,* 95–99.

Logan, G. D. (1988). Toward an instance theory of automatization. *Psychological Review, 95,* 492–527.

Malt, B. C., Ross, B. H., & Murphy, G. L. (1995). Making predictions using uncertain natural categories. *Journal of Experimental Psychology: Learning, Memory, and Cognition 21,* 646–661.

Markman, A. B., Yamauchi, T., & Makin, V. S. (in press). The creation of new concepts: A multifaceted approach to category learning. In T. B. Ward, S. M. Smith, & Vaid, J. (Eds.), *Conceptual structures and processes: Emergence, discovery, and change.* Washington, D.C.: American Psychological Association.

Medin, D. L., & Edelson, S. (1988). Problem structure and the use of base rate information from experience. *Journal of Experimental Psychology: General, 117,* 68–85.

Medin, D. L., Lynch, E. B., Coley, J. D., & Atran, S. (1995). *Categorization and reasoning among tree experts: Do all roads lead to Rome?* Manuscript under review.

Medin, D. L., & Schaffer, M. M. (1978). Context theory of classification learning. *Psychological Review, 85,* 207–238.

Medin, D. L., & Smith, E. E. (1981). Strategies and classification learning. *Journal of Experimental Psychology: Human Learning and Memory, 7,* 241–253.

Medin, D. L., & Smith, E. E. (1984). Concepts and concept formation. *Annual Review of Psychology, 35,* 113–138.

Medin, D. L., Wattenmaker, W. D., & Hampson, S. E. (1987). Family resemblance, conceptual cohesiveness, and category construction. *Cognitive Psychology, 19,* 241–279.

Murphy, G. L., & Medin, D. L. (1985). The role of theories in conceptual coherence. *Psychological Review, 92,* 289–316.

Murphy, G. L., & Ross, B. H. (1994). Predictions from uncertain categorizations. *Cognitive Psychology, 27,* 148–193.

Murphy, G. L., & Wright, J. C. (1984). Changes in conceptual structure with expertise: Differences between real-world experts and novices. *Journal of Experimental Psychology: Learning, Memory, and Cognition, 1,* 144–155.

Nosofsky, R. (1986). Attention, similarity, and the identification-categorization relationship. *Journal of Experimental Psychology: General, 115,* 39–57.

Nosofsky, R. (1988). Similarity, frequency, and category representations. *Journal of Experimental Psychology: Learning, Memory, & Cognition, 14,* 54–65.

Osherson, D. N., Smith, E. E., Wilkie, O., Lopez, A., & Shafir, E. (1990). Category-based induction. *Psychological Review, 97,* 185–200.

Reimann, P., & Chi, M. T. H. (1989). Human expertise. In K. J. Gihooly (Ed.), *Human and machine problem solving.* London: Plenum Publishing Corporation.

Rosch, E., Mervis, C. B., Gray, W., Johnson, D., & Boyes-Braem, P. (1976). Basic objects in natural categories. *Cognitive Psychology, 8,* 382–439.

Ross, B. H. (1984). The effects of remindings on learning a cognitive skill. *Cognitive Psychology, 16,* 371–416.

Ross, B. H. (1996). Category representations and the effects of interacting with instances. *Journal of Experimental Psychology: Learning, Memory, and Cognition, 22.*

Ross, B. H., & Murphy, G. L. (1996). Category-based predictions: The influence of uncertainty and feature associations. *Journal of Experimental Psychology: Learning, Memory, and Cognition, 22,* 736–753.

Ross, B. H., Perkins, S. J., & Tenpenny, P. L. (1990). Reminding-based category learning. *Cognitive Psychology, 22,* 460–492.

Ross, B. H., & Spalding, T. L. (1994). Concepts and categories. In R. Sternberg (Ed.), *Handbook of perception and cognition: Vol. 12. Thinking and Problem Solving* (pp. 119–148). San Diego, CA: Academic Press, Inc.

Schyns, P. G., & Murphy, G. L. (1994). The ontogeny of part representation in object categories. In D. L. Medin (Ed.), *The psychology of learning and motivation* (Vol. 28). Orlando, FL: Academic Press.

Sloman, S. A. (1993). Feature-based induction. *Cognitive Psychology, 25,* 231–280.

Smith, E. E., & Medin, D. L. (1981). *Categories and concepts.* Cambridge, MA: Harvard University Press.

Spalding, T. L., & Ross, B. H. (1994). Comparison-based learning: Effects of comparing instances during category learning. *Journal of Experimental Psychology: Learning, Memory, and Cognition, 20,* 1251–1263.

Spalding, T. L., & Ross, B. H. (1996). *Concept learning and feature interpretation.* Manuscript submitted for publication.

Tanaka, J. W., & Taylor, M. E. (1991). Categorization and expertise: Is the basic level in the eye of the beholder? *Cognitive Psychology, 23,* 457–482.

Waldmann, M. R., & Holyoak, K. J. (1992). Predictive and diagnostic learning within causal models: Asymmetries in cue competition. *Journal of Experimental Psychology: General, 121,* 222–236.

Ward, T. B., & Becker, A. H. (1992). Learning categories with and without trying: Does it make a difference? In B. Burns (Ed.), *Percepts, concepts and categories* (pp. 451–491). Amsterdam: Elsevier Science Publishers.

Ward, T. B., & Scott, J. (1987). Analytic and holistic modes of learning family-resemblance concepts. *Memory & Cognition, 15,* 42–54.

Wattenmaker, W. D. (1991). Learning modes, feature correlations, and memory-based categorization. *Journal of Experimental Psychology: Learning, Memory, and Cognition, 17,* 908–923.

Wattenmaker, W. D. (1992). Relational properties and memory-based construction. *Journal of Experimental Psychology: Learning, Memory, and Cognition, 18,* 1125–1138.

Wattenmaker, W. D. (1993). Incidental concept learning, feature frequency, and correlated properties. *Journal of Experimental Psychology: Learning, Memory, and Cognition, 19,* 203–222.

Wattenmaker, W. D., Dewey, G. I., Murphy, T. D., & Medin, D. L. (1986). Linear separability and concept learning: Context, relational properties, and concept naturalness. *Cognitive Psychology, 18,* 158–194.

Whittlesea, B. W. A. (1987). Preservation of specific experiences in the representation of general knowledge. *Journal of Experimental Psychology: Learning, Memory, and Cognition, 13,* 3–17.

Wisniewski, E. J. (1995). Prior knowledge and functionally relevant features in concept learning. *Journal of Experimental Psychology: Learning, Memory, and Cognition, 21,* 449–468.

Wisniewski, E. J., & Jung, T. (1996). *Differential feature interpretation in concept learning.* Manuscript under review.

Wisniewski, E. J., & Medin, D. L. (1994). On the interaction of theory and data in concept learning. *Cognitive Science, 18,* 221–282.

Yamauchi, T., & Markman, A. B. (1996). *Category-learning by inference and classification.* Manuscript under review.

BUILDING A COHERENT CONCEPTION OF HIV TRANSMISSION
A New Approach to AIDS Education

Terry Kit-fong Au
Laura F. Romo

I. Introduction

Adolescents are fast becoming a high-risk group for HIV infection (Brown, DiClemente, & Reynolds, 1991; Crawford & Robinson, 1990; Keller, Bartlett, Schleifer, Johnson, Pinner, & Delaney, 1991; Leland & Barth, 1993; Millstein, 1989; National Commission on AIDS, 1993; Sprecher, 1990). Almost a decade has elapsed since the Presidential Commission on the HIV Epidemic (Watkins et al., 1988) and the American Psychological Association Task Force on Pediatric AIDS (1989) have called for AIDS education programs—beginning in early childhood and extending through high school—that are appropriate to children's developmental and cognitive levels. How well have such calls been answered so far?

The overall picture seems to be that most children in the United States have acquired a fair amount of AIDS-related knowledge by late childhood and adolescence (e.g., Brown & Fritz, 1989; Fassler, McQueen, Duncan, & Copeland, 1990; Osborne, Kistner, & Helgemo, 1993). But the news is not all good: While most adolescents have a fair amount of AIDS-related knowledge, their knowledge does not seem to be related to their level of sex-related risk of becoming infected (e.g., Keller, 1993; Keller et al., 1991). To many who have heard this news, it seems that children's AIDS knowledge does not matter much in AIDS prevention. To us, such a sweeping antiknowledge stance does not make much sense.

Consider, if you will, the current approach to AIDS education. The basic messages are simple (perhaps to a fault): AIDS is deadly, and there is no cure; the best-documented ways of getting AIDS are through (a) sharing a needle, (b) sexual intercourse, and (c) getting contaminated blood in a transfusion. To children and adolescents, this may seem like a list of unconnected facts about AIDS, and it probably serves more as "food for memorization" than "food for thought." So, they might simply learn and then stow away these facts. How well they know these highly publicized facts, then, may not tell us much about the depth of their understanding, their interest in learning more about AIDS, or how concerned they are about getting AIDS. It therefore should not come as a surprise that adolescents' knowledge of these facts seems to have little to do with their sex-related AIDS risk.

II. Learning and Motivation Issues in Educating Children about AIDS

To educate children effectively about AIDS, health educators and researchers face several major challenges. First, how can we capitalize on children's natural curiosity to make sense of the world to get them to think about AIDS often, deeply, and sensibly? Second, how can we help children develop a coherent conception, rather than fragmented knowledge, of AIDS transmission that allows them to organize a considerable amount of information and to reason about what is safe and unsafe to do in situations that are not explicitly covered by AIDS education programs? Third, how can we explain to children about the seriousness of AIDS without incapacitating them with unjustified fear? Fourth, how can we explain AIDS transmission and prevention to children who do not yet know much or anything about sex?

A. GETTING CHILDREN TO LEARN AND THINK ABOUT AIDS

From age 2 or 3 on, children often ask their parents and other caregivers why things happen and how things work. Children's questions reflect curiosity about theorylike domains (e.g., naive biology, psychology, chemistry, and mechanics), and adults typically respond with causal explanations (e.g., Callanan & Oakes, 1992; Hood & Bloom, 1979). Such conversations are rich and full of natural, and at times intellectual, curiosity. Perhaps we can capitalize on children's curiosity to make sense of the world to get them to think about AIDS often and deeply.

If we can talk to children about the hows and whys of AIDS transmission coherently, instead of talking down to them by just telling them to learn some facts about AIDS, they may rise to this intellectual challenge by thinking often, coherently, and deeply about AIDS transmission—especially in connection with their self-protective behaviors. Moreover, if adolescents understand the causal mechanism for AIDS transmission, they may be less likely to have a false sense of security or invulnerability (e.g., thinking that "I won't catch it") than if they have only incorrect or vague ideas about the causal mechanism. Such knowledge may make it more salient to them that certain behaviors would indeed put them personally at risk for becoming infected. An important question is: How should we talk to children so that they can build a coherent conception of AIDS transmission?

B.   Coherent Conception of AIDS Transmission

Previous research suggests that children and teenagers are generally aware of some of the best-documented ways of getting AIDS. However, there also seem to be major gaps in their knowledge at all age levels regarding specifics about AIDS transmission (Osborne et al., 1993). For example, young children often overgeneralize that touching any needle puts someone at risk for getting AIDS (Fassler et al., 1990); older children correctly consider sex to be a main route of AIDS transmission, but often show great confusion about the relation between human reproduction and HIV transmission (e.g., "The AIDS goes into the sperm," Hoppe, Wells, Wilsdon, Gillmore, Morrison, 1994; this confusion might be related to another common misconception, namely, "whatever can prevent pregnancy can prevent AIDS"). Teenagers' common misconceptions include: AIDS could be acquired "by giving blood" and "kissing someone who has AIDS" (e.g., Brown & Fritz, 1989; Fassler et al., 1990). Even college students have some confusion about the infectiousness of various kinds of bodily fluids and the relative effectiveness of various preventive measures. In short, we need to do a better job and go beyond trying to teach children a few basic facts about AIDS. We have to get children to think coherently and deeply about what AIDS means to them in connection with their self-protective behaviors.

To understand better the role knowledge could play in AIDS prevention, it is crucial to distinguish between fragmented knowledge and a coherent conception of AIDS transmission (cf. Vosniadou & Brewer, 1992). A coherent belief system can be useful not only for organizing a considerable amount of information, but also for reasoning about novel situations. Because it is easier to remember things that make sense than to remember a number of unconnected facts (Dooling & Lachman, 1971), understanding the causal mechanism for AIDS transmission—and therefore the rationales for the "do's and don'ts" presented in AIDS education—should help children remember the recommendations better. Moreover, such understanding may help children decide what is safe and unsafe to do in situations that are not explicitly covered by health education programs (e.g., Walsh, 1995; cf. White, 1993). Such ability to reason about novel situations may also help children feel less helpless and less overwhelmed about what they do not yet know about AIDS transmission.

Our goal, then, is to help children build a coherent conception of AIDS with the understanding of a biological causal mechanism for HIV transmission at its core. An important question is whether children are ready to do so. Research on conceptual development reveals that children spontaneously and actively build intuitive conceptual frameworks about the world in their attempts to make sense of biological kinds, mental activities, physical objects, and substances (e.g., Au, 1994; Carey, 1985, 1995; Carey & Spelke, 1994; Gelman, 1996; Wellman & Gelman, 1992). There is evidence that preschoolers' naive mechanics and naive psychology are already quite theorylike because they outline the ontology and basic causal devices in those domains. However, it remains a hotly debated issue when children begin to construct their first autonomous biology. At issue is whether children know any causal mechanisms that are uniquely biological. Later in this chapter, we will take a closer look at children's understanding of biological mechanisms.

C. BALANCE BETWEEN EMPHASIZING THE GRAVITY AND PREVENTABILITY OF AIDS

Many teenagers do not appreciate how serious a disease AIDS is. For example, Slonim-Nevo, Ozawa, and Auslander (1991) found that about 40% of the teenagers they interviewed in youth centers thought that AIDS can be cured if treated early; Glenister, Castiglia, Kanski, and Haughey (1990) found that about two-thirds of the 9–16-year-olds in their study thought that AIDS can be cured. These findings underscore the importance of helping children and teenagers realize the serious consequences of becoming HIV positive.

On the other hand, researchers must help find ways to educate children and adolescents about the seriousness of AIDS without incapacitating them with unjustified fear. One reason why we must go beyond teaching children just the basic facts about AIDS is that knowing only a few facts about AIDS can be very frightening for children. For instance, when told that one cannot get AIDS through casual contact, children might wonder what counts as "casual contact." Simply giving them some positive and negative exemplars of casual contact will not do. Such a quick fix will place the burden of inducing the conceptual basis for deciding what is safe and unsafe in terms of AIDS prevention on the children. In other words, this amounts to hoping that children can induce the causal mechanism for HIV transmission from just a short list of "do's and don'ts."

This approach could be counterproductive because it could generate so much uncertainty and anxiety about this deadly and incurable disease that children and adolescents might cope by shunning all thoughts on this topic. In fact, by age 6 or 7, most children have already heard of AIDS, and many express unwarranted fears and misconceptions about catching AIDS (e.g., Fassler et al., 1990). During the early elementary school years (K–4), many children think that one can get AIDS in ways similar to how one can catch a cold or the flu—kissing, being coughed or sneezed on, sharing a drinking glass, touching, or being around someone who carries the virus/germ (e.g., Hoppe et al., 1994; Osborne et al., 1993; Sigelman, Maddock, Epstein, & Carpenter, 1993b; Walsh & Bibace, 1991). The fear of catching AIDS through casual contact was so prevalent among the fourth graders in our AIDS education study—to be reported in this chapter—that most of them thought it would be a good idea to set up "AIDS cities" for children and adults with the AIDS virus to live in. It is therefore important to teach children about AIDS early and coherently to help them understand the seriousness of AIDS without incapacitating them with unjustified fear.

Young adolescents seem to worry more about intimate contact than casual contact as an AIDS risk. A case in point: In our AIDS education study, about 50% of eighth graders (roughly age 13–14) independently asked us in writing whether there *will ever be* a cure for AIDS. An additional 20% wanted to know if there is a cure now (if detected early). By contrast, the younger children seemed more interested in how AIDS can be transmitted and prevented (e.g., "Can you get AIDS from animals?"). Perhaps the eighth graders wanted to know about a cure because they feel that, when they become sexually active, there is little they can do to prevent AIDS. In their AIDS curriculum guidelines, published by the National Catholic Educational Association (1992), condoms were described to have about a 10% failure rate. Also, a teacher told us that she had heard that 1 in 10 condoms has holes big enough for sperm—which are much bigger than the AIDS virus—to pass through. That is why she has been using an air-safety analogy as a teaching tool (recommended by an AIDS curriculum workshop for Catholic school teachers): "If you know that one in ten planes will crash, you probably won't fly either." This analogy seems to be quite widely used. In a separate research project, we found that a mother also used this analogy when she talked to her teenager daughter about AIDS and sexuality.

The intended message, of course, is abstinence. While many adults want adolescents to abstain from sex out of the best of intentions—e.g., religious beliefs, moral values, worries about AIDS, other sexually transmitted diseases, and teenage pregnancies—stressing the ineffectiveness of condoms may leave adolescents feeling that there is nothing they could do to prevent AIDS effectively when they become sexually active (whether in or out of marriage). Combined with the knowledge that to date there is no cure for AIDS, such feelings of helplessness may lead adolescents to repress or suppress any thoughts about AIDS transmission and prevention, and in turn, may lead to denial of their risks of getting AIDS.

A major challenge of educating children and adolescents about AIDS, then, is to educate them about the serious consequences of becoming HIV positive without scaring them into shutting out all thoughts about AIDS. A moderate level of perceived vulnerability to AIDS seems to lead to more self-protective behaviors than either extremely high or low levels (e.g., Emmons et al., 1986). Our approach to meet this challenge is to help children develop a deep understanding of the causal mechanism of AIDS transmission without resorting to fear tactics. Having a coherent basis for learning and reasoning about AIDS may actually encourage children and adolescents to think about AIDS often, deeply, and sensibly.

D.   AIDS EDUCATION BEFORE (OR APART FROM) SEX EDUCATION

Most preadolescents (age 10–12) learn about AIDS formally at school as part of sex education. Because many students around puberty—and some teachers, for that matter—find it very embarrassing to talk about sex and sexuality, students may listen without hearing. They may end up with bits and pieces of information that do not readily make sense. In trying to make the information fit together, they may develop serious misconceptions about AIDS prevention. Although many preadolescents may have heard that teenagers and young adults are at greater risk for AIDS because of sexual behaviors, many lack a correct understanding of how sexual activities might be related to AIDS transmission. It is perhaps not a coincidence that a common misconception among fifth graders is that whatever can prevent pregnancy (e.g., birth-control pills) can prevent AIDS (Hoppe et al., 1994). Given how emotionally charged and sensitive the topic of sexuality is, it may not be a good idea to introduce the topic of AIDS at school first in the context of sex education. It may be better to educate children about AIDS before they think, or know, much about sex and sexuality.

Another reason for introducing AIDS education before (or apart from) sex education is that parents generally find it very difficult to talk to their children about sex (e.g., Huston, Martin, & Foulds, 1990). Even parents who have open and smooth communication with their children often avoid this topic or discuss it clumsily. For instance, one of my colleagues simply left articles on condoms and AIDS on her refrigerator door for her teenager children to peruse. Another—when sent out to get summer-camp supplies for her teenage son—asked offhandedly whether she should also get some condoms. Her son responded with feigned exasperation, "Why can't I have normal parents?" That ended the discussion.

In the project on mother–adolescent communication mentioned earlier, some mothers (especially Latina mothers) were grateful for the opportunity to talk to their children about sexuality and AIDS. They told us that they somehow never managed to find time to talk to their children about these topics. When they managed to do so, as part of this project, how did they talk to their children? First, they were didactic, and they dominated the conversation (Lefkowitz et al., in press). Second, they tended to emphasize the "do's and don'ts" (e.g., Lefkowitz, 1995; see also Sigelman, Derenowski, Mullaney, & Siders, 1993a) rather than explanations for why those behaviors might be safe or unsafe. Such conversations are dramatically different from parent–child conversations on other topics. As noted earlier, children often ask their parents why things happen and how things work, and their parents typically respond with interesting causal explanations. It will be helpful if parents can draw on this kind of rapport when they talk to their children about AIDS. One possible application of our approach is to help parents talk to their children about AIDS on familiar territories—by talking about how things work and why things happen. If parents and children can begin a dialogue on AIDS by talking about the causal mechanism for AIDS transmission without even mentioning sex, they may stand a better chance later to have more meaningful and fruitful AIDS conversations.

To put it simply, our (rather radical) approach is to ask children to think about biology first, not sex. In other words, we want to explore an effective way of helping preadolescents develop a coherent conceptual framework for learning and reasoning about AIDS transmission first without complicating matters by talking about sex. We hope that such a conceptual framework will allow them to integrate and assimilate information about the relation between AIDS and sexual behaviors correctly when they later receive sex education.

III. A New Approach to AIDS Education: Building a Coherent Conception of HIV Transmission

In much of recent research on conceptual change and development, children have been characterized as theory builders eager to try to make sense of the world. As already mentioned, the naive theories that they try to construct are thought of as commonsense conceptual frameworks that cover a number of important domains: naive mechanics, psychology, chemistry, and biology. They outline the ontology and basic causal devices in their respective domains, thereby offering coherent bases for reasoning about relevant phenomena.

To develop a coherent set of beliefs in any domain, it is important to integrate information and individual concepts into the broader framework in that domain. So, why should we treat learning about AIDS any differently? To develop a coherent understanding of AIDS, why not integrate beliefs about AIDS into a framework that will offer a coherent basis for children to reason about AIDS transmission and prevention? Yet, a comprehensive review of AIDS education programs (experimental and otherwise) revealed that "most interventions have been based on an informal blend of logic and practical experience. Ten years into the AIDS epidemic, published AIDS-risk-reduction efforts that have been based on formal conceptualizations of any kind are exceedingly rare" (Fisher & Fisher, 1992, p. 463; see also Leviton, 1989). Moreover, existing AIDS education programs tend to focus on imparting factual knowledge to children rather than encouraging them to reason about novel situations (Walsh, 1995). When AIDS education programs are evaluated, children are rarely asked to reason about novel situations or asked about the causal mechanism for AIDS transmission (e.g., Ashworth, DuRant, Newman, & Gaillard, 1992; Schonfeld O'Hare, Perrin, Quackenbush, Showalter, & Cicchetti, 1995; see also Fisher & Fisher, 1992). Such lack of interest (and faith) in children's ability to reason coherently, and their conceptual basis for reasoning, is in stark contrast to what is going on in the field of conceptual development.

We propose that, in order to help children develop an understanding of AIDS that allows them to reason about AIDS transmission and prevention sensibly and coherently, it is crucial to embed beliefs about AIDS into children's intuitive biology. But do children have any intuitive theory about biological kinds? When do children begin to construct their first autonomous biology? These remain hotly debated questions.

A. When Do Children Construct Their First
     Naive Biology?

Young children, Carey (1985, 1991) proposed, probably begin with a naive mechanics and a naive psychology, and they may stretch these theories to domains about which they have not yet developed any theories. Carey marshaled considerable evidence that young children use their knowledge about people to reason about other biological kinds. Thus, a naive biology might emerge from a naive psychology, and children might not construct their first autonomous biology until age 10 or so. In response to this important and controversial proposal, substantial research efforts have been devoted to studying children's early knowledge about biological kinds. They focus generally on two kinds of biological knowledge: (a) the ontological distinction between biological and nonbiological kinds, and (b) biological processes, causal principles, and causal mechanisms.

1. The Ontological Distinction between Biological and Nonbiological Kinds

To date, there is rather compelling evidence that preschool children begin to distinguish plants and animals from human artifacts. For instance, 3- and 4-year-olds begin to appreciate that plants and animals, despite their salience differences, can grow and heal themselves without human intervention, whereas human artifacts cannot (e.g., Backscheider, Shatz, & Gelman, 1993; Hickling & Gelman, 1995; Keil, 1994). But important questions remain: How should we interpret preschool children's ability to distinguish plants and animals from human artifacts? Does it simply reflect the influence of input, namely, what children hear adults say about plants, animals, artifacts? Or, does it reflect an appreciation of an ontological distinction between biological kinds versus nonbiological kinds? One way to address these questions is to find out if, and how, children apply this distinction to novel entities such as germs.

Keil asked kindergartners, second graders, and fourth graders the following questions about poison (in powder or tiny pellets) and germs: Does it move on its own? Is it alive? Does it change size inside you? He concluded that there were "clear contrasts among biological and nonbiological agents in children as young as 5 years old, even though the agents are relatively unfamiliar and are invisible" (Keil, 1992, p. 124). However, because children's response rates were not compared to chance level, it remains unclear whether the children reliably attributed these properties to germs. In fact, the percentages of kindergartners answering Yes to each of these questions hovered around 50%; the percentages for the fourth graders hovered around 75%; those for the second graders lay somewhere in between. So, while these children seemed more likely to attribute these properties to germs than to poison, their tendency to attribute the properties to germs might not become above chance level until fourth grade (or roughly age 9 or 10). In some sense, we are back to Square One. Namely, we started with Carey (1985) arguing that children do not begin constructing an autonomous biological until age 9 or 10. Although there is some evidence that younger children can attribute growth and self-healing to familiar things, such as plants and animals but not artifacts, it remains unclear whether such ability reflects a conceptual distinction between biological and nonbiological kinds or merely piecemeal knowledge about these object categories.

To address this question, we asked 179 children individually whether an animal, a plant, an artifact, a mineral, and a germ "can grow bigger" and "will die someday" (Au & Romo, 1995). We chose these attributes because we wanted to focus children on particular relevant features rather than to ask about the more abstract concept "alive," which is known to be difficult for young children (e.g., Carey, 1985; Hatano, Siegler, Richards, Inagaki, Stavy, & Wax, 1993; Richards & Siegler, 1986; Stavy & Wax, 1989) or the less biologically relevant concept "will change size inside you" (see also Gelman, 1996). Each child was shown line drawings of, for instance, a dog, a tree, a chair, a rock, and a tiny speck (representing a germ)—one picture at a time. For each picture, the child would hear, "See this X? Can it grow bigger? Will it die someday?", where "X" was a label for the depicted object. The presentation orders of questions and stimulus objects were randomized and counterbalanced across children. The children ranged in age from 5 to 8; 76 of them attended an ethnically diverse university labora-tory school, and the remaining 103 attended two schools serving predomi-nantly low-income, Latino communities. They were tested individually at their school. Depending on their preference, the Latino children were tested in either English or Spanish. In addition, 53 college students at UCLA were asked individually "Can germs grow bigger?" and "Will a germ die someday?"

By age 5, about 75% of the lab school children consistently attributed the biological properties "can grow bigger" and "will die someday" to animals and plants but not artifacts and minerals. (To be credited as "consis-tently" correct, a child had to answer at least seven of the eight questions about these two properties for the four object categories correctly.) The low-income schoolchildren lagged by about 2 years. We were especially interested in what children would say about germs. Would they use their intuitions about core attributes of familiar living things (e.g., can grow bigger; will die someday) and nonliving things (e.g., cannot grow bigger; will not die) to categorize novel entities (e.g., a germ)? Because germs are not readily perceptible, children receive information about germs primar-ily—and probably exclusively—through language. If we can find out what they are likely to hear about germs, we can have a reasonably good charac-terization of the input to children about germs. We can then try to sort out which aspects of children's conception of germs can be easily accounted for by input from adults and which aspects have to be constructed by children.

"Will a germ die someday?" In our sample of 53 adults, 83% said Yes. Together with various television commercials for antibacterial soap, dish detergent, and mouthwash, these data suggest that most children probably have heard from adults and/or the media about killing germs. It would be straightforward for children to conclude that germs will die someday. But what about "Can germs grow bigger?" In our sample, only a small minority of adults (32%) answered Yes to this question. The rest said "No" (25%), "Don't know" (5%), or reinterpreted the question and said, "Yes, they can multiply/spread" (32%). In hindsight, we wish we had asked adults "Can *a germ* grow bigger?"—which would have been more similar to the question posed to the children—instead of "Can *germs* grow bigger?" The latter wording lends itself to the interpretation "Can a colony of germs grow bigger?" as well as the intended one, namely, "Can individual germs grow bigger?" Nonetheless, it seems that few adults endorse the idea that individual germs will grow bigger. Our guess is that even fewer adults would spontaneously tell children that individual germs can grow bigger. If children think that a germ can grow bigger in size, it is unlikely that they got this idea from adults.

Do children think that germs can grow bigger and will die someday? Before we could answer this question, we had to consider whether the children in our study understood the questions and felt at ease enough to tell us what they thought. Because the children from the two predominantly Latino schools typically came from working-class backgrounds or families of recently arrived immigrants, they may not have felt at ease in the testing situation (cf. Brice, 1983). In fact, both of our interviewers—who were native speakers of Spanish and of Latino heritage—noted that the youngest children in the two predominantly Latino schools tended to be more bashful and less talkative than their age peers in the lab school. Moreover, because modesty about the human body is quite prevalent in the Latino culture, Latino children may have fewer opportunities to hear adults at home talk explicitly about various biological functions in connection with the human body, which might be primarily how children to learn about the biological-nonbiological distinction (cf. Carey, 1985). This may in part account for the lag between the lab school children and the low socioeconomic status (SES) Latino children for the mastery of this distinction.

To deal with these concerns, we decided to focus our analysis on the 111 children who had a perfect or near-perfect response pattern (giving seven or more correct answers out of eight) for the animal, plant, artifact, and mineral items. We wanted to know whether, and how, children apply their conceptual distinction between familiar living things (e.g., plants and animals) and nonliving things (e.g., minerals and artifacts) to germs. For the germ questions, 22% of these 111 children gave the "adult" response pattern (i.e., "Germs will die but cannot grow bigger."). Interestingly, many more children seemed to have generalized the common differences between familiar biological and nonbiological kinds in thinking about germs. That is, 44% of the children, much more often than expected by chance, said that a germ could grow bigger as well as would die someday ("biological" response pattern; $p < .001$, 2-tailed binomial test, with chance level at 25%). Another 18% said that a germ would neither die nor grow bigger ("nonbiological" response pattern). The remaining 16% of the children, for some reasons not immediately clear to us, said that a germ can grow bigger but will not die ("other" response pattern). It seems, then, as children learn about the distinction between familiar biological and nonbiological kinds, they sometimes will overgeneralize what they know about familiar living and nonliving things to novel entities such as germs.

The distribution of children's response patterns varied as a function of age as well as cultural/socioeconomic background. As shown in Fig. 1, at age 5, both the lab school children and the low-income, predominantly Latino children favored the "biological" pattern and "adult" pattern roughly equally. In the lab school, children began to favor the biological pattern reliably from age 6 on ($p < .05$, 2-tailed binomial test, with chance level at 25%). By contrast, in the two low-income, predominantly Latino schools, the adult pattern was marginally favored by 43% of the 6-year-olds ($p < .06$, 1-tailed binomial test); the biological pattern was favored by the 7- and 8-year-olds over the other patterns only very slightly, and the preference was far from being reliable.

These results suggest that, even before school age, some children can apply their inchoate understanding of the biological-nonbiological distinction to novel entities as well as familiar ones. However, the age at which children begin to do so also seems to vary substantially across cultural/SES backgrounds. In our study, the low SES, Latino children lagged behind the lab school children by 2 to 3 years in their attribution of core biological properties and in their application of the distinction between familiar living and nonliving things to novel entities such as germs. Can input account for such substantial differences between these two school populations? How readily can such differences be reduced via educational intervention? What implications might such differences have for AIDS education?

To develop a coherent understanding of AIDS, as noted earlier, it is crucial to embed beliefs about AIDS in one's intuitive beliefs about biological kinds. From health educators' and researchers' perspective, it is critical to know more about (a) how the developmental course and/or timetable for children's beliefs about biological kinds might vary across cultural and socioeconomic backgrounds, (b) how the input provided to children might vary across backgrounds, and (c) how input might affect children's beliefs

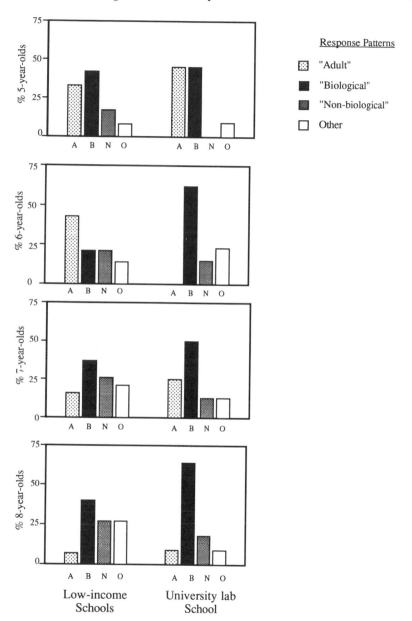

Fig. 1.   Percentages of children giving various patterns of attributing core biological functions (growth, death) to germs.

about biological kinds. Only by taking into account children's conception of biological kinds can we talk to them coherently about AIDS, or any biological phenomenon for that matter.

2. Biological Processes, Causal Principles, and Causal Mechanisms

In addition to outlining the ontology in a domain, a framework theory should also specify basic causal devices in that domain, thereby offering coherent bases for reasoning about relevant phenomena (e.g., Wellman & Gelman, 1992). It is no coincidence that basic causal devices or mechanisms constitute a major battleground for the debate on when children construct their first autonomous biology. At issue is whether young children know any causal mechanisms or devices that are uniquely biological. Researchers such as Hatano and Inagaki (1994), Keil (1992, 1994), and Springer (1995; Springer & Keil, 1991; Springer, Nguyen, Samaniego, in press; Springer & Ruckel, 1992) have argued that, prior to age 6 or 7, children understand some causal principles in the domain of biological kinds. On the other hand, Carey (1985, 1991, 1995; Carey & Spelke, 1994), Atran (1994), and Solomon (1995; Solomon & Cassimatis, 1995; Solomon, 1996 Johnson, Zaitchik, & Carey, 1996) have argued that children's early knowledge of biological kinds does not include explicit biological causal principles.

At first glance, underneath all the arguments between these two camps lies a consensus. Namely, most if not all participants of this debate seem to agree that, by age 6 or 7, children can understand some causal principles for explaining biological phenomena. Even Carey (1995, p. 299) now agrees that she "underestimated the age at which children construct their first autonomous biology (but not by much—I [i.e., Carey] would lower the age from 10 to 6–7)." Upon scrutiny, however, much of the research generated by this debate has focused on biological processes, input–output relations, causal agents (e.g., vital force, essence, innards), and so forth, rather than causal devices or mechanisms per se.

By age 4 or 5, children begin to distinguish *biological processes* from psychological ones. They seem to think that some processes (e.g., growth, breathing) cannot be stopped by intention alone. For instance, people cannot prevent an animal from growing, just because they want it to remain small and cute (Inagaki & Hatano, 1987). They also recognize that bodily processes and psychological processes tend to be modified by different means. For example, running speed can be modified by exercise and diet; forgetfulness can be modified by mental monitoring (Inagaki & Hatano, 1993).

Coley (1995) has found a dissociation of biological versus psychological properties among children as young as age 6. Kindergartners attributed biological properties such as "has blood" and "sleeps" to predatory and domestic animals at the same rate, but attributed psychological properties such as "can feel happy" and "can feel scared" more to domestic animals. By age 8, the pattern is even stronger and there is a double dissociation between biological and psychological processes. That is, 8-year-olds use taxonomic groups (e.g., mammals, birds, reptiles, fish) as a basis for attributing biological but not psychological properties. They use the predatory versus domestic distinction to attribute psychological (e.g., "can feel pain," "is smart," "can feel scared") but not biological properties.

Preschool children also seem to think that "growth" is a process unique to plants and animals. From age 6 on, children begin to extend its domain of application to germs (Au & Romo, 1995). Preschoolers also understand that growth and development are constrained in specific ways: Animals get bigger not smaller and become structurally more complex not simpler (e.g., from caterpillar to butterfly and not vice versa; Rosengren, Gelman, Kalish, & McCormick, 1991).

Children's early knowledge of parent–child resemblance goes beyond descriptions of how individual living things change. For instance, preschool children expect that animals of the same family, more so than unrelated but similar-looking animals, share certain properties (e.g., tiny bones, ability to see in the dark; Springer, 1992). They also expect that race is inherited and unaffected by upbringing. That is, a baby shares racial characteristics with the biological parents rather than adoptive parents (Hirschfeld, 1994). Whether children project novel characteristics (e.g., pink heart, tiny bones, can see in the dark) from birth parents but not adoptive parents to birth/adoptive children remains an open question (e.g., Solomon, 1995; Solomon et al., 1996; Springer, 1995). Nonetheless, children's inchoate understanding of parent–child resemblance seems to include some kind of causal relations. For lack of better terminology, we will call it an *"input–output" relations.* Simply put, input = some characteristics of the parents; output = similar characteristics in their baby. How the input is turned into the output—that is, the causal mechanism—however, remains unspecified (see also Carey, 1995). We will take up this issue again.

To date, there are several proposals about causal principles in children's intuitive conception of biological kinds: vitalistic causality (Hatano & Inagaki, 1994; Inagaki & Hatano, 1993), functional–teleological explanations (Keil, 1992, 1994), essence (S. Gelman, Coley, & Gottfried, 1994), and innards (e.g., R. Gelman, 1990). While each proposal has considerable empirical support, it remains unclear to what extent the proposed *causal agents* are uniquely biological. Are there analogs in the domain of nonbiological kinds? For instance, how different is "vital force" from "fuel" in getting some machinery (human and otherwise) to work? How different is the essence for biological kinds from that for chemicals? How do innards differ for biological versus nonbiological kinds? Perhaps, more importantly, none of the proposed causal principles offers any explicit causal mechanisms or devices. What might the causal chain of events look like? How do the proposed causal agents such as "vital force," "essence," or "innards" work?

B. Do Children Understand any Uniquely Biological Causal Mechanism or Causal Device?

Because we are interested in how to help children build a coherent conception of AIDS—with the understanding of a causal mechanism for HIV transmission at its core—we will take a close look at the few studies that explicitly examined children's beliefs about causal mechanisms for biological phenomena. Consider Inagaki and Hatano's (1993) attempt to compare children's preference for intentional, vitalistic, and mechanical causal explanations for biological phenomena. They asked children why we eat food every day. Children were asked to choose among three explanations: "Because we want to eat tasty food" (intentional); "Because our stomach takes in vital power from the food" (vitalistic); "Because we take the food into our body after its form is changed in the stomach and bowels" (mechanical). When asked why we take in air, children were asked to choose from: "Because we want to feel good" (intentional); "Because our chest takes in vital power from the air" (vitalistic); "Because the lungs take in oxygen and change it into useless carbon dioxide" (mechanical). The main findings were: Six-year-olds in the study chose vitalistic explanations as most plausible most often; they chose those explanations 54% of the time. Eight-year-olds chose vitalistic explanations only 34% of the time; they generally preferred mechanical explanations (62% of the choices). Adults overwhelmingly preferred mechanical explanations (96%).

Springer and Keil (1991) also found that, by age 6 or 7, children favored mechanical causality over other kinds of causal mechanisms (e.g., genetic, intentional) in explaining, for instance, how a baby flower may get its blue color or how a puppy may get its brown fur color. As in Inagaki and Hatano's study, children in this study were offered three kinds of possible explanations: "The mother flower wanted her baby to be blue just like her. Because she wanted the baby to be blue, she gave it some very tiny things that went into the seed and turned the baby flower blue" (intentional); "Some very tiny blue pieces went from the mother to the baby flower. These tiny blue pieces went into the seed and got all over the baby flower. Because they got into the baby flower's petals, the baby flower turned blue" (mechanical); "Some very tiny colorless things went from the mother to the baby flower. These tiny things put the blue color together in the baby flower. Even though these tiny things aren't any color, they could make the baby flower blue" (genetic).

The mechanical account (or what Springer and Keil [1991] called the "gemmulic account") was a clear winner among these possible explanations. It was judged best by the 6-year-olds nearly 80% of the time. Note that an important difference between the winner and the losers is that the mechanical account specify a simple mechanical transfer of color pigment, whereas the genetic and the intentional accounts did not. Together with Inagaki and Hatano's (1993) findings, it seems that mechanical causality is the mechanism of choice during middle childhood for explaining biological phenomena.

This is reminiscent of Carey's (1985) idea that children begin to see the human body as a machine sometime during middle childhood. One caveat: In both of the studies just described, children were asked to chose among two or three possible mechanisms, rather than to generate one on their own. As Carey (1995) pointed out, it is very difficult to make different explanations types comparable with respect to the informativeness of the explanation and familiarity with the information it contains. So, when children chose one type of explanation over another, it is no easy matter to figure out why they did so.

While we fully appreciate Carey's critique of Inagaki and Hatano's (1993) and Springer and Keil's (1991) methodology, we also think mechanical causality is probably indeed the mechanism of choice for young children trying to understand biological phenomena. For one thing, mechanical causality is something that young children are quite experts on. From infancy on, children know and rapidly learn quite a lot about physical objects. Their naive mechanics allows them to appreciate that objects (hidden and otherwise) will move in accordance with principles such as cohesion, solidity, contact, and continuity. In other words, they have considerable knowledge about how object and substances behave. Namely, objects are connected bodies that maintain their connectedness as they move; two objects cannot intersect in time and space; objects move together only if they are in contact; an object must move on a connected path (e.g., Carey & Spelke, 1994; Spelke & Hermer, 1996; Wellman & Gelman, 1992). So, before children understand any uniquely biological mechanisms, it seems reasonable for them to apply their naive mechanics—a rather well-worked-out belief system—to reason about living things as well as nonliving things.

Another obvious candidate for the job, of course, is naive psychology. In fact, Carey (1985, 1991, 1995) has suggested that young children use their knowledge about people to reason about other biological kinds. Thus, a naive biology might emerge from a naive psychology. But several findings argue against this proposal. First, as already noted, children appreciate the

ontological distinction between biological and nonbiological kinds by age
6 or so, if not earlier. By then, they also begin to differential psychological
processes and properties from biological ones (e.g., Coley, 1995; Inagaki &
Hatano, 1993; Springer & Keil, 1991).

An early differentiation between psychological and biological processes—20/20 hindsight—perhaps should not have come as a surprise.
There is considerable evidence that even preschoolers can distinguish mental and physical entities (e.g., a cookie in a dream vs. a cookie in real life)
and processes (e.g., thinking about eating a cookie vs. actually eating a
cookie; Wellman, 1990; Wellman & Estes, 1986). If children have to stretch
either their naive psychology or naive mechanics to reason about biological
processes, they might opt for naive mechanics because—like mechanical
processes—most biological processes (e.g., growth, healing, reproduction)
act on physical rather than metaphysical matter. That is, while both mechanical and biological processes typically have to do with changes in physical
matter, psychological processes typically affect thoughts, feelings, and at
times behaviors. So, before children understand any uniquely biological
mechanisms, it may be more natural for them to stretch their naive mechanics rather than naive psychology to explain biological phenomena.

If we are on the right track, we should find children using mechanical
causality to explain biological phenomena from early on. We have just
started collecting evidence for early use of mechanical causality to explain
reproduction, diseases, and so forth. We will begin with an anecdote that
inspired our hypothesis.

A child we know asked, at age 2 years 9 months, where she was when
her mother planted the orange tree in their backyard and was told that she
was in her mother's tummy. She then wanted to know where she was when
her mother planted the lemon tree in their front yard. The mother said,
"You weren't even in my tummy yet." The child was visibly upset about
her nonexistence once upon a time. The mother relented and explained,
"Half of you was in my tummy; the other half, in Daddy's tummy." The
child went away happy but came back in a few minutes to ask, "Were my
feet in Daddy's tummy?"

The mother was determined to help the child supplant this mechanical
explanation with a proper one, namely, a biological one. She explained
that the two halves did not have arms and legs; instead each half was like
a little egg (without the shell, she emphasized); the two little eggs mixed
together and then grew into a baby. The toddler nodded and talked about
this matter-of-factly a few times in the ensuing weeks. Her mother was
pleased with the progress until the child asked one day, "How did I get into
your tummy? Did Dr. Wilkinson cut open your tummy to put me inside?"

The notion of procreation is a tough nut for children to crack. How can children reconcile the concept of object permanence in their naive mechanics with the transition from nonexistence to existence in reproduction of biological kinds? The toddler in this case went with her intuitions about mechanical causality. We have seen other children do this too. In a study of children's beliefs about germs, we asked some 8- and 9-year-olds, "There are a few germs on a piece of fish inside a plastic bag. What will happen in a couple of days? Will there be more germs, fewer germs, or the same number of germs? Why?" 31% of the 13 8-year-olds and 22% of the 23 9-year-olds explained their predictions about the number of germs by invoking mechanical causality. Some examples are: "Same number of germs—because no germs can get through the plastic;" "More germs— because the fish will get more germs from the plain plastic bag. There might be dirt in that bag." Eight percent of the 8-year-olds and 22% of the 9-year-olds correctly explained that there would be more germs because the germs would divide or multiply.

We also asked these children to consider, "Some bad germs got inside a kid's body. She felt okay for a day. But then the next day she started to feel sick all over her whole body. Why did it take a whole day for her to feel sick after the germs got inside her body?" Sixty-two percent of the 13 8-year-olds failed to give any meaningful explanation. But 15% of them did explain that it took time for enough germs to get inside the girl's body. Eight percent of the 8-year-olds and 41% of the 22 9-year-olds explained that it took time for the germs to get to different parts of the girl's body. Only 9% of the 9-year-olds explained that it took time for the germs to multiply/reproduce inside the girl's body.

Together, this modest amount of data suggests that children invoke mechanical causality to explain biological phenomena from probably age 2 or 3 on. This tendency seems to persist into middle and late childhood, even though by that age children have a fair amount of biological knowledge. These findings, if proved to be robust, can have implications for both basic and applied research on conceptual changes in the domain of biology. First, if children's naive biology turns out to emerge from some other naive theory, as Carey (1985, 1991, 1995) suggests, it may well emerge from children's naive mechanics instead of (or in addition to) their naive psychology. Second, to date, no study has demonstrated that children understand any uniquely biological causal devices or mechanisms prior to age 9. Even counting our just-summarized findings of children's beliefs about food spoilage and infection incubation, only a small proportion of 8- and 9-year-old children spontaneously invoked a biological mechanism (e.g., germ reproduction) to explain biological phenomena in their everyday life. Despite the discovery of rather impressive and impressively early knowledge about biological kinds, we need to be cautious in attributing the status of an autonomous biology to such knowledge structure (see also Atran, 1994, 1995; Carey, 1995; Solomon et al., 1996). To credit children with an autonomous biology, we need to know what might its domain-specific causal devices and mechanisms look like.

This discussion also directly bears on applied issues such as science and health education. A case in point: A coherent understanding of AIDS transmission should include knowledge of a causal mechanism for AIDS transmission. To help children build such a coherent conception, we cannot take it for granted that they have the pertinent biological causal mechanism, or any biological mechanism for that matter, in their repertoire. This is precisely why we have made a causal mechanism for AIDS transmission the focus of our experimental AIDS curriculum.

IV. How to Help Children Understand a Basic Causal Mechanism for AIDS Transmission

In collaboration with a health specialist and a demonstration teacher at the UCLA Seeds University Elementary School, we developed a three-lesson plan for discussing several concepts relevant to understanding the causal mechanism for AIDS transmission. The discussion plan was used in the *Experimental* Condition. We have also consulted with biomedical experts on campus to make sure that the information presented in our AIDS curriculum was accurate.

In order to compare our experimental AIDS curriculum module to existing AIDS education offered in schools, we developed a parallel discussion plan for the *Control* Condition according to the AIDS curriculum published by the National Catholic Educational Association (1992), which was favored by the school in which this study was conducted. The discussion in both conditions was led by us (a faculty member and two graduate students at UCLA specializing in cognitive development). We tried to make the two conditions as similar as possible for aspects that are not central to the target concepts.

A.   EXPERIMENTAL CONDITION

1.   *Lesson 1: Germs Are Microscopic*

Children saw color slides of germs (viruses, bacteria, fungi), including the HIV. The narration emphasized that:

  1. Germs come in all shapes and sizes.

2. Some germs are good (e.g., certain yeast cells for making bread, certain bacteria for making yogurt), and some germs are bad (e.g., disease-causing germs).

3. Germs are so small that we cannot see individual germs with the naked eye.

4. When germs are in large numbers (e.g., in colonies), we can see them.

They also viewed germs (*E. coli* and, a kind of relatively large bacteria, *Bacillus megaterium*) and human blood cells through light microscopes (400 times magnification).

We began our experimental curriculum in this way because we wanted children to appreciate that the AIDS virus is just one kind of germ, and that they should reason about the HIV rationally just as they should about other kinds of germs. We also hoped that children would appreciate that, although extremely small and not readily perceptible, germs are nonetheless tiny organisms fundamentally similar to other bigger and more familiar living things. To try to convince children that germs are living things, we asked them to contribute germs to the nutrient agar in several petri dishes. We invited them to get their hands dirty (e.g., handling coins, touching the floor) and then touch the agar, to spit into the agar, or to use a cotton swab to scrape their teeth and then touch the agar with it. The petri dishes were then covered and kept at roughly 95° F (in a styrofoam cooler with a small light bulb) for a week until Lesson 2.

2. Lesson 2: Germs Can Reproduce and Die

Children visually inspected the yellow and white spots (bacteria colonies) and moldy spots on their agar culture from the previous week. We discussed the idea of how certain places are suitable or friendly environments for germs to live and reproduce. For example, many bacteria live and reproduce best in a warm and moist environment where there is plenty of food for them (e.g., nutrient agar gel kept in an incubator). That was why we found colonies of bacteria (i.e., the yellow and white spots) on the nutrient agar in our petri dishes. Children also saw color slides of different modes of reproduction for germs (with narration): mold spores, yeast cells budding, bacteria dividing, and HIV bursting out of a human white blood cell.

We also demonstrated how chlorine bleach can kill germs. We put a few drops of bleach on the bacteria and mold colonies in the petri dishes. The colonies were gone instantly, and the agar became clear again. We then talked about the notion that germs, like other living things, can die as well as reproduce.

Children then participated in a discussion on environments where the HIV can reproduce/multiply quickly (e.g., fresh human blood), where the

HIV will die quickly (e.g., air, water), and where it can live and possibly reproduce very slowly, if at all (e.g., human saliva). We also told children that the story with saliva is still unclear and that scientists are still working on it. We agonized over whether to talk about this element of uncertainty regarding saliva and decided to discuss it because we did not want to talk down to children by just telling them to learn a few facts. We wanted to challenge them by presenting to them the complexity of the issues.

Along with our discussion points about the uncertainty of the saliva as an ecological environment for the AIDS virus, we added some reassuring facts to help children think about this issue sensibly. Throughout the lesson, we emphasized that there is not a single documented case of HIV infection through saliva alone. (By contrast, there is at least one documented case of transmission through breast milk.) We repeatedly emphasized that the AIDS virus dies in air and water very quickly. So, there is no need to worry about saliva if it is exposed to air or water for a while. For instance, even if someone who has the AIDS virus sneezes or coughs, and the tiny droplets of their saliva have the AIDS virus, the virus will be dead on arrival and therefore can do no harm when it travels through the air to another person.

We, of course, still had to tackle the problem of how to talk to children about direct exchange of saliva (e.g., French kissing, mouth-to-mouth resuscitation). We decided to encourage caution for several reasons. First, we do know that the AIDS virus can live and perhaps reproduce slowly in human saliva. Second, while to date there is not a single documented case of transmission through saliva alone, there might be one in the future. Consider the case of breast milk. While scientists had known for some time that the AIDS virus can live and reproduce in human breast milk, they did not know that the virus can be passed from a mother to her baby through breast milk until the first well-documented case of such transmission (i.e., Elizabeth Glazer's case). Third, we need to think more broadly about our health and think about other infectious diseases besides AIDS. For instance, very serious infectious diseases such as hepatitis B can be passed readily through saliva from one person to another. So, we suggested to children that minimizing direct exchange of saliva seems like a good health practice.

3.   Lesson 3: Relating Ecological Environments for the HIV to AIDS Risks of Various Human Behaviors

The ecological environments for the HIV were reviewed: The HIV can reproduce rapidly in human blood (and probably breast milk); it can survive or reproduce slowly in saliva; it will die in air and water. The main idea is that different kinds of bodily fluids vary in how "friendly" they are to the AIDS virus. As children learn more about different kinds of bodily fluids, it is important that they find out how hospitable each fluid is to the AIDS virus. We then tried to help children link the information about ecological environments for the AIDS virus (i.e., friendly, hostile, or neutral environments) to the likelihood of transmission for various human behaviors or events. For instance, "You should not worry about getting AIDS from sharing a toilet seat with someone who carries the AIDS virus because the AIDS virus will die in the air quickly"; "You should avoid touching another person's cut because his/her blood—which might have live AIDS virus— could get into your body, if there are tiny cuts on your hands that you have not noticed."

We then asked children to come up with some safe and unsafe behaviors with respect to AIDS transmission. We also asked them to explain why each behavior is safe or unsafe. Children were encouraged to use the concepts of "friendly," "hostile," and "neutral" environment for the AIDS virus to reason about the AIDS risk of each behavior brought up in the class discussion.

4. The Core of the Curriculum

Together, these three lessons were designed to help children understand a basic causal mechanism for AIDS transmission. The mechanism can be summarized as follows: The AIDS virus is a living thing, and so it can reproduce, stay alive, and will die in various environments. For instance, it can reproduce rapidly in people's fresh blood; it can stay alive but perhaps reproduce slowly in people's saliva; it will die quickly in the air and water. Importantly, the AIDS virus is harmful (i.e., it can infect people to make them sick) only when it is alive, and the dead virus is harmless. This causal mechanism can potentially serve as a coherent basis for deciding about which behaviors are safe or unsafe with respect to AIDS transmission.

This mechanism is inherently biological because the biology of the AIDS virus is at its core. It matters a great deal what kind of ecological environment the AIDS virus has to travel through to get from an infected person to an uninfected one. So, the path the AIDS virus has to traverse—and the mechanical causality—is only part of the story. The ecology of the path and how it might affect the biology of the AIDS virus (e.g., reproduction, survival, death) is an equally important part of the story.

Like other explicit biological mechanisms, this simple causal mechanism for AIDS transmission is conspicuously absent from elementary school children's rather sophisticated belief systems about biological kinds. Consider, if you will, the domain of diseases. By age 4 or 5, most children know that germs can make people sick (e.g., Au et al., 1993; Kalish, in press; Springer & Belk, 1994). By age 6 or 7, many children attribute core biological properties (e.g., can grow bigger, will die someday) to germs (e.g., Au & Romo, 1995). However, even 9- and 10-year-olds seem to think that if a germ is chopped up into tiny pieces, it will still make people sick (e.g., Keil, 1992). In fact, the kindergartners, second graders, and fourth graders in Keil's study were as likely to say that chopped-up germs can make people sick as to say that chopped-up poison pellets can cause sickness. To jump a bit ahead of our story, we also found that the fourth, sixth, and eighth graders in the Control Condition of our study guessed at chance level when asked on the posttest, "Is the AIDS virus dangerous only when it is alive?" Only about 50% of the children in each grade responded Yes.

In short, we think that the core of our experimental AIDS curriculum— namely, a biological causal mechanism for AIDS transmission—is not in most elementary school or even junior high school students' repertoire of biological knowledge. On the other hand, we also think that it is simple enough that it can be readily taught to school-age children. Once they understand this causal mechanism, they might be able to use it as a coherent basis for deciding about which behaviors are safe or unsafe with respect to AIDS transmission.

B.   CONTROL CONDITION

1.   Lesson 1: Germs Are Microscopic

The lesson was similar to that of the Experimental condition except that the portion on germ reproduction was replaced with a "traveling germs" game. The game emphasized how germs—invisible to the naked eye, can be spread from one person to another in all sorts of ways. In short, it focused on the mechanical transfer rather than the biology of germs.

We then discussed how risky behaviors for catching a cold are very different from those for getting AIDS. For example, by the end of the discussion, children agreed that a cold virus could be spread from one person to another through coughing and sneezing, but the AIDS virus could not be spread in these ways.

2.   Lesson 2: Coping with AIDS

Children watched a videotape called "What's in the news: Coping with AIDS" (Swartz, 1989). The topics included: What does the acronym "AIDS" stand for? What are the most common ways of getting the AIDS virus? In what ways do people infected with the AIDS virus have to suffer socially (e.g., losing rights to choose where to live, attend school, and work) as well as physically? Children participated in a focused discussion on these topics.

3.   Lesson 3: AIDS Risks for Various Behaviors

We used the issues raised by the videotape in Lesson 2 as a context for children to talk about how people can and cannot get AIDS. We helped children reason about whether it is right or wrong to ban infected children from schools, or infected athletes from sports, by getting children to think about how risky various behaviors are with respect to getting the AIDS virus. For instance, children were told that they should not worry if a child with the AIDS virus attends their school because there is NO RISK of getting AIDS from casual contact such as shaking hands or sharing a toilet seat with someone who carries the AIDS virus. The same is true for sports participants. Because only casual contact is involved in sports, there is no need to worry. We did discuss that players should avoid touching another person's cut or wound because the AIDS virus has been found in human blood. So, touching another person's cut is a RISKY behavior because one may get AIDS this way.

As in the Experimental condition, we faced the challenge of how to discuss the risk of kissing with exchange of saliva, given the uncertainty of HIV infection through saliva. Again, we emphasized that there is not a single documented case of HIV infection through saliva alone. But we decided to classify French kissing as a VERY LOW RISK behavior instead of NO RISK behavior for reasons already discussed in our description of the Experimental condition.

To make sure that children in both the Experimental and Control condition received comparable information about the AIDS risk of various behaviors, we compiled a master list of high risk behaviors (e.g., sharing a needle, pregnant women with AIDS passing it on to their unborn babies), possibly low risk behaviors (e.g., kissing with exchange of saliva), and no risk behaviors (e.g., sharing a toilet seat, casual kissing, shaking hands, sharing a swimming pool) and talked about such behaviors in both conditions. The sixth and eighth graders in both conditions mentioned having sex with a person who has AIDS as a high-risk behavior. We acknowledged this fact without elaboration and directed the discussion to other topics.

C.   METHOD

1.   Subjects

The subjects were 87 children enrolled in a middle-class, predominantly Latino, parochial school. They included 30 fourth graders (11 girls, 17 boys, 2 did not report their gender), 30 sixth graders (12 girls, 18 boys), and 27 eighth graders (16 girls, 10 boys, 1 did not report the gender). Over 90% of the parents who had children enrolled in these three grades consented to their children's participation, perhaps because both the parents and the school administration believed that the children were in dire need of AIDS education. The school principal told us that he was concerned that most parents and teachers at his school were very reluctant to talk to children about AIDS transmission and prevention. Although he succeeded in convincing all the teachers at the school to participate in an in-service workshop on AIDS, many of them were still reluctant to talk to their class about AIDS. He had good reasons to be concerned: Latino adolescents are particularly at risk for HIV infection, even though the infection rates are lower for Mexican-Americans than for Puerto Ricans and Cuban-Americans (Crawford & Robinson, 1990; DiClemente, 1990; Scott, Shifman, Orr, Owen, & Fawcett, 1988). Fortunately for us, the school principal's concern translated into strong support for our project. We were invited to tell parents about this project in a parents' meeting at the school. Parents then received our letter describing the project, consent forms, and several reminders (in the school's newsletters) inviting them to support this project.

2. Design and Procedure

This study had a fully experimental design; individual children were randomly assigned to either the Experimental or the Control Condition. We (Au, Romo, and DeWitt) took turns leading the discussion in each condition. At the beginning of each lesson, we gave two name lists to each teacher for dividing his/her class into two groups according to the lists—Group A (the Control condition) and Group B (the Experimental condition). For each grade, the lessons for the two groups were conducted in separate rooms, and the teacher was free to stay in either room during a lesson or to divide his/her time between the two rooms. Children in both conditions participated in three 45-minute weekly lessons (as summarized in the preceding section). The children were asked not to discuss outside their discussion group what they talked about in their group during the project. At the end of the project, we asked the Control group children—in an offhand manner—what they knew about the activities and discussion in the other group. It seemed that they knew little about what had gone on in the Experimental Condition.

The children were given a 10-minute pretest and a 30-minute posttest. Both tests were paper-and-pencil tests; a researcher read each question aloud twice for the children. To put the children at ease and to protect their anonymity, we asked each child to make up a secret code name and to put down the code name instead of his/her real name on the pretest and posttest. To make sure that they would not forget their own code names at the time of posttest, we asked each of them to hide the code name in a sealed envelope to be opened at the posttest.

3. Pretest

The pretest included seven questions about the transmission, seriousness, treatment, and prevention of AIDS. Children saw these questions in a random order rather than the order used here. Children were asked to respond "Yes," "No," or "I don't know" to each question.

1. Can a person get AIDS by sharing a needle with a drug user who has AIDS?
2. Can a pregnant woman with AIDS give AIDS to her unborn baby?
3. Can doctors cure AIDS?
4. Will people with AIDS die from it?
5. Can doctors cure AIDS if they catch it early?
6. Can doctors now use a new vaccine to protect people from AIDS?
7. If people eat healthy foods, can they avoid AIDS?

After administering this short AIDS knowledge questionnaire, we asked children to tell us what they wanted to know most about AIDS. The sixth- and eighth-grade students wrote down their questions privately; the fourth graders told us their questions aloud in class, and we wrote down the questions verbatim. We collected children's questions because the questions may tell us not only what they wanted to know, but also something about their conceptions, misconceptions, and fears about AIDS.

4. Posttest

There were four sections:

a. Ecological Environments for the AIDS Virus Children were asked to consider nine environments: hair, skin, fresh blood, water, air, breast milk, dried blood, saliva, and orange juice. They were asked, "Which environments can the AIDS virus live in? Which environments can the AIDS virus reproduce in? Which environments will the AIDS virus die in?" In the Experimental condition, we discussed human blood, breast milk, saliva, air, and water as various ecological environments for the AIDS virus. This part of the posttest was designed to see if the children in the Experimental condition would be better at correctly classifying these environments than their peers in the Control condition. We were also interested in how children in the Experimental condition might classify environments not discussed in their lessons.

b. The Biology and the Virulence of the HIV Children were asked, "If the AIDS virus is in X, can it make someone sick?" (where X represents dried blood, skin, orange juice, fresh blood, hair, or saliva).

c. AIDS Transmission, Seriousness, and Treatment   The following 11 questions on AIDS transmission were added to, and mixed in randomly with, the seven questions on the pretest. The words in parentheses were not shown to the children; they indicate the ecology of the path traversed by the AIDS virus in each situation.

1. Is the AIDS virus dangerous only when it is alive?
2. Can someone get AIDS by sitting on a toilet seat? (air)
3. Can someone get AIDS by swimming in a small pond with a person who has AIDS? (water)
4. Can someone get AIDS by sharing an ice cream cone with a person who has AIDS? (saliva exposed to air and low temperature)
5. Is it easy to get AIDS if you kiss someone on the mouth who has AIDS? (saliva exposed to air)
6. Can someone get AIDS if they are coughed on or sneezed on by a person who has AIDS? (saliva exposed to air)
7. Can someone get AIDS by sharing a toothbrush with a person who has AIDS? (saliva exposed to air and water)
8. Can someone get AIDS by kissing and exchanging saliva with someone who has AIDS? (saliva with little exposure to air)
9. Can someone get AIDS by wiping a bleeding nose of a person who has AIDS? (blood)
10. Can someone get AIDS from tattooing? (blood)
11. Can someone get AIDS from ear-piercing? (blood, if done with a shared needle)

d. Children's Explanations   Children were asked to explain in writing their answers to five of the questions in the preceding section. Those five questions focused on reasoning about AIDS transmission in situations not widely covered by public AIDS education—tattooing, ear-piercing, wiping an infected person's bleeding nose, swimming in a small pond with an infected person, sharing a toothbrush with an infected person. This section was designed to explore children's reasoning about causal mechanisms for AIDS transmission.

D.   PRETEST RESULTS

1.   Knowledge of Well-Publicized Facts

Most of the fourth, sixth, and eighth grade children in this middle-class, predominantly Latino, parochial school knew several highly publicized facts about AIDS. In the pretest, all of the children in these grades said that a person can get AIDS by sharing a needle with a drug user who has AIDS. Most of them also knew that AIDS is deadly and incurable. Table I presents

TABLE I

PERCENTAGES OF CHILDREN GIVING A CORRECT RESPONSE ON
PRETEST ITEMS

Pretest items	Fourth grade		Sixth grade		Eighth grade	
	Expt (N = 14)	Control (N = 14)	Expt (N = 15)	Control (N = 15)	Expt (N = 11)	Control (N = 15)
1. Sharing a needle	100%	100%	100%	100%	100%	100%
2. Mom to unborn baby	57%	57%	73%	73%	100%	80%
3. No cure	86%	93%	67%	60%	100%	93%
4. Will die from AIDS	79%	64%	93%	80%	82%	93%
5. Cure if caught early	57%	36%	27%	13%	64%	73%
6. New vaccine	36%	14%	7%	0%	36%	27%
7. Healthy foods	21%	36%	80%	47%	100%	93%

the percentages of correct answers on the pretest for each grade and each condition.

2. Knowledge of Less Publicized Facts

Even though these children had learned that AIDS is deadly and there is no cure for it, there were still major gaps in their AIDS knowledge. Most of the fourth- and sixth-grade children did not realize that AIDS cannot be cured even if it is detected early; that there is no effective AIDS vaccine yet; that one cannot avoid AIDS by eating healthy foods. The eighth graders gave somewhat more correct responses, but even their correct response rates hovered about the 50% chance level (see Table I). Importantly, such gaps in AIDS knowledge might lead children to have an optimistic bias and to believe that they could protect themselves by eating healthy foods, getting vaccinated, and being tested for AIDS. Such unfounded optimism might distract them from effective ways of preventing AIDS. The younger children's responses to the question about mother–baby perinatal transmission also illustrates children's gaps in AIDS knowledge. Overall, the pretest results indicate that, once we go beyond well-publicized facts, many teenagers in our sample seemed to be at a loss in thinking about AIDS transmission.

3. What Children Want to Know about AIDS

a. "Give Me a Complete List of Risky Behaviors, Please!" While most sixth and eighth graders knew about some of the behaviors associated with

HIV infection (e.g., sharing a needle, having sex), some children seemed concerned that they did not know the whole story. About 13% of the sixth graders and 15% of the eighth graders asked questions such as: "How many ways can you get AIDS?" "What are the different ways you can get AIDS?" "How can you prevent AIDS?"

b. *"Can You Get AIDS If. . . ?"*   Instead of asking for a complete list, fourth graders asked many questions about the AIDS risk of specific behaviors:

1. Can you get AIDS by eating food?
2. Can you avoid AIDS by eating fruits and vegetables?
3. If you share a lollipop or drink, can you get AIDS?
4. Can you get sick by holding a pet or animal?
5. Can AIDS be spread around in the air?
6. If someone who has AIDS touches food at the grocery store, will I get AIDS if I touch what they touch?
7. If I borrow someone's clothes, can I get AIDS?
8. If you kiss someone, can you get AIDS?
9. Can you get AIDS on your own?
10. Are people born with AIDS?

Some sixth and eighth graders also wanted to know:

1. Can you get AIDS by an AIDS person coughing and sneezing on you? If someone has AIDS and sneezes into someone's mouth, could they get AIDS?
2. Can AIDS be transplanted through breast feeding? Can you get AIDS by hugging someone or touching what they touch?

As discussed earlier, knowing only a few facts about AIDS transmission can be very frightening for children. Simply giving them a short list of do's and don'ts does not help children decide what is safe and unsafe in novel situations in terms of AIDS prevention. Children's desire to know about situations not widely covered in existing AIDS education programs—or to get a complete list of risky behaviors, for that matter—probably reflects their unease about having just a partial list of risky behaviors and no conceptual basis to reason about novel situations.

c. *"Tell Me about AIDS and Sex!"*   Currently, most pre-adolescents learn about AIDS formally at school as part of sex education. This approach, we think, could create many misconceptions about AIDS transmission. One example documented in the research literature, as noted earlier, is that many fourth-graders believe that whatever can prevent pregnancy (e.g., birth control pills) can prevent AIDS (Hoppe et al., 1994). The questions raised privately by the sixth and eighth graders in this study further support our intuition that teenagers often have misconceptions about sex is related to AIDS.

1. How can you get AIDS from intercourse/sex?
2. Can you get AIDS the first time you have sex?
3. How can you get AIDS by intercourse because some people say it's from drinking saliva? (Note: Children from different local schools have told us that one has to drink a gallon of saliva from an infected person to get AIDS.)
4. If you have sex, and a girl or a guy has their period, do you get AIDS?
5. Can condoms protect you from AIDS? (Recall the widely circulated air-safety analogy about condom breakage.)
6. Why can the AIDS disease fit through the condom but a sperm can't?
7. Can you get AIDS by using protection?
8. If you have sex with different people, how many people until you get AIDS?
9. Can you get AIDS if you are a lesbian or are gay?

d. "How and Why?"   Some children also asked about the hows and whys—or the causal mechanisms—of AIDS transmission. However, these questions represented only a minority. One possible interpretation is that the children were not interested in the hows and whys. Another possibility is that they had been to some extent "brainwashed" by the current approach to AIDS education that emphasizes factual knowledge rather than reasoning; that is, most of them might as a result simply stop asking "Why?" and "How?" As mentioned earlier, about 50% of eighth graders simply asked us whether there *will be* a cure for AIDS, and an additional 20% wanted to know if there is a cure now (if detected early). Remarkably, none of the eighth graders asked any questions about causal mechanisms for AIDS transmission. Perhaps, as we conjecture, the emphasis of condom breakage in their prior AIDS education had led them to believe that there was little they could do to protect themselves from AIDS besides abstaining from sex forever. If this is true, it is no wonder that they stopped being curious about the whys and hows of AIDS transmission and prevention. By contrast, some of the 4th and 6th grades were still full of curiosity. They asked:

1. How does a person get AIDS by doing a slam dunk with Magic?
2. How does the AIDS virus get in your body?
3. How can you get AIDS from intercourse (because some people say it's from drinking saliva)?
4. Why can the AIDS disease fit through the condom but a sperm can't?
5. How can you get AIDS by having an open cut and exposing it to a person with a cut who has AIDS?
6. How come people get AIDS from sharing needles?

7. How would a pregnant woman who has AIDS give AIDS to her unborn baby?

8. How come mosquitoes can't carry the AIDS virus from a person they bite to another person they bite?

E. POSTTEST RESULTS

1. Ecological Environments for the AIDS Virus

Did children in the Experimental Condition learn anything about ecological environments for the HIV? Were they better than their peers in the Control Condition at deciding whether the AIDS virus can live, reproduce, and will die in these nine environments: hair, skin, fresh blood, water, air, breast milk, dried blood, saliva, and orange juice? Table II explains how we converted the patterns of children's responses to the questions about the biology of the HIV (i.e., "can live," "can reproduce," "will die") into categories of ecological environment for the HIV (i.e., "reproduce," "survive," "die"). For example, if a child indicated that the HIV can live and will not die but cannot reproduce in a certain environment, we would count the child as classifying that environment as one in which the HIV can survive.

The main findings are: The Experimental curriculum seems to help children correctly classify these ecological environments for the HIV. In each grade, the average percentage of correct classification was higher in the Experimental condition than in the Control Condition: 49% versus 30% (fourth grade), 47% versus 30% (sixth grade), and 58% versus 37% (eighth grade), all matched-$ts(10) > 3.5$, and all $p < .01$, 2-tailed. Table III presents the results on individual items.

2. The Biology and the Virulence of the HIV

Children were asked whether the AIDS virus can make someone sick if it is on a person's skin, in a person's hair, in fresh blood, in dried blood, in

TABLE II

CODING SYSTEM FOR THE
"ENVIRONMENT" QUESTIONS

Overall pattern	Individual questions		
	Reproduce	Live	Die
Reproduce	Yes	Yes	No
Survive	No	Yes	No
Die	No	No	Yes

TABLE III

PERCENTAGES OF CHILDREN CLASSIFYING EACH ENVIRONMENT CORRECTLY

Environments	Fourth grade		Sixth grade		Eighth grade	
	Expt (N = 16)	Control (N = 14)	Expt (N = 15)	Control (N = 15)	Expt (N = 12)	Control (N = 15)
REPRODUCE						
Fresh blood	81%	43%	100%	73%	100%	100%
Breast milk[a]	56%	29%	67%	33%	0%	7%
Saliva[a]	25%	21%	27%	27%	17%	20%
SURVIVE						
Saliva[a]	31%	36%	27%	0%	25%	0%
Breast milk[a]	31%	29%	33%	7%	42%	20%
DIE						
Air	75%	29%	87%	47%	100%	53%
Water	75%	50%	87%	80%	92%	47%
Hair	50%	14%	20%	7%	67%	27%
Skin	19%	7%	20%	0%	50%	20%
Dried blood	44%	21%	20%	13%	67%	47%
Orange juice	56%	50%	27%	40%	75%	60%

[a] The correct classification for "breast milk" and "saliva" is still uncertain. HIV may reproduce very slowly or not at all in these two environments.

saliva, and in orange juice. The Experimental curriculum seemed to help eighth graders appreciate that the AIDS virus cannot make someone sick if it is in dried blood ($p < .055$, Fisher's Exact test comparing the two conditions), orange juice ($p < .07$), and on people's skin ($p < .08$; see Table IV).

For some reason, the younger children (grades four and six) did not benefit from the experimental curriculum as much as the eighth graders,

TABLE IV

PERCENTAGES OF EIGHTH GRADERS MAKING A CORRECT JUDGMENT ON THE VIRULENCE OF HIV IN VARIOUS ENVIRONMENTS

	Fresh blood	Saliva	Dried blood	Orange juice	Skin	Hair
Experimental (N = 12)	100%	50%	91%*	100%*	90%*	100%
Control (N = 15)	100%	50%	50%	69%	54%	84%

*$p < .05$ (for each condition, binomial test against chance level = 50%).

as measured by this section of the posttest. It could be because the wording of these questions was somewhat confusing. Consider the question "If the AIDS virus is in X, can it make someone sick?" Some of the younger children seemed confused whether the question meant: (a) If the AIDS virus is on a person's skin, and so on, can that person become sick? or (b) Can someone else become sick? We know, in fact, that even the younger children in the Experimental Condition did learn something about the biology of the HIV and its virulence. When asked, "Is the AIDS virus dangerous only when it is alive?" children in the Experimental Condition performed better than chance at each grade level: 75% for fourth grade ($p < .04$, 1-tailed sign test), 93% for sixth grade ($p < .0005$), and 83% for eighth grade ($p < .02$). By contrast, children in the Control Condition seemed to guess randomly: 43%, 53%, and 53%, respectively (all $p > .3$).

Overall, the experimental curriculum seemed to help children appreciate three important things about the biology of the HIV. First, it helped children appreciate whether the HIV can survive, can reproduce, or will die in various environments (e.g., saliva, breast milk, blood, air, water). Second, it helped children make reasonable inferences about environments not explicitly covered in the experimental curriculum (e.g., dried blood, hair, skin, orange juice), perhaps because we had told those children that the HIV needs live human white blood cells to stay alive and reproduce. Third, the experimental curriculum also helped children understand that the HIV is dangerous only when it is alive. Together, these insights about the biology and virulence of the HIV might help children reason about the AIDS risk of various forms of human contact. For example, these concepts might help children understand why one cannot get AIDS by sharing a swimming pool with an infected person. That is, children might be able to reason that any AIDS virus traveling through the water will be dead, and therefore no longer dangerous, by the time it reaches anyone in the swimming pool. We will now turn to children's ability to reason about AIDS risks in novel situations.

3. Reasoning about AIDS Transmission in Novel Situations

a. Judgments on AIDS Risk   On the posttest, children were asked to consider the AIDS risk in 12 different situations. Because we are especially interested in how the biological causal mechanism for AIDS transmission discussed in the Experimental Condition might affect children's reasoning about novel situations, we will first look at the results on the five most novel situations. They include: tattooing, ear-piercing, wiping an infected person's bleeding nose, swimming in a small pond with an infected person, sharing a toothbrush with an infected person. (The answers according to our consultants should be Yes, Yes, Yes, No, No. See the highlighted items in Table V for the percentages of children responding Yes.)

To assess the benefits of understanding of a coherent causal mechanism for AIDS transmission, we computed each child's percentage of correct answers given to the five novel situations, and such percentages were sub-

TABLE V

PERCENTAGES OF CHILDREN GIVING A "YES" RESPONSE TO THE POSTTEST
ITEMS ON AIDS TRANSMISSION[a]

| Situations | Fourth grade | | Sixth grade | | Eighth grade | |
	Expt (N = 16)	Control (N = 14)	Expt (N = 15)	Control (N = 15)	Expt (N = 12)	Control (N = 15)
Via Air						
Sharing a toilet seat	6%	0%	0%	20%	0%	0%
Via Water						
Swimming in a pond	**6%**	**0%**	**7%**	**0%**	**0%**	**0%**
Via Saliva exposed to Air/Water						
Sharing an ice-cream cone	13%	7%	20%	20%	0%	0%
Kissing on mouth	31%	14%	27%	0%	0%	7%
Coughing or sneezing	6%	7%	33%	7%	0%	0%
Sharing a toothbrush	**38%**	**36%**	**40%**	**20%**	**0%**	**7%**
Average	22%	16%	30%	12%	0%	3%
Via Saliva						
French kissing	44%	50%	40%	13%	25%	20%
Via Blood						
Wiping a bleeding nose	56%	21%	73%	40%	75%	87%
Tattooing	38%	29%	40%	7%	75%	33%
Ear-piercing	**6%**	**0%**	**20%**	**7%**	**42%**	**33%**
Sharing I.V. needles	**100%**	**100%**	**100%**	**87%**	**100%**	**100%**
Mom to unborn baby	**88%**	**86%**	**100%**	**60%**	**92%**	**73%**
Average	58%	47%	67%	40%	77%	65%

[a] Boldfaced items represent the five most novel situations.

mitted to a Condition by Grade analysis of variance (ANOVA). There was a main effect of Condition, favoring the Experimental Condition ($F(1,81) = 9.2$, $p < .005$). There was no Condition by Grade interaction ($F(2,81) = .03$, $p > .97$), suggesting that the effect holds across grades. The percentages of correct responses for the Experimental and Control Condition were, respectively: 48% versus 34% (fourth grade), 55% versus 39% (fifth grade), 75% versus 60% (eighth grade). There was also an expected improvement with age; the main effect for Grade was substantial ($F(2,81) = 10.7$, $p < .001$). (In this and other analyses on the pretest and posttest data, we found no reliable sex differences.)

b. Children's Explanations We also asked children to explain their yes/no answers concerning the five novel situations. A main finding is that children in the Control Condition were marginally more likely to offer irrelevant or no explanations at all ($F(1,81) = 3.3$, $p < .08$). Some examples of irrelevant or uninformative explanations are: "You cannot get AIDS by ear-piercing because it does not affect the AIDS virus at all;" "No, I don't think so because my ears are pierced, and I don't have AIDS." The percentages of irrelevant/no explanations for the Experimental and Control conditions were, respectively: 34% versus 43% (fourth grade), 16% versus 36% (sixth grade), 10% versus 12% (eighth grade). There was, again, an expected decline with age in children's tendency to offer irrelevant or no explanations (main effect for Grade: ($F(2,81) = 7.5$, $p < .005$). There was no Condition X Grade interaction ($F(2,81) < 1$).

Recall that one reason we wanted to help children build a coherent basis for reasoning about AIDS transmission had to do with motivating children to think about AIDS more deeply. It seems that our experimental curriculum motivated children to do just that. When asked to explain their judgments on the AIDS risk in various novel situations, children in the Experimental Condition were somewhat more likely to offer thoughtful explanations than their peers in the Control Condition.

c. Explanations Mentioning the Biology of HIV Another measure of the effectiveness of our experimental curriculum is how often children thought about the biology of HIV when they reasoned about AIDS transmission. Table VI presents the percentages of children mentioning the biology of HIV (i.e., reproduce, survive, die) in their explanations for each of the five novel situations.

On average, children in the Experimental Condition invoked the biology of HIV in reasoning about AIDS transmission in five novel situations once or twice. The percentages of biological explanations were 26% (fourth grade), 24% (sixth grade), and 35% (eighth grade). As can be seen in Table VI, they were more likely to do so when they reasoned about the AIDS

TABLE VI

PERCENTAGES OF CHILDREN PROVIDING A BIOLOGICAL EXPLANATION FOR
VARIOUS NOVEL SITUATIONS

Novel Situations	Fourth grade		Sixth grade		Eighth grade	
	Expt (N = 16)	Control (N = 14)	Expt (N = 15)	Control (N = 15)	Expt (N = 12)	Control (N = 15)
Swimming in a pool	63%	7%	80%	60%	73%	17%
Sharing a toothbrush	44%	0%	40%	13%	53%	0%
Wiping a bleeding nose	6%	7%	0%	0%	7%	0%
Tattooing	13%	0%	0%	0%	0%	0%
Ear-piercing	6%	0%	0%	0%	7%	0%

virus in saliva and water. They were less likely to do so when asked to think about the AIDS virus in fresh blood, perhaps because they considered the knowledge that "the AIDS virus is alive and dangerous when it is in fresh human blood" to be in the common ground and not worth talking about. Consider how one child explained the AIDS risk of wiping an HIV infected person's bloody nose: "Because if you wipe a person who has a bloody nose and you have a cut on your hand, the infected blood can get into you." This child did not explicitly mention that the AIDS virus in the infected blood was alive and dangerous probably because the child took this to be old news and not worth mentioning.

Another reason why children rarely talked about the AIDS virus surviving and reproducing in blood when they reasoned about tattooing and ear-piercing is that many of the children did not even know that blood is involved in these two situations. (One caveat: While ear-piercing, when done professionally, is virtually AIDS-risk free, the practice of do-it-yourself body- or ear-piercing among teenagers in some communities is not. In the latter case, needles are probably reused without adequate cleansing.) This finding highlights the importance of explaining to children about the mechanics and the path of how the AIDS virus might go from one person to another. If children do not even know that blood and tiny open wounds are involved in tattooing or body/ear-piercing, no amount of knowledge about the biology of HIV would help them appreciate the AIDS risk of tattooing. Consider this explanation given by one of the children: "No, because in tattooing, you don't bleed, so the AIDS virus can't be living on any needles." Likewise, when adults educate children about AIDS transmission through sex or about using condoms in AIDS prevention, they must not shy away from telling them exactly how things work. In fact, as already reported, some of the children privately asked us in writing for precisely such information.

As expected, children in the Control condition rarely invoked the biology of HIV to explain their judgments of AIDS risk of various novel situations. There is one exception: Some sixth graders talked about water killing the AIDS virus to explain why it is safe to swim in a small pond with someone who has AIDS. We have a good—but embarrassing—explanation for it. One of us (who shall remain nameless) mistakenly told the sixth graders in the Control Condition several times that the AIDS virus will die quickly in water when the children asked us about the Olympic Gold Medalist Greg Louganis's disclosure of his HIV status. This bit of novel information impressed the students enough that they remembered it two weeks later when reasoning about a similar situation on the posttest (i.e., swimming in a small pond with someone who has the AIDS virus). But interestingly, presented in isolation without being embedded in a coherent framework, this information did not encourage them to think about the biology of HIV in reasoning about other ecological environments (e.g., saliva, blood).

To compare the extent to which children mentioned the biology of HIV in their explanations in the two conditions and three grades, we submitted individual children's percentages of such explanations to a Condition by Grade ANOVA. First, children in the Experimental Condition were more likely to offer this kind of explanations than children in the Control Condition ($F(1,81) = 42.4, p < .001$). The percentages of such responses for the Experimental and Control Condition were, respectively: 26% versus 3% (fourth grade, $p < .05$, by Tukey's HSD test), 24% versus 15% (sixth grade, N.S.), 35% versus 3% (eighth grade; by Tukey's HSD test). There was also a Condition X Grade interaction, mainly due to our mistake made in the sixth-grade Control condition ($F(2,81) = 4 p < .05$).

Interestingly, there was no reliable main effect of Grade ($F[2,81] < 1$). It seems, then, children do not spontaneously develop, during their teenage years, the insight that the biology of HIV is relevant to AIDS transmission. This finding supports our idea that the core of our experimental AIDS curriculum—namely, a biological causal mechanism for AIDS transmission—is not in most elementary and junior high school children's repertoire of biological knowledge. But at the same time, this causal mechanism is simple enough that it can be readily taught to school-age children.

d. Benefits of Thinking about the Biology of HIV   Once children understand how the biology of HIV can play a crucial role in AIDS transmission, will they be better at deciding about which behaviors are safe or unsafe?

If this is the case, when children mention the biology of HIV in their explanations, they should be more likely to decide correctly about the AIDS risk of a behavior than when they do not mention it. This is exactly what we found.

For each child, we computed two percentages of correct judgments of AIDS risk in novel situations—one for the instances where children mentioned the biology of HIV in their explanations, and one for those instances where children did not do so. Of the 87 children in this study, 45 gave at least one explanation mentioning the biology of HIV. The average percentage of correct judgments of AIDS risk in a novel situation associated with this kind of explanation was 90%, with a 95% confidence interval between 84% and 96%. As it turned out, all 87 children gave some other kind of explanation (or no explanation at all) for at least one of the five novel situations. The average percentage of correct judgments of AIDS risk associated with this latter kind of explanation was 45%, with a 95% confidence interval between 39% and 51%.

This pattern by and large holds for all three grades, although it was somewhat weaker in the fourth grade. In the 23 instances that the biology of HIV was mentioned in an explanation, fourth graders correctly judged the AIDS risk of the novel situation in question 65% of the time. Fourth graders made correct AIDS risk judgments in only 37% of the 127 instances that the biology of HIV was not mentioned. The corresponding percentages for the sixth graders were 93% (out of 29 instances) and 36% (out of 121 instances); those for the eighth graders were 91% (out of 23 instances) and 62% (out of 112 instances). In other words, when children mentioned the biology of HIV in explaining their AIDS risk judgment, their judgment was almost always correct. Moreover, it was much more likely to be correct when they explicitly talked about the biology of HIV than when they did not. This finding suggests that children in the Experimental Condition reasoned about AIDS transmission in novel situations better—i.e., making more correct judgments of AIDS risk and giving more meaningful explanations for their judgments—probably because they made use of what they had learned about the biological causal mechanism of AIDS transmission in the Experimental curriculum. The benefit of the Experimental Condition over the Control Condition seems to come directly from the core of our Experimental curriculum, rather than due to some peripheral variables such as differences in hands-on activities (e.g., culturing germs with nutrient agar in the Experimental Condition) or our enthusiasm in leading class discussion.

e. Mechanical Causality Because of children's precocious understanding of mechanical causality, and because biological phenomena often involve transfer of physical matter, we have suggested that children would be inclined to use mechanical causality to explain biological phenomena. To explore this possibility, we divided children's explanations for their judgments of AIDS risk in the novel situations into four categories. The percentages of agreement between two independent coders were uniformly high for individual categories, ranging from 91% to 97% (Cohen's Kappa for each category ranged from .86 to .95). The four categories are:

1. Mentioning the biology of the AIDS virus (die, survive, or reproduce), e.g., "I said no because the saliva on the toothbrush bristles connected with air, so the AIDS in the saliva are dead"; "No, because it dies in the water. We always rinse with water and it [the AIDS virus on a toothbrush] dies"; "No, because AIDS can die in water."

2. Mentioning the mechanical path traversed by the AIDS virus, e.g., "Because if you wipe a person who has a bloody nose and you have a cut on your hand, the infected blood can get into you"; "The AIDS virus can get from the needle to the other person."

3. Mentioning the media (substances surrounding the AIDS virus), e.g., "No, because there is no blood involved"; "Yes, because you can only get AIDS through blood."

4. No or irrelevant/uninformative explanation, e.g., "I said no because you can't get AIDS by tattooing anywhere, maybe something else."

The most prevalent kind of explanation was mechanical causality. Children talked about the path traversed by the AIDS virus 46% of the time. They mentioned the biology of the AIDS virus only 17% of the time and just the media of the virus only 11% of the time. For the remaining 26% of the time, children gave no or some irrelevant explanations. Interestingly, children's tendency to offer a mechanical causal explanation did not vary much across grades or conditions. A Condition X Grade ANOVA revealed no main effects and interaction. This pattern is unique among the four explanation categories. Briefly, there is a main effect of Condition for "biological explanations" and "mentioning media," a main effect of Grade for "mentioning media" and "no/irrelevant explanations," and a Condition X Grade interaction for "biological explanations" and "mentioning media."

In short, these results suggest that children's tendency to think about mechanical causality in reasoning about a biological phenomenon such as AIDS transmission is very robust. It seems to be the causal framework of choice for children of this (fairly wide) age range—age 9 to 14. This finding is in line with the suggestive evidence that children tend to choose, in forced-choice tasks, mechanical causal explanations over other kinds of explanations (e.g., genetic, intentional, or vitalistic) for biological phenomena from age 6 or 7 on (according to Springer & Keil, 1991) or from age 8 on (according to Inagaki & Hatano, 1993).

f. Appropriate Caution and Unwarranted Fear A main goal of the experimental curriculum was to help children develop appropriate caution about AIDS transmission without causing unwarranted fear. For children and adolescents who are not yet sexually active, the most dangerous kind of bodily fluid—in terms of infectious diseases such as AIDS—is blood. We wanted to know if the children in the Experimental Condition were more aware of the danger of blood—no matter how minute the amount might be, as in the case of tattooing and car-piercing—than children in the Control Condition. To address this issue, we computed each child's percentage of Yes responses given to the five relevant questions (i.e., sharing a needle in drug use, from a mother to an unborn baby, tattooing, ear-piercing, wiping someone else's bloody nose). The percentages of correct responses to these questions for the Experimental and Control Condition were, respectively: 58% versus 47% (fourth grade), 67% versus 40% (sixth grade), 77% versus 65% (eighth grade). There is an expected improvement with age in awareness of the AIDS risk of coming into contact with another person's blood, Grade effect: $(F[2,81] = 9.0, p < .001)$. Importantly, the main effect for Condition was reliable $(F[1,81] = 16.5, p < .001)$, and it held across the three grades (Condition by Grade interaction, $(F[2,81] = 1.8, p > .17)$. It seems, then, our experimental curriculum succeeded in enhancing fourth to eighth graders' appropriate caution about HIV transmission through blood.

What is the story about saliva? Recall that we mentioned our agony over whether to tell children in the Experimental Condition that the AIDS virus can survive and perhaps reproduce slowly in human saliva. Our concern was that this might cause unwarranted fear about becoming infected through being sneezed or coughed on, kissing, sharing food, sharing eating or drinking utensils, and so forth. But as noted earlier, we decided to discuss it because we did not want to talk down to children by just telling them to learn a few facts, and because we wanted to challenge them by presenting to them the complexity of the issues. Along with our discussion about the uncertainty of the saliva as an ecological environment for the AIDS virus, we emphasized repeatedly that: (a) the AIDS virus dies in air and water very quickly, so there is no need to worry about saliva if it is exposed to air or water for a while, and (b) there is not a single documented case of HIV infection through saliva alone. In the Control Condition, we simply told children that scientists are still not sure about the story with saliva. There is some evidence that the AIDS virus can be found in human saliva, but there is not a single documented case of HIV infection through saliva alone.

To see if our conceptually rather challenging discussion in the Experimental Condition increased children's unwarranted fear of saliva-related everyday human contact, we compared the percentages of Yes responses given to the four "saliva exposed to air/water" questions in the two conditions (see Table V). The percentages for the Experimental and Control Conditions were, respectively: 22% versus 16% (fourth grade), 30% versus 12% (sixth grade), 0% versus 3% (eighth grade). The level of fear about casual contact involving saliva was generally quite low, and there was no reliable differences between the two conditions at any grade level (For fourth and sixth grades, $ts(28) < 1.1$, $p > .29$, 2-tailed; no statistical test was performed on the eighth graders' data because of the clear floor effect in both conditions). In short, the children in the Experimental Condition were as unlikely as those in the Control Condition to think that one can get AIDS through saliva-related causal contact.

However, while our experimental curriculum did not cause true misconceptions about saliva, it may have nonetheless caused unwarranted anxiety by leaving children with overwhelming uncertainty about saliva. To examine this possibility, we compared the percentages of correct responses (i.e., No) to the same four "saliva exposed to air/water" questions in the two conditions. The percentages for the Experimental and Control Condition were, respectively: 63% versus 67% (fourth grade), 59% versus 66% (sixth grade), 90% versus 85% (eighth grade). So, the majority of children in each condition in each grade knew that one cannot get AIDS through casual contact involving saliva, and there was no reliable difference between the two conditions at any grade level ($ts < .6$, $p > .5$, 2-tailed; dfs = 28 for fourth and sixth grades; dfs = 25 for eighth grades).

The story about saliva is so far so good. But what about French kissing? Note that, in that case, the saliva being exchanged is less exposed to air or water than in the case of kissing on the mouth, sharing a toothbrush or ice-cream cone, or being sneezed or coughed on. As it turned out, the Experimental and Control did not differ reliably in the tendency to judge French kissing to be unsafe (see Table V), regardless of whether the three grades were considered separately or together ($ps > .1$, 1-tailed, by Fisher's Exact tests). Moreover, about 43% of the children judged this behavior to be safe; the percentages ranged from 29% to 60% for individual grades in each condition. Again, the two conditions did not differ reliably whether the three grades were considered separately or together ($ps > .1$, 1-tailed, by Fisher's Exact tests). So even in the case when children were most likely to be anxious about AIDS transmission through saliva, their anxiety was far from overwhelming. Together, these findings suggest that our experimental curriculum managed to enhance children's appropriate caution without increasing unwarranted fear about AIDS transmission.

F. POSTSCRIPT

We went back to the school to debrief the children about the differences between the two conditions and to answer whatever questions they might still have about AIDS. Naively, we planned to spend about 20 minutes reviewing the core concepts of the experimental curriculum and about 25 minutes answering questions in each class (with children in both conditions together). Because we brought no props—no color slides, videotapes, microscopes, specimen slides, agar plates—but just ourselves, we thought that the children might become bored well before our allotted time (45 minutes) was up. Well, we ended up staying for an hour and a half in each classroom and had to tear ourselves away despite children's entreaties for us to stay longer. What was the secret ingredient of our success and popularity? The answer: Children's natural curiosity to learn.

What we did in the question-and-answer session was to ask children whether they had any more questions about AIDS transmission. We turned every question raised by the children to the whole class and asked them to vote by hand whether or not the situation described in each question was an AIDS risk. We then asked children to explain their votes. For instance, a child might ask, "Can you get AIDS by using a shower stall or bathtub that has been used by someone who has AIDS?" Some of the children in the class voted Yes, and others voted No. When we asked representatives on each side to explain their opinions, one of the children explained that AIDS cannot be transmitted by sharing a shower stall or bathtub because the AIDS virus will die quickly in air and water. This was a typical question-and-answer sequence in each classroom. The questions of course varied from grade to grade, but the children's insistence on continuing the Q-&-A session was the same in each grade. And insist they did. We wanted to kick ourselves for not tape-recording these question-and-answer sessions. Fortunately, the teachers were present at those sessions, and they could bear witness.

And bear witness they did—in other ways too. After we finished the debriefing sessions, we went to thank the school principal for his support for the project. We said we wanted to give the school a gift to express our gratitude for their cooperation and help; we asked the principal what we could buy for the school—art supplies? science class supplies? books for the school library? The principal said if we really wanted to give the school a gift, he would like it very much if we could hold an in-service workshop for the teachers on our Experimental curriculum. We suspected that he had heard good things about our curriculum from the teachers (and his son who was in the Experimental Condition in the sixth-grade class). We knew that the principal wanted us to spark discussions about AIDS at his school. Perhaps he had heard through the grapevine that our Experimental curriculum had done that, if nothing else. So, even before he knew about our posttest results, he wanted us back to serve as a catalyst for more AIDS discussion among the teachers and in the classrooms.

We are optimistic that we can be of help in that regard, because both the teachers and the students seemed very receptive to our approach. After each lesson, the teachers warmly thanked us for generating so much discussion in their class on such a difficult topic. Two teachers who observed the experimental curriculum even wanted to take our posttest to see how much they had learned about AIDS transmission. The eighth-grade teacher told us that he wanted to continue to talk about AIDS in his sex education class, because he was impressed by how his students asked so many thoughtful questions about sex-related AIDS transmission without embarrassment during the debriefing session. (We were especially pleased by this turn of events considering that all the eighth graders wanted to know mainly before the curriculum was whether there would ever be a cure for AIDS.)

V. Conclusions

While we are still working on improving our experimental curriculum to educate children about AIDS (and, in another project, infectious diseases in general), we have already learned several things about children's naive biology and health education.

A. Naive Biology and Causal Mechanisms

Children want to know why things happen and how things work. When they try to understand biological phenomena, they naturally want to figure out the underlying causal mechanisms for such phenomena. However, as Carey (1985) argued, children do not begin to understand any uniquely biological causal mechanisms until age 9 or 10. Carey (1995; Carey & Spelke, 1994; Solomon et al., 1996) has since revised the probable age onset to 6 or 7 to accommodate recent evidence of early inchoate biological knowledge (e.g., S. Gelman, 1996; Inagaki & Hatano, 1993; Keil, 1992; Springer & Keil, 1991). We actually want to go against the tide by arguing that an understanding of any true biological causal mechanism is not something children pick up intuitively in everyday life. Even what Carey and her colleagues are willing to accept as evidence for such understanding— such as, knowing that one inherits traits such as eye color from birth parents but not adoptive parents—is not about causal mechanisms per se. Rather, it is about causal input-output relations.

In our study, we have seen that while mechanical causal mechanisms are often invoked by 9- to 14-year-olds to explain AIDS transmission, they invoked biological causal mechanisms only infrequently. More importantly, only those children who had been explicitly taught a biological causal mechanism did so. One might argue that AIDS transmission is a relatively novel domain to children; that children might use biological causal mechanisms to make sense of more familiar biological phenomena. This is a distinct possibility, but the burden of proof is on those who argue for this position.

B. Learning and Motivation

To say that children do not spontaneously develop an intuitive understanding of biological mechanisms is not the same as to say that children cannot learn them readily. Quite the contrary, children readily learned a biological causal mechanism for AIDS transmission introduced in our experimental curriculum. Their grasp of the mechanism seemed to help them reason about novel situations and enhance their prudent caution without engendering unwarranted fear. As for AIDS prevention, what might turn out to be crucial is that such a causal mechanism offers children a coherent basis for thinking about AIDS transmission. Coupled with children's natural curiosity to make sense of the world—of which unfortunately AIDS is a part—such a coherent conceptual framework may actually get children to think about AIDS more often, deeply, and sensibly.

Acknowledgments

We thank the children, staff, and parents of Our Lady of Lourdes Elementary School, St. Didacus School, St. Thomas Aquinas Elementary School, and UCLA Seeds University Elementary School for their support and cooperation. We are grateful to Muriel Ifekwunigwe and Ann De la Sota at Seeds University Elementary School of UCLA for their valuable input to the experimental curriculum used in this study. Three biomedical experts on campus, Marcus Horwitz, Ralph Frerichs, and Jeffrey Ohmen, taught us much about AIDS and infectious diseases in general. Remaining misconceptions are of course ours. We are grateful to Albert DeLeon, Wendy Francis, Karla Izquierdo, Marlene Martinez, Lauralyn Miles, Sharon Peri, Denise Piñon, and especially Jennifer Dewitt for their invaluable assistance in data collection and coding. This work was supported in part by the UCLA AIDS Institute and the Urban Education Studies Center.

References

Ashworth, C. S., DuRant, C. N., & Gaillard, G. (1992). An evaluation of a school-based AIDS/HIV education program for high school students. *Journal of Adolescent Health,* *13,* 582–588.

Atran, S. (1994). Core domains versus scientific theories: Evidence from systematics and Itza-Maya folkbiology. In L. A. Hirschfeld and S. A. Gelman (Eds.), *Domain specificity in cognition and culture* (pp. 316–340). New York: Cambridge University Press.

Atran, S. (1995). Causal constraints on categories and categorical constraints on biological reasoning across cultures. In S. Sperber, D. Premack, & A. J. Premack (Eds), *Causal cognition* (pp. 205–233). Oxford: Clarendon Press.

Au, T. K. (1994). Developing an intuitive understanding of substance kinds. *Cognitive Psychology, 27,* 71–111.

Au, T. K., & Romo, L. F. (1995). What are germs? Biological or nonbiological kinds? Poster presented at SRCD, Indianapolis.

Au, T. K., Sidle, A. L, & Rollins, K. B. (1993). Developing an intuitive understanding of conservation and contamination: Invisible particles as a plausible mechanism. *Developmental Psychology, 29,* 286–299.

Backscheider, A. G., Shatz, M., & Gelman, S. A. (1993). Preschoolers' ability to distinguish living kinds as a function of regrowth. *Child Development, 64,* 1242–1257.

Brice, S. H. (1983). *Ways with words: Language, life, and work in communities and classrooms.* Cambridge, England: Cambridge University Press.

Brown, L. K., DiClemente, R. J., & Reynolds, L. A. (1991). HIV prevention for adolescents: Utility of the health belief model. *AIDS Education and Prevention, 3,* 50–59.

Brown, L. K., & Fritz, G. K. (1989). Children's knowledge and attitudes about AIDS. *Journal of the American Academy of Child and Adolescent Psychiatry, 27,* 504–548.

Callanan, M. A., & Oakes, L. M. (1992). Preschoolers' questions and parents' explanations: Causal thinking in everyday activity. *Cognitive Development, 7,* 213–233.

Carey, S. (1985). *Conceptual change in childhood.* Cambridge, MA: M.I.T. Press.

Carey, S. (1991). Knowledge acquisition: enrichment or conceptual change? In S. Carey and R. Gelman (Eds.), *The epigenesis of mind: Essays on biology and cognition* (pp. 257–291). New Jersey: Erlbaum.

Carey, S. (1995). On the origin of causal understanding. In S. Sperber, D. Premack, & A. J. Premack (Eds), *Causal cognition* (pp. 268–302). Oxford: Clarendon Press.

Carey, S., & Spelke, E. (1994). Domain specific knowledge and conceptual change. In L. A. Hirschfeld and S. A. Gelman (Eds.), *Domain specificity in cognition and culture* (pp. 169–200). New York: Cambridge University Press.

Coley, J. D. (1995). Emerging differentiation of folkbiology and folkpsychology: Attributions of biological and psychological properties to living things. *Child Development, 66,* 1856–1874.

Crawford, I., & Robinson, W. L. (1990). Adolescents and AIDS: Knowledge and attitudes of African-American, Latino, and Caucasian midwestern U.S. high school seniors. *Journal of Psychology and Human Sexuality, 3,* 25–33.

DiClemente, R. J. (1990). The emergence of adolescents as a risk group for human immunodeficiency virus infection. *Journal of Adolescent Research, 5,* 7–17.

Dooling, D. J., & Lachman, R. (1971). Effects of comprehension on retention of prose. *Journal of Experimental Psychology, 88,* 216–222.

Emmons, C.A., Joseph, J.G., Kessler, R.C., Wortman, C.B., Montgomery, S.B., & Ostrow, D.G. (1986). Psychosocial predictors of reported behavioral change in homosexual males at risk for AIDS. *Health Education Quarterly, 13,* 331.

Fassler, D., McQueen, K., Duncan, P., & Copeland, L. (1990). Children's perception of AIDS. *Journal of the American Academy of Child and Adolescent Psychiatry, 29,* 459–462.

Fisher, J. D., & Fisher, W. A. (1992). Changing AIDS-risk behavior. *Psychological Bulletin, 111,* 455–474.

Gelman, R. (1990). First principles organize attention to and learning about relevant data: Number and the animate-inanimate distinction as examples. *Cognitive Science, 14,* 79–106.

Gelman, S. A. (1996). Concepts and theories. In R. Gelman & T. K. Au (Eds.), *Handbook of perception and cognition: Volume 13: Perceptual and cognitive development,* (pp. 117–150). New York: Academic Press.

Gelman, S. A., Coley, J. D., & Gottfried, G. M. (1994). Essentialist beliefs in children: The acquisition of concepts and theories. In L. A. Hirschfeld and S. A. Gelman (Eds.), *Domain specificity in cognition and culture* (pp. 169–200). New York: Cambridge University Press.

Glenister, A. M., Castiglia, P., Kanski, G., & Haughey, B. (1990). AIDS knowledge and attitudes of primary grade teachers and students. *Journal of Pediatric Health Care, 4,* 77–85.

Hatano, G., & Inagaki, K. (1994). Young children's naive theory of biology. *Cognition, 50,* 171–188

Hatano, G., Siegler, R. S., Richards, D. D., Inagaki, K., Stavy, R., & Wax, N. (1993). The development of biological knowledge: A multi-national study. *Cognitive Development, 8,* 47–62.

Hickling, A. K., & Gelman, S. A. (1995). How does your garden grow? Evidence of an early conception of plants as biological kinds. *Child Development, 66,* 856–876.

Hirschfeld, L. A. (1994). The child's representation of human groups. In D. Medin (Ed.), *The psychology of learning and motivation: Advances in research and theory: Vol. 31.* (133–185) New York: Academic Press.

Hood, L., & Bloom, L. (1979). What, when, and how about why: A longitudinal study of the early expressions of causality. *Monographs of the Society for Research in Child Development, 44* (6, serial No. 181).

Hoppe, M. J., Wells, E. A., Wilsdon, A., Gillmore, M. R., & Morrison, D. M. (1994). Children's knowledge and beliefs about AIDS: Qualitative data from focus group interviews. *Health Education Quarterly, 21,* 117–126.

Huston, R. L., Martin, L. J., & Foulds, D. M. (1990). Effect of a program to facilitate parent-child communication about sex. *Clinical Pediatrics, 29,* 626–633.

Inagaki, K., & Hatano, G. (1987). Young children's spontaneous personification as analogy. *Child Development, 58(4),* 1013–1020.

Inagaki, K., & Hatano, G. (1993). Young children's understanding of the mind-body distinction. *Child Development, 64(5),* 1534–1549.

Kalish, C. (in press). Preschoolers' understanding of germs as invisible mechanisms. *Cognitive Development.*

Keil, F. C. (1992). The origins of an autonomous biology. In M.R. Gunnar & M. Maratsos (Eds.), *Modularity and constraints in language and cognition. Minnesota Symposia on Child Psychology: Vol. 25,* (pp. 103–137). Hillsdale, NJ: Erlbaum.

Keil, F. C. (1994). The birth and nurturance of concepts by domains: The origins of concepts of living things. In L. A. Hirschfeld and S. A. Gelman (Eds.), *Domain specificity in cognition and culture* (pp. 234–254). New York: Cambridge University Press.

Keller, M. L. (1993). Why don't young adults protect themselves against sexual transmission of HIV? Possible answers to a complex question. *AIDS Education and Prevention, 5,* 220–233.

Keller, S. E., Bartlett, J. A., Schleifer, S. J., Johnson, R. L., Pinner, E., & Delaney, B. (1991). HIV-relevant sexual behavior among a healthy inner-city heterosexual adolescent population in an endemic area of HIV. *Journal of Adolescent Health, 12,* 44–48.

Lefkowitz, E. S. (1995). "Sharing needles, having sex": Mother-adolescent conversations about AIDS. Poster presented at SRCD, Indianapolis.

Lefkowitz, E. S., Kahlbaugh, P., & Sigman, M. D. (In press). Turn-taking in mother-adolescent conversations about sexuality and conflicts. *Journal of Youth and Adolescence.*

Leland, N. L. & Barth, R. P. (1993). Characteristics of adolescents who have attempted to avoid HIV and who have communicated with parents about sex. *Journal of Adolescent Research, 8,* 58–76.

Leviton, L. C. (1989). Theoretical foundations of AIDS-prevention programs. In R. O. Valdiserri (Ed.), *Preventing AIDS: The design of effective programs* (pp. 42–90). New Brunswick, NJ: Rutgers University.

Millstein, S. G. (1989). Adolescent Health: Challenges for behavioral scientists. *American Psychologist, 44,* 837–842.

National Catholic Educational Association AIDS Education Task Force. (1992). *AIDS: A Catholic educational approach to HIV (human immunodeficiency virus).* Teacher's Manual. Washington, D.C.: National Catholic Educational Association.

National Commission on AIDS (1993). *Behavioral and social sciences and the HIV/AIDS epidemic.* United States of America, Washington, D.C.

Osborne, M. L., Kistner, J. A., & Helgemo, B. (1993). Developmental progression in children's knowledge of AIDS: Implications for education and attitudinal change. *Journal of Pediatric Psychology, 18,* 177–192.

Richards, D. D., & Siegler, R. S. (1986). Children's understandings of the attributes of life. *Journal of Experimental Child Psychology, 42(1),* 1–22.

Rosengren, K. S., Gelman, S. A., Kalish, C. W., & McCormick, M. (1991). As time goes by: Children's early understanding of growth in animals. *Child Development, 62,* 1302–1320.

Schonfeld, D. J., O'Hare, L. L., Perrin, E. C., Quackenbush, M., Showalter, D. R., & Cicchetti, D. V. (1995). A randomized, controlled trial of a school-based, multi-faceted AIDS education program in the elementary grades: The impact on comprehension, knowledge and fears. *Pediatrics, 95,* 480–486.

Scott, C. S., Shifman, L., Orr, L., Owen, R.G., & Fawcett, N. (1988). Hispanic and Black American adolescents' beliefs relating to sexuality and contraception. *Adolescence, 23,* 667–688.

Sigelman, C. K., Derenowski, E. B., Mullaney, H. A., & Siders, A. T. (1993a). Parents' contributions to knowledge and attitudes regarding AIDS. *Journal of Pediatric Psychology, 18,* 221–235.

Sigelman, C., Maddock, A., Epstein, J., & Carpenter, W. (1993b). Age differences in understanding of disease causality: AIDS, colds, and cancer. *Child Development, 64,* 272–284.

Slonim-Nevo, V., Ozawa, M. N., & Auslander, W. F. (1991). Knowledge, attitudes and behaviors related to AIDS among youth in residential centers: Results from an exploratory study. *Journal of Adolescence, 14,* 17–33.

Solomon, G. E. A. (1995). Against the claim that preschoolers already know biology as an autonomous conceptual domain. Paper presented at the symposium on "Characterizing young children's knowledge of biology" at Society for Research in Child Development, Indianapolis.

Solomon, G. E. A., & Cassimatis, Nicholas L. (1995). On young children's understanding of germs as biological causes of illness. Poster presented at Society for Research in Child Development, Indianapolis.

Solomon, G. E. A., Johnson, S. C., Zaitchik, D., & Carey, S. (1996). Like father, like son: Young children's understanding of how and who offspring resemble their parents. *Child Development, 67,* 151–171.

Spelke, E. S., & Hermer, L. (1996). Early cognitive development: Objects and space. In R. Gelman & T. K. Au (Eds.), *Handbook of perception and cognition: Volume 13 Perceptual and cognitive development,* (pp. 71–114). New York: Academic Press.

Sprecher, S. (1990). The impact of the threat of AIDS on heterosexual dating relationships. *Journal of Psychology and Human Sexuality, 3,* 3–23.

Springer, K. (1992). Children's awareness of the biological implications of kinship. *Child Development, 63(4),* 950–959.

Springer, K. (1995). The role of factual knowledge in a naive theory of biology. Paper presented at the symposium on "Characterizing young children's knowledge of biology" at Society for Research in Child Development, Indianapolis.

Springer, K., & Belk, A. (1994). The role of physical contact and association in early contamination sensitivity. *Developmental Psychology, 30,* 864–868.

Springer, K., & Keil, F. C. (1991). Early differentiation of causal mechanisms appropriate to biological and non-biological kinds. *Child Developmental, 62,* 767–781.

Springer, K., Nguyen, T., & Samaniego, R. (in press). Early awareness of decomposition as a distinctive property of biological kinds: Evidence for a naive theory. *Cognitive Development.*

Springer, K., & Ruckel, J. (1992). Early beliefs about the cause of illness: Evidence against immanent justice. *Cognitive Development, 7,* 429–443.

Stavy, R., & Wax, N. (1989). Children's conceptions of plants as living things. *Human Development, 32(2),* 88–94.

Swartz, Timothy E. (Producer and Director), (1989). *What's in the news: Coping with AIDS* [video]. Pennsylvania State University, The Center for Instructional Design and Interactive Video. Philadelphia, PA: The Pennsylvania State University.

Task Force on Pediatric AIDS, American Psychological Association. (1989). Pediatric AIDS and Human Immunodeficiency Virus Infection. *American Psychologist, 44,* 258–264.

Vosniadou, S., & Brewer, W. F. (1992). Mental models of the Earth: A study of conceptual change in childhood. *Cognitive Psychology, 24,* 535–585.

Walsh, M. E. (1995). Conceptions of illness in children and adults. Paper presented at SRCD, Indianapolis.

Walsh, M. E., & Bibace, R. (1991). Children's conceptions of AIDS: A developmental analysis. *Journal of Pediatric Psychology, 16,* 273–285.

Watkins, J. D., Conway-Welch, C., Creedon, J. J., Crenshaw, T. L., Devos, R. M., Gebbie, K. M., Lee, B. J., Lilly, F., O'Connor, J. C., Primm, B. J., Pullen, P., Servaas, C., & Walsh, W. B. (1988). *Report of the Presidential Commission on the HIV Epidemic* (Publication No. 0-214-701-:QL3). Washington, D. C.: U. S. Government Printing Office.

Wellman, H. M. (1990). *The child's theory of mind.* Cambridge, MA: MIT Press.

Wellman, H. M., & Estes, D. (1986). Early understanding of mental entitics: A reexamination of childhood realism. *Child Development, 57,* 910–923.

Wellman, H. M., & Gelman, S. A. (1992). Cognitive development: Foundational theories of core domains. *Annual Review of Psychology, 43,* 337–375.

White, B. Y. (1993). Intermediate causal models: A missing link for successful science education? In R. Glaser (Ed.) *Advances in instructional psychology* (Volume 4, pp. 177–252). Hillsdale, New Jersey: Erlbaum.

SPATIAL EFFECTS IN THE PARTIAL REPORT PARADIGM
A Challenge for Theories of Visual Spatial Attention

Gordon D. Logan
Claus Bundesen

I. Introduction

Cognitive theories explain the mind as the interaction of mental representations and the processes that operate on them. Neither representation nor process is sufficient by itself. Representations do not do anything without processes to operate on them and processes do not do anything without representations to operate on. But put them together and they "execute" like the running of a program. The "steps" they go through are the mind in action, manifest in various behavioral and biological measures, from reaction time and accuracy to event-related electrical brain potentials and functional magnetic resonance imagery.

There is an important balance between representation and process. Representations must provide the information that is necessary to support the processing, and the processes must be able to exploit the information available in the representation. Theories that attempt to specify one without the other or focus on one more than the other are incomplete and underdeveloped.

In our view, the balance between representation and process is far from optimal in current theories of visual spatial attention. Spatial selection has been a central topic in attention research for 35 years (Averbach & Coriell,

1961; Sperling, 1960) and a dominant paradigm in attention research for the last 15 (Bundesen, 1990; Cave & Wolfe, 1990; Duncan & Humphreys, 1989; Nissen, 1985; Treisman & Gelade, 1980; Treisman & Gormican, 1988; van der Heijden, 1992, 1993; Wolfe, 1994). Theories abounded, processes flourished, but little was said about the representation of space.

This reticence about representation of space limits the theories in important ways. For one thing, the meager representations of space available in current theories of attention are not sufficient to support the computation required to direct attention from a cue to a target, which is an essential ability in many attention paradigms (Logan, 1995). For another, the meager representations in current theories do not provide accounts of several distance and grouping-by-proximity effects that pervade the literature on visual spatial attention (Logan, 1996). It seems to us that a theory of spatial attention should explain the effects of space on selective attention.

The purpose of this chapter is to propose a theory that strikes what we hope is a better balance between representation and process in visual spatial attention, and to use that theory to explain distance and grouping effects in the Sperling (1960) and Averbach and Coriell (1961) partial report paradigm. The theory is an extension of Bundesen's (1990) Theory of Visual Attention (TVA), which already provides an excellent account of temporal factors, load effects, and similarity between targets and distractors in partial report tasks, but does not account for the distance effects. We extend the theory by combining it with van Oeffelen and Vos (1982, 1983) COntour DEtector theory of perceptual grouping by proximity, which parses the display into regions that TVA samples. The theory, which we call the CODE Theory of Visual Attention (CTVA), is explained in detail and applied to several paradigms in Logan (1996). Our purpose here is to apply it to the partial report paradigm, fitting an important data set, reported by Mewhort, Campbell, Marchetti, and Campbell (1981), that shows a variety of spatial effects.

II. Partial Report Paradigm

A. BACKGROUND

In the partial report paradigm, introduced by Sperling (1960), subjects are presented with a brief display containing many forms—usually letters or digits—and they are required to report a subset of them. The items to be reported are distinguished from the items to be ignored by a property called the *selection attribute.* Most often, the selection attribute is location (e.g., "report the items in the top row" or "report the item next to the bar marker"), but many other attributes have been investigated, including color, size, and alphanumeric category (Sperling, 1960; von Wright, 1968, 1970). The partial report task requires subjects to report a property of the selected items that is different from the selection attribute. This property, called the *reported attribute,* is usually letter identity (or digit identity), but it can be any property other than the selection attribute (see, e.g., Clark, 1969; Nissen, 1985). The display is usually presented briefly (for about 50 ms), and in many cases, a cue indicating the relevant value of the selection attribute (e.g., which row to report) is presented at some delay (usually less than 1,000 ms) following the display.

In 1961, Averbach and Coriell introduced an important variation of the partial report task, called the *bar-probe* task. In the bar-probe task, subjects are required to report only a single item, which is (usually) the one adjacent to a bar marker or probe. The bar probe is presented at various delays relative to the display, and the decay functions observed with the bar probe are very similar to those observed in Sperling's (1960) multitarget version of the partial report task. The bar-probe version of the task is the focus of the modeling effort in the present chapter.

The partial report paradigm is used for two primary purposes: to study visual selective attention and to study sensory or "iconic" memory, which lasts for a brief time after the display is turned off. Students of selective attention usually manipulate the nature of the selection attribute (e.g., Bundesen, 1987; Bundesen, Pedersen, & Larsen, 1984; Bundesen, Shibuya, & Larsen, 1985; Nissen, 1985; Shibuya, 1993; Shibuya & Bundesen, 1988; von Wright, 1968, 1970); students of sensory memory usually manipulate the delay between the display and a cue that tells the subject the relevant value of the selection attribute (Averbach & Coriell, 1961; Gegenfurtner & Sperling, 1993; Sperling, 1960). The modal view of sensory memory, from 1960 to 1980 or so, accounted for the delay effects in terms of a rapidly fading image. Information about the identity of the display items—information about the reported attribute—is lost in half a second or so (Rumelhart, 1970; for reviews, see Coltheart, 1980; Dick, 1974; Long, 1980).

There are a number of grouping and proximity effects that complicate the picture. In the multitarget version, Fryklund (1975) found that report was more accurate if the target items (i.e., the items that possessed the relevant value of the selection attribute) were clustered together in a coherent pattern than if they were dispersed randomly about the display. Also in the multitarget version, Merikle (1980) found that report was more accurate if the selection attribute was compatible with the perceived organization of the display than if it was incompatible with it. For example, subjects reporting the top row of a 3 × 3 display were more accurate if the display was organized into rows (by the Gestalt principle of proximity) than if it was organized into columns. In the single-target version, Snyder (1972) found that when subjects made errors, the items they reported were likely to have appeared adjacent to the cued item in the display. These results suggest that spatial information plays an important role in accessing sensory memory and argue for a more explicit representation of space in theories of the paradigm.

B.   Mewhort, Campbell, Marchetti, and Campbell (1981)

In 1981, Mewhort, Campbell, Marchetti, and Campbell published an important set of experiments on location errors in the bar-probe task that challenged the modal view of sensory memory. Mewhort et al. (1981) argued, from their data, that decay in sensory memory resulted from the loss of spatial information rather than the loss of item information, as the modal view assumed. Their experiments are important because the data are very clear, the key results have been replicated (see Mewhort, Butler, Feldman-Stewart, & Tramer, 1988), and the implications, drawn out by Mewhort et al. (1981), are provocative. Moreover, the data from all the experiments were reported in detail (numerically) in an appendix, so the article is especially useful for our purposes.

The Mewhort et al. (1981) experiments included six conditions, which are depicted in Fig. 1. In each condition, the target display contained eight letters and the task was to report the identity of the letter that was cued by a bar probe presented adjacent to it. A response was required on each trial. Condition 1 was the standard Averbach and Coriell (1961) bar-probe task. A target display was presented for 30 ms followed by a 30-ms bar probe that appeared 0, 40, 80, 120, or 160 ms after the target display terminated. Conditions 2–6 presented a masking stimulus at some duration following the display.

In Condition 2, the mask and the bar probe appeared simultaneously 0, 40, 80, 120, or 160 ms after the target display terminated. Condition 3 was a replication of Condition 2, except that the display was exposed until the mask and probe appeared. Mewhort et al. (1981) noted that this condition confounded delay with the intensity of the target display (due to temporal summation on their display screen) but they included it anyway because it replicated the procedure of a previously published experiment that they found interesting. In Condition 4, the probe always appeared immediately after the display, but the mask was delayed, appearing 0, 40, 80, 120, or 160 ms after the display. Condition 5 was a replication of Condition 4, except that the probe was exposed for 190 ms. Condition 6 was a conceptual replication of Conditions 4 and 5, in which the probe appeared simultaneously with the target display but remained on for 600 ms (whereas the

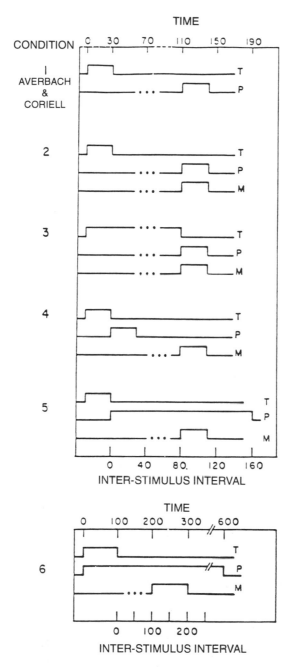

Fig. 1. Schematic description of the timing of events on a representative trial in each condition of the experiment by Mewhort, Campbell, Marchetti, and Campbell (1981). T, P, and M refer to the target display, probe, and mask, respectively. The dots indicate those timings that vary for other cases within the condition. Reprinted from Mewhort et al. (1981) by permission of The Psychonomic Society.

target display was terminated after 100 ms), and the mask, which appeared on 80% of the trials, was presented 0, 50, 100, or 150 ms after the target display terminated.

There were four replications of each condition, differing from each other in the sequential constraints imposed on the selection of letters for the target displays. The sequential constraints reflected various "orders of approximation to English" ($-2, 0, 2,$ and 4th order). In an Nth order approximation to English, sequences of N letters have a high probability of occurring in printed English text (-2nd order is 2nd order reversed). These sequential constraints have important effects on accuracy, which provide valuable information about the elementary processes underlying reading, but they did not interact with the major variables relevant to our present purposes, so we will not discuss them further.

Mewhort et al. (1981) distinguished *correct reports* from two kinds of errors, *location errors,* in which subjects reported an item that was not cued but was nevertheless present in the target display, and *item errors,* in which subjects reported an item that was not presented in the target display. In the standard Averbach and Coriell (1961) condition (Condition 1), they found a trade-off between correct reports and location errors: Correct reports declined as probe delay increased, and location errors increased in a compensatory fashion. Item errors remained relatively constant over probe delay. A similar trade-off was observed in an analysis of serial position effects. Correct reports were a W-shaped function of position in the display, with high accuracy on the end and middle items, while location errors were a complementary M-shape, being low for the end and middle items and high for the items in between (also see Mewhort & Campbell, 1978).

Mewhort et al. (1981) also analyzed the spatial distribution of location errors and found that they came primarily from items immediately adjacent to the probed item (conceptually replicating Snyder, 1972). They interpreted this pattern as evidence of a location confusion: The attention system failed to resolve space properly and selected an adjacent item instead of the correct one.

The trade-off between correct reports and location errors and the spatial distribution of location errors led Mewhort et al. (1981) to challenge the modal view, proposing that location information rather than item information was lost as "iconic memory" decayed. This is an important hypothesis that changed many researchers' views about the nature of sensory memory (cf. Chow, 1986; but see Mewhort et al., 1988). Part of our purpose in modeling the Mewhort et al. (1981) data set was to see if this proposal was warranted.

Mewhort et al. (1981) used the remaining conditions (2–6) to converge on the conclusions they reached in the first condition. They argued that the modal view predicted that masking and delaying the bar probe should have the same effects—on item errors primarily. By contrast, they found that masking affected item errors primarily, whereas probe delay affected location errors primarily, suggesting a dissociation that supported an alternative two-buffer account that they proposed (also see Mewhort, Marchetti, Gurnsey, & Campbell, 1984).

III.   Theoretical Analysis of the Partial Report Task

A.   THEORY OF VISUAL ATTENTION

Bundesen's (1990) theory of visual attention (TVA) models selective attention as a race between alternative perceptual categorizations of display items. The rate at which the different items in the display "run" in the race depends on three parameters, $\eta(x,i)$, which is the quality of sensory evidence that item x is a member of category i, w_x, which is the attention weight allocated to item x, and β_i, which is the person's bias to categorize display items as members of i. The quality of sensory evidence is determined by bottom-up perceptual factors and by the person's history of learning. The attentional weight and the bias are set by the person's homunculus in accord with task set and task instructions. The three parameters combine in Equation 1 to produce the processing rate, $v(x,i)$, which determines how quickly x races to be categorized as i:

$$v(x,i) = \eta\,(x,i)\,\beta_i\,\frac{w_x}{\sum\limits_{z \varepsilon S} w_z} \qquad (1)$$

The attentional weight on item x (w_x) is normalized by dividing it by the sum of the attentional weights on the other items in the display set, S. The weight itself is set by manipulating a pertinence parameter, π_j, which reflects the importance of selecting items with the property j. The attentional weight is the product of the pertinence parameter and the quality of sensory evidence that the item possesses the relevant property, j; items are given more weight the more clearly they possess the relevant property. In some cases, items may be selected on the basis of more than one property (e.g., "select the red items or the green ones"), so attentional weight is summed over all of the relevant properties in the set $\mathbf{R}$:

$$w_x = \sum\limits_{j \varepsilon R} \eta\,(x,j)\,\pi_j \qquad (2)$$

In TVA, the attentional weights are used to select a particular item and the bias is used to select a particular categorization for the selected item. The property, j, that determines the attentional weight is the *selection attribute*, and the property i that receives the bias is the *reported attribute*. In a typical partial report paradigm, j might be a particular location in the display (e.g., the one cued by a bar marker) and i might be the identity of the letter in that location. In all applications, TVA assumes that selection operates in parallel over the entire visual field. This imposes a constraint on the kinds of attributes that can serve as selection attributes and reported attributes: They must be the kinds of attributes that can be computed in parallel by local parallel processes. Attributes that cannot be computed in parallel cannot drive selection in TVA (see e.g., Ullman, 1984).

In partial report tasks, TVA selects the first K items to finish processing, where K is the capacity of visual short-term memory. Suppose the items are letters and the reported attribute is letter identity. If β values are $\beta_1 > 0$ for letter identities but 0 for any other categories, then all perceptual categorizations that enter the short-term store are categorizations of letters with respect to identity. In this case, a stimulus letter finishes the race if and when a categorization of the letter with respect to identity finishes the race. The identity of the letter represented in visual short-term memory is given by the first-finishing categorization of the letter. Thus, the accuracy of report depends on (a) the number of targets among the letters that enter visual short-term memory, and (b) the probability that the first-finishing categorization of a target letter gives the correct identity of the letter.

In the single-target partial report task developed by Averbach and Coriell (1961), the target is reported correctly if (a) the letter is among the letters that enter short-term memory, and (b) the first-finishing categorization of the target gives the correct identity of the target. If the exposure duration is sufficiently long, K items from the display finish the race, so that short-term memory is filled with display items. In other cases (e.g., if the display is masked), fewer than K runners may finish. In those cases, report can only be accurate to the extent that the target item is among those that finish.

The mathematics of the selection process can be found in Bundesen, Pedersen, and Larsen (1984), Bundesen, Shibuya, and Larsen (1985), Bundesen (1987, 1990), and Shibuya and Bundesen (1988), along with fits to a variety of data sets. Bundesen (1990) extended them to include decay of item information when the probe follows the display. Here, we extend them to include the idea that it takes time to switch attention to the cued location.

Response probabilities in the partial report task depend on the storage capacity, K, of visual short-term memory, the processing capacity, C, of the system, the exposure duration, τ, of the display, and the time constant, μ, for the decay of the η values. The processing capacity, C, is defined as the sum of the $v(x,i)$ values over all categorizations ($i \ \varepsilon \ \mathbf{R}$) of all display items ($x \ \varepsilon \ \mathbf{S}$), given by

$$C = \sum_{x \varepsilon S} \sum_{i \varepsilon R} v(x,i) \tag{3}$$

(see Bundesen, 1990, pp. 524-525).

We assume the stimulus is presented from Time 0 to time τ, and the probe is presented at time t_c, where $t_c \geq 0$. We assume further that the time taken to switch attention to the cued location, or *attention reaction time* (a_{RT}), is greater than zero, but constant. Research by Eriksen and colleagues (Colegate, Hoffman, & Eriksen, 1973; Eriksen & Collins, 1969; Eriksen & Hoffman, 1972) suggests that performance reaches asymptote when the cue precedes the display by 150–300 ms. This asymptote represents the maximum time taken to switch attention (i.e., the upper tail of the distribution of a_{RT}), whereas a_{RT} represents the mean switching time (Sperling & Weichselgartner, 1995).[1]

The brief exposures and probe delays complicate the analysis of the partial report task. The processing rate for a given item changes when the display turns off and changes again when attention switches to the item after the probe is presented. And masking stimuli terminate processing, setting the rate to zero. The probability of a correct response (and the probability of the various kinds of errors) depends on all the different processing rates that are effective throughout the duration of the trial.

The v value for an item is the sum of the v values for all of the perceptual categorizations of that item. The v value for a target is a function of time, t. When the probe is presented after the target terminates, the function is given by

$$v(t) = \begin{cases} 0 \; for \; t \leq 0 \\ C/(T+D) \; for \; 0 < t \leq \tau \\ [C/(T+D)] \exp[-(t-\tau)/\mu] \; for \; \tau < t \leq t_c + a_{RT} \\ (C/T) \exp[-(t-\tau)/\mu] \; for \; t_c + a_{RT} < t \end{cases} \tag{4}$$

[1] Coltheart and Coltheart (1972) criticized Rumelhart's (1970) model of partial report performance because it assumed that attention switched to the probed position immediately, as soon as the probe was presented (i.e., $a_{RT} = 0$). They pointed out that many data suggest that it takes time to switch attention, and they regarded Rumelhart's (1970) model as unrealistic because it failed to account for this fact. We included attention reaction time (a_{RT}) as a free parameter to avoid this criticism. It turns out that the fits were not very sensitive to this parameter. They improved when it was added, but not by much. When the data were fitted without this parameter, the negative log likelihood measure was 40.99 for the random-response-rule TVA fit, 38.15 for the random-response-rule CTVA fit, 40.85 for the spatial-response-rule TVA fit, and 38.05 for the spatial-response-rule CTVA fit. These values are larger but close to the values for the fits that included a_{RT} as a parameter (see Table I). Perhaps Coltheart and Coltheart (1972) overstated their case.

where T is the number of targets (1 in this case) and D is the number of distractors. The v value for a distractor is

$$u\ (t) = \begin{cases} v(t) \ for \ t \le t_c + a_{RT} \\ 0 \ for \ t_c + a_{RT} < t. \end{cases} \tag{5}$$

In other words, capacity is divided equally among targets and distractors until attention is switched to the target after the probe appears, and then it is focused entirely on the probed position (a similar assumption was made by Rumelhart, 1970). The remainder of the mathematics, adapted from Bundesen (1990), can be found in this chapter's Appendix.

Note that TVA assumes sensory memory decay is based on the loss of item information rather than location information. In this respect, it is more similar to the modal view than to Mewhort et al.'s (1981).

B. COntour DEtector Theory of Grouping by Proximity

The COntour DEtector (CODE) theory of grouping by proximity was proposed first by van Oeffelen and Vos (1982, 1983) and modified subsequently by Compton and Logan (1993). The theory assumes that item locations are represented as distributions rather than as points in space, as illustrated in the top panel of Fig. 2 (also see Maddox, Prinzmetal, Ivry, & Ashby, 1994). Location information for the different items in the display is combined by adding together the distributions to form a *CODE surface*, as illustrated in the middle panel of Fig. 2. Perceptual grouping by proximity is accomplished by applying a *threshold* to the CODE surface, dividing it into a number of above-threshold and below-threshold regions. Items that fall within the same above-threshold region are perceived as belonging to the same perceptual group. The bottom panel of Fig. 2 illustrates three different groupings of a three-item display. The low threshold includes all three items in one group; the middle threshold groups two items together and splits off the third; and the high threshold divides the display into three separate items. The theory assumes that the threshold is under the control of the subject (or the subject's homunculus), in order to account for the role of top-down processes (attention) in choosing between alternative organizations of the same display.

Van Oeffelen and Vos (1982) tested one version of CODE by exposing it to textbook demonstrations of grouping by proximity (e.g., a matrix of dots organized into rows by proximity) and comparing the groups produced by CODE with those produced by human subjects. The agreement between CODE and human subjects was nearly perfect. Compton and Logan (1993) tested many versions of CODE by exposing it to random dot patterns and comparing the groups it produced with those of human subjects. Agreement

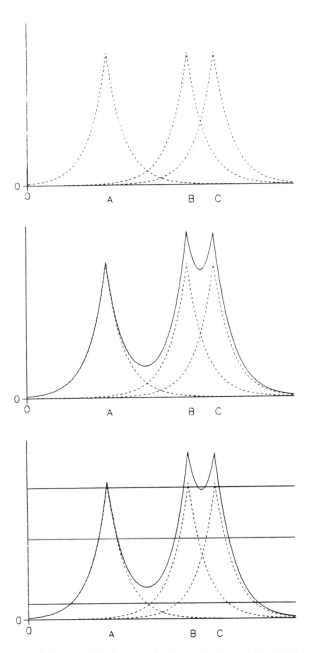

Fig. 2. *Top panel:* Feature distributions for items A, B, and C. *Middle panel:* CODE surface and feature distributions for items A, B, and C. *Bottom panel:* Three thresholds applied to the CODE surface for items A, B, and C. The low threshold includes all three items in one group; the middle threshold groups B and C together and separates A; the high threshold separates all three items.

was less than perfect but well above chance and close to subjects' agreement with each other's grouping judgments.

Compton and Logan (1993) compared several versions of CODE, varying the form of the distribution (normal, as in the original version, vs. Laplace), how the distributions were combined (by addition, as in the original version, vs. taking the maximum), and how the variability of the distributions was determined (depending on the distance to the nearest neighbor, as in the original version, vs. holding it constant for all items in the display). They found that adding Laplace distributions with the same variability produced fits that were as good as the best and significantly better than the original CODE fits. The constant-variability, additive, Laplace version of CODE is the most tractable, so it was the one we used here in combination with TVA (also see Logan, 1996).

C.   CODE THEORY OF VISUAL ATTENTION

The CODE theory of visual attention, proposed by Logan (1996), integrates Bundesen's (1990) TVA theory with the CODE theory of perceptual grouping by proximity. CODE provides the perceptual input to TVA, and TVA transforms the input to output. The two theories together are called the CODE theory of visual attention (CTVA), and CTVA accounts for many effects of distance, density, and proximity that were problematic for TVA and other theories of attention.

CTVA goes beyond CODE in interpreting the distributions of location information as distributions of information about the features of the items; CTVA assumes that feature information is spread over space (also see Ashby, Prinzmetal, Ivry, & Maddox, 1996; Ratcliff, 1981; Wolford, 1975). CTVA assumes further that TVA samples information from one or more above-threshold regions of the CODE surface. An above-threshold region of the CODE surface in CTVA is the same as an element in the visual field in TVA. At any point in time, the set of regions (elements) from which information is being sampled by TVA is called the *field of spatial attention,* **A.** The field of spatial attention can be (a) a singleton set (e.g., a single letter in a multiletter display) or (b) a set of items that make up a single higher-level element (e.g., a subset of letters in a multiletter display that are seen as a single perceptual group). This idea is illustrated in Fig. 3, which portrays a threshold applied to a CODE surface. Vertical lines are drawn from the intersection of the CODE surface to the abscissa to represent the boundary of the above-threshold region. As can be seen in Fig. 3, a single above-threshold region contains information about the items that lie within it but it also contains information about adjacent items.

CTVA formalizes this idea in what is called the *feature catch.* Suppose that a threshold is applied to the CODE surface for a multi-item display so that

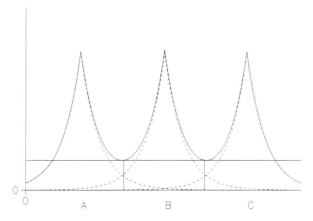

Fig. 3   A CODE surface for three items with a threshold applied to it. Vertical lines extending from the threshold to the abscissa represent the limits of integration in computing the feature catch. Note that some portions of the feature distributions for the peripheral items are included in the sample even though attention is focused on the central item.

each item in the display forms a separate above-threshold region. Let x and y be items in the display with corresponding above-threshold regions $\mathbf{A}x$ and $\mathbf{A}y$. The feature catch, $c_{x|Ax}$, is the likelihood of sampling features of item x from region $\mathbf{A}x$, and the feature catch, $c_{y|Ax}$ is the likelihood of sampling features of item y from region $\mathbf{A}x$. In the one-dimensional case,

$$c_{x|Ax} = \int_{lo}^{hi} \frac{1}{2}\lambda_x \exp\left[-\lambda_x|u-\theta_r|\right]\,du \qquad (6)$$

where $\frac{1}{2}\lambda_x\exp[-\lambda_x|u-\theta_x|]$ is a Laplace distribution (with location parameter θ_x and scale parameter λ_x) representing the spatial spread of the features of item x.

The feature catch modulates the information input to TVA. We represent this formally by replacing the eta values, $\eta(x,i)$, by *effective eta values*, $\eta_e(\mathbf{A}x,i)$, in Equations 1 and 2 of TVA. The effective eta value for the categorization that items in region $\mathbf{A}x$ are members of category i is given by

$$\eta_e(Ax,i) = \sum_{y\in S} c_{y|Ax}\,\eta(y,i) \qquad (7)$$

Equation 7 reflects the CTVA assumption that attention samples from a region—$\mathbf{A}x$—rather than an item. When attention is focused on region

Ax it samples all items in the display in proportion to the area of their feature distributions that falls within the region (i.e., in proportion to their feature catches, $c_{y|Ax}$). Thus, Equation 1 becomes

$$v(Ax,i) = \eta_e(Ax, i)\beta_i \frac{w_{Ax}}{\sum\limits_{Az \varepsilon S} w_{AZ}} \tag{8}$$

Substituting effective eta values in Equation 2 and assuming that the attentional weight of an element is 0 if it is outside the field of spatial attention **A,** yields the CTVA equation

$$w_{Ax} = \begin{cases} \sum\limits_{Z \varepsilon S} \sum\limits_{j \varepsilon R} C_{z|Ax} \, \eta \, (z,j) \, \pi_j \text{ if } Ax \, \varepsilon \, A \\ 0 \text{ if } Ax \, \bar{\varepsilon} \, A \end{cases} \tag{9}$$

CTVA does not assume that attention samples above-threshold regions serially. Serial processing is possible, but so is parallel processing. If subjects process above-threshold regions in series, then the effective attention weight, $w_{Ax}/\Sigma w_{Az}$, in Equation 8 equals 1 (because Ax is the only attended area, so $w_{Ax} = \Sigma w_{Az}$). If subjects process above-threshold regions in parallel, then the effective attention weight in Equation 8 is less than one (because $w_{Ax} < \Sigma w_{Az}$).

The mathematics of CTVA are the same as the mathematics of TVA. CTVA becomes identical to TVA when (a) **A = S** (i.e., subjects attend to the whole display at once, so that the field of spatial attention coincides with the set of items in the display), and (b) $c_{x|Ax} = 1$ for every item x but $c_{y|Ax} = 0$ when x is different from y. In some partial report experiments, it seems plausible that (a) subjects attend to all the items in the display at once, and (b) interitem distances are so large that feature catches from adjacent items can be neglected. In such cases, an analysis based on CTVA reduces to an analysis based on TVA (e.g., an analysis in terms of the fixed-capacity independent race model of Shibuya and Bundesen, 1988). Thus, CTVA can be viewed as a generalization of TVA, and TVA can be viewed as a special case of CTVA. CTVA "inherits" the successes of TVA (see Bundesen, 1990) and TVA is largely responsible for the successes of CTVA (see Logan, 1996).

The CTVA analysis of partial report differs from the TVA analysis in an important respect. TVA treats target location as a primitive category, computed by local parallel processes, whereas CTVA treats target location as a complex (compositional) category that cannot be computed by local parallel processes. In the partial report task, target location is defined relative to the location of the probe. Theory (Logan, 1995; Ullman, 1984) and data (Logan, 1994) suggest that relative location is not a primitive category that can be apprehended in parallel. The probe and the target locations have to be apprehended separately and a further act of attention is necessary to compute the location of one relative to the other. Apprehension of the location of the target relative to the cue involves processes that are outside CTVA (Logan, 1996; for details of the process of apprehending relative location, see Logan & Sadler, 1996). This makes CTVA less elegant and less complete than TVA, but we feel it is a necessary step on logical and empirical grounds.

From a psychological perspective, CTVA can be viewed as a spotlight theory of attention, with the "beam" of the spotlight corresponding to an above-threshold region of the CODE surface. CTVA can also be viewed as an object-based theory of attention, with the objects defined in terms of the perceptual groups created by applying a threshold to the CODE surface. CTVA integrates space-based and object-based approaches to attention: The above-threshold region is both a region of space and a perceptual object. In CTVA, space-based and object-based attention are different perspectives on the same thing.

CTVA provides TVA with a representation of space that has sufficient power to account for a variety of distance, density, and proximity effects in attention tasks (for a review, see Logan, 1996), as well as accounting for perceptual grouping by proximity. We feel that CTVA provides a better balance of representation and process than TVA by itself or CODE by itself, and we feel that that balance is responsible for CTVA's successes. As we shall see in the upcoming fits, the balance of representation and process in CTVA provides a better account of the Mewhort et al. (1981) data set than TVA by itself.

Note that CTVA, like TVA, interprets sensory memory decay in terms of loss of item information rather than location information, and in this respect, it differs from the Mewhort et al. (1981) proposal. It would be possible to model decay of spatial information in CTVA in terms of an increase in the variance of the feature distributions (a decrease in λ) over time. Preliminary investigations suggested that a linear increase in variance over time would account for the data nicely. However, we leave that for future development of the model and restrict our present analysis to the decay of item information.

IV. Fitting Theory to Data

We fitted TVA and CTVA to the data of Mewhort et al. (1981). We fitted all conditions except Condition 3, which confounded display duration with display intensity. In order to model this, we would have let the $\eta(x,i)$ values increase with exposure duration, and we wanted to keep the fits as simple as possible. We fitted the probability of correct reports, near location errors ($\pm$ 1 item from the target position), far location errors (more than $\pm$ 1 item from the target position), and item errors as functions of probe and mask delay in Conditions 1–2 and 4–6. Note that we broke Mewhort et al.'s (1981) location errors down into two categories, where they used only one. We did this to be able to assess the effects of distance and delay simultaneously.

We collapsed the data across order of approximation to English and across stimulus position. We restricted our analysis to trials in which the target had at least two neighboring items on each side (therefore including target positions 3–6 in our averaging and ignoring positions 1, 2, 7, and 8).

We did not attempt to model the serial position effects that Mewhort et al. (1981) observed. TVA predicts no position effects, unless we build them into the model. CTVA predicts the increase in correct reports and decrease in location errors in the end positions (i.e., the tails of the M and W shapes) because end items have only one neighbor that falls in their feature catch, whereas middle items have two or more (i.e., at least one on each side). We could model the increase in correct reports and decrease in location errors in the middle two positions (i.e., the middle of the W and M shapes) by assuming that the variability of the feature distributions increases with eccentricity. This is a reasonable assumption because visual receptive fields increase in size with eccentricity. Moreover, Mewhort and Popham (1991) made a similar assumption (an acuity function with an inverted U shape) in modeling similar data. However, we decided to ignore the serial position effects to keep the fitting simple.

We fitted TVA and then CTVA to the data for two reasons. First, we wanted to see how well TVA would account for the data without special assumptions about the representation of space. TVA has provided a good account of a large body of partial report data in the past and we wanted to see whether the same model would work with this data set. Second, we wanted to use the TVA fits as a baseline against which to evaluate the CTVA fits so we could see which parts of the fits were due to TVA and which parts were due to the extra spatial assumptions in CTVA.

We tried two kinds of fits for both TVA and CTVA, one with a *random response rule* and one with a *spatial response rule*. With both rules, the response is based on the target if a (correct or incorrect) categorization of the target is present in visual short-term memory. If the target is not in short-term memory, and the model follows the random response rule, then the subject reports a letter identity selected at random from those in short-term memory rather than guessing an identity not stored in short-term memory. If no identities have been stored, the subject guesses a letter identity at random.

If the model follows the spatial response rule, a letter identity is guessed at random if, and only if, no letter within a distance of ± 2 letters from the bar probe is stored in visual short-term memory. If any letters within a distance of ± 2 letters from the bar probe are found in visual short-term memory, then the subject reports an identity stored in short-term memory at a location as near as possible to the bar probe.

In all the fits reported below, we held the capacity, K, of short-term memory constant at a value of 5 items.

A. TVA FITS

1. Random Response Rule

The TVA fit for the random response rule involved four parameters, the processing capacity of the race, C, the capacity of short-term memory, K, the rate parameter for the exponential decay, μ, and the attention reaction time, a_{RT}. The details of the fitting procedure are provided in the Appendix to this chapter. The values that provided the best fit were $C = 11.19$ items per second, $K = 5$ items, $\mu = 139$ ms, and $a_{RT} = 35$ ms. The estimates of processing capacity and short-term memory capacity are close to the values Bundesen (1990) obtained in fits to Sperling's (1960) data. The exponential decay parameter, μ, is smaller than the value from Bundesen's (1990) fits to Sperling's (1960) data, but is generally consistent with the literature.

How reasonable is the estimate of attention reaction time? Eriksen and colleagues showed that the improvement in performance when the probe precedes the display reaches asymptote when the probe appears some 150–300 ms before the display (Colegate et al., 1973; Eriksen & Collins, 1969; Eriksen & Hoffman, 1972). Sperling and Weichselgartner (1995) argue that this asymptotic delay does not represent attention reaction time directly, but instead represents the upper tail of the distribution of attention reaction times (i.e., the point at which almost all switches of attention would have had time to finish). In order to convert our estimates of attention reaction time to asymptotic probe delays, we assumed that the distribution of a_{RT} was exponential (i.e., $F(t) = 1 - \exp[-(1/a_{RT})t]$) and solved for the value of t at the 99th percentile of the distribution.[2] With $a_{RT} = 35$ ms, the

---

[2] The assumption that the distribution of attention reaction times is exponential and the choice of the 99th percentile as the asymptotic value are somewhat arbitrary, and should not be interpreted as part of TVA or CTVA. We made these assumptions so that we could evaluate the plausibility of the fitted parameters in a crude and tentative fashion. We do not intend the reader to interpret the estimated asymptotes as predictions of our models.

asymptotic cue delay would be 161 ms, which is within the range observed by Eriksen and colleagues.[3]

The fits, plotted in the second row of Figs. 4 and 5, can be compared with the Mewhort et al. (1981) data, which are plotted in the top row of Figs. 4 and 5. Figure 4 contains the probabilities of correct reports, location errors (summed over near and far location errors), and item errors as functions of the delay of the probe or the mask or both (see Fig. 1 for a key to the conditions). Figure 5 plots the distribution of responses around the correct position (i.e., it compares correct reports, in position 0, with near location errors, in positions ± 1, and with far location errors, in positions $> +1$ or < -1).

Overall, the fit was quite good, especially considering that four parameters were fitted to 150 data points. Measures of goodness of fit are presented in Table I. The fit minimized the negative log likelihood measure

$$-\ln \left(\prod_{i=1}^{150} P_{theoretical} (i)^{P_{observed}(i)} \right)$$

(see chapter Appendix). The value for this fit was 39.83. For comparison, the value for a perfect fit would be 36.24 and the value for an imperfect fit, in which the same probability was assigned to each condition, would be 44.79. Table I also contains more traditional measures of goodness of fit—the correlation (r) between predicted and observed values and the root mean squared deviation $(rmsd)$ between predicted and observed values—for comparison.

Note that TVA was able to account for the trade-off between location errors and correct reports in Condition 1 (the standard bar-probe task introduced by Averbach & Coriell, 1961) and for the (relative) constancy of item errors over delay. This is important because Mewhort et al. (1981) interpreted the trade-off between location errors and correct reports and the constancy of item errors as evidence that forgetting in sensory memory was due to decay of location information rather than decay of item information. TVA accounts for the same pattern of data assuming that item information decays and location information does not. Because our conclusion is opposite to that of Mewhort et al. (1981), it deserves some explanation.

[3] The same analysis can be applied to the exponential decay parameter, μ, which represents the loss of item information over time. The poststimulus delay at which partial report performance reaches asymptote can be viewed as the upper tail of an exponential distribution of durations of sensory memory. The asymptotic delay can be estimated as the value of t corresponding to the 99th percentile for a given a value of μ. For $\mu = 139$, the estimated asymptotic delay would be 640 ms, which is within the range of observed asymptotic delays in the partial report paradigm (250–1,000 ms; see Sperling, 1960).

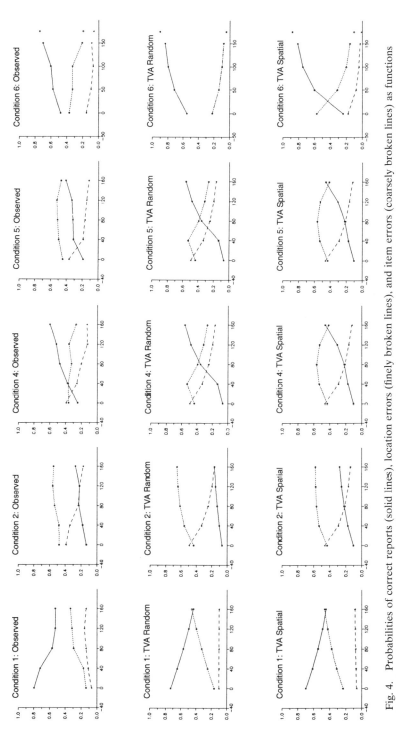

Fig. 4. Probabilities of correct reports (solid lines), location errors (finely broken lines), and item errors (coarsely broken lines) as functions of the delay of the probe and the mask. *Top row* = observed data from Mewhort, Campbell, Marchetti, and Campbell (1981); *middle row* = theoretical fits for the random-response-rule version of TVA; *bottom row* = theoretical fits for the spatial-response-rule version of TVA. The columns represent the different conditions described in the text and in Fig. 1. Horizontal axes = delay in MS; vertical axes = response probability.

TABLE I

MEASURES OF GOODNESS OF FIT FOR THE
RANDOM-RESPONSE-RULE AND
SPATIAL-RESPONSE-RULE VERSIONS OF
TVA AND CTVA

	Random		Spatial	
Response rule:	TVA	CTVA	TVA	CTVA
NLLM[a]	39.83	37.99	37.96	37.67
r	.905	.933	.917	.936
rmsd	.076	.059	.063	.057

[a] NLLM = negative log likelihood measure (for a definition, see chapter Appendix); r = product-moment correlation between predicted and observed values; rmsd = root
mean squared deviation between predicted and observed
values.

TVA assumes that attention is spread evenly over the display until the probe is presented (i.e., each position in the display receives the same attentional weight, w). When attention is reallocated in response to the probe, all attentional weight is concentrated at the probed position (i.e., all distractors get attentional weights of 0). These assumptions lead to a trade-off between location errors and correct reports in Condition 1. Processing the target is speeded up once attention is concentrated on the target, so correct reports are inversely related to probe delay. Why do location errors increase with probe delay? Because increasing probe delay increases the time during which the display is processed with equal attention to each item and decreases the time during which the display is processed with attention concentrated entirely on the target. The longer the time the display is processed with equal attention to each item and the shorter the time the display is processed with attention concentrated on the target, the greater the probability that short-term memory will contain distractors without containing a target, so the greater the probability of a location error.

With the random response rule, item errors occur only when no display items enter short-term memory. Intuitively, the probability that no items finish processing before a certain time t should be largely independent of the point in time at which target processing is speeded up at the expense of distractor processing. Mathematically, it can be shown that the probability of the event depends on processing capacity C, but the probability is independent of the way in which the capacity is distributed among the items in the display. Thus, with the random response rule, the probability of item errors in Condition 1 is strictly independent of the delay of the probe.

It is should be noted that Rumelhart (1970) made the same assumptions about the distribution of attention over time in his mathematical model of sensory memory, so his model could make similar predictions about the trade-off between location errors and correct reports (if it were equipped with a response rule that deals with single-target partial report). His model, like TVA, assumed that forgetting in sensory memory was due to loss of item information, not location information.

The random-response-rule version of TVA did a good job of accounting for the relations between correct reports, location errors, and item errors as functions of probe and mask delay (see Fig. 4), but it was less successful in accounting for the spatial distribution of responses (see Fig. 5). Basically, TVA predicts more reports from the probed position than for the non-probed positions, but it predicts an equal number of reports from positions near to and far from the probed position, and that is not apparent in the data, particularly in Condition 1 (the standard Averbach & Coriell, 1961, condition). This is because TVA does not include a representation of space like the one in CTVA.

2. Spatial Response Rule

The TVA fits for the spatial response rule also involved four parameters. The best-fitting values were $C = 21.49$ items per second, $K = 5.00$, $\mu = 118$ ms, and $a_{RT} - 109$ ms. Processing capacity was about twice the value for the random response rule, and the estimate of a_{RT} tripled, but μ was roughly the same (leading to a predicted poststimulus asymptotic probe delay of 543 ms). The value of a_{RT} predicts an asymptotic predisplay probe delay of 501 ms, which is beyond the range of observed values in the bar-probe task (Colegate et al., 1973; Eriksen & Collins, 1969; Eriksen & Hoffman, 1972).

The fits, plotted in the bottom rows of Figs. 4 and 5, can be compared with the Mewhort et al. (1981) data, which are plotted in the top row, and with the fits with the random response rule, which are plotted in the middle row. The spatial response rule improved the TVA fit, relative to the random response rule, reducing the negative log likelihood measure (which we tried to minimize) and *rmsd* while increasing *r* (see Table I).

The spatial-response-rule version of TVA still captured the trade-off between location errors and correct reports over delay in Condition 1, as the random-response-rule version did (see Fig. 4). In addition, it was able to capture more of the spatial distribution of responses than the random-response-rule version (see Fig. 5) because the spatial rule let it report an item adjacent to the probed position rather than one farther removed if the target item was not available for report. This is important because

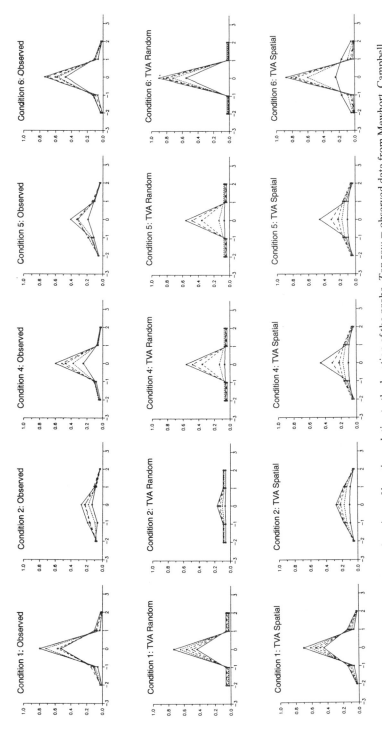

Fig. 5. Probabilities of report as functions of location relative to the location of the probe. *Top row* = observed data from Mewhort, Campbell, Marchetti, and Campbell (1981); *middle row* = theoretical fits for the random-response-rule version of TVA; *bottom row* = theoretical fits for the spatial-response-rule version of TVA. The columns represent the different conditions described in the text and in Fig. 1. Delay increases from the top line to the bottom line in Condition 1; delay increases from the bottom line to the top in Conditions 2–6. Horizontal axes = position; vertical axes = response probability.

both of these effects led Mewhort et al. (1981) to propose that location information decayed. This version of TVA accounts for them both, albeit not perfectly, by assuming that item information decays, without assuming that location information decays.

B.   CTVA FITS

1.   Random Response Rule

The CTVA fit involved five parameters, the processing capacity of the race, C, the capacity of short-term memory, K, the rate parameter for the exponential decay, μ, attention reaction time, a_{RT}, and the feature catch, P_c, which reflects the probability of selecting an item in the probed position versus one immediately adjacent to it. The details of the fitting procedure are provided in the Appendix to this chapter. The values that provided the best fit were $C = 12.06$ items per second, $K = 5$ items, $\mu = 160$ ms, $a_{RT} = 15$ ms, and $P_c = 0.79$. The estimate of processing capacity is similar to the random-response-rule TVA fit and to Bundesen's (1990) fits to Sperling's (1960) data. The decay parameter is similar as well (leading to a predicted asymptotic poststimulus probe delay of 767 ms). The estimate of a_{RT} is quite small. It predicts an asymptotic predisplay probe delay of 69 ms, which is much shorter than the range observed in the bar-probe experiments of Eriksen and colleagues (Colegate et al., 1973; Eriksen & Collins, 1969; Eriksen & Hoffman, 1972).

The parameter P_c, which represents the feature catch, $c_{x|Ax}$, is related to the distance between the items and the variability of the Laplace feature distributions. If the distance between the means of the feature distributions is d and the threshold is placed at the local minimum halfway between the means (see Logan, 1996), then

$$P_c = \int_{-d/2}^{d/2} \frac{1}{2} \lambda \exp\left[-\lambda |x|\right] dx$$
$$= 1 - \exp\left[-\lambda d/2\right]$$

From this expression, we can derive the ratio of the distance between items to the standard deviation of the feature distribution, d/SD. CTVA assumes Laplacean feature distributions with a standard deviation of $\sqrt{2}/\lambda$, so

$$d/SD = \lambda d/\sqrt{2}$$
$$= -\sqrt{2} \ln\left[1 - P_c\right]$$

where SD = standard deviation. With P_c = 0.79, d/SD is 2.21, which is close to the ratios Logan (1996) used in fitting CTVA to other tasks.

The fits are plotted in the middle rows of Figs. 6 and 7. They can be compared with the Mewhort et al. (1981) data, which are replotted in the top row, or the TVA fits in Figs. 4 and 5.

The CTVA fits with the random response rule were better quantitatively than the TVA fits with the random response rule (see Table I) and they were better qualitatively as well. Specifically, CTVA captured the spatial distribution of responses much better than TVA did, predicting more near location errors than far location errors (see Fig. 7; cf. Fig. 5). This improvement in fit reflects the effect of CTVA's assumptions about the representation of space and, consequently, the intrusion of adjacent items into the feature catch from the probed position. Again, in contrast with Mewhort et al. (1981), CTVA accounts for these effects and for the trade-off between location errors and correct reports (see Fig. 6, Condition 1) by assuming that only item information is lost over time, without assuming any decay of location information.

2. Spatial Response Rule

The CTVA fits for the spatial response rule also involved five parameters. The best-fitting values were C = 17.67 items per second, K = 5.00 items, μ = 129 ms, a_{RT} = 61 ms, and P_c = 0.86. The fits were only slightly better than the fits with the random response rule (see Table I). Processing capacity increased by half and the exponential decay constant, μ, decreased slightly, as it did with the TVA fits. The estimate of attention reaction time was more reasonable, producing an estimated asymptotic prestimulus delay of 281 ms, which is within the range observed by Eriksen and colleagues (Colegate et al., 1973; Eriksen & Collins, 1969; Eriksen & Hoffman, 1972). The ratio of the distance between items to the standard deviation of the feature distributions, d/SD, was 2.78, still close to the values that Logan (1996) used in fitting other tasks and paradigms.

Once again, CTVA captured the qualitative pattern of the data as well as the quantitative pattern. There was a trade-off between location errors and correct reports in Condition 1 (see Fig. 6) and location errors were more likely to be items adjacent to the probed position than items farther removed (see Fig. 7). Again, these patterns were produced without assuming a loss of location information over time. All that decayed was item information.

V. Other Distance and Density Effects in Partial Report Tasks

Several other investigators reported distance and density effects in partial report tasks that are problematic for models like TVA that do not propose

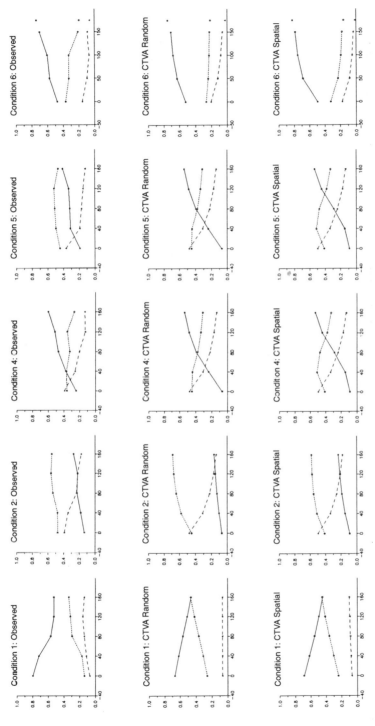

Fig. 6. Probabilities of correct reports (solid lines), location errors (finely broken lines), and item errors (coarsely broken lines) as functions of the delay of the probe and the mask. *Top row* = observed data from Mewhort, Campbell, Marchetti, and Campbell (1981); *middle row* = theoretical fits for the random-response-rule version of CTVA; *bottom row* = theoretical fits for the spatial-response-rule version of CTVA. The columns represent the different conditions described in the text and in Figure 1. Horizontal axes = delay in MS; vertical axes = response probability.

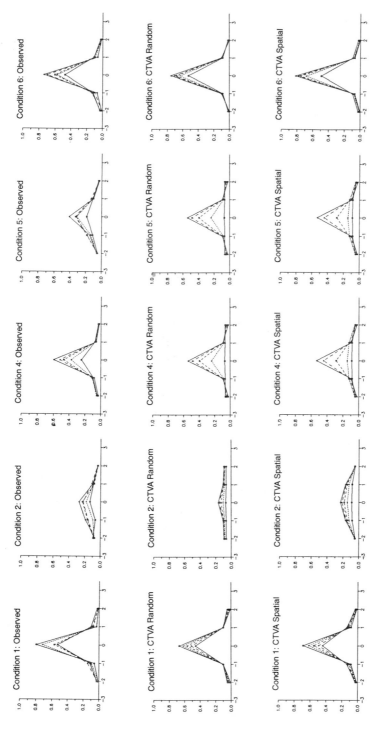

Fig. 7. Probabilities of report as functions of location relative to the location of the probe. *Top row* = observed data from Mewhort, Campbell, Marchetti, and Campbell (1981); *middle row* = theoretical fits for the random-response-rule version of CTVA; *bottom row* = theoretical fits for the spatial-response-rule version of CTVA. The columns represent the different conditions described in the text and in Fig. 1. Delay increases from the top line to the bottom line in Condition 1; delay increases from the bottom line to the top in Conditions 2–6. Horizontal axes = position; vertical axes = response probability.

explicit representations of space. We suggest that the CTVA analysis of partial report can be extended to account for these other effects. A full quantitative account is beyond the scope of this chapter, but we would like to provide a sketch of the kind of account CTVA would provide. It is based primarily on the analysis of the Mewhort et al. (1981) data set.

A. SNYDER (1972)

Snyder (1972) reported that errors in a partial report task were more likely to be correct reports of letters adjacent to the target than letters in other positions in the display. Instead of a bar probe, Snyder used properties of the letters themselves (color, inversion, fragmentation into parts) to cue the position of the target letter, but his results can be explained with the same principles that accounted for the spatial distribution of location errors in the bar-probe task. We would argue that subjects focused attention on an above-threshold region of the CODE surface corresponding to the location of the target and sampled features of items adjacent to the target as well as features of the target item. The shape of the feature distribution (peaked at the center, trailing off at the edges) makes it more likely that items immediately adjacent will be sampled than items farther removed, so location errors will be clustered around the target's position.

B. FRYKLUND (1975)

Fryklund (1975) showed that performance in a multitarget partial report task was better when the target items were clustered together than when they were spread randomly throughout the display. The CTVA analysis would account for these results with the same principles it used to account for the Mewhort et al. (1981) data and for Snyder's (1972) data. We would argue that subjects are likely to report items adjacent to the one on which attention is currently focused. When adjacent items are also targets, those reports are considered correct responses rather than errors; when adjacent items are distractors, reports of adjacent items are considered to be location errors. In Fryklund's (1975) procedure, items adjacent to the currently attended item are more likely to be targets when the targets are clustered close together than when they are spread far apart. Reports of adjacent items would add to the number of correct responses when targets were clustered, but they would add to the number of location errors when targets were spread throughout the display. In fact, correct report (of letters) was positively correlated ($r = .60$) with the number of neighboring targets and negatively correlated ($r = -.61$) with the number of neighboring distractors in Fryklund's (1975) data (when distractors were also letters).

C. MERIKLE (1980)

Merikle (1980) showed that performance in a multitarget partial report task was better when the perceptual organization (by proximity) of the array into columns or rows was compatible with the organization of report (i.e., reporting columns in displays perceived as columns or reporting rows in displays perceived as rows) than when it was incompatible (i.e., reporting columns in displays perceived as rows or reporting rows in displays perceived as columns). The CTVA analysis here is the same as in Fryklund (1975) and derived from the CTVA analysis of Mewhort et al. (1981) and Snyder (1972): When the organization of report is compatible with the perceived organization of the display, the near neighbors that would intrude on the feature catch of an attended item are more likely to be targets than distractors, and that would inflate correct reports. When the organization of report is incompatible with the perceived organization of the display, the near neighbors of an attended item are likely to be distractors, and that would inflate errors.

VI. Conclusions

The fits to the Mewhort et al. (1981) data set illustrate the importance of specifying both representation and process explicitly. The processing assumptions of TVA (and Rumelhart, 1970) turned out to be sufficient to account for an important aspect of the Mewhort et al. (1981) data set—the trade-off between location errors and correct reports. This is an important contribution because that trade-off led Mewhort et al. (1981; also see Mewhort et al., 1988) to conclude that decay in sensory memory was due to loss of spatial information rather than item information, as had been assumed traditionally. The TVA analysis shows that the trade-off can be accounted for with the traditional assumption that sensory memory decay reflects the loss of item information. This does not falsify the Mewhort et al. (1981) account. Instead, it shows it is not unique. Thus, the trade-off does not necessarily require theorists to assume that location information is lost when sensory memory decays.

The CTVA fits illustrate the utility of combining the powerful processing assumptions of TVA with an explicit representation of space. The CTVA fits were able to account for the major effects in the five conditions we modeled. CTVA, like TVA, accounted for the trade-off between location errors and correct reports. In addition, CTVA accounted for the spatial distribution of location errors, which is something that TVA by itself was not able to account for. Logan (1996) describes further examples of effects in the literature on visual spatial attention that TVA by itself cannot account for but CTVA (i.e., TVA plus CODE) can.

The accounts of the other data sets (Fryklund, 1975; Merikle, 1980; Snyder, 1972) further demonstrate the power of the representation-process pairing in CTVA. They encourage further exploration of CTVA. More generally, the qualitative accounts of those data sets and the quantitative accounts of the Mewhort et al. (1981) data set encourage further investigation of theories of selective attention in which powerful processing mechanisms are coupled with powerful representations of space.

Appendix

This appendix presents the mathematics underlying the TVA and CTVA predictions for the single-target partial report paradigm (Averbach & Coriell, 1961), which we used to fit the data from Mewhort et al. (1981). After preliminary analyses common to both response rules, we analyze the random response rule and the spatial response rule separately.

A. STIMULUS PROCESSING

Let the stimulus array of eight letters be presented from Time 0 to time τ, let the bar marker (probe) be presented at time t_c, and let a_{RT} (attention reaction time) be the time taken to reallocate attention in response to the bar marker. Our model assumes that the eight letters in the stimulus array are processed in parallel with equal attentional weights from Time 0 to time $t_a = t_c + a_{RT}$. At time t_a, attention has been reallocated to the probed position, and after time t_a, only the letter indicated by the bar marker has a positive attentional weight.

From Time 0 to time τ, η values caused by any stimulus letter are assumed to be η_1 for the correct identity of the letter, but 0 for other letter identities. After time τ, η values decay exponentially with time constant μ, but all η values are set to 0 if and when the mask is presented. Beta values are β_1 for letter identities, but 0 for any other categories. Thus, all perceptual categorizations that enter visual short-term memory (VSTM) are categorizations of letters with respect to identity.

B. RESPONSE RULES

Two versions of the model are considered. In one version of the model, a *random response rule* is assumed. By the random response rule, the response is based on the target letter whenever a (correct or incorrect) perceptual categorization of the target is found in VSTM. If no categorization of the target has entered VSTM, but categorizations of other letters have entered the store, the subject reports a randomly chosen identity code present in VSTM rather than guessing an identity not coded in VSTM. If no identities have been stored in VSTM, the subject guesses an identity at random.

The other version of the model assumes a *spatial response rule*. By the spatial response rule, the subject guesses a letter identity at random if, and only if, no letter within a distance of ± 2 letters from the bar probe is found in VTSM. If any letters within a distance of ± 2 letters from the bar probe have entered VSTM, the subject reports an identity coded in VSTM at a location as near as possible to the bar probe.

C. PARAMETER P_c

For the task at hand, the CTVA analyses differ from the TVA analyses by including an additional parameter, P_c. Parameter P_c was arrived at as follows: Assume feature distributions are so narrow that, at the location of any particular letter x (a particular above-threshold region of the CODE surface), feature catch factors are vanishingly small for features extracted from other letters than x and the letters immediately adjacent to x. If special conditions pertaining to end elements are neglected, then the perceptual identification of any letter in the array is determined by a race among three possible perceptual categorizations: one categorization that represents the correct identity of the letter and two others that represent identities of letters immediately adjacent to the given letter. Let the effective η value for the correct identity of the given letter be η' from Time 0 to time τ, and let each of the effective η values for the two incorrect identities be η'' from Time 0 to time τ. Then the conditional probability that the correct identity of the letter wins the processing race, given that at least one of the three categorizations completes processing, equals

$$P_c = \frac{\eta'}{\eta'' + \eta' + \eta''}$$

The conditional probability that a particular one of the two incorrect identities wins the processing race, given that at least one of the three categorizations completes processing, equals

$$P_e = \frac{\eta''}{\eta'' + \eta' + \eta''}$$
$$= \frac{(1 - P_c)}{2}$$

Probabilities P_c and P_e are independent of the time at which the race is completed by the winner. This stochastic independence simplifies computations dramatically. The stochastic independence is found because the hazard rates of the completion times of the three categorizations (i.e., the v values of the three categorizations) are mutually proportional functions of time (cf. Bundesen, 1993; Marley & Colonius, 1992).

Note that if P_c equals 1, then P_e equals 0, and predictions by CTVA become identical to predictions by TVA. Thus, TVA may be regarded as the special case of CTVA in which P_c equals 1.

D.   DENSITY AND DISTRIBUTION FUNCTIONS

Let the v value of an element x be the sum of the v values of all perceptual categorizations of x. Then the processing capacity C equals the sum of the v values across all elements x in the display. The v value for the target (the cued letter) is a function of time t. If $t_a \geq \tau$ then

$$v(t) = \begin{cases} 0 \ for \ t \leq 0 \\ C/8 \ for \ 0 < t \leq \tau \\ (C/8) \ \exp \ [- \ (t - \tau) \ /\mu] \ for \ \tau < t \leq t_a \\ C \ \exp \ [- \ (t - \tau) \ /\mu] \ for \ t_a < t \end{cases}$$

except that $v(t)$ is set to zero if and when a mask is presented. If $t_a < \tau$, then

$$v(t) = \begin{cases} 0 \ for \ t \leq 0 \\ C/8 \ for \ 0 < t \leq t_a \\ C \ for \ t_a < t \leq \tau \\ C \ \exp \ [- \ (t - \tau) \ /\mu] \ for \ \tau < t \end{cases}$$

except that $v(t)$ is set to zero when a mask is presented. In any case, the v value for a distractor (one of the seven uncued letters) is given by

$$u(t) = \begin{cases} v(t) \ for \ t \leq t_a \\ 0 \ for \ t_a < t. \end{cases}$$

The probability that (a correct or incorrect categorization of) the target finishes processing at or before time t $(t \geq 0)$ is given by

$$F(t) = 1 - \exp\left[-\int_0^t v(s) \, ds\right]$$

which is readily solved analytically (see, e.g., Bundesen, 1990, p. 547). The corresponding density function is

$$f(t) = v(t) \, [1 - F(t)]$$

The probability that (a correct or incorrect categorization of) any given distractor finishes processing at or before time t is

$$G(t) = \begin{cases} F(t) \text{ for } 0 \leq t \leq t_a \\ F(t_a) \text{ for } t_a < t \end{cases}$$

and the corresponding density function is

$$g(t) = \begin{cases} f(t) \text{ for } 0 \leq t < t_a \\ 0 \text{ for } t_a < t. \end{cases}$$

We show below how functions $F(t), f(t), G(t)$, and $g(t)$ were used in calculating probabilities of correct reports, item errors, and location errors with both the random response rule and the spatial response rule.

I. Random Response Rule

For ease of reference, let the stimulus array of eight letters include a substring of letters,

$$\ldots z_2 \, z_1 \, x \, y_1 \, y_2 \ldots ,$$

where element x is the target, elements z_1 and y_1 are distractors immediately adjacent to the target, and elements z_2 and y_2 are distractors removed one element from the target.

Let P_1 be the probability that the target (element x) is selected, but the total number of selected elements is less than the storage capacity of VSTM (K elements). If $K < 2$, then $P_1 = 0$, else

$$P_1 = F(\infty) \times \sum_{m=0}^{Min(K-2,\,7)} \binom{7}{m} G(\infty)^m [1 - G(\infty)]^{(7-m)}$$

Let P_2 be the probability that the total number of selected elements equals short-term storage capacity K, and the target is the Kth element to be selected. If $K < 1$ or $K > 8$, then $P_2 = 0$, else

$$P_2 = \binom{7}{K-1} \int_0^\infty G(t)^{(K-1)} [1 - G(t)]^{(8-K)} f(t)\, dt$$

Let P_3 be the probability that the total number of selected elements equals short-term storage capacity K, and the target is selected, but the Kth element to be selected is a distractor. If $K < 2$ or $K > 8$, then $P_3 = 0$, else

$$P_3 = 7 \times \binom{6}{K-2} \int_0^\infty F(t)\, G(t)^{(K-2)} [1 - G(t)]^{(8-K)} g(t)\, dt$$

A. THREE WAYS OF REPORTING

Reports can be produced in three ways. In Case 1, the target is selected, and the report is based on the target. In Case 2, the target fails to be selected, but one or more distractors are selected. In this case, the report is based on one of the selected distractors; by symmetry, the report is equally likely to be based on any one of the seven distractors in the stimulus. In Case 3, no letters are selected, and the report is made by guessing. The probabilities of the three cases are given by

$$p(Case\ 1) = P_1 + P_2 + P_3$$
$$p(Case\ 3) = [1 - F(\infty)] \times [1 - G(\infty)]^7$$
$$p(Case\ 2) = 1 - p(Case\ 1) - p(Case\ 3)$$

B. CORRECT REPORTS

Correct reports can occur in each of the three cases: (a) by selecting the target element x and reporting its identity correctly, (b) by failing to select the target, but selecting an immediately adjacent element (y_1 or z_1) and misidentifying it as a letter of the same type as the target, and (c) by guessing. Let N be the number of letters in the alphabet (i.e., $N = 26$). Then the overall probability that the subject makes a correct report equals

$$p(Case\ 1)P_c + p(Case\ 2)\left(\frac{2}{7}\right)P_e + p(Case\ 3)\left(\frac{1}{N}\right)$$

C. ITEM ERRORS

A subject who makes an item error reports a letter that was not presented in the display (Mewhort et al., 1981). The probability that the subject makes an item error is

$$p(Case\ 3)\frac{(N-8)}{N}$$

D. LOCATION ERRORS

A subject who makes a location error reports a letter that was presented in the display but not in the target position. The probability that a subject makes a location error is the complement of the sum of the probabilities of correct reports and item errors.

1. Near Location Errors

Near location errors are reports of letters immediately adjacent to the probed, target position (i.e., y_1 or z_1). Consider the probability that the subject reports the identity of, say, y_1. As with correct reports, reports of y_1 can occur in each of the three cases we have considered: (a) by selecting the target element x and misidentifying the target as y_1, (b) by failing to select the target, but either selecting, correctly identifying, and reporting y_1 or selecting, misidentifying, and reporting y_2 as y_1, and (c) by guessing. The overall probability of reporting y_1 equals

$$p(Case\ 1)P_e + p(Case\ 2)\left[\left(\frac{1}{7}\right)P_c + \left(\frac{1}{7}\right)P_e\right] + p(Case\ 3)\left(\frac{1}{N}\right)$$

2. Far Location Errors

Far location errors are reports of letters more than one position away from the probed, target position. The probability of far location errors equals the difference between the probability of location errors and the probability of near location errors.

II. Spatial Response Rule

A. CORRECT REPORTS

As with the random response rule, some correct reports occur because the target is selected and correctly identified. The probability that the subject makes a correct report that is based on selecting the target is given by

$$(P_1 + P_2 + P_3) P_c$$

Other correct reports occur in cases in which the target fails to be selected. Some of these correct reports are based on selecting a distractor that is immediately adjacent to the target and misidentifying this distractor. The probability that the subject makes a correct report that is based on selection of element y_1 (i.e., a particular one of the two distractors that are immediately adjacent to the target) equals

$$[Q_1 + Q_2 + .5(Q_3 + Q_4)] P_e$$

Here, Q_1 is the probability that x fails to be selected, y_1 is selected, z_1 fails to be selected, and the total number of selected elements is less than short-term storage capacity $K;$ if $K < 2$, then $Q_1 = 0$, else

$$Q_1 = [1 - F(\infty)] \, G(\infty)[1 - G(\infty)] \times \sum_{m=0}^{Min(K-2, 5)} \binom{5}{m} G(\infty)^m [1 - G(\infty)]^{(5-m)}$$

Q_2 is the probability that x fails to be selected, y_1 is selected, z_1 fails to be selected, and the total number of selected elements is $K;$ if $K < 1$ or $K > 6$, then $Q_2 = 0$, else

$$Q_2 = \binom{5}{K-1} K \int_0^\infty [1 - F(t)]G(t)^{(K-1)} [1 - G(t)]^{(7-K)} g(t) \, dt$$

Q_3 is the probability that x fails to be selected, both y_1 and z_1 are selected, and the total number of elements selected is less than $K;$ if $K < 3$, then $Q_3 = 0$, else

$$Q_3 = [1 - F(\infty)] \, G(\infty)^2 \times \sum_{m=0}^{Min(K-3, 5)} \binom{5}{m} G(\infty)^m [1 - G(\infty)]^{5-m}$$

Q_4 is the probability that x fails to be selected, both y_1 and z_1 are selected, and the total number of elements selected is equal to K; if $K < 2$ or $K > 7$, the $Q_4 = 0$, else

$$Q_4 = \left(K \frac{5}{-} 2\right)K \int_0^\infty [1 - F(t)]G(t)^{(K-1)}[1 - G(t)]^{(7-K)}g(t)\, dt$$

Finally, correct reports can be obtained by pure guessing. The probability that the subject makes a correct report which is based on pure guessing is

$$[1 - F(\infty)]\, [1 - G(\infty)]^4/N$$

B. ITEM ERRORS

The probability that the subject makes an item error is

$$[1 - F(\infty)]\, [1 - G(\infty)]^4\, \frac{(N - 8)}{N}$$

C. LOCATION ERRORS

As with the random response rule, the probability that a subject makes a location error is the complement of the sum of the probabilities of a correct report and an item error.

1. *Near Location Errors*

Consider the probability that the subject reports the identity of y_1 (i.e., a particular one of the two distractors that are immediately adjacent to the target). Four cases must be considered. First, the report can be based on misidentification of the target as y_1. The probability of this event is

$$(P_1 + P_2 + P_3)\, P_e$$

Second, the report can be based on correct identification of distractor y_1. The probability of this event is

$$[Q_1 + Q_2 + .5(Q_3 + Q_4)]\, P_c$$

Third, the report can be based on misidentification of distractor y_2 as y_1. The probability of this event is

$$[R_1 + R_2 + .5(R_3 + R_4)] \, P_e$$

Here, R_1 is the probability that target x fails to be selected, distractors y_1, z_1, and z_2 also fail to be selected, but y_2 is selected, and the total number of selected elements is less than K; if $K < 2$, then $R_1 = 0$, else

$$R_1 = [1 - F(\infty)] \, [1 - G(\infty)]^3 G(\infty) \sum_{m=0}^{Min(K-2, 3)} \binom{3}{m} G(\infty)^m [1 - G(\infty)]^{(3-m)}$$

R_2 is the probability that target x fails to be selected, distractors y_1, z_1, and z_2 also fail to be selected, but y_2 is selected, and the total number of selected elements is equal to K; if $K < 1$ or $K > 4$, then $R_2 = 0$, else

$$R_2 = \binom{3}{K-1} K \int_0^\infty [1 - F(t)] G(t)^{(K-1)} [1 - G(t)]^{(7-K)} g(t) \, dt$$

R_3 is the probability that target x fails to be selected, distractors y_1 and z_1 also fail to be selected, but both y_2 and z_2 are selected, and the total number of selected elements is less than K; if $K < 3$ then $R_3 = 0$, else

$$R_3 = [1 - F(\infty)] \, [1 - G(\infty)]^2 G(\infty)^2 \sum_{m=0}^{Min(K-3, 3)} \binom{3}{m} G(\infty)^m [1 - G(\infty)]^{(3-m)}$$

R_4 is the probability that target x fails to be selected, distractors y_1 and z_1 also fail to be selected, but both y_2 and z_2 are selected, and the total number of selected elements equals K; if $K < 2$ or $K > 5$, then $R_4 = 0$, else

$$R_4 = \binom{3}{K-2} K \int_0^\infty [1 - F(t)] \, G(t)^{(K-1)} [1 - G(t)]^{(7-K)} g(t) \, dt$$

Finally, the report can be based on pure guessing. The probability of this event is

$$[1 - F(\infty)] \, [1 - G(\infty)]^4 / N$$

2. Far Location Errors

As with the random response rule, the probability of far location errors equals the difference between the probability of location errors and the probability of near location errors.

III. Fitting Procedure

The equations described above were fitted to the observed probabilities of six types of events (viz., correct reports, near location errors to the left of the target, near location errors to the right of the target, far location errors to the left of the target, far location errors to the right of the target, and item errors) in five of the six conditions reported by Mewhort et al. (1981). We excluded Condition 3, in which stimulus intensity was confounded with mask delay. All of the conditions were fitted simultaneously with the same set of parameters. The CTVA fits involved five parameters: C (processing capacity in items/s), K (short-term storage capacity), μ (time constant for decay of η and v values), P_c (probability of correct identification rather than confusion with an adjacent item), and a_{RT} (attention reaction time) TVA was fitted with the same parameters, except that P_c was fixed at a value of 1.

The data were fitted using STEPIT and a maximum-likelihood criterion, maximizing

$$y = \prod_{i=1}^{150} p_{\text{theoretical}} (i)^{p_{\text{observed}}(i)}$$

by minimizing its negative logarithm, $-ln(y)$.

Acknowledgments

This research was supported by National Science Foundation Grant No. SBR 94-10406 to Gordon Logan and a grant from the University of Copenhagen to Claus Bundesen.

Correspondence concerning this chapter may be addressed to Gordon D. Logan, Department of Psychology, University of Illinois, 603 East Daniel Street, Champaign, Illinois, 61820, U.S.A., or to Claus Bundesen, Psychological Laboratory, University of Copenhagen, Njalsgade 90, DK-2300 Copenhagen S., Denmark. Electronic mail may be addressed to glogan@s.psych.u-iuc.edu or bundesen@axp.psl.ku.dk.

References

Ashby, F. G., Prinzmetal, W., Ivry, R., & Maddox, W. T. (1996). A formal theory of feature binding in object perception. *Psychological Review, 103,* 165–192.

Averbach, E., & Coriell, A. S. (1961). Short-term memory in vision. *Bell System Technical Journal, 40,* 309–328.

Bundesen, C. (1987). Visual attention: Race models for selection from multielement displays. *Psychological Research, 49,* 113–121.

Bundesen, C. (1990). A theory of visual attention. *Psychological Review, 97,* 523–547.

Bundesen, C. (1993). The relationship between independent race models and Luce's choice axiom. *Journal of Mathematical Psychology, 37*, 446–471.

Bundesen, C., Pedersen, L. F., & Larsen, A. (1984). Measuring efficiency of selection from briefly exposed visual displays: A model for partial report. *Journal of Experimental Psychology: Human Perception and Performance, 10*, 329–339.

Bundesen, C., Shibuya, H., & Larsen, A. (1985). Visual selection from multielement displays: A model for partial report. In M. I. Posner & O. S. M. Marin (Eds.), *Attention and performance XI* (pp. 631–649). Hillsdale NJ: Erlbaum.

Cave, K. R., & Wolfe, J. M. (1990). Modeling the role of parallel processing in visual search. *Cognitive Psychology, 22*, 225–271.

Chow, S. I. (1986). Iconic memory, location information, and partial report. *Journal of Experimental Psychology: Human Perception and Performance, 12*, 455–465.

Clark, S. E. (1969). Retrieval of color information from preperceptual memory. *Journal of Experimental Psychology, 82*, 263–266.

Colegate, R. L., Hoffman, J. E., & Eriksen, C. W. (1973). Selective encoding from multielement visual displays. *Perception and Psychophysics, 14*, 217–224.

Coltheart, M. (1980). Iconic memory and visible persistence. *Perception and Psychophysics, 27*, 183–228.

Coltheart, M., & Coltheart, V. (1972). On Rumelhart's model of visual information processing. *Canadian Journal of Psychology, 26*, 292–295.

Compton, B. J., & Logan, G. D. (1993). Evaluating a computational model of perceptual grouping by proximity. *Perception and Psychophysics, 53*, 403–421.

Dick, A. O. (1974). Iconic memory and its relation to perceptual processing and other memory mechanisms. *Perception and Psychophysics, 16*, 575–596.

Duncan, J., & Humphreys, G. W. (1989). Visual search and stimulus similarity. *Psychological Review, 96*, 433–458.

Eriksen, C. W., & Collins, J. F. (1969). Temporal course of selective attention. *Journal of Experimental Psychology, 80*, 254–261.

Eriksen, C. W., & Hoffman, J. E. (1972). Temporal and spatial characteristics of selective encoding from visual displays. *Perception and Psychophysics, 12*, 201–204.

Fryklund, I. (1975). Effects of cued-set spatial arrangement and target-background similarity in the partial-report paradigm. *Perception and Psychophysics, 17*, 375–386.

Gegenfurtner, K. R., & Sperling, G. (1993). Information transfer in iconic memory experiments. *Journal of Experimental Psychology: Human Perception and Performance, 19*, 845–866.

Logan, G. D. (1994). Spatial attention and the apprehension of spatial relations. *Journal of Experimental Psychology: Human Perception and Performance, 20*, 1,015–1,036.

Logan, G. D. (1995). Linguistic and conceptual control of visual spatial attention. *Cognitive Psychology, 28*, 103–174.

Logan, G. D. (1996). The CODE theory of visual attention: An integration of space-based and object-based attention. *Psychological Review.*

Logan, G. D., & Sadler, D. (1996). A computational analysis of the apprehension of spatial relations. In P. Bloom, M. Peterson, L. Nadel, & M. Garrett (Eds.), *Language and space.* Cambridge MA: MIT Press.

Long, G. M. (1980). Iconic memory: A review and a critique of the study of short-term visual storage. *Psychological Bulletin, 88*, 785–820.

Maddox, W. T., Prinzmetal, W., Ivry, R., & Ashby, F. G. (1994). A probabilistic multidimensional model of location information. *Psychological Research, 56*, 66–77.

Marley, A. A. J., & Colonius, H. (1992). The "horse race" random utility model for choice probabilities and reaction times, and its competing risks interpretation. *Journal of Mathematical Psychology, 36*, 1–20.

Merikle, P. M. (1980). Selection from visible persistence by perceptual groups and category membership. *Journal of Experimental Psychology: General, 109,* 279–295.

Mewhort, D. J. K., Butler, B. E., Feldman-Stewart, D., & Tramer, S. (1988). "Iconic memory," location information, and the bar-probe task: A reply to Chow (1986). *Journal of Experimental Psychology: Human Perception and Performance, 14,* 729–737.

Mewhort, D. J. K., & Campbell, A. J. (1978). Processing spatial information and the selective masking effect. *Perception and Psychophysics, 24,* 93–101.

Mewhort, D. J. K., Campbell, A. J., Marchetti, F. M., & Campbell, J. I. D. (1981). Identification, localization, and "iconic memory": An evaluation of the bar probe task. *Memory and Cognition, 9,* 50–67.

Mewhort, D. J. K., Marchetti, F. M., Gurnsey, R., & Campbell, A. J. (1984). Information persistence: A dual-buffer model for initial processing. In H. Bouma & D. G. Bouwhuis (Eds.), *Attention and performance X* (pp. 287–298). London: Erlbaum.

Mewhort, D. J. K., & Popham, D. (1991). Serial recall of tachistoscopic letter strings. In W. E. Hockley & S. Lewandowsky (Eds.), *Relating theory and data: Essays on human memory in honor of Bennet B. Murdock* (pp. 425–443). Hillsdale, NJ: Erlbaum.

Nissen, M. J. (1985). Accessing features and objects: Is location special? In M. I. Posner & O. S. M. Marin (Eds.), *Attention and performance XI* Hillsdale NJ: Erlbaum.

Ratcliff, R. (1981). Theory of order relations in perceptual matching. *Psychological Review, 88,* 552–572.

Rumelhart, D. E. (1970). A multicomponent theory of the perception of briefly exposed visual displays. *Journal of Mathematical Psychology, 7,* 191–218.

Shibuya, H. (1993). Efficiency of visual selection in duplex and conjunction conditions in partial report. *Perception and Psychophysics, 54,* 716–732.

Shibuya, H., & Bundesen, C. (1988). Visual selection from multielement displays: Measuring and modeling effects of exposure duration. *Journal of Experimental Psychology: Human Perception and Performance, 14,* 591–600.

Snyder, C. R. R. (1972). Selection, inspection, and naming in visual search. *Journal of Experimental Psychology, 92,* 428–431.

Sperling, G. (1960). The information available in brief visual presentations. *Psychological Monographs, 74,* 1–29.

Sperling, G., & Weichselgartner, E. (1995). Episodic theory of the dynamics of spatial attention. *Psychological Review, 102,* 503–532.

Treisman, A., & Gelade, G. (1980). A feature-integration theory of attention. *Cognitive Psychology, 12,* 97–136.

Treisman, A., & Gormican, S. (1988). Feature analysis in early vision: Evidence from search asymmetries. *Psychological Review, 95,* 14–48.

Ullman, S. (1984). Visual routines. *Cognition, 18,* 97–159.

van der Heijden, A. H. C. (1992). *Selective attention in vision.* New York: Routledge.

van der Heijden, A. H. C. (1993). The role of position in object selection in vision. *Psychological Research, 56,* 44–58.

van Oeffelen, M. P., & Vos, P. G. (1982). Configurational effects on the enumeration of dots: Counting by groups. *Memory and Cognition, 10,* 396–404.

van Oeffelen, M. P., & Vos, P. G. (1983). An algorithm for pattern description on the level of relative proximity. *Pattern Recognition, 16,* 341–348.

von Wright, J. M. (1968). Selection in visual immediate memory. *Quarterly Journal of Experimental Psychology, 20,* 62–68.

von Wright, J. M. (1970). On selection in immediate memory. *Acta Psychologica, 33,* 280–292.

Wolfe, J. M. (1994). Guided search 2.0: A revised model of visual search. *Psychonomic Bulletin and Review, 1,* 202–238.

Wolford, G. (1975). Perturbation model for letter identification. *Psychological Review, 82,* 184–199.

STRUCTURAL BIASES IN CONCEPT LEARNING
Influences from Multiple Functions

Dorrit Billman

I. Introduction

Taking a limo into town from an airport is a simple thing. To do this, one must identify something as being a limo, discriminating it from shuttle buses, private limos, and taxis. In short, one has to classify. But even such a simple interaction with an object requires more than classification. It might involve reasoning about such matters as where to find one, relative costs, expected travel time, and even variability of actual from announced departure time. The same concept is used in many more processes than classification.

Concepts are responsible to the ecology of the world for capturing the predictive structure of the entities in a domain and for organizing this information in a manner to support classification. For the purpose of assigning instances to categories, the relations *between instances and concepts* are central. However, concepts are also responsible to the ecology of mind and must be easily recruited in a variety of thinking tasks. Concepts are used in problem solving, planning, conceptual combination, induction, deduction, and so forth. For the purposes of reasoning, relations *among concepts* are paramount.

Concepts serve both functions facing "outward" to the ecology of the world and those facing "inward" to the ecology of mind. These different types of functions place distinct pressures on concept formation. On the one hand, a system of concepts should divide entities in the world into groups that preserve relevant characteristics of those entities and should support reliable classification of both novel and familiar items into these groups. Systems of categories that serve these outward-facing functions well can be characterized as corresponding well to important structure in the world. On the other hand, a system of concepts should support sound and useful reasoning. By mapping entities or states of affairs in the world onto concepts, and reasoning about these concepts, one should be able to produce coherent plans, explanations, predictions, and projections. Systems of concepts that serve these inward-facing functions well afford sound reasoning and can be characterized as coherent. In addition, concepts also underlie the ability to communicate about these relations of correspondence and coherence.

Concepts support many functions and the goodness or value of a system of concepts will be influenced by how well it serves these multiple tasks. In understanding any learning problem the broad function of what is learned should be considered. By considering a broad set of functions of concepts, we can gather clues about multiple constraints or biases of the concept-learning mechanism. Jointly these might constrain models/theories more than considering just one type of function which categories serve.

In this paper I will argue that analysis of concept use should inform research on concept learning, but more broadly than it traditionally has. First, I review work on concept learning, which focuses on the outward-facing uses of concepts in classification. Second, I consider why concept-learning models *should* simultaneously be tuned to pressures from inward- and outward-facing uses of concepts. Third, I consider how adequate concept-learning models developed with a focus on classification will be for understanding concept learning more broadly. Finally, I consider how work on concept learning might shift if internal as well as external functions of categories are given more consideration. Two lines of research investigating structural biases relevant to internal as well as external functions are summarized.

II.   The Role of Concept Use in Concept-Learning Research

Research on concept learning is deeply influenced by the goals and functions concepts are assumed to serve. This influence guides the kinds of learning tasks studied, and the mechanisms proposed in learning models. Research has not, however, been guided by a diverse mix of inward- and outward-facing uses. Rather, concept-learning research has assumed, implicitly or explicitly, a single, primary use: prediction of properties in the world. When researchers have asked how the function of concepts might influence the learning process, it is this external function that has been the focus of analysis (Anderson, 1991; Brunswick, 1955; Rosch, 1978). The idea that the purpose of concepts is to predict properties in the world plays out differently for models that focus on supervised versus unsupervised learning.

Early research on concept learning (e.g., Bruner, Goodenow, & Austin, 1956) assumed the goal of the learner was to match externally provided categories. Here supervised concept-learning tasks were used and "predicting structure in the world" meant prediction of a relatively isolated and arbitrary function identified by the feedback. The goal of knowing a category was directly and narrowly linked to the category definition or criteria: One wants to know how to categorize poisonous versus nonpoisonous mushrooms to avoid being poisoned; one wants to know how to identify objects in an experiment so one can be correct. This perspective fits with the view of categories as represented by definitions constructed to pick out an arbitrary but important class. So the purpose of concepts here is to capture predictive structure in the environment—but one aspect of the environment per category. This research focuses on the human ability to discover successfully a wide range of rather arbitrary classification schemes. Many models of supervised classification adhere to this view of the purpose of concepts: The learning algorithm is designed to recover sufficient information to allow successful classification of novel instances of the category (Hayes-Roth & Hayes-Roth, 1977; Holland & Reitman, 1978; Kruschke, 1992; Medin & Schaffer, 1978; Nosofsky, 1984, 1987).

Rosch (1978) changed perspective on the function of categories and on what makes a good category: Natural categories, or at least good ones, capture rich correlational structure in the world, not an isolated function. Rather than considering each concept as an arbitrary classification rule, the Roschian notion of concepts suggests that each concept should reflect richer correlational structure underlying the input. Brunsick (1955) and Garner (1974) provided related, important ideas about capturing information in the environment, but Rosch addressed the issue in the context of naturally occurring categories. The world does have a great deal of correlational structure, and Rosch pointed out that most natural categories capture multiple aspects of this structure; knowing something is a dog versus horse tells you a great deal about it, as knowing a mushroom is poisonous versus nonpoisonous does not.

Rosch did not talk much about how this should affect learning (but see Mervis & Cristafi, 1982), but some morals are straightforward. Learners should be biased to learn more informative sets of categories over relatively uninformative ones. Further, if the world provides rich structure it makes sense that a learner could discover this without the aid of a teacher's feedback. In contrast, of course, it would not be possible to learn an arbitrary partition of instances without an "oracle" or teacher to identify which function the learner should be using. The idea that good or preferred concepts should capture rich correlational structure has been particularly influential in research on unsupervised concept learning, and models that treat supervised concept learning as a special case of unsupervised. In psychology, early computational models of unsupervised learning treated concept learning as discovery of predictive rules or patterns among attributes in input (Billman & Heit, 1988). In machine-learning models, unsupervised algorithms were formulated to try to maximize the predictive utility of each category formed using recursive hierarchical clustering (Fisher's COBWEB, 1987; Martin's TWILIX, 1992). Anderson's (1991) rational-analysis model treats supervised learning as a special case of unsupervised learning and uses a nonhierarchical version of the clustering algorithm. For both hierarchical and nonhierarchical versions, the learning algorithm maximizes a metric tracking predictive utility.

Most research on concept learning has focused on the outward-facing, predictive functions of concepts. However, the inward-facing functions of concepts (in reasoning) take center stage in research on one key phenomenon: Match to prior beliefs and theories influences ease of concept learning and what is learned (Murphy & Medin, 1985). Research here has provided information about how existing beliefs influence new classification learning (Murphy & Allopenna, 1994; Wisniewski & Medin, 1994). Prior theoretical beliefs are included as influences determining how easily a new classification problem will be learned.

The theory-based approach, however, has not addressed how the *future* role of the new categories in thinking might influence their acquisition. Learners may be biased to construct categories to be easy to reason with, as well as categories likely to predict properties in the world accurately. In particular, the relations among new concepts and attributes will be important, as well as the relations to old beliefs.

Research on conceptual change in development (Carey & Spelke, 1994; Keil, 1991) or in science (Nersessian, 1993; Thagard, 1992) does focus on the relations among the new concepts and their role in thought. Connotations of conceptual change vary, but researchers mean, at least, cases of conceptual learning where the resulting state of knowledge is quite different from the preceding ones. The central concern in research on conceptual change is the change in a concept's relations to other theoretical concepts: Relations among concepts and the role of concepts in thought are paramount, while concept-instance relations are secondary. If research on concept learning considered the internal as well as external roles of concepts, better integration of concept learning with conceptual change would be possible. In turn, this would connect what we know about learning from observation of examples with learning from conceptual combination, causal reasoning, and instruction.

In sum, the fundamental assumption within concept-learning research has been that the purpose of categories is to capture predictive structure in the input—either narrowly as in supervised classification or more broadly in unsupervised concept learning. This approach has provided good insights about biases guiding concept learning: Concept learners should be biased to form concepts that capture a great deal of information about the world and selection of relevant information for classification can be guided by existing beliefs and theories. However, this perspective has led to the formation of models that seem lacking as broad models of concept learning, and even of classification learning. In particular, many models seem insensitive to factors that are probably very important for the inward-facing roles of concepts. The exclusive focus on classification in concept-learning research has also resulted in a schism between research on concept learning and research on conceptual change, even though both are concerned with the ongoing acquisition of concepts.

III. The Need For A Broader Perspective on Function in Concept Learning

Science necessarily proceeds by decomposing complex issues into simpler and more easily investigated ones. However, I suggest that looking at the "external" functions of classification in isolation from the "internal" ones is insufficient for understanding concept learning. The internal and external functions of concepts need to be addressed simultaneously. Two broad and intuitive phenomena highlight the need for considering both together. These two phenomena are the pervasiveness of concepts throughout cognition and the flexibility with which any individual concept can be used across many cognitive processes. I will argue that while these phenomena are widely assumed, their import for understanding concept learning has not been appreciated.

A. PERVASIVENESS

Every aspect of cognition involves concepts and reliance on concepts is incorporated in any account of cognitive processes. Memory research may focus on the organizing relations among concepts (Anderson & Bower, 1973, Collins & Quillian, 1969, Mandler 1962) or on effects of the content of a particular schema, concept, or stereotype (Anderson & Pichert, 1978; Bransford, 1979). Phenomena from reconstructive memory to encoding specificity can be seen as effects of established concepts on the encoding or retrieval of new material. Research on memory blends into research on reasoning, as reasoning tasks often involve making explicit the knowledge which had been indirectly represented in memory.

Research on reasoning, both inductive and deductive, depends on the organization of concepts. Much of the research on simple deductive reasoning has been done using "sentence verification" tasks. While experiments used some sentences that were assertions participants would have heard and hence could remember directly, for example "Birds can fly," many sentences were novel and required simple inferences to make implied knowledge explicit, for example "No typhoons are wheat" or "All snails can breathe" (Meyer 1970; Smith, Shoben, & Rips, 1974). Accounts differed in claims about where particular information was stored or what the access procedure was, but all assumed the availability of (richly interrelated) concepts. Research on more complicated inductive reasoning has focused directly on how conceptual organization influences the strength of an inductive argument (Osherson, Smith, Wilkie, Lopez, & Shafir, 1990; Rips, 1975; Shipley, 1993).

Language-comprehension theories assume a rich conceptual base of knowledge to carry out any comprehension from the direct to inferential (Bransford, Barclay, & Franks, 1972; McKoon & Ratcliff, 1986). Most simply, words are assumed to correspond to concepts, or sets of possible concepts, but more complicated relations between conceptual content and syntax are certainly also involved (Cabrera & Billman, 1996; Fisher, Gleitman, & Gleitman, 1991; Talmy, 1985).

Problem-solving research typically investigates how problem-solving procedures are learned, while assuming the availability of the concepts needed for the procedures. This available conceptual vocabulary can then be used in the conditions or actions of productions that represent steps in the procedure. A few studies have addressed changes in classification, such as types of problems (Chi, Feltovich, & Glaser, 1989), or effects of problem solving on classification (Blessing & Ross, 1996).

Conceptual change through development or instruction (Carey, 1985; Chi, Slotta, & DeLeuuw, 1994; Inhelder & Piaget, 1964; Smith, Carey, & Wiser, 1985) is one area of cognitive psychology that addresses learning new or altering old concepts. In contrast to the concept-learning literature, here concepts are treated in their relation to a system of other concepts, not in relation to the instances they classify.

In summary, a fundamental and striking phenomena is that concepts permeate every aspect of cognition. And many, many of these concepts are learned. These two facts impose a simple but important constraint on theories of concept learning: Accounts of concept learning should eventually be responsible for explaining how concepts supporting each of these uses come to be learned.

B. FLEXIBILITY

A second key phenomenon about concept use is the flexibility with which the same concept can be used across the full range of cognitive processes. Since this second point is fundamental to motivating the choices made in the present research, a bit more elaboration is called for. Accounts of cognition (at least symbolic theories) assume that a particular concept, be it *anteater, auto,* or *acceleration,* can be invoked in any number of contexts and any number of tasks. This flexibility of use of concepts contrasts with the encapsulation of skills and is one of the most fundamental differences motivating the distinction between declarative and procedural knowledge.

The same concept can be implicated in judging certainty of an induction, in framing effects in decision making, as a retrieval cue in remembering, as a source of predictions in planning, as an element in problem solving, and so on. Researchers refer to a given concept (be it *bear* or *birthday*) with the same name across all these tasks and the assumption is that the same concept is being referred to whenever it is talked about. Of course, the information about a given concept that is accessed does vary from one occurrence to another and one context to another (Barsalou, 1987). But there is never an assumption that distinct concepts are used for distinct tasks: a BEAR1 concept for induction, a BEAR2 for language comprehension, a BEAR3 for memory retrieval, and so on. Indeed, assuming different concepts for different cognitive operations would lead to incoherence in thought and action. If a person is making inductions about whether or not bears have spleens, or problem solving about how to lure a bear away from camp, that reasoning had better be linked together with any other cognitive process from decision making to language comprehension to whatever classification knowledge allows identification of bears. Lacking this, the person would have no way of constructing even a locally consistent mental model, or of mapping the mental model constructed in thinking about bears, onto the world to make use of the product of thought. The same concept can be flexibly reused in many cognitive tasks.

I believe this assumption about the reusability of concepts is exactly right. It deserves more overt recognition, as fundamental both to the coherence of thought and to the correspondence between the mental worlds developed by thinking and the external world. The fact that concepts in general serve so many functions, inward as well as outward facing, and the fact that an individual, particular concept must be recruitable in a variety of functions (or cognitive processes) puts concept learning in a different light. A well-adapted organism would be influenced by multiple functions and multiple criteria of "goodness."

We might ask how well such criteria happen to converge by asking how well models developed with one function in mind—successful clasification—might do as the basis for understanding concept learning more generally. To anticipate, I will argue that while models of concept learning based on classification have many strengths, they do not provide an adequate account of what must be learned for the variety of functions that concepts serve in addition to classification.

IV. Models Focus on External Functions

I briefly review how a focus on classification has shaped concept-learning models. Models of supervised learning usually take the goal of concept learning to be representing information that will allow optimal discrimination between two (occasionally more) classes. Models of unsupervised concept learning usually take the goal of learning to be capture of correlational (or predictive) structure in the input. Several approaches to accomplishing these predictive goals can be used: instance and composite trace models, rules, and schemas. These models vary in the degree of abstraction of the representations formed and in the flexibility of accessing the information represented. I summarize what I am referring to by each of these classes of models and then consider the strengths and weaknesses of each, as a foundation for models addressing a broader set of purposes.

Instance and composite trace (Gluck & Bower, 1988; Hintzman, 1986; Kruschke, 1992; Medin & Shaffer, 1978; Nosofsky, 1984, 1987; Schyns, 1991) models preserve and are *influenced by* essentially all information in the input; thus they do not build or rely on representations that isolate a subset of information deemed relevant. One approach for these broad-information models is to store instances and make comparisons by whatever similarity metric the system has initially. A more sophisticated approach, suitable for supervised concept learning, is to store instances but change the similarity metric to maximize discrimination between externally provided categories (Kruschke, 1992). Parallel distributed processing (PDP) systems and holographic models such as MINERVA (Hintzman, 1986) store a composite representation of instances and, in the PDP case, also reweigh what properties or combinations of properties (in models with hidden units) should be weighted most heavily to produce good discrimination.

A second approach is to construct rules. By rule I mean something informationally the same as a production rule with a condition specifying properties to be matched (perfectly or partially) for the rule to apply and an action specifying a decision if the rule is selected. In supervised concept learning, the action is the classification of an instance matching the condition. Rules may vary widely in their specificity. Rule-learning models of supervised learning attempt to construct a set of rules that allow successful discrimination of categories (Anderson, Kline, & Beasley, 1979; Holland & Reitman, 1978; Miller & Laird, in press; Miller & Laird, in press; Nosofsky, Palmeri, & McKinley's RULEX, 1994). While rule models can be reduced to instance-level specificity if the task can only be done as paired associate learning, rule-learning mechanisms are designed to extract regularities if regularities are present. The learning process may move either from initially "instance-like," very specific conditions to more general rules, or from general to specific.

Application of rule models to unsupervised learning provides some additional challenges. While the task structure itself in supervised learning divides the predictor properties (represented in the condition) from the predicted properties (represented in the action), the task structure of unsupervised learning does not provide this decomposition and does not identify a single property to be predicted. The Internal Feedback (Billman & Heit, 1988; Chalnick & Billman, 1988) rule-learning model of unsupervised learning constructed rules that capture the predictive structure of input such as "If covering = feathers, then mouth = beak." Often, rule systems for supervised or unsupervised learning do not form any unitary representation of a concept, particularly if the structure of the concept is disjunctive.

A third approach is to construct schemas. By schemas I mean a structure (a) that can vary in the specificity or abstraction of information (though a particular model might use just one level of specificity), and (b) that does not separate the information controlling access to the schema from information guiding action following access (in contrast to rules). However, schemas may be organized in a structured way and this structure may guide access, as in decision trees. Schemas, at least in concept-learning models, can be considered declarative knowledge, in the standard procedural–declarative contrast. Schema models, in the declarative sense used here, have been least developed as current psychological models. This is in part due to the failure of early schema models—prototype models that represented average or modal feature values. Models that constructed a single prototype per category proved empirically inadequate because a schema constructed from modal or average properties does not preserve information about the distributions of or relations between properties (Hayes-Roth & Hayes-Roth, 1977; Medin, Altom, Edelson, & Freko, 1982; Neumann, 1977). The most well-known contemporary schema model in the psychological literature is Anderson's rational analysis (1991; see also Clapper & Bower, 1994). This model deals with capturing relations between properties by splitting its categories into increasingly specific groupings until the significant correlational structure has been split into a partition of separate categories. In contrast, research in machine learning has focused heavily on schema models. Work from our lab (TWILIX, Martin, 1992) draws on the machine-learning tradition of recursive, hierarchical clustering algorithms that grow a hierarchy of concepts (COBWEB for unsupervised, Fisher, 1987; ID3 for supervised, Quinlan, 1986). Unlike rule and instance models, schema models seem capable of functioning in very much the same way for supervised and unsupervised learning. Our unsupervised concept-learning model forms hierarchies of concepts based on capturing predictive structure. Unlike the flat model of Anderson, relations of set inclusion at different levels of concept generality, as well as contrast at a single level, are represented. TWILIX includes mechanisms for identifying attribute importance, with respect to some type of concepts.

Within each of these three broad representational formats, we can ask how the representations constructed by these systems would serve the uses of concepts in reasoning. Successful reasoning seems to depend on three properties: (a) explicit representation of information about what groups instances together as members of a category, (b) flexible access to information particularly to information about commonalities, and (c) explicit representation of information about the relations between concepts. These properties are different from those most important for successful classification of instances, that is for use in the external functions of concepts. Thus, a learning model designed to learn concepts useful in reasoning might prioritize learning about concept commonalities and about relations between concepts over learning about the properties that best discriminate between a pair of concepts in classification.

Instance models (Kruschke, 1992; Medin & Shaffer, 1978; Nosofsky, 1984, 1987) do not form summarized or integrated representations of what makes a dog a *dog* or a case of TB *tuberculosis*. Where instance models do include abstraction, it is in the form of attentional learning or a global reweighting of attribute importance. This form of abstraction is not designed for flexible access, nor very explicit. Further, the basis for attentional learning is discrimination between categories, not commonalties within them. Instance models preserve no information about relations between concepts. These models are far from providing the main sorts of abstractions apparently needed for reasoning. Instance models do, however, preserve much information about the input and this information should be available for reanalysis for any purpose. Thus, while the product of instance learning is relatively far from what is needed for reasoning, its representations could be used as input for some other learning mechanism.

Connectionist (Gluck & Bower, 1988; Rummelhart & Zipser, 1986) and composite models (Hintzman, 1986) derive a summary representation (in the process losing information about instances) and one that is useful across novel input, as any serious model of classification must be. Connectionist models may be designed to have asymmetrical access, with one set of properties in input and another set in output, or symmetrical access where the same properties are represented as input and output. But connectionist models of concept learning are very weak on showing how information learned in one task might be accessible to another. While connectionist systems are open with respect to new inputs from the same space and for the same task, they provide few tools for explaining how the knowledge resulting from a classification could be used in any new, unanticipated *task,* let alone productive reasoning. All response alternatives for all tasks must be specified in the design of the network. Even models that encompass two related tasks (Schyns model of concept formation and concept labeling, 1991), have those two tasks built into the fundamental architecture of the model; there is no open or unanticipated reusability of resulting concepts. A fundamental challenge for using connectionist classifiers or pattern recognizers in reasoning, would be to allow this flexibility, not just across novel input, but across novel tasks (see Clark, 1993, for discussion).

How do rule models fare as far as providing explicit representation of within concept commonalities, flexible access to this information, and explicit representation of relations between concepts? Representations constructed by rule-learning systems typically include knowledge of what is common to a category. If rules are constructed from specific to general, this will preserve common as well as distinguishing properties in the rules. Often, of course, the attributes that differentiate between categories will also be those that are common within category. So rule-learning systems are good at building explicit abstractions of the properties that predict category membership, and these abstractions will reflect concept commonalities to a greater or lesser degree depending on the domain structure and the details of the learning algorithm. Second, access to this knowledge in rule systems is an interesting mix of flexibility and rigidity. Matching of any one production is usually independent of other knowledge in the system, and this provides a kind of locality and hence flexibility. However, only information in the condition of a rule allows accessing the rule, and only the information in the action of a rule specifies the decision. Access is inherently asymmetrical in rule systems. As a result, the same knowledge cannot be directly used even in tasks so similar as producing a category label given an instance and producing an instance description given a category label. Finally, rule models of concept learning do not directly represent relations among concepts. Representing relations between concepts is difficult to do in rule models, particularly models of unsupervised learning, because rule models often do not construct a unitary representation of concepts at all. Without a unitary representation of a concept, representation of relations between concepts is much more difficult.

The fact that relations between concepts are (only) represented implicitly in rule systems is sometimes cited as a virtue: Set inclusion-like phenomena can sometimes be produced from the priority in which rules are applied, for example, application of a more general rule when a more specific rule is missing (Miller & Laird, in press). However, lack of clear representation of relations makes reasoning problematic. Thus, while rule-learning models may include explicit representation of concept commonalties, representation of relations between concepts is a challenge.

As with instance models, we can ask how the input derived from a rule-learning system might support analysis or reuse by some further learning mechanism. Rules might be chained together to form more complex reasoning; rather than giving the category name as output, the system could classify internally in reasoning chains. However, the learning mechanisms for constructing such category-based chains have been little been developed, either in concept learning or in reasoning research (but see bucket brigade mechanisms in Holland et al., 1986).

Schema models directly represent information about commonalities within concepts, as rule models do. Schema models can be organized hierarchically, allowing both a unitary representation of a concept (e.g., dog) and subcategories which capture the more disjunctive correlational structure within the superordinate. Some schema models (e.g., TWILIX) represent a variety of relations between concepts explicitly, such as inclusion in a parent category, contrast with a sister category, or overlap with a differently organized set of concepts. These strengths in explicit representation of information common to a concept and of relations between concepts are an important virtue. An important issue for these hierarchical schema models as psychological accounts is how information is accessed. As in early, and incorrect, models of semantic memory (Collins & Quillian, 1969), access of information follows the logical structure of the information. Access of a given concept is based on recursive classification starting at the top of a tree and following increasingly specific partitions. The TWILIX model allows multiple trees, but still within any one tree, access is hierarchical. As a decision tree, this has great advantages, but it cannot be taken as a serious model of how access to an individual concept in memory is made. Recognition is both more parallel, and more pitched to some concept level of intermediate specificity than a literal construal of this process would suggest. Thus while decision-tree-like structures may represent the information structure used in classification or reasoning, it should not be taken as a model of the time course of accessing information.

In summary, models of concept learning derived in the context of classification have serious shortcomings modeling how concepts as elements of thought are learned. First, instance, connectionist, and rule models all have difficulties in that they do not learn to represent relations between concepts explicitly. Second, connectionist models and rule models also lack flexible access and reuse of information about the concept for different tasks. Third, instance models and connectionist models lack a useful characterization of the commonalties of instances in the same concept. For each of these approaches substantial extensions to current models would be needed to expand the scope of these models to even quite simple tasks involving reasoning and use. Schema models provide some powerful assets for studying concept learning in the context of concepts' roles in reasoning as well as classification. Their promise for extending the scope of concept-learning models derives from these properties, typical of schema models:

1. They abstract out commonalties of a concept and represent this in a unitary form.
2. This in turn allows easy representation of relations between concepts.
3. They allow flexible reuse of information across tasks as well as across novel instances.

V. Concept Learning As Serving Internal and External Functions

Looking at concept learning with a broader set of uses in mind suggests a different set of learning principles and casts a different perspective on old questions. First, it casts abstraction and selection of information in a somewhat different light. Second, it casts the need to capture predictive structure in input, or relations between attributes, in a different light. Third, it raises questions about what sorts of relations among concepts, and between concepts and attributes, contribute to a "good" system of concepts.

First, human concept learning is selective in the information that influences classification. A subset of information is preferentially used, call it attentional learning or abstraction. Abstraction or attentional learning might be viewed as a necessary evil: Although classification would be best given retention and use of all the information in input, this is impossible because of people's limited encoding abilities, and so attentional learning strategically allocates the limited available capacity. Alternatively, this selectivity may be a desirable benefit for reasoning, rather than an undesirable cost from limited encoding capacity. From the perspective of concept use in reasoning, abstraction is a virtue needed even for a system with an unrestricted bandwidth for encoding. Abstraction of the information relevant to a concept, or what makes a dog a *dog,* is needed to use a concept in reasoning and for construction of a coherent system of concepts.

Second, while a fundamental purpose of concepts is to capture predictive structure in the world, learners may seek to learn and to organize concepts in a way that aids reasoning. As well as being biased to recover predictive structure, learners are biased to construct locally coherent systems of knowledge. The first set of experiments we will review here investigated a bias for *value systematicity.* These experiments ask how the structure in input affects success in discovering the relations among attributes, and how learning biases contribute to the formation of a coherent set of concepts.

Third, while research on classification focuses on the relations between a concept and its instances, research addressing the role of concepts in reasoning will need to focus on concept–attribute relations and concept–concept relations. The coherence of a concept is central to its role in reasoning and coherence cannot be judged in isolation, or in terms of concept–instance relations. Rather, coherence depends on relations with other concepts. There are probably several relational structures that are the basis for highly coherent systems of concepts. Causal chains, part–whole hierarchies, and set inclusion hierarchies are plausible candidates. An important property of good relational structures may be that they are constrained and have considerable redundancy to allow reconstruction or generation of information. The second set of experiments investigates the effect on learning of hierarchical set-inclusion relations among concepts, and particularly the interaction of hierarchical relations with attribute relevance.

VI. Value Systematicity Experiments: Effects on Learning Predictive Structure

One line of research done in our laboratory investigates the idea that learning the correlational structure in input is fundamental to concept learning, but that not all predictive structure is created equal. If any progress is to be made capturing useful predictive structure from a limited sample of experience, the learner must be biased, that is, must indeed come equipped for prioritizing what to learn. Learning biases are required for learning with feedback and are still more important for learning without feedback. When the environmental constraint of feedback is unavailable, the learner must rely still more on internal principles.

Our experiments investigate one structural bias in concept learning. Learning biases or constraints may specify the content or the structure of what is to be learned. Content biases are expectations about relevant content in the domain. These might identify the aspects of input germane to the task, such as relative versus absolute pitch in language acquisition (Gleitman & Gleitman, 1992) or surface texture for distinguishing animates from inanimates (Gelman, 1990). Alternatively, content biases might prioritize relations or theories constructed during learning, such as preference for one cause over another: For rats, nausea is attributed to distinctive tastes rather than shock (Garcia & Koelling, 1966); for people, learning new vehicle categories is guided by expectations about what jungle or arctic vehicles should be like (Murphy & Allopenna, 1994). Psychological research on learning has focused on content biases; they are discussed in the developmental literature as constraints or principles and in the concept-learning literature as effects of prior theory or belief.

Structural biases do not specify content, but rather the format or organization of the resulting knowledge. Keil's M and W constraints (1979) are perhaps the most familiar examples of structural constraints, though Keil focused on the resulting knowledge rather than the learning process. A bias to construct 1-to-1 mappings is a structural bias that has been proposed both for mapping between words and meanings in word learning (Markman, 1989) and for mapping between analogs in analogical learning (Holyoak & Thagard, 1989; Gentner, 1989). Machine learning has focused largely on structural or formal biases.

The correlational systems approach analyzes the organization of correlations among attributes and hypothesizes learning biases that guide discovery of correlational structure. Our experiments investigate value systematicity, one hypothesized structural learning bias. *Value systematicity* is a bias to learn predictive relations between attributes which are part of a set of mutually relevant attributes. This bias should direct learning toward that correlational structure in input likely to be most coherent and useful in reasoning. We look at the system of relations in the domain to be learned and ask how the organization of that whole system might affect learning.

We will use the term *value systematicity* to refer both to a bias in the learner and to structure in input that matches this bias. As a property of the input domain, high value systematicity means that (a) there are predictive attribute values in the domain (i.e., there is information there), and (b) attribute values that predict one attribute predict others (i.e. information is highly concentrated in a proper subset of values). Value systematicity refers to the amount *and* organization of correlational information in a domain. Two domains can have the same total redundancy or correlation, but differ in the degree of value systematicity. In domains with high value systematicity, correlations are not widely distributed across attributes, but cluster in a few. As a learning principle, the claim is that structure in a domain with high attribute systematicity will be learned faster than structure in a domain with lower attribute systematicity. If one attribute value (e.g., limb = wing) predicts the value of a second attribute (locomotion = fly), this relation will be discovered more quickly when that same first attribute co-varies with the values of still other attributes (covering = feathers). A particular relation between two properties will be discovered faster when it occurs in the context of other predictive attributes than when it occurs without additional relations. Further, this benefit from a relevant context will be found even when comparing learning about systems that differ in value systematicity but are equal in number of total rules or amount of total information.

To illustrate, suppose that in the domain of animal kinds in our actual world, having a beak, flying, having feathers, singing, and having wings all co-vary. If this characteristic of having the information carried by interrelated cues is widely true, the domain would have high value systematicity. A bias for learning structures with high value systematicity predicts learning that a mouth-type of beak co-occurs with a vocalization of singing would be easier to learn in this world than in one where beak and singing were unrelated to other properties. This bias could be realized in several learning mechanisms. Most directly, this bias was implemented as an attentional learning process in a model of unsupervised learning (Billman & Heit, 1988; Chalnick & Billman, 1988). As the estimate of the predictive utility of a property increases, additional sampling is directed to that attribute.

A value systematicity bias in learning would be useful because it simultaneously (a) capitalizes on a structural property of input identifying information valuable for later reasoning while, (b) also accommodating limited processing capacity. It uses attention as a selective guide to aspects of structure that are likely to matter most. Correlations that form part of a system of interlocking correlations will be more useful than the same amount of information distributed among a more scattered set of attributes. Rich sets of correlations will produce a smaller set of more informative concepts. Richer concepts will be more likely to be consequential, reflect a common underlying cause, or be a more profitable locus for theorizing.

A. Value Systematicity Experiments with Object Categories

Three experiments tested and found evidence for a bias for value systematicity in learning animal concepts: People are biased to capture systems of mutually relevant correlations (Billman & Knutson, 1996). These studies used college student participants exposed to pictures of novel animals in an unsupervised learning task. Animal pictures were composed from seven three-valued attributes: head, body shape, texture, leg, tail, time-of-day, and habitat. Figure 1 shows examples. Participants were introduced to the task as one on visual memory and then saw a set of 27 pictures of alien animals, repeated in each of four learning blocks.

Conditions differed in the correlational structure available in input, specifically, in what attributes co-varied. Following the unsupervised learning phase, participants moved to the test phase. Here participants were shown pairs of novel animals, and picked which of the two pictures best "matched with" the animals seen in the learning phase. Each experiment tested multiple rules to ensure that any difference between conditions was not an idiosyncrasy of the specific attribute combinations being tested.

Value Systematicity (VS) Experiments VS1 and VS2 compared learning a given target rule between values of a pair of attributes, when that rule occurred in isolation versus as part of a structured, mutually relevant system of correlations. In the Isolating Condition, just two attributes co-varied,

Fig. 1. Example learning stimuli used for the Value Systematicity Experiments VS1–VS3. The same seven attributes (head, body, texture, tail, legs, habitat, and time-of-day) were used in all three experiments; values differed for Experiments VS1 and VS2 versus VS3. Copyright © from Billman & Knutson (1996) by the American Psychological Association. Reprinted with permission.

providing a single target rule and there were no further correlations in input. In the Structured Condition, four attributes co-varied so that the two attributes of the target rule also co-varied with two more attributes. For example, head type and time of day co-varied (forming the target rule) for one group of participants in the Isolating Condition, and only values of these two attributes carried any predictive information about the stimulus structure; assignments of all other attribute values were counterbalanced to ensure they were uninformative. In the comparable participant group of the Structured Condition, head type and time of day co-varied in the identical way, but tail and texture co-varied with each other and with head and time as well. The identical target rule was always compared in Isolating and Structured Conditions, and multiple configurations of rules were used. Experiments VS1 and VS2 differed in the rules and configurations used. Figure 2 shows details of the stimuli design for the structured and isolating conditions of Experiment VS2.

Test stimuli were novel instances that either preserved or disrupted the pairings of the target rule. Thus, one head type might be combined with the incorrect time of day in one member of the forced choice pair and with the correct time of day in the other. To ensure a fair test of the same knowledge across conditions, we needed to use test items with missing attributes rather than intact items. For intact items, if the wrong head was paired with a particular time of day, this would also disrupt the pairings of head with tail and of head with texture in the Structured Condition, producing multiple rule violations for those subjects. To ensure that we were testing knowledge specifically of the target rule in both conditions, attributes that might provide additional information for Structured Condition participants (e.g. tail and texture) were deleted. All test items in both conditions had two attributes deleted, or "covered up," to make the test items visually similar and to provide equivalent information about the target rule. Structured and Isolating participants saw the identical sets of test items.

In both experiments, participants were better at learning the identical target rule when that rule occurred in a more systematic context than when it occurred in isolation (Experiment VS1: Structured mean = 75.9%, SD = 19%; Isolating mean = 65.5%, SD = 21%; $F[1,114] = 14.98$, MSe = 88.67, $p<.001$. Experiment VS2: Structured mean=73.4%, SD=23%; Isolating mean = 61.8%, SD = 22%; $F[1,108] = 7.89$, MSe = 136.53, $p<.006$). Figure 3 shows the results for Experiment VS2, broken down by each rule.

Experiments VS1 and VS2 demonstrated better unsupervised learning of an individual correlational rule or pattern when it occurred in a structured rather than in an isolating context. The system of correlations present across the whole input domain influenced the learning of the relation between

Structured Condition

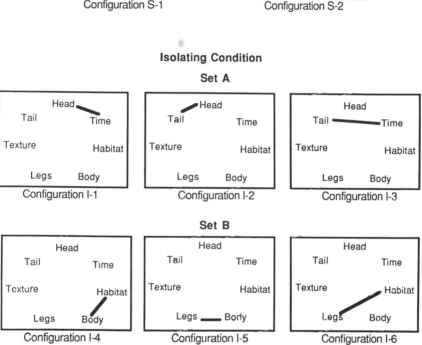

Set A

Set A — Configuration S-1

Set B

Set B — Configuration S-2

Isolating Condition

Set A

Configuration I-1

Configuration I-2

Configuration I-3

Set B

Configuration I-4

Configuration I-5

Configuration I-6

Fig. 2. Design diagram for Value Systematicity Experiment VS1. Each box shows the stimuli configuration for one group of participants. Lines mark correlations between pairs of attributes. In the Structured Condition (top panel) four of the seven attributes co-varied, in each of two configurations (Set A or B). In the Isolating Condition one of the correlations present in the Structured Condition occurs alone. Copyright © from Billman & Knutson (1996) by the American Psychological Association. Reprinted with permission.

particular pairs of attribute values. Specifically, learning a particular "target" correlational rule or pattern (such as the pairings of each of three head types with a corresponding type of tail) was learned more easily when other attributes co-varied with the attributes in the target rule than when

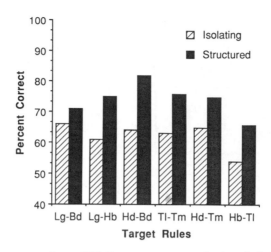

Fig. 3. Results of Experiment VS2. Percent correct on the forced choice Missing Parts test. Chance is 50%. Lg = Leg, Bd = Body, Hb = Habitat, Tl = Tail, Tm = Time, Hd = Head. Rules are Leg–Body; Leg–Habitat; Head–Body; Tail–Time, Head–Time, and Habitat–Tail. Copyright © from Billman & Knutson (1996) by the American Psychological Association. Reprinted with permission.

the target rule occurred in isolation. Rather than finding blocking or competition among rules, as has sometimes been found for supervised learning (Chapman & Robbins, 1990; Gluck & Bower, 1988), we found facilitation.

Experiment VS3 was designed to separate the effects of the amount of predictive structure from its organization. In Experiments VS1 and VS2, the Isolating Condition differed from the Structured in that it had a smaller amount of total information and smaller total number of rules, as well as differing in the organization of those rules. Experiment VS3 introduced an Orthogonal Condition which had more total information and an equal number of rules to the Structured Condition, but still had lower value systematicity. The design of Experiment V3S is shown in Fig. 4. In the Orthogonal Condition, multiple correlational rules are present, but they are unrelated to each other. Here again we found better learning of a target rule when that rule was part of a mutually relevant set of correlational rules. Participants in the Structured Condition averaged 77.2% (SD 20.5%) correct, compared to the Orthogonal Condition average of 66.2% (SD = 20%; $F[1,46] = 5.39$, MSE = 27.07, $p<.03$). Even when organization was separated from the total amount of information and the total number of pair-wise rules, the structured organization of correlational rules benefited learning.

B.   VALUE SYSTEMATICITY EXPERIMENTS WITH EVENT CATEGORIES

A second series of experiments (Kersten & Billman, 1995) tested the correlational systems approach in learning event categories. Our event categories

Structured Condition

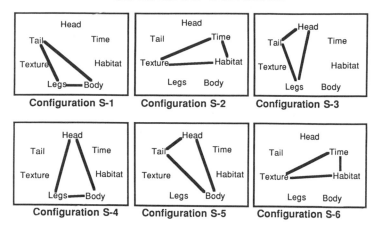

Configuration S-1   Configuration S-2   Configuration S-3

Configuration S-4   Configuration S-5   Configuration S-6

Orthogonal Condition

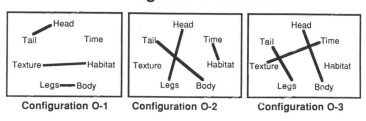

Configuration O-1   Configuration O-2   Configuration O-3

Fig. 4.   Design diagram for Experiment VS3. Each box shows the stimuli configuration for one group of participants. Heavy lines mark correlations between pairs of attributes. In the Structured Condition (top panel) three of the seven attributes co-varied producing three pairwise correlations, in one of six configurations (one repeated). In the Orthogonal Condition each participant saw three correlations, but they were unrelated to each other. Each pair-wise correlation is used equally often in the Structured and Orthogonal Conditions. Copyright © from Billman & Knutson (1996) by the American Psychological Association. Reprinted with permission.

grouped "verb-sized," transitive motion events that varied in properties such as manner of motion, state change, property of the agent, and so on. Our event categories were designed to form plausible referents for a verb meaning, though no language was used in any of these experiments. Learning of event categories has been little studied, but analysis of verb structure (Gentner, 1981) and verb learning (Huttenlocher & Lui, 1979) suggests that verbs and perhaps the event categories to which they refer, may not be primarily organized around capturing correlational structure in the world. Thus the learning bias found for object categories might not generalize to events. However, here too we found that predictive relations were learned more quickly when part of a system of mutually relevant correlations. These experiments again looked for evidence of facilitation learning an individual correlational rule when the attributes in that target rule also co-vary with other attributes.

In four event experiments college students watched animated events of transitive interactions. In each event an agent character approached and contacted a patient character, producing a state change in the patient and movement away by the patient. The attributes we used for the events were motivated by the properties that are frequently relevant to verb meaning and included agent path, patient path, state change, environment, agent or patient appearance, orientation of movement, and limb movement. Across the four experiments, multiple rules were assessed; Environment with Manner of Motion, Agent Path with Patient Path, and Patient Appearance with Agent Path are examples of target rules.

The procedure was similar to that in the experiments on learning object categories. Participants were told that they would be watching interactions between characters on another planet and should be learning about the kinds of events that could take place. After this unsupervised learning phase, participants began the test phase. During test, some novel instances preserved the correlation of the target rule and some disrupted the correlation. In three experiments participants judged an individual event as belonging or not belonging on the planet using a 5-point rating scale; the fourth used forced choice rather than rating. As in the animal-category experiments, test items obscured information that might allow correct responses based on information other than the target rule. While the learning phase differed between conditions, test items were always identical for conditions within an experiment.

Three different designs assessed the effects of rich correlational structure on learning a target rule. These designs are summarized in Fig. 5. All compare learning a given rule when part of a cluster of mutually relevant attributes with learning that rule when no other attributes covaried with the attributes of the target rule. Multiple event rules were used both within and across experiments.

The first two event experiments used designs analogous to those used for studying object categories. The design for the first event experiment, shown in Panel A of Fig. 5, is analogous to the design used in Experiment VS3. For example, for some subjects the target correlational rule was type of agent path with manner of motion. For these subjects in the structured condition, state change and environment also correlated perfectly with agent path and manner of motion. In the comparison condition there were multiple correlations but each correlation, on which a category could be based, was unrelated or orthogonal to the others. This forms a matrix-like

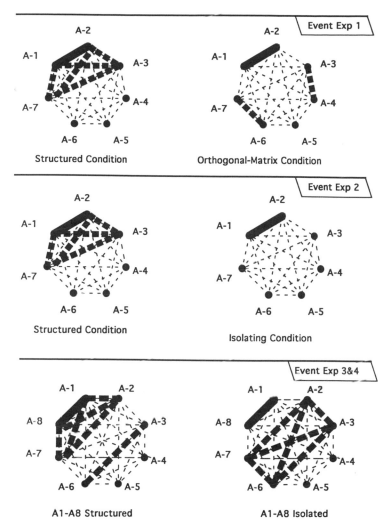

Fig. 5. Design diagrams for the event category experiments. Dots labeled "A-*n*" represent the *n* attributes, which varied. Heavy solid lines indicate the target correlational rule, present in both conditions. Heavy dashed lines indicate additional correlations; conditions differed in what additional correlations were available in input. Light, dashed lines indicate pairs of unrelated attributes. Not shown are the multiple configurations, testing different target rules.

organization, such as that which has sometimes been suggested for verb meanings. The design for the second event experiment, shown in Panel B of Fig. 5, is analogous to the design used in object category Experiments VS1 and VS2. Learning of a target rule in the structured condition is compared to learning the rule when it is the only correlational rule in the input. In both experiments, participants were significantly more likely to learn a target rule about event categories when it occurred in the structured context, as shown in Fig. 6.

The third and fourth event experiments used a new design based on a within-subject comparison. Each subject had the opportunity to learn two target rules, one part of a cluster of related rules, and one in isolation. Each subject was tested on the two rules, while across subjects we counter-balanced the number of times a given rule was in a cluster versus in isolation. This design, showing that the same rule was in a cluster for some subjects but isolated for others, is shown in the bottom panel of Fig. 5. Again, subjects learned a target rule significantly better when its attributes were part of a cluster of mutually relevant properties, than when the rule occurred in isolation.

The object category (Billman & Knutson, 1996) and event category experiments (Kersten & Billman, 1995) compare learning from input with high-value systematicity to learning in a variety of control conditions with lower value systematicity. These controls compared performance of learning a target rule when part of a mutually relevant set of rules to learning the same rule (a) when it was the only regularity in input, (b) when other unrelated regularities were present, and (c) when an unrelated rule and a rule in a mutually relevant set were both available in the same input. Across these varied comparisons and domains learners showed facilitation in learning those aspects of correlational structure which were related to other

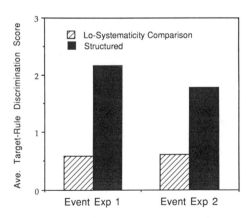

Fig. 6. Summarized results of event Experiments 1 and 2. Discrimination score is the difference between ratings of correct test events (consistent with the target rule) and incorrect test events (violating the target rule). A discrimination score of zero indicates failure to learn the target rule.

regularities. While capturing correlational structure is central to unsupervised learning, people's data-driven learning is still biased to recover aspects of structure which are coherent and hence might be a more useful locus for reasoning, explaining, or theorizing.

VII. Experiments on Consistent Contrast and Hierarchical Inclusion Relations

Value systematicity is a structural bias emphasizing relations between attributes. Consistent contrast is a structural bias emphasizing relations between concepts, specifically relations between concepts in set inclusion hierarchies. We address relations within set inclusion hierarchies because of their pervasive importance in virtually every inward-facing cognitive process of reasoning, comprehension, or problem solving. Natural concepts seem to be organized into collections of local hierarchies, each consistent within a sphere of activity, but producing overlap when the same concept plays a role in multiple spheres or domains (e.g., cooking and botany). Relations among concepts are important both as products of learning and as factors influencing the process of acquisition.

I claim that the psychologically relevant relations within a taxonomic hierarchy are those of *inclusion* (animal–dog) and *contrast* (cat–dog). Indirect relations within a hierarchy are composed from these. Inclusion is the more familiar relation. Concept A *includes* another, Concept B, if B is represented as a type of A. If A includes B, all Bs are represented as being As, or the description of A subsumes the description of B. Two or more concepts are in a *contrast* relation if they are represented as mutually exclusive and mutually relevant. A common parent category establishes mutual relevance among daughter categories, but mutual relevance could arise from a contextually specified superordinate, such as "the categories for this experiment." Classes that are not mutually relevant do not contrast, even if they are mutually exclusive; *things smaller than a bread box* does not contrast with *mature featherless bipeds*. Contrast sets differ in the consistency with which the attributes important for one category are important for other categories in the set; we call this *consistency of contrast.*

In sets of concepts with *consistent contrast* the attributes that are homogeneous within one category assume homogeneous (though usually distinct) values in other categories. That is, in a set with consistent contrast the same attributes matter across the categories. We predict that people are biased to learn sets of categories that contrast consistently and hence that learning will be easier when the target categories have consistent contrast.

Attentional learning mechanisms are related to a bias to learn consistently contrasting concepts. Both often benefit from concentrating the important information in a small number of attributes. Attentional mechanisms produce fastest learning when the information from a small number of attributes is sufficient to distinguish between categories, and this will usually be the case for consistently contrasting categories. There are three somewhat subtle differences, however.

First, consistency of contrast assumes a representation using multivalued attributes: Contrast is consistent if each type of bird assumes a homogeneous and distinctive type of beak, or if each type of farm animal has its own homogeneous vocalization. In contrast, attentional learning can be directed to presence or absence of any property, be it a particular value such as *red* versus not-red, or an attribute, such as color versus shape. The idea of consistency of contrast is most germane when a set of common attributes can be assumed for instances in multiple categories. If instances were represented just as presence or absence of particular properties, the informativeness of any individual property would not be very great across a set of several categories, and almost any contrast set with multiple categories would have rather low consistency of contrast.

Second, consistency of contrast directly measures homogeneity of an attribute within a category, not discrimination between categories, while attentional learning is usually driven by discrimination between categories. Consistent contrast is a generalization of a particular learning bias, variability bias, implemented in TWILIX (Martin, 1992; Martin & Billman, 1991). Variability bias was used to influence construction of new categories when instances assumed novel values on attributes previously homogeneous within the familiar categories. Variability bias and consistent contrast are particularly useful in determining when an instance does not belong to an old category, and in inductions from a single instance. If all observed jays have been blue, all canaries yellow, and all robins red breasted, witnessing a black bird is very good evidence that the creature belongs to none of the old categories and requires a new one.

Third and most importantly, consistency of contrast is local to one contrast set, or to the subordinates of a single superordinate. A hierarchy can have maximum consistency of contrast even if different properties matter within each of several branches. Learning biases sensitive to this will learn about the local relevance of an attribute within a branch of a hierarchy. This differs from attentional learning, which is a global shift in what properties are preferentially encoded or used. Probably global shifts in what is attended in encoding (attentional learning) occur as well as local shifts in what information is judged relevant to a particular type of category (learning sensitive to consistent contrast). Consistency of contrast makes use of information from hierarchical relations in a way that attentional learning does not.

A.   INITIAL CONSISTENCY OF CONTRAST EXPERIMENTS

Experiment C1 looked for as direct and substantial an effect of consistency of contrast in learning a system of categories as we could devise (Billman & Davila, 1995). We again used animal stimuli, which had six attributes. We used supervised rather than unsupervised learning to teach three animal categories. The organization of the attributes that would allow successful classification differed for the consistent and inconsistent conditions. In the consistent contrast condition each category had homogeneous values on two attributes (e.g., vocalization and movement), and these attributes were the same two for all three categories. In the inconsistent contrast condition, each category differed in which pair of attributes mattered.

Fifty college students participated. They were instructed that they would be touring the Saturn zoo, learning about different animals, and would be tested later. During learning they viewed animated, alien animals, schematically represented in Table I. In the Consistent Condition the same attributes marked each of the three categories; for example, in Configuration 1 all *yodlars* croaked and flew, *ralfazes* bleated and walked, while *muntogs* roared and jumped; the remaining attributes, A3–A6, (shown with Xs in Table I), were randomly assigned. In the Inconsistent Condition, a different

TABLE I

STIMULUS SCHEMA FOR CONSISTENT CONTRAST EXPERIMENT C1[a]

	Consistent Contrast Condition		
	Configuration 1	Configuration 2	Configuration 3
Category 1	11 xx xx	xx 11 xx	xx xx 11
Category 2	22 xx xx	xx 22 xx	xx xx 22
Category 3	33 xx xx	xx 33 xx	xx xx 33
	Inconsistent Contrast Condition		
	Configuration 1	Configuration 2	Configuration 3
Category 1	11 xx xx	xx 11 xx	xx xx 11
Category 2	xx 22 xx	xx xx 22	22 xx xx
Category 3	xx xx 33	33 xx xx	xx 33 zx

[a] Stimulus schema for the three categories for each of six participant groups are shown schematically. Numbers indicate the value of an attribute that was consistently assigned to members of a given category. Xs indicate random attribute values for members of the category. Each column indicates an attribute (A1–A6), ordered as sound, movement, habitat, color, head-type, and body/leg.

pair of attributes was homogeneous in each category, so the same attribute did not matter for more than one category; for example, for Configuration 1, Category 1 used sound and movement, Category 2 used habitat and color, and Category 3 used head and body. For each category the remaining four attributes varied randomly, as in the Consistent Condition. For each category 15 instances were generated and, across configurations, the identical 15 instances were used for a given category (i.e. the set of fifteen xx xx 22 instances) whether the category contrasted consistently or inconsistently with alternatives (i.e., shown in the top or bottom panel of Table 1).

During supervised learning (45 trials) participants viewed animal pictures and clicked the label they thought appropriate (*yodlar, ralfaz,* and *muntog*). The correct label was then highlighted. At the beginning of the Fit Test, participants were told they would see displays, some of which would be like what they had seen and some of which would be different. They were told to click a Yes button if the event was "like something you had seen before" and No otherwise. Neither labels nor feedback were provided during the test. The 15 correct, familiar displays were normal but novel members of one of the three categories used during learning. Incorrect test items scrambled up the assignments of the defining attribute pair (e.g., 12 xx xx rather than the correct 11 xx xx). Thus, participants needed to know about relations between cues to perform perfectly, not just the relation between an individual cue and the category label. This tests knowledge of within category correlations. Finally, participants filled out a questionnaire about what they noticed.

The average number correct over learning was 86.9% in the Consistent and 49.5% in the Inconsistent Condition. Participants in the Consistent Condition jumped to high, asymptotic classification in the first 10 trials. The effect of Condition, $F(1,44) = 269$, $p < .001$, but not Configuration, $F(4,44) = 2.27$, was highly significant. Scores on the Fit Test were higher in the Consistent Contrast Condition, mean of 75.1% correct, than those in the Inconsistent Contrast Condition, mean of 55.3% (Condition $F[1,44] = 14.03$, $p = .001$; Configuration $F[4,44] =. 87$). Thus, participants learned much faster in the Consistent Condition, and also were much better at noticing the correlational structure within category.

This dramatic effect prompted more controlled separation of effects of consistent contrast from confounds of similarity. In Experiment C1, the completely unconstrained assignment of random attributes allowed occasional generation of ambiguous items such as 11 12 xx or even 1122xx in the Inconsistent Condition; thus the similarity structure might favor the Consistent Condition and contribute to the improved learning there.

Experiment C2 tested for benefit from consistent contrast, when similarity favored the inconsistent condition. Experiment C2 introduced two changes in the assignment of random attributes. This made the within-category similarity higher and the between-category similarity lower in the Inconsistent Condition than in the Consistent Condition, thus stacking the deck against the predicted benefit from consistency. Inspection of Table II shows that the formerly random attributes were assigned to be partially predictive in the Inconsistent Condition: In the xx22xx category, no 1s were assigned to the A1 or A2 and no 3s were assigned to A5 or A6. This makes the category *distinctiveness* greater in the Inconsistent Condition. Further, two of the four members in each category in the Consistent Condition had a closely matched "foil" in one of the other categories: *11*1312 matches *33*1312 and *11*3121 matches *22*3121 on four of six attributes. In the Inconsistent Condition the strongest between category match is only two of six attributes. This makes the category *confusibility* greater in the Consistent Condition.

Experiment C2 used a Generalization Test; at test participants continued to classify instances into the three categories rather than make yes/no judgments about belongingness. Experiment C2 also introduced an Induction Task after the Generalization Test. An instance with all new values (44 44 44) was presented as a new kind of animal, and the participant judged if other target animals were the same kind as the source animal. The target animals differed in whether they matched the source on the relevant or irrelevant attributes (e.g., 44 55 55 vs. 55 44 55). Two source animals representing two new categories were used, each followed by six target animals. Participants in the Consistent Condition who learned about what properties were important for the contrast set would have a systematic basis for induction to a new category in the set: If an attribute had been homogeneous within three familiar categories, it should be homogeneous for a fourth. Stimuli in the Inconsistent Condition did not provide a reliable basis for induction. Thus participants there could only draw on the more idiosyncratic properties of attribute salience or preference.

TABLE II

LEARNING STIMULI FOR CONFIGURATION 1: EXPERIMENT C2

Consistent Condition			Inconsistent Condition		
Category 1	Category 2	Category 3	Category 1	Category 2	Category 3
11 11 11	22 22 11	33 13 12	11 11 11	22 22 11	22 11 33
11 13 12	22 31 21	33 33 22	11 13 12	23 22 12	23 13 33
11 31 21	22 22 23	33 22 23	11 31 21	32 22 21	32 31 33
11 33 22	22 32 33	33 32 33	11 33 22	33 22 22	33 33 33

Participants in the Consistent Condition learned significantly faster, reflected in a significant interaction of condition with learning block and a main effect of condition (p's < .05). For example, in the second block (trials 10–18) the Consistent Condition averaged 76% versus the Inconsistent's 56%. The Consistent Condition scored significantly higher on Generalization (67% vs. 50%, $F[1,32] = 6.07$, $p = .019$) and Induction (76% vs. 40%. $F[1,32] = 19.17, p = .0001$) as well. Figure 7 shows the learning curve.

Both Experiments C1 and C2 (Billman & Davila, 1995) found that a set of three contrasting categories was learned much faster when the same attributes were important for each of the three categories than when different attributes mattered for different categories. Performance on the Fit Text in Experiment C1 showed that participants also learned to detect violations in the correlations between two predictive cues better in the consistent than inconsistent condition. Performance on the induction task in Experiment C2 showed that participants also were better able to generalize their knowledge to novel categories and novel attribute values. Experiment C2 showed that the benefits of consistently informative attributes

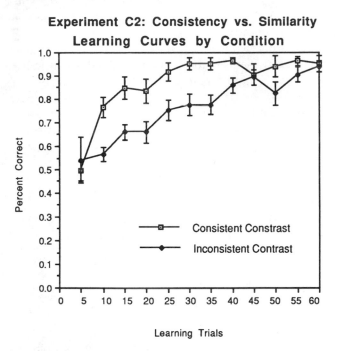

Fig. 7.   Results from Experiment C2. Percent correct over learning in conditions where three categories contrasted consistently or inconsistently.

outweighed the costs of reduced within-category similarity and increased between-category confusibility.

These results are inconsistent with concept-learning models that do not allow dynamic reweighting of attribute importance based on its informativeness (e.g. Anderson's RA, 1991). Predictions based on benefit from consistent contrast are not the same as predictions based on global informativeness of attributes, but these experiments did not distinguish benefit from global attentional learning from benefit from consistent contrast local within a hierarchy. Since these experiments did not have multiple contrast sets under different superordinates, the effects of global versus local informativeness of attributes could not be distinguished. Experiment C3 investigated whether participants use hierarchical structure to delimit the scope for assessing attribute informativeness.

B.   HIERARCHY AND CONSISTENT CONTRAST

To show that participants are sensitive to an attribute's role within a hierarchy requires separating the global informativeness of an attribute from its local significance within a constrast set. We sought to do this by presenting hierarchically organized concepts where concepts within different branches of the hierarchy relied on different attributes. To provide hierarchically organized input, we made one general partition of the instances, based on the most salient property. Then within each of these general, superordinate categories, other less distinctive properties partitioned each superordinate into subordinates. Conditions differ in whether membership in the superordinate allows prediction of which attribute(s) will be important for the subordinate categories. In the Consistent Contrast Condition, all the categories under the same superordinate are distinguished by the same properties. In the Inconsistent Contrast Condition the global informativeness of each attribute is the same as in the Consistent Condition, but its informativeness is distributed across the superordinates; knowing the superordinate tells one nothing about what attributes will distinguish the subordinate categories there. Does consistent contrast, within a hierarchy, aid learning?

A four-category pilot experiment with two subordinate categories nested within each of two superordinates was very easy and produced no difference between Consistent and Inconsistent Conditions during learning or test. However, participants did show sensitivity to consistent contrast in a surprising way. Their explanations at the end of the experiment suggested they had also adopted an A versus not-A strategy for classification, in comments such as "a shoosa jumps and makes a croaking noise, while a lonkar jumps and makes any noise except croaking." These protocols suggested that participants were imposing consistent contrast and using a single attribute to distinguish categories within a superordinate, even when an alternative, positive description (e.g., "has an antenna-head") was available. This pilot highlighted the importance of using multiple lower-level categories so that participants could not "convert" inconsistently contrasting categories in input to a consistently represented pair of categories by recoding a set of attributes to an A versus not-A format.

A follow-up experiment used a more difficult nine-category system to see if consistency within a hierarchy aided learning. The stimuli again were alien animals as in the simple contrast experiments, but seven attributes were used, each assuming three values: sound, habitat, color, head shape, face type, body shape, leg type. The nine categories were hierarchically grouped into three groups of three. Sound always distinguished the superordinate categories. Category labels were two words (e.g., FLARNO GOFNAR), the first referring to the superordinate (e.g., things making a whisking sound), and the second to the subordinate (e.g., red things making a whisking sound). Instances within each of the nine categories shared values of two attributes common to only that subordinate plus a third common across the superordinate. Conditions differed in whether the same pair of attributes mattered for all three categories within a superordinate, or whether different values were relevant for each.

Table III shows stimuli schema for the Consistently and Inconsistently Contrasting Hierarchy Conditions. In the consistently contrasting hierarchy

TABLE III

STIMULI SCHEMA FOR EXPERIMENT C3[a]

Consistently Contrasting Hierarchy					
Superordinate 1		Superordinate 2		Superordinate 3	
Category 1	1 11xxxx	Category 4	2 xx11xx	Category 7	3 xxxx11
Category 2	1 22xxxx	Category 5	2 xx22xx	Category 8	3 xxxx22
Category 3	1 33xxxx	Category 6	2 xx33xx	Category 9	3 xxxx33
Inconsistently Contrasting Hierarchy					
Superordinate 1		Superordinate 2		Superordinate 3	
Category 1	1 11xxxx	Category 4	2 xx11xx	Category 7	3 xxxx11
Category 2	1 xx22xx	Category 5	2 xxxx22	Category 8	3 22xxxx
Category 3	1 xxxx33	Category 6	2 33xxxx	Category 9	3 xx33xx

[a] Numbers represent the values used for each attribute and Xs represent values assigned with constrained randomization. Columns within a schema represent attributes. The first attribute, marking the superordinates, is sound. Assignments of other attributes to columns varied across three configurations of stimuli. Each superordinate category groups together the three subordinate categories, i.e., categories 1–3, 4–6, and 7–9.

the same attributes mattered for all three categories within one superordinate; a different pair mattered for each of the three superordinate sets. In the inconsistently contrasting hierarchy, a different pair of attributes mattered for each of the three categories within a given superordinate. Note that the overall informativeness of each of the six nonsound attributes is the same within and between conditions. The difference is solely in whether the three categories that use the same attributes are in the same or different superordinates. Three different configurations varied the assignments of real attributes to columns in the schema.

In the Consistent Hierarchy Condition, the random attributes could take on any value 1–3. In the Inconsistent Hierarchy Condition, assigning values of the random attributes was constrained to preclude the construction of ambiguous items: No items such as 1 11 22 xx, which would match both the Category 1 and Category 2 schema, were generated. That is, if an attribute (e.g., column 4) was "random" within a category (e.g., category 1), it could only take on the two values not relevant to a category within that superordinate; 1 11 11 xx or 1 11 33 xx might be generated, but not 1 11 22 xx. Notice that this increases the within-category similarity of the Inconsistent Hierarchy Condition, which should aid learning there. A different set and order of learning stimuli were generated for each participant.

In sum, in the Consistent Hierarchy Condition, knowing the superordinate category specifies which attributes will be important in distinguishing subordinates, but this is not the case in the Inconsistently Contrasting Hierarchy Condition. For example, in the Consistent Hierarchy Condition, if a particular Sound 1 (chirping) were heard this would indicate which two attributes (e.g., habitat and color) are predictive of category membership. In the Inconsistent Hierarchy Condition, however, the superordinate provides no information about attribute relevance, as all six are informative in each superordinate.

Test stimuli were additional category instances generated from the same schema as the learning stimuli. In addition, some test stimuli included one value of one attribute that had not been seen during learning. At test, the nine category labels plus an "other" label were displayed.

Induction stimuli used novel values of familiar attributes. The purpose of the induction task was to measure whether participants had learned about attribute importance within the hierarchy and used this to guide inductions about novel kinds of animals. The design of the induction items was guided by what properties had been important in the Consistent Hierarchy Condition. Induction stimuli consisted of a source and a set of target items. These items used the sounds from the learning phase, but values of all other attributes had not appeared in learning. Because the same sounds were used, participants could classify the induction source item as a novel type of animal within a particular superordinate. The target items matched the source item on some but not all values. "Correct" target items matched the source item on those attributes that were important in differentiating categories within the particular superordinate to which the source item belonged. Three different source items were used, one from each superordinate, and 10 target items were constructed to assess generalization from each source item. The same stimulus set was used for both conditions.

The procedure consisted of the learning phase, generalization phase, induction task, and debriefing. During the 81-trial learning phase, participants saw an animal with nine possible labels displayed below the picture, selected the label they thought correct, and got feedback. Participants were told at the beginning that the nine categories were grouped into three broader categories and that listening to the sounds would help them learn those three broad categories. At test, participants continued to classify instances, but a 10th button labeled "other" was added, and no feedback was provided.

For the induction phase, participants saw three blocks of items, one block for each of the three source animals. Participants were told they would see an animal that also belonged in the alien zoo, that it would make a familiar sound but have novel attribute values otherwise. Participants were to judge whether each of a set of target items fit with the source item. (Participants had printed images of the source animals to refer to during the task.)

Participants in the Consistent Hierarchy Condition had a higher average learning score, of 51%, than did participants in the Inconsistent Condition, with 40% correct, chance performance = 11%, $F(1,28) = 7.22, p = 0.12$. The mean test scores for Consistent Hierarchy Condition was 71%, significantly greater than the mean of 37% for the Inconsistent Hierarchy Condition, $F(1,28) = 39.43, p < .0001$. The induction means of 61% for the Consistent Hierarchy versus 55% for the Inconsistent Hierarchy did not differ significantly, however, $F(1,28) = 1.50, p = .23$.

VIII. Conclusions

When researchers have sought to understand the forces guiding concept learning, they have turned to the external functions of categories. In supervised learning paradigms this function is analyzed as learning to predict a particular property of instances: Is it poisonous? What is its label? In unsupervised tasks, concept learning is usually analyzed as learning to predict a broad set of properties from a variety of initial information. The importance of learning the predictive structure of the input is indeed central to concept learning. But concepts function in an internal ecology of mind as well, and utility for reasoning is important as well as veracity of predictions. I suggest that the need for manageable reasoning produces organizational biases that (a) select aspects of correlational structure most likely to be learned and (b) guide how that structure is organized.

The experiments summarized here provide evidence for two structural biases. The first set of experiments (Billman & Knutson, 1996) found evidence for value-systematicity bias. A bias for value systematicity will guide the learner to discover selectively those aspects of predictive structure that are mutually relevant. This will bias the learner toward a smaller number of more informative categories. These categories should be more promising seeds for theorizing, explanation, or other interpretive and less data-driven learning processes. This learning bias influenced learning of event as well as object categories (Kersten & Billman, 1996).

The second set of experiments found effects of the relations among new concepts on their acquisition, specifically of consistency of contrast and of inclusion by same or different superordinate. People are biased to learn consistently contrasting categories. One of the most interesting types of evidence that hierarchies are both learned and important would be the interaction of hierarchical relations with other factors affecting learning. While the first two contrast experiments (Billman & Davila, 1995) showed an effect of consistent use of the same attributes in providing information about multiple categories, the third experiment showed how this interacted with hierarchical structure. This experiment investigated a system of categories of sufficient complexity such that the organization of the new categories might be expected to affect learning significantly. This study provides initial evidence for the importance of hierarchical inclusion relations, and for the modulation of benefits of consistency by the hierarchical relations among concepts.

The heart of learning is induction, or going beyond the given data in useful and productive ways. It has long been recognized that learners need constraints on induction to prioritize some possibilities over others. Characterization of the constraints, principles, or biases guiding learning is very important to understanding the underlying processes. A description in terms of principles and constraints is more general than any particular computational or mental-mechanism model, but provides a (partial) specification of the properties necessary for a successful model. Characterization in terms of constraints also allows clear formulation of questions about domain specificity or generality of learning. Analysis of constraints has many of the advantages of rational analysis without requiring as strong assumptions about the purpose of a particular type of learning or what the optimal performance would be.

In this chapter I have made two suggestions for how learning principles might usefully be sought. First, whereas much work has focused on constraints or principles stated in terms of the content of what is being learned, it is also useful to seek structural biases. Second, although it is useful to seek learning principles by analyzing the learner's goals and the uses of what is learned, there are frequently multiple uses and divergent goals. As a result, learning may typically be under multiple and partially conflicting pressures. In particular, concept learning is likely to be simultaneously driven by the need to form organized, coherent ideas that are easy to think with and to form groups which capture predictive structure in the environment. The experiments presented in this chapter assume learning correlational structure is very important, but critically modulated by pressures for coherence and organization. The experiments are presented as steps toward linking the ecology of mind and the ecology of the external world in understanding concept learning.

Acknowledgments

I would like to thank David Dávila, Alan Kersten, and Jim Knutson for their collaboration on the empirical work summarized in this chapter and Ángel Cabrera, David Dávila, and Alan Kersten for extended discussions of some of the issues addressed.

References

Anderson, J. R. (1991). The adaptive nature of human categorization. *Psychological Review, 98,* 409–429.

Anderson, J. R., & Bower, G. H. (1973). *Human associative memory.* Hillsdale, NJ: Erlbaum.

Anderson, J. R., Kline, P. J., & Beasely, C. M. (1979). A general learning theory and its application to schema abstraction. In G. H. Bower (Ed.). *The psychology of learning and motivation* (Vol. 13). New York: Academic Press.

Anderson, R. C., & Pichert, J. W. (1978). Recall of previously unrecallable information following a shift in perspective. *Journal of Verbal Learning and Verbal Behavior, 17,* 1–12.

Barsalou, L. W. (1987). The instability of graded structure: Implications for the nature of concepts. In U. Neisser (Ed.), *Concepts and conceptual development: Ecological and intellectual factors in categorization.* Cambridge, England: Cambridge University Press.

Billman, D., & Davila, D. (1995). Consistency is the hobgoblin of human minds: People care but concept learning models do not. J. D. Moore & J. F. Lehman (Eds.), *Proceedings of the Seventeenth Annual Conference of the Cognitive Science Society.* Hillsdale, NJ: Erlbaum.

Billman, D., & Heit, E. (1988). Observational learning from internal feedback: A simulation of an adaptive learning method. *Cognitive Science, 12* 587–625.

Billman, D., & Kersten, A. (1991). Learning event categories: Effects of correlational structure. Paper presented at the Psychonomics Society, San Francisco, November, 1991.

Billman, D., & Knutson, J. (1996). Unsupervised concept learning and value systematicity: A complex whole aids learning the parts. *Journal of Experimental Psychology: Learning, Memory, and Cognition, 22,* 459–476.

Blessing, S. B., & Ross, B. H. (1996). The effect of problem content on categorization and problem solving. *Journal of Experimental Psychology: Learning, Memory, and Cognition, 22,* 792–810.

Bransford, J. D. (1979). *Human cognition: Learning, understanding, and remembering.* Belmont, CA: Wadsworth.

Bransford, J. D., Barclay, J. R., & Franks, J. J. (1972). Sentence memory: A constructive versus interpretive approach. *Cognitive Psychology, 3,* 193–209.

Bruner, T. S., Goodnow, T. J., & Austin, G. A. (1956). *A study of thinking.* New York: Wiley.

Brunswick, E. (1955). Symposium on the probability approach in Psychology: Representative design and probabilistic theory in a functional psychology. *Psychological Review, 12(3),* 103–217.

Cabrera, A., & Billman, D. (1996). Language-driven concept learning: Deciphering "jabberwocky." *Journal of Experimental Psychology: Cognition, Learning, and Memory, 22,* 540–556.

Carey, S. (1985). *Conceptual change in childhood.* Cambridge, MA: MIT Press.

Carey, S., & Spelke, E. (1994). Domain-specific knowledge and conceptual change. In L. A. Hirschfeld & S. A. Gelman (Eds.), *Mapping the mind: Domain specificity in cognition and culture.* Cambridge, England: Cambridge University Press.

Chalnick, A., & Billman, D. (1988). Unsupervised learning of correlational structure. In *Program of the tenth annual conference of the cognitive science society* (pp. 510–516). Hillsdale, NJ: Erlbaum.

Chapman, G. B., & Robbins, S. J. (1990). Cue interaction in human contingency judgment. *Memory & Cognition, 18,* 537–545.

Chi, M. T. H., Feltovich, P. J., & Glaser, R. (1989). Categorization and the representation of physics problems by experts and novices. *Cognitive Science, 5,* 121–152.

Chi, M. T. H., Slotta, J. D., & DeLeuuw, N. (1994). From things to processes: A theory of conceptual change for learning science concepts. *Learning and Instruction, 4,* 27–43.

Clark, A (1993). *Associative Engines: Connectionism, Concepts, and Representational Change.* MIT Press: Cambridge, MA.

Clapper, J. P., & Bower, G. H. (1994). Category invention in unsupervised learning. *Journal of Experimental Psychology: Learning, Memory, and Cognition, 20,* 443–460.

Collins, A. M., & Quillian, M. R. (1969). Retrieval time from semantic memory. *Journal of Verbal Learning and Verbal Behaivor, 8,* 240–247.

Fisher, C., Gleitman, H., & Gleitman, L. R. (1991). On the semantic content of subcategorization frames. *Cognitive Psychology, 23,* 331–392.

Fisher, D. (1987). Knowledge acquisition via incremental conceptual clustering. *Machine Learning, 2,* 139–172.

Garcia, J., & Koelling, R. A. (1966). The relation of cue to consequence in avoidance learning. *Psychonomic Science, 4,* 123–124.

Garner, W. R. (1974). *The processing of information and structure.* Hillsdale, NJ: Erlbaum.

Gelman, S. A. (1988). The development of induction within natural kind and artifact categories. *Cognitive Psychology, 20,* 65–95.

Gelman, R. (1990). First principles organize attention to and learning about relevant data: Number and the animate-inanimate distinction as examples. *Cognitive Science, 4,* 79–106.

Gentner, D. (1981). Some interesting differences between verbs and nouns. *Cognition and Brain Theory, 4,* 161–178.

Gentner, D. (1989). The mechanisms of analogical learning. In S. Vosniadou & A. Ortony (Eds.), *Similarity and analogical reasoning* (pp. 199–241). Cambridge: Cambridge University Press.

Gleitman, L. R., & Gleitman, H. (1992). A picture is worth a thousand words, but that's the problem: The role of syntax in vocabulary acquisition. *Current Directions in Psychological Science, 1,* 31–35.

Gluck, M. A., & Bower, G. H. (1988). Evaluating all adaptive network model of human learning. *Journal of Memory and Language, 27,* 166–195.

Hayes-Roth, B., & Hayes-Roth, F. (1977). Concept learning and the recognition and classification of exemplars. *Journal of Verbal Learning and Verbal Behavior, 16,* 321–338.

Hintzman, D. L. (1986). Schema abstraction in a multiple-trace memory model. *Psychological Review, 93,* 411–428.

Holland, J. H., Holyoak, K. J., Nisbett, R. E., & Thagaard, P. R. (1986). *Induction.* Cambridge, MA: MIT Press.

Holland, J. H., & Reitman, J. S. (1978). Cognitive systems based on adaptive algorithms. In D. A. Waterman, & F. Hayes-Roth (Eds.), *Pattern directed inference systems.* New York: Academic Press.

Holyoak, K., & Thagard, P. (1989). Analogical mapping by constraint satisfaction. *Cognitive Science, 13,* 295–355.

Huttenlocher, J., & Lui, F. (1979). The semantic organization of some simple nouns and verbs. *Journal of Verbal Learning and Verbal Behavior 18:* 141–162.

Inhelder, B., & Piaget, J. (1964). *The early growth of logic in the child.* New York: Norton.

Keil, F. C. (1979). *Semantic and conceptual development: An ontological perspective.* Cambridge, MA: Harvard University Press.

Keil, F. C. (1991). The emergence of theoretical beliefs as constraints on concepts. In S. Carey & R. Gelman (Eds.), *The epigenesis of mind: Essays on biology and cognition.* Hillsdale NJ: Erlbaum.

Kersten, A., & Billman, D. (1995). *Learning of event categories.* Manuscript submitted for publication.

Kruschke, J. K. (1992). ALCOVE: An exemplar-based connectionist model of category learning. *Psychological Review, 99,* 22–44.

Mandler, G. (1962). From association to structure. *Psychological Review, 61,* 235–236.

Markman, E. M. (1989). *Categorization and naming in children: Problems of induction.* Cambridge, MA: MIT Press.

Martin, J. D. (1992). Direct and indirect transfer: Investigations in concept formation. (Tech. Rep.). GIT-CC-92/58 Atlanta, GA: Department of Computer Science, Georgia Institute of Technology.

Martin, J., & Billman, D. (1991). Variability bias and category learning. In L. A. Birnbaum & G. C. Collins (Eds.), *Proceedings of the Eight International Workshop on Machine Learning,* (pp. 90–94). San Mateo, CA: Morgan Kaufman.

McKoon, G. & Ratcliff, R. (1986). Inferences about predictable events. *Journal of Experimental Psychology: Learning, Memory, and Cognition, 12,* 82–91.

Medin, D. L., Altom, M. W., Edelson, S. M., & Freko, D. (1982). Correlated symptoms and simulated medical classification. *Journal of Experimental Psychology: Learning, Memory, and Cognition, 8,* pp. 37–50.

Medin, D. L., & Schaffer, M. M. (1978). A context theory of classification learning. *Psychological Review, 85,* 207–238.

Mervis, C. B., & Crisafi, M. A. (1982). Order of acquisition of subordinate-, basic-, and superordinate-level categories. *Child Development, 53,* 258–266.

Meyer, D. E. (1970). On the representation and the retrieval of stored semantic information. *Cognitive Psychology, 1,* 142–300.

Miller, C. S., & Larid, J. (in press). Accounting for graded performance with a discrete search framework. *Cognitive Science.*

Murphy, G. L., & Allopenna, P. D. (1994). The locus of knowledge effects in concept learning. *Journal of Experimental Psychology: Learning, Memory, and Cognition, 19*, 203–222.

Murphy, G. L., & Medin, D. L. (1985). The role of theories in conceptual coherence. *Psychological Review, 92*, pp. 289–316.

Nersessian, N. (1993). How do scientists think? Capturing the dynamics of conceptual change in science. In R. Giere (Ed.), *Minnesota studies in the philosophy of science: Vol. 15: Cognitive models of science.* Minneapolis, MN: University of Minnesota Press.

Neumann, P. G. (1977). Visual prototype information with discontinuous representation of dimensions of variability. *Memory & Cognition, 5*, 187–197.

Nisbett, R. E., Krantz, D. H., Jepson, C., & Kunda, Z. (1983). The use of statistical heuristics in everyday inductive reasoning. *Psychological Review, 90*, 339–363.

Nosofsky, R. M. (1984). Choice, similarity and the context model of classification. *Journal of Experimental Psychology: Learning, Memory, & Cognition, 10*, 104–114.

Nosofsky, R. M. (1987). Attention and learning process in the identification and categorization of integral stimuli. *Journal of Experimental Psychology: Learning, Memory, & Cognition, 13*, 87–108.

Nosofsky, R. M., Palmeri, T. J., & McKinley, S. C. (1994). Rule-plus-exception model of classical learning. *Psychological Review, 101, No. 1*, 53–79.

Osherson, D. N., Smith, E. E., Wilkie, O., Lopez, A., & Shafir, E. (1990). Category-based induction. *Psychological Review, 97*, 185–200.

Quinlan, J. R. (1986). Induction of decision trees. *Machine Learning, 1*, 81–106.

Rips, L. J. (1975). Inductive judgments about natural categories. *Journal of Verbal Learning and Verbal Behavior, 14*, 665–681.

Rosch, E. H. (1978). Principles of Categorization. In E. H. Rosch & B. B. Lloyd (Eds.), *Cognition and categorization.* Hillsdale, NJ: Erlbaum.

Rumelhart, D. E., & Zipser, D. (1986). Feature discovery by competitive learning. In D. E. Rumelhart & J. L. McClelland (Eds.), *Parallel distributed processing* (Vol. 1). Cambridge, MA: MIT Press.

Schyns, P. G. (1991). A modular network model of concept learning. *Cognitive Science, 15*, 461–508.

Shanks, D. R. (1985). Forward and backward blocking in human contingency judgment. *Quarterly Journal of Experimental Psychology, 37B*, 1–21.

Shipley, E. F. (1993). Categories, hierarchies, and induction. *The Psychology of Learning and Motivation, 30*, 265–301.

Smith, C., Carey, S., & Wiser, M. (1985). On differentiation: A case study of the development of the concepts of size, weight, and density. *Cognition, 21*, 177–237.

Smith, E. E., Shoben, E. J., & Rips, L. J. (1974). Structure and process in semantic memory: A featural model for semantic decisions. *Psychological Review, 81*, 214–241.

Talmy, L. (1985). Lexicalization patterns: Semantic structure in lexical forms. In T. Shopen (Ed.), *Language typology and syntactic description: Vol. 3. Grammatical categories and the lexicon.* Cambridge: Cambridge University Press.

Thagard, P. (1992). *Concepts and conceptual systems.* Princeton, NJ: Princeton University Press.

Wisniewski, E. J., & Medin, D. L. (1994). On the interaction of theory and data in concept learning. *Cognitive Science, 18*, 221–281.

INDEX

CONTENTS OF RECENT VOLUMES